SIKKIM

REQUIEM FOR A HIMALAYAN KINGDOM

SIKKIM

REQUIEM FOR A HIMALAYAN KINGDOM

Andrew Duff

BIRLINN

First published in 2015 by
Birlinn Limited
West Newington House
10 Newington Road
Edinburgh EH9 1QS

www.birlinn.co.uk

ISBN 978 1 78027 286 3

British Library Cataloguing-in-Publication Data
A catalogue record for this book is available from the British Library

Typeset in 12¾ on 15pt Adobe Arno Pro by Iolaire Typesetting, Newtonmore
Printed and bound by Gutenberg Press, Malta

For my parents
Ronald and Jane Duff

And in memory
Martha Steedman

Contents

List of Illustrations

Black-and-white plates

1 The author's grandfather in the Himalayas, *c.* 1928
2 Crown Prince Thondup as a young man with his family, *c.* late 1940s
3 Princess Coocoola on her wedding day, 1941
4 The Dalai Lama riding through Sikkim (travelling from Tibet to India), 1956
5 Crown Prince Thondup with Nari Rustomji (Dewan of Sikkim), *c.* late 1950s
6 Martha Hamilton with Crown Prince Thondup and Hope Cooke, *c.* 1963
7 PNG schoolchildren digging trenches against the Chinese threat, 1965
8 Chinese and Indian soldiers facing off on the Sikkim-Tibet border, 1967
9 Chogyal Thondup Namgyal and Hope Cooke (Gyalmo), late 1960s
10 Hope Cooke (Gyalmo) dancing, late 1960s
11 Nehru and his daughter, Indira Gandhi, with the Kennedys, 1961
12 *Hindustan Times* cartoon mocking Indira Gandhi, 1974
13 Letter (extract) from Chogyal Thondup Namgyal to Martha Hamilton, 1974
14 The Kazi and Kazini with B.B. Lal, late 1970s
15 The Kazi and Kazini, mid 1970s
16 Beleaguered monarch – Thondup Namgyal, *c.* 1981

Colour plates

A Note on Romanisation

For non-English words in the main text, I have used what I consider to be the most usual up-to-date romanised forms and focused on consistency rather than following one particular system. Where different spellings are included in quoted text, I have left these as they stand.

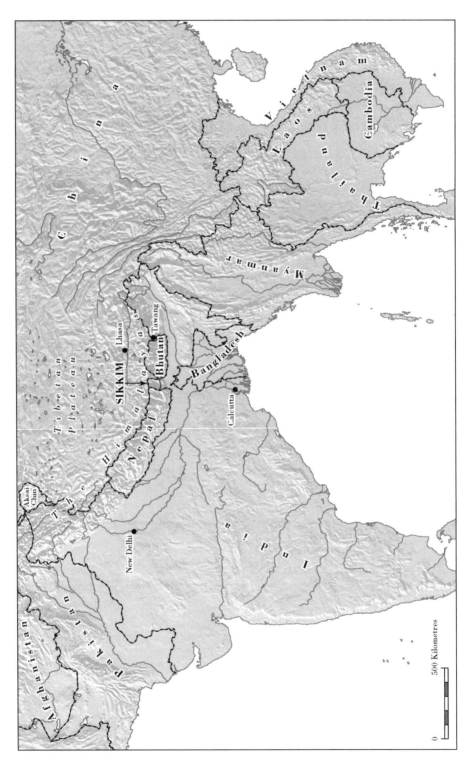

Sikkim: at the heart of Asia

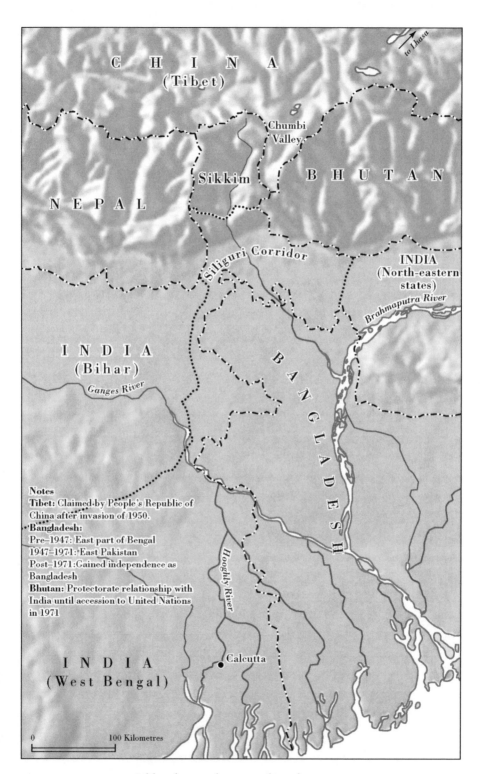

Sikkim's complex geopolitical position

C H I N A
(Tibet)

C H I N A
(Tibet)

NEPAL

▲ Khangchendzonga
8586m

S I K K I M

Teesta River

Chumbi Valley

● Yatung

Nathu La

Jelep La

Rangeet River

Pemayangtse
Monastery ■

● Gangtok

BHUTAN

● Singtam

● Namchi

Chakung ●

Teesta River

Rangeet River

Darjeeling ●

● Kalimpong

I N D I A

Teesta River

NEPAL

● Siliguri

·········· Author's journey in 2009
retracing his grandfather's
1922 journey

BANGLADESH

0   20 Kilometres

Sikkim

Introduction

April 2009, Pemayangtse Monastery, Sikkim

'How much do you know about Sikkim?'

The monk looked at me through the fading light, across the low table in his home on the grounds of Pemayangtse Monastery. A single bulb flickered as the electricity struggled up from the valley thousands of feet below. His maroon robes, trimmed with blue and gold brocade around the cuffs and buttoned front, contrasted with the peeling paint on the window behind him. He left the question hanging in the air as he picked up his soup bowl and slurped its contents. Through the window I could hear Buddhist chants floating out over the sounds of cymbals, horns and drums.

The words, spoken in an accented English unlike any I'd heard elsewhere in India, were the first he had spoken for some minutes. I shifted uncomfortably in my bench-seat as I thought of my sparse knowledge. On the table between us I had placed a blue plastic folder from which spilled my grandfather's notes and photographs of the trek he made through Sikkim to this monastery in 1922. I supposed, wrongly, that my inheritance gave me permission to discuss Sikkim with the monk. Now it was clear I had miscalculated.

'Not much,' I admitted. 'But I would like to learn . . .'

His hooded eyes rested on me impassively. The chanting had stopped and I could hear the steady sound of his breathing above the hum of electric current trying to feed the bulb. He picked up a book from beside him. I could just see its title: *Smash and Grab: Annexation of Sikkim*.

He tossed the book to me. 'Read this. It is banned in India. We speak tomorrow.'*

Looking back now, it seems a bit odd that I didn't know more about Sikkim. By the time I met the monk, the place had been in my consciousness for over two decades.

My journey to the beautiful hilltop monastery of Pemayangtse started in the 1980s. I was a teenager, living in Edinburgh. As my paternal grandparents' minds began to fade, my parents moved them from St Andrews to live five doors down the road from us. I was happy: as their youngest grandchild, I had become close to them. Besides, they had around them the glow of something other, something different: they had spent most of their lives in India.

The move prompted a house clearance in St Andrews. Among the belongings that found their way into our house were a number of albums of photographs from India. I was captivated by all of them, but there was one album in particular that I would spend hours poring over. There was something physically pleasing about the weight and feel of this album. It was large and sturdy, about 18 inches wide by 12 inches tall. Inside the stout mid-brown leather cover, marked with over half a century of scratches, were two and a half inches of bound grey linen pages. It was, as my grandfather explained in a short note inside the front cover, 'strong rather than artistic' on account of its provenance: it had been made in Gourepore, the jute mill outside Calcutta where he worked in the 1930s.

The photographs inside were absorbing: most were from my grandfather's early bachelor years in Calcutta. Others showed by grandparents newly married in the 1930s. My father and aunt also featured, as small children soon to be sent home to Scotland as the prospect of war loomed.

I wanted to talk to my grandparents about the stories behind the photographs. I felt there was something deeply unfair about the way they were declining just as I became a curious teenager. It was clear that my grandfather cared deeply for India, in his own way. Every image on every page had been carefully outlined in ink with hand-drawn geometric designs. But it was the carefully inscribed titles for each photograph that fired my imagination. I wanted to know what it felt like to jump from the

---

* In fact, the book was never banned, although, as the author Sunanda Datta-Ray explains in a new 2014 edition of the book, it was cleverly sidelined by the Indian authorities.

back of a canoe and swim in the river at Falta, to watch the monsoon break at Parasnath, to mess around burying his best friend J. E. Osmond in sand to look like Tutankhamun at Gopalpur. I wanted him to tell me about the elephants on the tea estate in Bhooteachang, about bathing naked and picnicking on fish in the Sunderbans. I wanted to ask him about the Garhwal Himalayas, the Pindari Glacier, about places with strange names like Shillong, Kalimpong, Darjeeling, Ranchi, Phalut.

But there was one word I wanted to ask him about more than anything else: Sikkim.

Each time I opened the album, it was the first word that confronted me. On the right-hand page, encased in elaborate stencils, was a single black-and-white photograph of a river rushing under a flimsy-looking bridge. On one side of the photo in large letters was written 'Sikkim'; on the other, 'Pujahs 1922'. On the facing page six typewritten sheets of yellowing note-paper had been carefully glued by their edges so that they overlapped. At the top of the first sheet: 'Notes on a Tour in Sikkim Oct. 1922'. The notes contained an account of a journey – a holiday – walking a ten-day circular route into the Sikkim Himalaya. The first eight pages were photographs of that journey, made when my grandfather was only 22 and had been in India for less than two years, but there had been other journeys through Sikkim, too, after my grandparents had married in 1929. There was a trip in 1932, again in 1934, and – perhaps most remarkably – one in 1938, when they trekked together over a 14,000-foot pass into Tibet.

But it was the 1922 journey that captured my imagination most. I must have read the matter-of-fact opening a hundred times: 'Our party consisted of four: Sinclair, who made most of the arrangements, Ewan, Ryrie and myself. We left Darjeeling after tiffin on October 15th, and arrived back there on the 25th.' There were details of costs, kit, the maps they used, even the stores they took (supplied by the Army and Navy stores in Calcutta). As I read the notes and built an impression from the photographs, I felt as if I was venturing with them deep into the Himalayas. Soon I knew the route description by heart. Place names such as Chakung, Rinchenpong and Dentam became embedded in my memory. I loved reading about the physically challenging landscape: there were constant reminders of 'steady tiring climbing', 'steep descents', more 'stiff climbs', descents of 5,000 feet that were described as 'likely to be very tiring to the walker'. But the rewards were spelled out, too: rows and rows of tea plantations ('very pleasing after Bengal'), roaring rivers with 'the jade green water rushing amid massive boulders between the mountainous banks on either side', 'the snows peeping over the hills to the north' and finally, as they progressed deeper into the Himalayas, 'a magnificent view of the sun peeping over the whole range'.

It was the description and the photographs of the hilltop monastery that was their final destination – Pamionchi – that took the firmest hold on my mind. After five days of arduous trekking, the final approach at dusk– 'through dark and eerie woods, wind and silent', with monkeys 'the only animal life of any kind' – had clearly spooked my grandfather and his companions. That night they had been able to see 'the twinkling of the lights in Darjeeling . . . a pretty sight'. But it had not been till the following morning that they had fully appreciated the spectacular location of the monastery. They could see for miles in every direction. Most spectacularly, to the north, not more than a dozen miles, lay the peaks of the third-highest mountain in the world, Khangchendzonga, sacred to the lamas of Sikkim. The monastery, too, had made an impression – of a slightly different kind. They had found the temple a 'weird place' and the wall paintings 'extremely crude and pagan'. Nevertheless, it was clear from the black-and-white pictures that the imposing building, the monks and their houses had sparked the young men's curiosity – although there were limits: the monks failed in their effort to entice them into the upper floors of the monastery to see the 'treasures' for a fee of ten rupees: 'Remembering we were Scotch, and had a reputation to keep up, we contented ourselves with seeing downstairs only.'

The four men spent two days at the monastery before returning together to Darjeeling, staying in the Government of India-owned dak bungalows that the British had built across the Himalayas to allow a sufficient level of control. It had taken less than a fortnight. But the notes and photographs survived to fire my imagination more than half a century later. When my grandparents died within three months of each other in 1988, a seed was planted in my mind.

It took two decades for that seed to germinate.

In late 2008, I decided it was time. The first thing I needed to do was to look for Sikkim once again in the atlas. I almost missed it.

Nestled in between Nepal and Bhutan, Sikkim is tiny, about a third of the size of Wales. In most atlases, the space is not even big enough to hold the six letters of Sikkim's name. It lies about two-thirds of the way along the Himalayas, the great white crescent of mountains that stretches for more than 1,800 miles from the steppes of central Asia to the tropical forests of Myanmar and South-east Asia. As I peered at the atlas I could see one very good reason why it had appealed to my grandfather: Sikkim lies almost due north of Calcutta.

In early 2009, I packed photocopies of the notes and photographs into my rucksack and set off for northern India. From Calcutta I travelled up to Siliguri, the junction town from where the Darjeeling Himalayan Railway snakes up into the hills, chugging gently into the mountains, covering no more than 50 miles in six hours. By the time we reached Darjeeling, the heat of the plains had been replaced by a persistent drizzle and a penetrating chill in the air, part of the attraction for the inhabitants of steamy Calcutta. Today the hill station still retains a few signs of its colonial past, managing somehow to stay just the right side of faded grandeur.

It took me a few days to arrange for an Inner Line Permit* and to establish that I would be able to follow my grandfather's route into Sikkim. Numerous guides tempted me with offers of trekking along the Nepali border to see Mount Everest, but slowly I started to piece things together. There was one thing that still puzzled me, though. I could not find any reference to the monastery that had been the apex of their journey: Pamionchi.

The turning point came when I found a 1917 book that mentioned it. I cross-referenced the book's map with a 1981 military one I had acquired in Calcutta. Everything fell into place: Pamionchi, I realised, was an early twentieth-century effort to anglicise the word Pemayangtse – this was the modern name for the monastery that was now my destination. The following day I met a guide willing to help me find accommodation along the way. I knew there was little chance of staying in the government-owned dak bungalows that my grandfather and his friends had used.

The landscape turned out to be even more spectacular than I'd expected. The first day and a half consisted of a steep knee-crunching descent of over 5,000 feet to reach the river Rangeet, which separates modern West Bengal from Sikkim. Crossing the river, the footbridge that I had looked

---

* Regulations governing access to Sikkim today are remarkably similar to those introduced by the British in 1873.

at so many times in my grandfather's album was still there, spanning the glacial water. I used the photocopied notes and photographs that I carried with me to help navigate my way into the Himalayan foothills. After following the river upstream for a few miles, I finally entered Sikkim on 4 April 2009.

Over the next three days I covered more than 50 miles on foot, ascending and descending a few thousand feet each day to cross the concertina of ridges that define the southern area of Sikkim. As I passed through every hill pass, I could see, less than 30 miles away, the magnificent massif of Mount Khangchendzonga and the other snow-capped ranges than separate India from the Tibetan plateau.

It was hard not to feel a sense of destiny as I retraced my grandfather's footsteps from 87 years before. At times the challenging terrain almost defeated me. His party had numbered more than 20 (including all the porters). They had even taken a pony – my grandfather had made an aside that 'it is a help in climbing to hang on to the pony's tail if someone else is riding'. As I zigzagged up steep slopes by myself, I could understand what he meant.

Finally, as dusk fell on the fifth day, I walked high along the side of the Kulhait Valley, climbing up the steep road to the hilltop monastery of Pemayangtse, and my meeting with the monk.

For the first four days of the trek, my guide had managed to procure rooms in the most unlikely of places: among others, a concrete cell-like room above a village bank, and a bed in the house of a local postmaster. In the village below the monastery, I struck gold. I was told that a former monk, who now ran a school offering a Buddhist-based curriculum, was willing to let me stay in his house, right by the monastery. It was on the first evening in his house that he tossed me the book, telling me we would speak the following day.

That night, in a small wood-panelled room at the top of his house, I opened the book and began reading. At first I found the story hard to follow – it seemed to be an account of the funeral of the king, or 'Chogyal', of Sikkim. One thing was clear: the author was convinced that a great wrong had taken place against the king in the 1970s. Tiredness began to get the better of me. With the freezing air making the skin on my face feel numb, my eyes drooped and I struggled to focus on the page.

Then I suddenly became alert. A few pages in, amid an account of the funeral procession, I read the following: 'Finally [came] Sonam Yongda, the Sikkim Guards captain who had paid dearly for his patriotism, and returned to the monastery whence he began. . .clad in the lama's maroon.'

At first I told myself it was a coincidence. I had learnt in Pelling, the small village below the monastery, that my host's name was Yongda. Surely there must be more than one Yongda with connections to a monastery in Sikkim. But curiosity took me to the index. There were multiple references under 'Yongda, Captain Sonam'. I turned to the first:

Captain Sonam Yongda. . . had passed out with distinction from the Indian Military Academy and had trained for more than a year with an Indian Gurkha regiment. The son of a senior lama at Pemayangtse Monastery, where he himself had also been ordained, Yongda came of sturdy Bhutiya stock.

The odds were narrowing: this Yongda had been at Pemayangtse too. Another passage hinted at a man of some courage: 'With Yongda behind bars, the Sikkim Guards were deprived of the only officer who could have forged commitment and fervour into resistance.'

Curious, I returned to the main story and read on. It was obvious that the author held the king in high regard and was convinced that he had been badly mistreated, abandoned by all but a few loyal supporters, including this 'Captain Yongda'. It was a compelling story of tragedy and intrigue. Even the piercing cold could not stop me reading till the small hours of the morning.

I woke early and dressed quickly, donning fleece layer after fleece layer. I told myself again it must simply be a coincidence: the military man in the book *must* be a different Sonam Yongda, a brother or a cousin of the monk who was my host at Pemayangtse, nothing more.

I made my way downstairs and into the kitchen area, past the wooden bed frames, towards the low tables and benched seating. Three girls were bustling around the kitchen, filling bowls and pouring tea. The monk was at the table, hunched over a bowl of porridge. He was dressed in an extraordinary outfit – it was hard to reconcile him with the maroon-clad monk of the previous evening. His monastic robe was gone, replaced by a turquoise shellsuit over which he wore a thick, dark-blue down bodywarmer. He had a bulky woollen hat pulled down over his brow. He glanced up from the bowl of porridge and nodded a greeting to me. I took a seat beside him. One of the girls brought over a mug of steaming tea and a bowl of porridge sprinkled with chilli flakes. The three girls also took seats at one end of the low table with their own bowls. I tucked in to the delicious porridge and, with no idea what to say, I waited for the monk to open the conversation.

'So. How you sleep?'

'Yes, well, thank you.'

'Did you like the book?'

I looked over at him but couldn't read his face in the morning gloom.

'Yes, I did.' I decided to chance it. 'I came across references to someone called Yongda from this monastery. I wondered if he might be a relative of yours.'

I noticed that the girls were all suppressing giggles. I glimpsed the slightest of smirks as Yongda looked over at them.

'You?' is all I could think to say.

He nodded, the hint of a shy smile on his lips, which quickly disappeared. It seemed barely believable that this was the man in the book. I could not hide my curiosity. I blurted out, 'So you were the King of Sikkim's personal bodyguard?'

He nodded again, then looked up at me. 'You must read the whole book. It is a very important story. A terrible story, terrible what they did to the Chogyal.'

His face turned impassive again. 'But that was a long time ago. And I am now late,' he said, standing up. He gathered his things and left.

When I set out on the journey, my intention had been to write about my reconnection with my grandfather's years living in India and his love for the Himalaya, particularly Sikkim. But the book that the monk gave me contained such an extraordinary story of political intrigue and wonderful characters in the 1950s, 1960s and 1970s that my horizons soon broadened. I stayed in the monastery for a further three days, talking to Yongda about his memories of the king, and reading the account of the final days of the Himalayan Kingdom of Sikkim. I read how this tiny part of the world had survived as an independent entity after India gained its own independence; how King Thondup, the last Chogyal, had married an

American woman, Hope Cooke, once talked of in the same breath as Grace Kelly, and how together they had believed they could revive the ancient kingdom; how (the author of *Smash and Grab* alleged) Indira Gandhi had used her intelligence services to bring that dream to a close, surrounding the palace with troops as she annexed the kingdom in 1975. And as if the drama of the story were not enough, the cast of supporting characters had names worthy of a James Bond novel: the Kazini, a shadowy Scottish woman who orchestrated events on behalf of her husband, the leading politician in Sikkim who harboured a lifelong grudge against the king; the improbably nicknamed Princess Coocoola, the king's sister, who Heinrich Harrer (of *Seven Years in Tibet* fame) believed to be the most beautiful woman in the world. The most astonishing revelation was that Sonam Yongda, the monk who had given me the book, had played an important part in the climax of the story as a captain in the Sikkim Guards, the small body of military men who protected the king. In hour-long sessions, he slowly revealed the details of his role in this remarkable tale.

It took me four days to trek back to the Sikkimese border. At one point I found myself walking along old moss-covered cobbled bridleways through ancient forests of deodar. Finally, I reached the river and climbed 5,000 feet back up to the ridge that Darjeeling straddles, returning to where I had started a fortnight before. I spent a week trying to process what I had read, looking for other accounts of Sikkim's story in the best bookshop in the hill town, the Oxford Stores. I discovered that Sikkim's name stemmed from a word meaning 'happy home'. But in the few slim volumes that mentioned the events of 1975 most referred to it as a 'merger' between Sikkim and India, a triumph for 'democratic forces', the culmination of a popular rising by the Sikkimese people themselves – against a feudal monarch. Some even referred to Hope Cooke as a CIA agent. And of the few people I found willing to talk about their recollections of the time, none gave me the same account. The story seemed slippery, full of nuance and complication. Versions seemed to proliferate like subdividing cells.

From Sikkim, I travelled through Nepal and into Tibet, where I began to understand the delicate political and religious connections and tensions between the countries across the Himalayan region. But it was Sikkim's tale that now obsessed me. When I eventually returned to my home in Scotland, I immersed myself in finding out what I could about the place. I discovered that there was a small group of academics researching its early history. I learnt that Sikkim's ties to Tibet and its position alongside the biggest chink in the Himalayan massif had made it geopolitically valuable for centuries.

Most importantly, I understood that the history of Sikkim's demise could not be seen in isolation. The British involvement in Sikkim and Tibet in the early twentieth century had set up many of Sikkim's problems. After the British left in 1947, the Himalayan region had been at the centre of a period of international intrigue across Asia, a second front for the Cold War. I began to realise that Sikkim never stood a chance.

But I still felt I was some distance from getting under the skin of what happened in Sikkim. *Smash and Grab* was a valuable first-hand account, but the author was open about his close friendship with the Chogyal. I wondered if that had coloured his narrative. I longed for another perspective. My first break came when I was introduced to Martha Steedman (née Hamilton) by a friend of my parents. Martha, a bright, energetic Scottish woman in her late seventies with a distinguished teaching career behind her, had been headmistress of the main girls' school in the Sikkimese capital, Gangtok, between 1959 and 1966. Sikkim was a small place, and she had direct access to the Palace. She showed me extraordinary photographs of the royal couple, of their wedding and coronation. The turning point came when she asked if I'd like to see the weekly letters she had written to her parents from Sikkim. Far from being 'of little interest', as she had suggested, the pale blue aerogrammes provided a unique perspective on the world of Sikkim. Life in the palace burst into full Technicolor. I began to discover references to Sikkim in travel memoirs and articles in magazines such as *Time, Newsweek, National Geographic* and *Paris Match* that illuminated matters further.

With the help of Martha Hamilton's letters, I started to piece together the story. But she also gave me my second break. Perhaps, she suggested, I might like to speak to her successor as headmistress at the school, Ishbel Ritchie, another Scot, who had served in Sikkim between 1966 and 1996. A fortnight later I was walking out of Ritchie's home in Dunfermline laden with another box of weekly letters home. As I put them into order, I realised I had stumbled across another treasure trove. Ritchie's letters (which she had to hide from the Indian censors operating in Sikkim) were just as insightful as Hamilton's. I now had first-hand, contemporaneous accounts of the years from 1959 to 1975, during which Thondup and his queen, Hope Cooke, had tried to reinvigorate the Kingdom of Sikkim.

A project that I thought would take a year had already taken 18 months. But there was one big problem. I was now so immersed in the local story of Sikkim in the 1960s and 1970s that I had missed the other vital part of the story – the geopolitical context within which Sikkim had existed, located on the frontier between India, which had emerged from British rule in 1947, and Tibet, occupied by China since 1950. I began to delve into the motivations of the Indian and Chinese governments in this period, understanding that they were deeply influenced by the Cold War politics swirling around Asia at the time. I realised that understanding the motivations of one woman in particular – Indira Gandhi, the Indian Prime Minister from 1966 to 1977 and then again from 1980 to 1984 – was critical in telling the story of Sikkim.

Suspecting that official records of the UK government might also shed light on the story, I turned to the Foreign Office records in the National Archives. Every year, under what is called the '30-year-rule', the UK government releases secret files from three decades previously. I realised that files from the 1970s would be available. I discovered a remarkable set of documents demonstrating that the UK government had shown a keen interest in the events in Sikkim, a place that was clearly dear to many Foreign Office mandarins, some of whom had been intimately connected to Sikkim's royal family. Secret reports and memos added to the sense of intrigue in the story.

Meanwhile I returned to Sikkim on a number of occasions, tracking down some of those who had been involved in the events I was writing about. As they entered their seventies and eighties, some welcomed the opportunity to unburden themselves, talking openly of their role in the events of the time, often admitting to a sense of embarrassed guilt.

Finally, in early 2013, just as I thought I had completed the final draft of the book, Wikileaks released a tranche of US government cables from the early to mid-1970s. With some trepidation (I had by now had enough of 'revelations') I decided to do a word search within the documents for 'Sikkim'. The computer revealed 500 secret cables that brought to life the extraordinary Cold War background to Sikkim's demise. It was the last piece of a complex puzzle, putting the events of Sikkim into their proper global context.

At last, I felt I had a complete story to write.

The story of Sikkim is a cautionary tale of what can happen when a small kingdom tugs at the tailcoats of the Great Powers. But it is also an intensely human story – about King Thondup and his wife Hope Cooke. He was the scion of a Buddhist ruling family; she, 17 years his junior and a teenager when they first met, the orphaned granddaughter of a New York shipping company president. That they met at all was remarkable enough; the way their relationship developed – often in the public eye – I found fascinating. As I researched their story in Sikkim, no one I spoke to was shy about giving an opinion. Navigating through those opinions was never easy.

Thondup died in 1982, but Hope Cooke still lives in New York today. I contacted her in 2010. At first she offered to talk about the 'cultural context' to Sikkim, but then decided (after consulting with her children) that she should leave her 1981 biography to stand as her record of the period. Although this was initially disappointing, as time passed I understood that decision. I was pleased that we reestablished contact in 2015. Her enthusiasm for Sikkim remains undiminished.

This tiny piece of land, no more than 70 miles by 40 miles, has dominated my life for five years. The pursuit of the story has taken me back to Sikkim and India many times, drawing me into fascinating corners and cul-de-sacs I never dreamed of visiting. I have researched in Gangtok's Institute of Tibetology, the Tibetan Government-in-Exile's archive in Dharamsala in northern India, the Bodleian Library, the British Library and the London Library. I have interviewed former Indian diplomats in Delhi, and former (and current) Sikkimese politicians in Gangtok. But the keys to unlocking this story were the letters of Martha Hamilton and Ishbel Ritchie. Both have been unfailingly generous.

On my desk as I write this, there is a small cardboard head-and-shoulders cut-out picture of my grandfather taken in India. He is wearing a shirt and pullover, a pipe hanging out of his mouth. It may even have been taken in Sikkim. It is strange for me to think that without him none of this would have been written.

To him, and to my parents, enormous thanks.

Prologue

On 15 May 1975 a curious letter appeared in the pages of *The Times*. The title was 'Chogyal of Sikkim' and it was signed by 'JOHN CLARKE, G8KA, Tanyard, Frittenden, Kent'. Clarke's letter was in response to a flurry of correspondence about Sikkim that had appeared in *The Times* over the past month, which had caused him to recall a bizarre conversation he had overhead a month earlier in April.

Clarke was a 56-year-old local solicitor and county coroner, looking forward to an early retirement. It was common knowledge that he would slip away for odd afternoons in the local garden centre to catalogue the rhododendrons,[1] but his other hobby, amateur radio communications, was less well known to his colleagues and friends. The G8KA in his signature on the letter was his callsign.

At 15:18 hrs GMT on 11 April he had just finished chatting with a fellow enthusiast in Australia, callsign VK2DA, when another station broke in saying there was an 'AC3' station on 14151 kilocycles making a distress call. Clarke could not resist returning to his radio set.

As he honed in on the right frequency he could hear a conversation fading in and out. He could only just make out the callsign of one side of the conversation: AC3PT. He immediately looked it up in his amateur radio callbook. Establishing that AC3 was the country code for Sikkim, he saw that only one name was listed, PT Namgyal. The address: 'The Palace, Gangtok, Sikkim'.

Intrigued, Clarke refocused on the signal. Through the static, he strained to hear the high-pitched voice speaking accented but very good

English at considerable speed. It was a weak signal, but the message was unmistakeable.

AC3PT was saying that his country was being invaded and urgently requested that someone tell the 'International League for the Rights of Man'.

Then suddenly the signal faded to nothing. Wondering if AC3PT had moved to another frequency, Clarke called his Australian friend VK2DA back on the line. Both tried to re-establish contact with the signal, but to no avail.

It was very strange. At 15:54 GMT it was just as if callsign AC3PT had vanished into thin air.

Four and a half months later on 26 August, Oliver Forster, Acting British High Commissioner in New Delhi, put the finishing touches to a report on the events in Sikkim. The report had been urgently requested by the Foreign Secretary, Jim Callaghan, in London. With a state of Emergency still in place across India, it wasn't exactly priority number one, but it did present an opportunity for Forster to demonstrate his ability to see through the confusing mire of politics on the subcontinent. He titled it 'The Indian Takeover of Sikkim'.

His closing paragraph read:

All in all, the world may be a little worse off for the loss of a Shangrila, ruled benignly but in the interests of a small minority by a Buddhist prince with an American wife and a liking for alcohol. The Indian action may seem a little crude and Indian self-justification somewhat nauseating, but no British interests were involved, no deep moral issues were at stake and only one life was lost, probably accidentally. In the days of British India we would have done just the same, and frequently did with recal-citrant Maharajahs, though one may hope a little earlier and with fewer exclamations at our own virtues. In the event, we successfully kept out of the whole business and such support as the Chogyal has received in the correspondence columns of *The Times* has not been sufficient to offend Indian sensitivities.[2]

Sikkim, he reflected, was history.

CHAPTER ONE

A British Legacy

1941–9

-1-

In late December 1941, 18-year-old Prince Palden Thondup Namgyal, second son of the Ninth Chogyal of Sikkim, returned to his family's modest palace in Sikkim's capital, Gangtok, with a spring in his step. Coming home to his family's Himalayan kingdom always gave him a thrill, climbing steadily along the steep-sided valleys to the palace perched on a ridge above the tiny capital of Sikkim. But that December it felt particularly good to be back. Finally, after seven years at the Bishop Cotton School in Simla, he was free. He had enjoyed his time at the prestigious boarding school with its regimented life modelled on those in England; he had taken an active part in school life, showing academic promise and playing sports. But it had not all been easy. With his shy nature and slight stammer, he had been an easy target for the bullies. He had found it hard, too, not to fall under the shadow of his elder brother, Crown Prince Paljor, 18 months his senior. Now that Paljor was training with the Royal Indian Air Force, it was exciting to think that, at last, he might be able to carve his own path.

As he settled back into life in Gangtok, he started to think about what might come next. His teachers at Bishop Cotton had already helped him explore the possibility of studying science at Cambridge; perhaps, if the war eased, he might be able to travel in Europe or in the United States. If not, he could still travel across the mountain passes into Tibet, maybe visit the remote monastery on the Tibetan plateau where he had spent three years as a child living with his uncle, training as a Buddhist monk. He could even visit Lhasa, the Tibetan capital, where his mother's family lived and where his younger sister had just got married. He could pay his respects to the six-year-old boy recently identified as the Dalai Lama, the spiritual head of his family's Buddhist faith. But first he decided just to relax and enjoy feeling genuinely carefree for the first time in his life.

It was only days after arriving home that the telegram arrived. The news contained in it – that Paljor had been killed while serving with the Royal Indian Air Force – changed everything. Over the following few days the details of what had happened filtered up the official channels to the British political officer in Gangtok, Basil Gould, who relayed them immediately to the Palace. It had happened on 20 December, he told the grieving family. They could be proud of their son. Number 1 Squadron, based in Peshawar, had been training in Westland Lysanders as they prepared to transfer to Burma, where they would fight the expected Japanese advance. Paljor's plane had crashed while coming in to land, bursting into flames on impact. The Crown Prince had been the Squadron's first casualty.

Thondup watched as his father, Sir Tashi, now 48 years old, tried to cope with this latest family tragedy. Some believed the Namgyals were cursed: in the family's 300-year history, the firstborn had rarely succeeded. A quarter of a century earlier, in 1914, Sir Tashi himself had been thrust unwittingly into the position of Chogyal after the untimely death of his own brother. Now, as he helped make the preparations for Paljor's funeral, Thondup knew the wheel had turned once more.

His life, he realised, was no longer his own.

The immediate problem facing Sir Tashi Namgyal, the Chogyal of Sikkim, was how to prepare Thondup for the role that he knew would now define his young son's life. He remembered how hard he had found it when he had been in the same situation. Sikkim was a more stable place now than it had been then; nevertheless, he wanted to give Thondup the best possible chance of success. As usual in matters of state, he turned to Basil Gould, the Political Officer.

Gould was one of a remarkable group of no more than a few dozen

men, known collectively as the 'Frontier Cadre'*, who had run the operations of the Empire in this region since an official British Residency had
been established in Gangtok in 1890. By 1941 he was already in his late
fifties and had known Tashi Namgyal for nearly three decades; he had
briefly been political officer in Sikkim in 1913, when he had been the
leader of an extraordinary social experiment, taking four sons of Tibetan
nobles to England to be educated at Rugby School. The project had not
been a success (one of the boys had died of malaria and the careers of the
other three were somewhat blighted by their involvement in the project
when they returned to Tibet), but it was an indication of the underlying
attitude of the British in the region. The Residency in Gangtok acted as
the political officer's base, but it was the desire to open trade relations
with and gain political influence in Tibet that was the primary reason
behind Britain's presence in the Himalayas.

Nevertheless, successive British political officers had got to know the
Namgyals well. Gould, who had been appointed to Gangtok as political
officer for a second time in 1935, had developed a particularly close
relationship with the children. Shortly before Gould's return, relations
between Sir Tashi and his wife had reached breaking point; she had
recently returned from a visit to Tibet pregnant with the child of a monk.†
It had fallen to Gould to shield the children from the fallout of the scandal.
He had done so by taking them to the sea for the first time and allowing
them to travel with him on official journeys to Bhutan, becoming something akin to an uncle to them. 'I remember a hot afternoon,' he wrote
later in his memoirs, 'when, bumping along a dusty track on the Bhutan
border in a motor lorry, we passed the time singing "Ten Green Bottles", a
hymn, "The Grand Old Duke of York" and a carol or two.'[1]

Gould felt qualified, therefore, to help Tashi, who now wore curious
round, tinted glasses on account of his myopia, to decide on the best route
for Thondup's future. The aim of the political officer in an Indian state,
one of his colleagues had once said, was to be 'the Whisper behind the
Throne, but never for an instant the Throne itself'. Gould agreed whole-
heartedly: he believed his job to be 'to interfere as little as possible, but

---

* A term coined by historian Alex McKay in his book *Tibet and the British Raj*.
† Thondup's mother lived in a separate house in Gangtok for the rest of her life, where she
brought up the child who over time became an integral part of the extended family.

to be able to give sensible advice if it was asked for'. The present situation was one in which he felt he could offer such sensible advice. Thondup, he suggested to Sir Tashi, was certainly an able boy, but he might benefit from attending the Indian Civil Service administrative course. It just so happened, Gould reminded Sir Tashi, that Thondup's cousin Jigme Dorji, a member of the family who held the hereditary post of prime minister in neighbouring Bhutan, was due to attend the course starting in February.

It seemed too good an opportunity to miss.

A few weeks later Thondup arrived at the ICS school in Dehradun. Renowned as the training ground for aspirant Indian bureaucrats with an eye on the day the British would finally hand over the reins of the administration of their country, the school had also become popular with rulers of India's Princely States keen to ensure their children learnt the 'fundamentals of administration'.[2]

The tented camp, situated in the Doon Valley not more than a couple of hundred miles from Bishop Cotton in Simla that he had left only a few weeks earlier, was very different from the spires of Cambridge that Thondup had been hoping to attend. There was one consolation: his cousin Jigme Dorji would be on the course with him. Thondup loved Jigme, or 'Jigs' as he had been known at Bishop Cotton, where he had excelled, earning a place as a member of the school's hallowed 'Spartan' club.

As the two settled down in the mess tent for lunch on the first day, they found themselves sitting next to a young Indian diplomat, Nari Rustomji. Rustomji, like Thondup and Jigme, had a strong affinity for the British Indian heritage. A ramshackle young man with an innate sense of fun and a deep love for European culture, Rustomji had been educated at Bedford School in England, and then at Cambridge, before passing the ICS exams in London. 'My early influences were Plato and Beethoven,' he wrote later. 'It was through Beethoven, I think, that I was prepared, made ripe, for receiving the Compassionate Buddha's message.'[3]

The three men immediately struck up a friendship. Jigme, Rustomji noticed immediately, was an 'out-and-out extrovert', but it was the young Crown Prince of Sikkim to whom he felt more 'temperamentally akin'. For Rustomji, Thondup appeared an endearingly 'shy, timorous fawn, lost and lonely in the vast Indian subcontinent';[4] for Thondup, Rustomji's love of antics and buffoonery was just what he needed. The two soon became firm friends. They spent most of the course riding and listening to Mozart and Beethoven on Rustomji's old gramophone. Thondup was, Rustomji recalled, 'quickly infected by my passion for music . . . It was not long before he asked me to select a nucleus for a collection of classical records of his own.' In the evenings Thondup would regale Rustomji with tales of Sikkim's colourful history; Rustomji in turn would conjure up the dreaming spires of his years as a Classical scholar at Christ's College, Cambridge. Together they constructed a life of 'little extravagances' ('I confess,' Rustomji later wrote, 'it used to give me quite a thrill to smoke his gold-tipped State Express 999's'), as they made their way through the course. It was the start of a close 30-year friendship during which Thondup would often turn to 'Uncle Rusty' (so-called because he was the older of the pair by a year) for advice and guidance.

During the summer break of 1942 the Prince invited Rustomji back up to Sikkim. They took the train to Siliguri, where Thondup, bursting with pride, picked up his gleaming new Sunbeam Talbot and drove his friend through the foothills of Sikkim to Gangtok. Rustomji was immediately struck by the unpretentious lifestyle of the Palace, where the two men listened to music, read, wrote letters and relaxed. No less striking were Thondup's two beautiful and improbably nicknamed younger sisters, Coocoola and Kula, who 'captured every heart, mine included'.

But it was the wilderness of Sikkim's peaks that Rustomji loved most. As the pair trekked through deep valleys and up steep mountains, there was, he noted, 'none of the pomp and fanfare of the "democratic" leaders of today. We slept in bamboo shacks hastily erected within minutes of our arrival at our halting-place and ate the homely fare provided by the villagers amongst whom we happened to be travelling.'

Rustomji was utterly captivated by the simple lifestyle of the people of Sikkim and the Tibetan traders who passed through on 'gaily decorated mules with tinkling bells' heading up into the mountains with their goods bound for Lhasa. The troubles of the European war seemed a distant nightmare.

At the end of the summer the two returned to continue their course, this time to an army base in Lahore. Word had got around the city about the handsome 'young Sikkim' who 'was considered, in the matrimonial market, to be quite a catch'. Rustomji noticed that all too frequently 'objects of delight were put in his way, with studied casualness, and he had to tread warily to steer clear of entanglement'.[5]

At the end of the course the two bid each other a sad farewell. Twelve years would pass before Rustomji would be reunited with Thondup, serving as dewan (prime minister) in the tiny Himalayan kingdom at Thondup's request; by that time, Sikkim would be in very different circumstances – the British would be gone, replaced by representatives of a very different India; and there would be a communist regime on Sikkim's doorstep.

But in 1942, as Rustomji headed for a posting in Assam,* Thondup returned to Gangtok a more confident young man.

-2-

Life for Sikkim's royal family in Gangtok in the 1940s was, as Italian writer Fosco Maraini† put it, something of a 'fairy tale'.

The place had an otherworldliness that captivated and entranced the 'travellers, mountaineers, geologists and plant-hunters' – Americans, British, Italians, German and French – who made their way up to the Sikkimese capital. Even if they were just passing through, perhaps heading to Tibet via the neighbouring Chumbi Valley (at that time the preferred approach to Mount Everest), they invariably dined at the Palace with the Namgyals. It was hard not to be fascinated by the combination of a simple lifestyle and complex religious beliefs set against the awe-inspiring beauty of the landscape.

Most could not help noticing the inherent contrasts and contradic-tions in Sikkim. 'In this Himalayan landscape, with its dizzy extremes and excesses,' Maraini wrote, 'it is appropriate that by way of contrast there should be a toy capital, with a toy bazaar, toy gardens and toy houses, set among tree-ferns and wild orchids on a hillside among the clouds.'[6]

Gangtok in 1942 was, indeed, still tiny, a suitable capital for a miniature kingdom. The town, nestled into a hillside against a majestic landscape,

---

* A state in India's north-east, south of Bhutan, and not far from Sikkim.

† Maraini, author of *Secret Tibet*, visited Sikkim twice in the 1930s and 1940s on his way to explore Tibet.

consisted of not much more than a few hundred buildings and a bazaar strung out across one side of a wooded valley. A smattering of houses crept up to a low-slung ridge that stretched up towards the mountains on one side and ended in a promontory on the other, beyond which the ridge fell away steeply.

The highest building on the mountainside, set back in the trees looking down over the ridge and the promontory, was the British political officer's Residency, deliberately emphasising the pecking order in the Kingdom over which the British had established a loose protectorate. The role of political officer in Sikkim was a complex one (the officer was responsible for relations with Tibet and Bhutan as well as Sikkim), but it was never taxing. As a result, it was highly sought after by a certain type of British administrator. Sikkim itself was the attraction: one PO, Arthur Hopkinson, thought the Kingdom 'altogether too good to be true, with its lovely country, its charming people, including such a charming family at the palace . . . such friendly relations between the communities.'[7]

But it was the Residency – and its garden in particular (recognised as one of the finest in British India) – that made the posting so unique. The brick-built house, constructed in the 1890s by local labourers under the guidance of Sikkim's first political officer, looked as if it could have been transported to Sikkim from England's Home Counties. To the political officers, it was a 'divine place . . . beautifully furnished, terraced garden, full of lovely trees, trim beds, all sorts of roses, hydrangeas, a wild cherry in blossom . . . ponds with fountains and goldfish, a lovely aviary full of shrubs, a peculiar brace of geese, Dalai Lama birds, grouse, partridges, pheasants.'[8] By the early 1940s it was even possible to get BBC broadcasts in the isolated Residency, when they weren't 'distorted by atmospherics'.[9]

Further down the ridge, on the promontory below the Residency, sat the 'small and rather simple' Royal Palace of the Namgyals. Constructed in the 1920s, it was, at first glance, no less 'a corner of old England', with its 'fine great timber beams, panelled walls, period furniture and lovely garden stocked with the homely flowers of England'. By contrast, the rooms inside were full of Buddhist decoration. The walls of the formal entertaining rooms downstairs were lined with vivid Tibetan tangkas from Kham in Eastern Tibet (the Namgyals had migrated to Sikkim in the 13th century and were established as rulers in the 1640s). The floors were covered with a large beige carpet, 30 by 35 feet and bearing the Namgyal arms, in the centre of which stood an 'exquisite . . . small, round white lacquer table, supported by three finely carved male skeletons, thirty inches high'.[10] Even in this Himalayan Buddhist atmosphere, however, British influence had deeply permeated. Life in the Palace was run 'on European lines – morning tea in bed, with breakfast, lunch and dinner as family meals in the dining room . . . Hot scones, strawberries and cream, Cheddar cheese, apple sauce and the illusion was complete.'[11]

By 1942, this curious mix of Tibetan and British influences was considered perfectly normal. During his reign Thondup's father, Sir Tashi, had developed into the perfect example of a submissive British Indian ruler, presiding over a gradual blurring of the lines between his own position and that of the British political officer. The British had maintained a constant presence in Sikkim since 1890 and increased cooperation had evolved naturally between two parties whose interests had unexpectedly converged. The British needed an acquiescent ruler in this vital part of the Himalayas; Tashi had learnt to value the protective cover and stability that the British presence provided. Successive political officers treated the Namgyals with respect and affection, while Tashi and his family in turn admired (and adopted) many elements of the British imperial system, and the lifestyle that went with it. The king's birthday was celebrated each year; the dead from the Great War were commemorated with two minutes' silence; a large hall had been built to commemorate the first British political officer in the region. Just as in other Indian Princely States, Sir Tashi was showered with honours to bring him further into the fold. In 1918, he was made a Commander of the Indian Empire; in 1923, he was elevated to a Knight Commander. On the eve of the Second World War he received the Star of India, the highest honour available in the Indian imperial honours system. Relations between the Palace and the Residency were warm, friendly and civilised. Tashi positively encouraged Thondup and his brothers and sisters to develop an understanding of the British way of life to complement their Buddhist heritage. There was an English governess; they all attended British-run boarding schools; Thondup and his sisters had even attended a college run by Jesuits in the late 1920s. 'Their parents took the view,' Gould wrote in his memoirs, 'that if they went to chapel services at school they would be all the better Buddhists.'

It was a satisfactory arrangement for all concerned and, for the British political officers, represented the very best of what could be achieved through laissez-faire rule. Each year the incumbent PO would file a short report on the progress in the kingdom. It always contained the same short paragraph. The system of governance in Sikkim, the report stated with some admiration, was 'based on the good old patriarchal monarchy of ancient days of oriental civilisation where subjects stand as children of the Ruler; and with the simple hill people unaffected by the virus of democracy and elections, the system works excellently'.[12]

For the ruling family of Sikkim, and for the political officers in Gangtok, life in Sikkim in 1942 was, as Fosco Maraini put it, 'something of a fairy tale'.

It was this 'fairy tale' kingdom to which Thondup returned from Dehradun in 1942. But underneath the surface it soon became clear that Tashi had been deeply affected by his eldest son's death. This small, thin, delicate man, who had coped so admirably with becoming Chogyal unexpectedly in 1914 when he was only 21 years old, now retreated into himself, finding comfort only in meditation and painting. By the time Maraini dined with him in the late 1940s he was 'small, thin and elderly, as delicate as a little bird and as noble as a coat of arms, draped magnificently in his brown silk Tibetan robe'. The Italian watched the Chogyal 'bend over his plate, peer through his spectacles, and follow – with notable ability, it cannot be denied – some peas which tried to escape the point of his fork'.

In this 'exquisite, microscopic struggle' lay the seeds of a sad, gradual withdrawal from public life in the last two decades of Tashi's life, during which he spent much of his time painting visions of Khangchendzonga, the mountain worshipped by the people of Sikkim.

Almost immediately on his return, therefore, Thondup took over the reins of power in Sikkim. He had matured quickly in Dehradun and now felt ready to act as head of the State Council, the unelected body that ran the affairs of the country. In 1943, when the Scottish missionary-run girls' school in Gangtok was renamed the Paljor Namgyal Girls' School (known as the PNG), it was Thondup who gave the address. 'I happened to make my speech quite well,' the 23-year-old prince wrote to his friend Rustomji. 'No boasting and long words – and did not stutter more than twice.'

In 1945, a new British Political Officer, Arthur Hopkinson, arrived in

Gangtok to replace Basil Gould. He could not help but think of the parallels between Thondup and his own King George VI. Both men had reacted with great maturity when thrust into a role they had never expected. It seemed uncanny, too, that both men were able to suppress their stammers when in front of a microphone. But it was Thondup's open and generous manner that Hopkinson admired more than anything, as he recorded in a letter home:

> The charming Maharajkumar,* in his purple Chuba, spent most of the evening playing bridge with the old folk in the bridge room – not because he didn't want to romp, but to get the bridge going and help the old people too. He is so nice, he reminds several people of our King. In a way in looks. Young & pleasant, clean and keen looking, with a charming smile. Young-minded and youthful, but intensely keen on his work. Tactful, doesn't rub up the old state servants. A slight stammer. Very intelligent face, & good features. Charming manners, & v considerate. Well groomed, always nicely dressed, and not ostentatious.[13]

All these qualities, Hopkinson felt, would assist the young prince as he tried to modernise Sikkim, something that Hopkinson noticed Thondup seemed painfully aware he needed to do. But what impressed Hopkinson most was that he seemed willing to roll his sleeves up and do something about it personally. In early 1946 he expressed his pleasure at seeing Thondup and his cousin Jigme, the heir in Bhutan, spend 'two whole days sweating in Tata's scrap-yard scrounging all the scrap iron required for road shovels etc, personally. Not many Indian "Maharaj Kumars" elsewhere would get down to it with personal sweat like that.'

-3-

Apart from Paljor's tragic death, the war had not greatly affected Sikkim. Its end, however, brought with it the prospect of great change.

The Second World War had merely postponed the inevitable British retreat from Empire. In late 1945 the new prime minister in London, Clement Attlee, confirmed via the King's Speech that the UK government

---

* This was the Indian name for the Crown Prince in common usage in Sikkim at the time.

planned 'the early realisation of full self-government in India'.[14] The words were carefully chosen. How it would happen was by no means clear. Less than half of India was directly administered by the British government; the rest of the country consisted of a patchwork of independent kingdoms, known collectively as the Princely States. These states – around 600 of them – played a vital part in Britain's imperial rule in India, but their status was a legal minefield. While each was nominally sovereign, each also accepted the principle that the British Raj rule over them was 'paramount'. In return the British provided public services on their behalf and collected taxes. It was an arrangement that generally worked well for the Princes and for the British, but everyone knew that, since no two agreements with Princely States were alike, the transition to 'full self-government' in these semi-autonomous areas would be far from simple. Thus, while India's leading politicians – Mahatma Gandhi, Jawaharlal Nehru and Mohammed Ali Jinnah – led discussions with the British about what a successor Indian government might look like, the rulers of the Princely States looked very carefully at their own arrangements in preparation for the inevitable negotiations to come.

When Sikkim had been admitted to the Indian 'Chamber of Princes' in 1935 it had been expressly recognised that Sikkim was a 'special case'. The reason noted was that, unlike any other Princely State, Sikkim was 'bounded on three sides by foreign territory and only on one side by British India'.[15] But there were other reasons that Sikkim could be considered an exception. Religiously and culturally, Sikkim was very different from the other Princely States. Across the subcontinent the Princely rulers were mostly Hindu or Muslim. Sikkim, like neighbouring Bhutan, was a Buddhist state with strong religious ties to the theocracy of Tibet and its spiritual leader, the Dalai Lama.

Most importantly of all, the historical process by which Sikkim had become part of British India had – astonishingly – left the British presence with no formal footing for being in Sikkim at all.

Sikkim had only ever been a means to an end for the British. The country had first come to the attention of the British while they were looking for allies around the fringes of Nepal during the Anglo-Gurkha war of 1814–16. They had discovered the tiny Kingdom of Sikkim, nestling conveniently between Nepal and Bhutan. The Sikkimese, who had suffered harassing raids from the Gurkhas for most of the previous century, had readily assisted the British in the hope of regaining lost territory. When the Gurkhas were defeated in 1816, the British and the Sikkimese signed the mutually convenient Titalia Treaty in 1817: the Namgyals regained the land they wanted, while the British gained political influence through asserting that they would arbitrate in the case of further disputes with the Gurkhas, which they found cause to do a number of times.

In 1835, the British had secured a permanent presence in the region by persuading the Chogyal at the time, Thondup's great-grandfather, to sign over a small ridge of Sikkimese land, Darjeeling, nominally as a sanatorium or 'hill station'. The initial deal was undoubtedly underhand (the renegade British Officer had deliberately ignored the Chogyal's request for land in exchange), but by the time the Chogyal and his advisers realised they had been misled it was too late. They lodged a formal complaint to Calcutta, who accepted in 1846 that Darjeeling had been 'acquired in a very questionable and unsatisfactory manner', but by then the town was already a thriving hub of commercial activity in the hills. For the British, it was the start of a concerted effort to open up trade through the land trading route that they had discovered lay alongside Sikkim: the Chumbi Valley.

Although his great-grandfather had been granted an annual payment in recompense, the 'Darjeeling Grant' remained a bone of contention for Thondup's ancestors and their advisers. Matters soon came to a head. The Namgyals had always relied on strong dewans, chosen from the Sikkimese nobility, to complement their own role as defenders of the Buddhist faith in Sikkim. In 1849, the so-called 'Pagla' ('Mad') Dewan kidnapped two British travellers (one of them the renowned botanist Joseph Hooker) near the Tibetan border. The kidnap caused a major panic in Darjeeling. Although the two were released within a few weeks, the British immediately sought to avenge the insult. Lord Dalhousie, the Governor-General in Calcutta, felt that his government had been put in 'a very humiliating position' with regards to 'the hill savage'. Military retaliation, however, was quickly ruled out on account of the mountainous terrain. Instead the British had settled for the banishment of the Pagla Dewan and the cessation of the annual payment to the Namgyals for Darjeeling.

For a decade, there was an uneasy peace. But in 1860 the Pagla Dewan returned, harassing the British once more. This time the British did not hold back. A force of 1,800 troops marched into Sikkim and enforced a punitive treaty in 1861, the Treaty of Tumlong, by which the British won trading rights through Sikkim. They now focused on opening up Tibet to trade. A succession of moustachioed trade commissioners made their way up to windswept 14,000-foot passes between Sikkim and the Tibetan Chumbi Valley to try and open the way for British manufactured goods. Time and again they were rebuffed: the influential Tibetan monasteries (who largely controlled trade in and out of Tibet) jealously guarded the secrecy and privacy of Tibet and did not want the British in their country. The Namgyals in Sikkim found themselves caught in the middle between the British pushing to open the Chumbi Valley, and the Tibetans seeking to keep it closed.

In 1888, the Tibetans occupied a small part of Sikkim, just across the 14,000-foot Jelep La pass on the Sikkim–Tibet frontier, to try and halt what they saw as steady encroachment by the British in the region. By now Darjeeling, not more than 30 miles from the pass, had become the centre of an extremely valuable British Indian tea industry. The British therefore decided they could not countenance such Tibetan insolence and sent a force trudging up to fight a minor war. The Tibetans were routed in what one British officer called 'a unique and rather tiresome hill war'.*

The British were now determined to consolidate their gains. Rather than negotiate with the Tibetans, they signed a convention with the Chinese government, who claimed a vague overlordship of the Tibetans. The Anglo-Chinese Convention was very significant for Sikkim. In it, the two governments effectively agreed to recognise each other's rights in, respectively, Sikkim and Tibet.† Clause Two specifically recognised the

---

* It was not a popular war with the troops; Lt Iggulden's account continues: '... unique because it took place at altitude and under climactic conditions unparalleled in the history of British frontier wars, and irksome on account of its long duration and the negative and indecisive action of the British government, due to fear of complications with China.'

† The 1890 Anglo-Chinese Convention and a subsequent 1893 Sikkim–Tibet Convention have a good claim to represent the nadir of British imperial influence. Remarkably, the negotiators for both sides were British: Henry Durand, the Government of India's Foreign Secretary, represented the British interests in India; James Hart represented the Chinese Maritime Imperial Customs service that managed the Chinese government's relations with the Treaty Ports and other frontiers. Durand and Hart agreed that the two empires they represented (Indian and Chinese) would respect the other's claims to 'suzerainty' over Sikkim and Tibet respectively.

British government's 'protectorate over the Sikkim State' and acknowledged that the British had 'direct and exclusive control over the internal administration and foreign relations of that state'. Although nothing had been signed directly between Sikkim and the British, there was now an international treaty stating that Sikkim was a British protectorate.

The convention marked a turning point in the British relationship with Sikkim. They sent a political officer to establish a Residency in Gangtok and temporarily banished the Chogyal (who had absconded to Tibet during the conflict) to live in British India. By the time the Chogyal returned in 1895, the British had set up a new administration packed with nobles to act as a counterbalance to the Namgyals.

By now the British had convinced themselves that there was another more strategic reason for establishing relations with Tibet. In the western Himalayas, the shady battle with the Russians for control of Afghanistan known as the 'Great Game' had reached something of a stalemate. But the bogey of Russian expansionism remained. Lord Curzon, appointed as Viceroy in 1899, was worried by rumours that the Russians had begun to forge relations with the Tibetan leadership in Lhasa. In response he mounted the extraordinary Younghusband Expedition, which bludgeoned its way to Lhasa, via Sikkim, in 1904.* The mission found little evidence of the supposed Russian threat, but they did manage to enforce a treaty, this time directly with the Tibetan leadership (with the Chinese as a signatory), which secured limited British influence in Lhasa.

Gangtok now became the main base for British attempts to influence Tibet and create it into a 'buffer state' to exclude Russian, and later Chinese, influence. Sikkim's importance in this respect was further emphasised after the Dalai Lama, escaping a final bid to subdue Tibet by the collapsing Chinese Empire, fled into the British political officer's arms in Gangtok in 1911. For nearly two years the Dalai Lama lived in Darjeeling, where the British carefully cultivated him; by the time he returned, he had become convinced of the value of British influence in Tibet – as a counterbalance to the Chinese.

---

* Despite Francis Younghusband's expedition being touted as a political mission, it had a military escort of 1,150 men. Younghusband was obsessed with getting to Lhasa and frequently and wilfully misinterpreted orders from London counselling restraint. In one terrible confrontation nearly 700 Tibetans were massacred with Maxim guns.

Nearly a quarter of a century had now passed since Britain had established the Residency in Gangtok. During that period the political officers had carefully brought the Namgyal family under their control. The eldest Namgyal son and heir, who had refused to return from Tibet, had been deftly sidelined by simply changing the succession; his younger brother, Sidkeong, had been educated at the best British Indian boarding school, sent for a year at Oxford in 1906 and taken on an extraordinary round-the-world tour to expand his horizons. The family were honoured at the Imperial Durbar of 1911 and officially given a 15-gun salute. In 1914, there had been a slight hiccup to the plans when Sidkeong had died after only ten months on the throne, but his replacement, Tashi, had proved equally malleable. In 1918, the British had restored full powers to him; in 1935, he had become an official member of the Indian Chamber of Princes.

During the 1920s and 1930s, no one had thought it necessary to consider the oddities of the nebulous relationship between Sikkim and the British Indian government. The British, who, as one post-independence diplomat would later put it, were 'past masters at manipulation without definition', were certainly not concerned.

But with the British announcement in 1945 that they were going to leave, Thondup realised that some sort of 'definition' was urgently needed.

-4-

In early 1946, the British sent a Cabinet Mission to Delhi to decide on the future of India after independence. Thondup immediately realised that Sikkim's membership of the Chamber of Princes might be used to argue that Sikkim should be lumped in with every other Indian Princely State. For Thondup that was anathema: Sikkim was an independent Buddhist state and, despite the administrative and political connection with the British, had little if any cultural connection with India itself. His own family were Tibetan, and Sikkim's historical links were clearly to the north, with Tibet, rather than with India.

Thondup therefore wrote to Lord Pethick-Lawrence, the 70-year-old head of the mission, asking that:

no decision directly affecting Sikkim will be taken without due consideration of the position of Sikkim as a border state and without giving the Sikkim representative an opportunity of setting forth the peculiarities of the case before the Right Honorable the Cabinet ministers and seeking their advice.

He also politely requested a meeting with Pethick-Lawrence to discuss these matters. But for the commission, sweating under the Delhi heat as they tried to reconcile opposing factions in India, the Himalayan Kingdom of Sikkim was hardly a priority. The request was equally politely rebuffed.

Unperturbed, Thondup lobbied hard that summer, joining forces with his cousin Jigme in Bhutan, who faced a similar problem. In the Residency, British Political Officer Arthur Hopkinson looked on benevolently as 'the Sikkim heir-apparent charged off to Delhi' on a regular basis. Hopkinson felt that there would be consequences if Sikkim's status was not clarified, but knew he was no longer in a position to help. 'President Nehru,' he wrote in his diary that summer, 'if he is not careful, will have the Chinese Empire within three hundred miles of Calcutta. . . the Sikkim and Bhutan people are very worried, and I am not in a position to give them any comfort.'

Thondup was determined to ensure that Sikkim's separate identity was respected. He therefore turned his efforts to Nehru and the Indian Constituent Assembly that had been given the responsibility for shaping the future of India in 1946. As a Kashmiri, Nehru had some sympathy with the position of both Sikkim and Bhutan as Himalayan states. In early 1947 he therefore pushed through a resolution agreeing that Sikkim and Bhutan were 'not Indian States' and acknowledging that, since they constituted a 'special problem', their future should be negotiated separately.

For Thondup, still only 23, this felt like a major victory – all his hard work had paid off. Not only was it now in writing that Sikkim was different from the rest of the Princely States, but also Sikkim was to be classified alongside Bhutan. Unlike Sikkim, Bhutan had signed a specific 'treaty of perpetual friendship and peace' with the British Indian government and was thus in a stronger position to assert its international identity (legally speaking) than Sikkim. If the two countries were treated as broadly similar, that could only help his cause.

In June 1947, faced with a deteriorating situation in India, the British decided to bring forward the date for the transfer of power from Britain to India. Originally planned for 1948, the Viceroy, Lord Mountbatten, decided that Britain needed to quit India by the end of August – within three months.

Across India the impact was immediate. Until that point the focus of negotiations had been on the main body of India and the question of partition or otherwise. Suddenly the unresolved question of the future of the Princely States became pressing. For Mountbatten the issue became something of a personal priority, a chance to demonstrate the Crown's ability to fulfil its promises in the face of intense criticism over their handling of the problems between India's core communities. He decided that, at the very least, he would deliver what he called 'a full basket of apples'[16] (i.e. a solution that dealt with every one of the 600-plus Princely States) by 15 August, the date now set for Independence.

During July 1947, Delhi therefore became a feverish and colourful place, as hundreds of Indian princes were ferried back and forth to open (and sometimes closed) meetings. Thondup again travelled to Delhi to state his case, and again won a reiteration from officials in the External Department that Sikkim's position was 'different from that of any other ruler'.[17]

But Sikkim was not the only outlier. Four other states made their desire for independence clear, the most important being Kashmir and Hyderabad, both huge states with proud histories. As Mountbatten began to realise that he might end up with something considerably less than the 'full basket of apples' he had promised, he looked for short-term solutions. When it came to Sikkim and Bhutan, he told Hopkinson to inform them that it would be in their best interests to accept a continuation of existing arrangements: Hopkinson should stay in Gangtok after 15 August; he would be merely 'changing masters'. This, Hopkinson was advised, would be the best guarantee of continued recognition of Sikkim's 'special position'. Hopkinson passed the message on but remarked in a private letter that he felt sympathy for Sikkim, which he thought was being 'deserted' by the British.

Nevertheless, Thondup left Delhi for Gangtok satisfied. Although nothing had actually been agreed, Sikkim's special position had been recognised, giving hope that he could maintain a Sikkim outside of India.

In Sikkim, few people took to the streets to celebrate or commemorate the handover of power to India in 1947. Gangtok was significantly closer to Lhasa than to Calcutta – let alone Delhi. In fact, the town was so removed from the world of Indian politics that it took quite some time to locate the solitary Indian flag that was in the town.[18]

There were some Sikkimese, however, who recognised the momentous shift that had taken place. One such person was 22-year-old Chandra Das Rai, who was in Darjeeling at the time of the handover and felt a great sense of excitement at this new dawn.[19] Born into a poor family in a small village near Namchi Bazaar in south of Sikkim in 1925, he had been sent to Darjeeling, paid for by a local kazi,* to be educated. As political consciousness grew in the hill town, Rai was swept up in the excitement. The hill town had become a symbol of the Raj and was an easy target for those seeking to highlight the excesses of the colonial project. In the central market the Union Jack was 'thrown down'[20] and the Indian tricolor proudly raised.

In late 1947, after witnessing the celebrations in Darjeeling, Rai set off back to his home town of Namchi Bazaar to help his comrades in Sikkim celebrate throwing off the shackles of British rule. What he found left him 'thunderstruck! There was nothing going on!' Despite being only a few miles from Darjeeling, Namchi Bazaar was almost entirely isolated from the political feelings being expressed there, so Rai moved on to the Sikkimese capital.

In Gangtok he found that a more urgent local political problem had sparked the agitation he sought. During the 1940s the antiquated system of land laws in Sikkim had come under pressure. The system was based on a simple feudal hierarchy: all land was ultimately owned by the Chogyal, who leased land to the kazis, who collected taxes and ran the estates on his behalf. At the bottom of the heap were the landless tenants, with few rights and many obligations.

---

* A Bhutia-Lepcha term for the local landowners in Sikkim.

Most of these tenants were Nepalis who had been brought in as part of a mass programme during the late nineteenth century. The British had made no bones about the purpose: at a time when relations with the Buddhist Namgyal ruling family were at a low ebb, the advent of the Nepalis had one purpose: 'Hinduism will assuredly cast out Buddhism and the praying wheel of the Lama will give place to the sacrificial implements of Brahman.'[21] They were also said to be more industrious workers. In 1873, there was reportedly not a single Nepali in Sikkim. By the 1940s they constituted 75 per cent of the population, outnumbering the Bhutias (those who had come to Sikkim with the Namgyals) and the Lepchas (who were considered to be close to 'indigenous' in Sikkim), who together constituted the ruling minority.

Thondup had inched towards a process of reform of the land laws,[22] but the basics of a feudal system remained.* In 1946–7, while Thondup had been darting back and forth to Delhi, the discontent had boiled over with a wide-scale 'no-rent' campaign involving the mostly Nepali tenant population of southern Sikkim. The kazis, many of whom in the south-west of Sikkim were Lepchas, came under intense pressure and were unable to perform their basic duties as tax collectors, provoking a minor crisis in finances in the country.

When Rai arrived in December 1947, therefore, he found a number of nascent political movements coalescing around the no-rent campaign. It was hardly an insurrection, but Rai was pleased to find that some of the leaders thought that the 'good old patriarchal monarchy of ancient days of oriental civilization' that the British had so consciously supported should be replaced with a system more akin to a democracy. A small group approached the British Political Officer, Arthur Hopkinson (who had 'stayed on' as directed, and was still regarded as holding sway), in the hope that he might support their call for change. But Hopkinson disappointed them: for years the British had upheld Sikkim's autocratic government, run by a small cabinet responsible only to the Chogyal, with not even a nod to the 'virus of democracy'. With no wish to upset what he saw as a perfectly

---

* One obligation that was nominally curtailed in 1945 was the despised *jharlangi*. This obliged locals to provide free porterage for Sikkim government or British officials on tour.

good system, Hopkinson steered well clear of an awkward situation.* The small group turned their attention to the palace, organising a picnic gathering in Gangtok on the hillside near the top of the ridge, which quickly turned into a minor political rally. Rai wasted no time in getting involved. Someone read out a small tract entitled 'A few facts about Sikkim', which questioned the legitimacy of the current system of government. Rai, as one of the few educated Nepalis present, was asked to translate it into Nepali. He clambered onto a table and read it out. The very act of translation was political, bringing the disenfranchised ordinary Nepalis into the political arena in a way that had previously been unthinkable.

Thondup was astute enough to come out and meet the protestors, promising to consider reform. It was enough to break up the small meeting. But a flame had been ignited. In the days following the picnic, a political party took shape: the Sikkim State Congress (SSC) emerged, designed to be more representative of the real ethnic make-up of Sikkim – Nepalis, Bhutias and Lepchas. A new, more pointed memo was sent to the Palace with three more specific demands: first that 'landlordism' should be abolished; second that a 'responsible government' should be formed as a precursor to democracy; and third that Sikkim should agree to accede to India.

For 24-year-old Thondup the demands posed an irritating challenge. He could accept the first demand: he knew that the land laws needed to change, but he also knew that the problem was deeply ingrained and could not be addressed overnight.

As for the second demand, he was willing to consider change, but he also had grave concerns. For decades the ethnic make-up of Sikkim had been altered with the wide-scale immigration from Nepal. Any move towards more representative government would give the Nepalis more power. Thondup was deeply concerned by the obvious implication – that

---

* Fosco Maraini recalls a conversation with Hopkinson around this time, which brilliantly captures the mentality of the British withdrawal. In reply to an enquiry as to what he might do next, Hopkinson replied: 'My dear fellow, these are difficult times for us all. Now they are dismantling the British Empire, and I shall have to look for a job, what can one do when one is nearly half a century old and has spent the best years of one's life among official documents? I know several Indian languages, and I know Tibetan, but is that of any use? Do you think you could find me a job teaching in Italy, for instance? Just look at what we are reduced to, after being lords of half the earth! Apart from that I feel old already. You see India is a great lady, but she sucks the life out of you.'

his Buddhist community might lose its strong connection with the land in the face of the growing Nepali, and largely Hindu, population. Conferring with Hopkinson, the Namgyals came up with a clever compromise that seemed to promise much but in reality changed little. The Palace suggested that the new political party should send three representatives, one from each community – the Bhutias, Lepchas and Nepalis – to function as official 'secretaries' to the Chogyal. It was a shrewd move by Thondup and his father, calculated to ensure that the Nepalis (who were now more than 50 per cent of the population) remained in minority representation and that truly representative government was parked as an issue. It seemed to be enough to satisfy those who sought change – for now.

It was the third demand, however – that Sikkim should join India – that Thondup found most frustrating. He was certain that such a move was incompatible with Sikkim maintaining its identity separate from India. For Sikkimese Nepalis like Rai on the other hand, the demand made perfect sense: many were Hindus and did not feel the same sense of religious and cultural separation from India. Moreover, if accession to India would bring economic benefits – and increase the likelihood of political reform and more representative government – then most of the new members of the SSC believed this was in Sikkim's interest.

For Thondup, it was quite different. Over the last five years he had become utterly convinced that he was laying the foundations for a strong Sikkim, and that its best chance of success lay in gradual political reform within the current monarchical system.

In the event, the issue was conveniently postponed. With the blood flowing from the tragedy of Partition, the Indian government was quite willing to put off engaging with the complexities of the issue of Sikkim's future. On 27 February 1948, the governments of India and Sikkim signed a standstill agreement stating that existing arrangements would continue 'pending the conclusion of a new agreement or treaty' in due course.

None of the three issues raised by the SSC had actually been addressed, but, with the appointment of the three secretaries, the Palace had effectively bought off the leaders of the campaign for reform. Many in the SSC, including Rai, realised that the new set-up was nothing more than a sop and grew frustrated and distrustful of the situation. They were even more concerned by the emergence of what looked like a

Palace-sponsored political party, the National Party, the leaders of which wasted no time in issuing a declaration that 'Sikkim shall not under any circumstances accede to the dominion of India.' A further statement that the party intended by all means available to them 'to maintain intact the indigenous character of Sikkim and to preserve its integrity' was seen by some in the SSC as a thinly veiled anti-Nepali-immigrant platform. As a result, the SSC were able to attract sizeable crowds to a rally in the southern Sikkimese town of Namchi Bazaar in October.

In December, representatives from the SSC decided to approach Nehru himself (now undisputed head of the Indian polity following the assassination of Gandhi) to maintain some momentum. Three young politicians, including Rai, travelled to Delhi to meet with Nehru and present him with the same three demands.

Nehru received the three petitioners personally. He quickly brushed aside 'landlordism' as irrelevant: he was, he said, in the process of dealing with much larger landlords; there was no need to worry – as British influence receded so the influence of unscrupulous Sikkimese landlords would gently fade away. As for 'responsible government', he told the three men that he had been fighting for it his whole life and would happily continue doing so on Sikkim's behalf. But it was on the demand for accession to India that Nehru's response was unexpected. He told them not to push for accession to India. If accession was rushed through, Nehru said, 'we will be accused by international opinion that a small state like Sikkim has been coerced to join India. Sikkim, Bhutan and Nepal should all grow according to their own genius.' The three men, somewhat overawed by being in Nehru's presence at all, thanked him profusely and headed back to Gangtok none the wiser. Nehru had once more postponed any decisions on Sikkim's future.

Back in Sikkim the situation deteriorated in early 1949. Further demonstrations broke out in the south, leading to the temporary arrest of Rai and others, piling the pressure on Thondup and his three hapless secretaries. Thondup, aware of the mission to Delhi, was suspicious about the disturbances. Hopkinson had by now been replaced by a new Indian political officer, Harishwar Dayal; Thondup wondered if Dayal had a hidden agenda to promote political change that would threaten his own position. In April 1949 he wrote to his friend Nari Rustomji, now an adviser to the government in nearby Assam, another equally troubled north-eastern state, revealing his frustrations:

> I am in a hell of a spot as you may have learnt from your intelligence people. Sikkim is not what she used to be. These damn exploiters are raising hell. I am all for fulfilling the wishes of our Bhutia-Lepchas, the real wishes. But I will sooner be damned than let these mean conspirators and job-hunters have their way if I can. We are on the verge of getting independence of sorts like Bhutan and I think we have achieved a miracle in not having had to accede. Our greatest drawback is that the PO and the GoI seem to favour the other side, and we have to proceed so that we give you people no chance to butt in. The second trouble which I feel is common is the unruly Nepalese element against whom I cannot take action like I would like to have.[23]

On 1 May the SSC organised a demonstration outside the palace. This time, far from the banal picnic of 18 months earlier, 5,000 agitators moved on the Palace. Thondup sensed real trouble. Running out of options, he approached the Indian Political Officer, Harishwar Dayal, for protection. Two companies of Indian Army soldiers in the state were able to disperse the troublemakers, but now the balance had tilted. Dayal advised Thondup to declare a new form of government. Thondup hurriedly agreed to a new arrangement – three SSC members and two appointees from the Palace would form a small ministry with a degree of independence from the Palace itself – hoping that it would bring some measure of calm to the state.

This 'popular ministry', set up on 9 May 1948, was a disaster. None of the members trusted each other. Meanwhile some in the SSC continued their agitation. Within days the divisions between the factions were severe enough to concern the Indian government, who had one eye on a tense regional situation. In West Bengal to Sikkim's south, the political situation was so dire that the state government had taken the extreme step of banning the communist party. To Sikkim's west, the Indians were also worried about the emergence of communism in Nepal. An official in the Indian government told a British official that they were 'classing Sikkim with Nepal as an area of communist activity'. Worst of all, the situation in Tibet, to Sikkim's north, was also unclear; with the Chinese communists all but victorious in the mainland, no one knew what might happen next.

The Indian government decided it could take no chances. In late May they sent the External Affairs Minister to visit the state and make an assessment. At the beginning of June, Dayal dismissed the government that had been formed only a few weeks earlier. It had lasted 28 days. Instead, Dayal announced, an Indian dewan, or prime minister, in Sikkim was to be appointed as a 'temporary' solution, pending a full-blown treaty between India and Sikkim. Thondup and his father were persuaded that this was the only way to guarantee stability – and the survival of the existing order. But for the young Crown Prince the whole episode smacked of underhand tactics. The Palace had requested assistance from the Indians to restore order in Gangtok. Instead they now had an Indian-appointed prime minister at the heart of the state. Thondup was convinced that the Indian political officer was working alongside the politicians in a bid to challenge Sikkim's separate identity from India. The official press organ in Sikkim, with Thondup's knowledge, put out an angry piece, emphasising what they called India's 'fascist policy'. Meanwhile the leaders of the SSC were equally suspicious of Dayal and the Indian actions but for different reasons – they were convinced that Dayal and Thondup were in cahoots, and that the new government had been dismissed in order to bolster the Namgyal family's position.

In London, the Foreign Office (which now had sole responsibility for policy towards India, Sikkim and Tibet) found it hard to keep up with events. At first they presumed that the Indian deployment in Sikkim meant that the state had been 'persuaded' to accede to the Indian Union; it was hard not to think of the forced accession of Hyderabad the previous year. In June, one baffled British diplomat wrote disdainfully of the Indian action:

> It would now appear that Sikkim has *not* acceded to the Indian Union. If this is so, the action of the Government of India is a considerable extension of the theory of intervention which they have been developing during the past two years in relation to acceding states.

One thing was for certain: the British government no longer had the right nor the inclination to intervene.

Meanwhile the question of Sikkim's real constitutional status remained as elusive as ever.

CHAPTER TWO

Under the Shadow of Tibet

1949–59

-1-

The events in Sikkim in 1949 had not taken place in a vacuum. The rapidly developing regional situation in Tibet – and elsewhere in Asia – had been a major factor behind India's firm actions. Over the next decade, the situation in Tibet would cast a long shadow over events in Sikkim.

Tibet posed a headache for India's diplomats. For more than 30 years, Britain had supported the 'de facto' independence of Tibet, believing it acted as a 'buffer', protecting the British Empire's possessions in India. From their base in Gangtok, British political officers had maintained close relations with elements within the Tibetan leadership. During the 1920s they had funded and trained a Tibetan army who paraded in uniforms based on British designs. In 1936 they even managed to establish a permanent 'Residency' in the Tibetan capital of Lhasa. It was, at its heart, a policy of realpolitik designed to keep the Chinese at arms length from British Indian possessions. As such, it had worked.

When the new Indian government took over in 1947, the question of how to deal with Tibet created significant divisions in the cabinet. Sardar Patel, the hawkish Indian Home Affairs Minster, felt strongly that Tibet was a vital buffer against the Chinese. It was imperative that India continue to support the idea of autonomy for Tibet. Nehru held a quite different view. His vision was for a pan-Asia federation, with China and India as close partners in a post-imperial world. The Indian presence in

Tibet was a hangover of British imperial policy; he saw no reason to make a firm commitment to Tibet's autonomy, something that he knew would cause unnecessary tensions with the Chinese. During 1947–9, as the Chinese civil war between Chiang Kai-shek's nationalists and Chairman Mao's communists had played out, it had not been clear which of the Indian views would prevail.

The Tibetan leadership, aware that they could not rely on Indian support, sent a trade mission trooping through Britain and the USA during 1948 and 1949 in an attempt to gain support for their independent status and forge relations with the major trading nations.[1] In London they found the British government alarmingly disengaged, unwilling to take any position on its former imperial obligations.

The response in Washington was slightly more positive. A new administration, determined to back the concept of self-determination, expressed mild support for the Tibetan cause. This support strengthened when, in October 1949, only months after the Indian intervention in Sikkim, Mao's communists declared victory over the nationalists, announcing the formation of the People's Republic of China. The US administration was determined to combat the growing threat of global communism: it did not take long for the State Department to identify Tibet as a potential front for 'checking Chi Commie advances'.[2]

The issue assumed greater urgency when, on 1 January 1950, Radio Peking announced 'the tasks for the People's Liberation Army for 1950 are to liberate Taiwan, Hainan and Tibet'. Within weeks, units of the People's Liberation Army started to move rapidly across the mountainous terrain of western China's Sichuan Province towards the Tibetan border.[3] The Indian action to assert some control in Sikkim six months earlier suddenly looked very prescient.

In Gangtok, Sikkim, Crown Prince Thondup had watched events unfold in Tibet during 1950 with some concern. Sikkim's royal family shared more than a belief in Buddhism with their northern neighbour; they considered the Tibetan nobility as their kin. Familial ties with Tibet had been strengthened in the 1940s by his sister Coocoola's marriage to the governor of Gyantse, son of one of the four ministers of Tibet. Thondup himself was also about to get married – he wrote to Rustomji that 'my parents have at last caught up with me and they have made me agree to marriage . . .' The bride chosen for him – a beautiful Tibetan girl, Sangey Deki – was from an important Tibetan family. He already had two children through a Lepcha mistress,[4] but at 27, marriage, his father felt, would confer responsibility on the Crown Prince.

During 1950 Thondup knew that his focus had to remain on the survival of Sikkim itself. In August 1949, John Lall, a tall Indian ICS officer with a clipped British accent, had been appointed as the new Indian dewan. Lall had set about his task with an alarming gusto, 'inspired by a sense of mission to clean the Augean stables'[5] of Sikkim. He immediately stripped the landowning kazis of their feudal rights, from tax collection to judicial privileges, and set about a rapid modernisation of the state, reshaping Sikkim 'along the lines of an Indian state or district'.[6] 'Everything and everybody existed, or so it appeared, on the sufferance of the Dewan Omnipotent,' wrote one observer.[7]

Faced with such an onslaught, Thondup headed down to Delhi in early 1950 determined to clarify Sikkim's nebulous status with the Nehru administration. Sikkim was now the only one of the three Himalayan states whose status was still under review. There was no question that Nepal would remain independent; meanwhile Bhutan's treaty of the previous year had guaranteed the country internal autonomy and conceded only that India should 'guide' its foreign affairs. But, with the Chinese assertion of its rights in Tibet highlighting the pressures on India's northern border, Sikkim's negotiating position was significantly weaker. Nevertheless, Thondup recalled, the appointment of an Indian dewan had been only temporary. He hoped he could achieve a status analogous to Bhutan.

Despite the actions of the previous year, Nehru's government was still divided about how to deal with the Sikkim issue. Sardar Patel, Minister of Home Affairs, was highly sensitive to the threat posed by the new Chinese government to the north and advocated a clear assertion of Indian control in Sikkim. On the other side stood Nehru with his Himalayan bias, still fixated on the idea of a new Asia rising out of the ashes of colonialism, a 'Third Way' encompassing shades of different opinion under one pan-Asia umbrella. Why, Nehru asked Patel, was there any need to change the status of Sikkim, particularly now that Thondup had sanctioned an Indian dewan to assist with Sikkim's administration? Sikkim could continue to flourish as a buffer state alongside Bhutan, with a similar status to that which they'd both had before 1947, he argued. As Thondup left Delhi, he declared in a letter to his friend Rustomji that he was confident 'there is going to be a Sikkim on the map and outside the grip of Sardar Patel'.[8]

But events to the north of Sikkim were moving fast.

In March, as Chinese communist troops headed towards Tibet, the Tibetans turned to their nearest neighbours, the new Indian government, for support. The British had regularly supplied arms to the Tibetans; they hoped the Indians would maintain the commitment. They made a request for 38 two-inch mortars with 14,000 bombs, 63 three-inch mortars with 14,00 bombs, 150 Bren guns, and a million rounds of rifle ammunition – enough for a single brigade. But India refused – Nehru, an ardent anti-imperialist, did not want to be seen as siding with the USA and the UK against China. He was also still convinced that an accommodation with Mao and the Chinese communists was possible.

But the picture across Asia was changing rapidly. The invasion of the south of Korea in June 1950 was a further sign of the new confrontational geopolitics in the region. With Chiang Kai-shek's nationalists now also established in Taiwan, it looked like a new Asian dimension to the emerging Cold War could be opening up, with the potential for multiple fronts to the east and west of China.

When a large earthquake struck Eastern Tibet in August, the Tibetans had no doubt that it was a deadly omen, compounding the appearance of a comet streaking across the sky the previous year. There were still those old enough to remember that a similar comet had been seen in 1910 just before the Chinese invasion that had led to the 13th Dalai Lama's flight from Tibet into Sikkim and into the arms of Charles Bell, the British Political Officer in Gangtok.*

On 7 October 1950 all the prophecies came true, as Chinese troops once more marched into Tibet. There were pockets of resistance, but the training and weaponry on the Chinese side gave them an overwhelming advantage. The result was a foregone conclusion: the Chinese were now back in Lhasa, and in broad control of Tibet.

---

* The 13th Dalai Lama subsequently spent more than a year in exile in Darjeeling, during which time Bell carefully developed the British government's relations with Tibet.

The Tibetan leadership refused to give up hope. In November, they made an appeal to the newly formed United Nations to restrain the Chinese aggression, but few countries were willing to stand up for Tibet. It fell to the tiny nation of El Salvador to demand a debate in the UN. The British representative at the UN, Sir Gladwyn Jebb, summed up the evasive British position: 'Politically, I have no doubt at all that what we want to do is to create a situation which does not oblige us in practice to do anything about the Communist invasion of Tibet.'[9] In Delhi, Nehru was not willing to do anything for the Tibetans either. The government in Washington, knee deep in the quagmire of the Korean War, also held their counsel – for the time being. Urgent telegrams from the Dalai Lama and his Kashag to all three governments went unanswered. The lack of response from the British was especially galling. The Dalai Lama recalled later in *My Land and My People*:

The replies to these telegrams were particularly disheartening. The British Government expressed their deepest sympathy for the people of Tibet and regretted that owing to Tibet's geographical position, since India had been granted independence, they could not offer help. The Government of the United States also replied in the same sense, and declined to receive our delegation. The Indian Government also made it clear that they would not give us military help, and advised us not to offer any armed resistance, but to open negotiations to a peaceful settlement on the basis of the Simla Agreement of 1914. So we learned that, in military matters, we were alone.

Meanwhile, the Chinese troop presence in Lhasa was growing daily. On 15 November the Dalai Lama, still only 15 years old, was declared temporal ruler of Tibet in an effort to bolster the spirits in the capital. But as December passed it became clear that, for his own safety, the Dalai Lama would have to leave Lhasa. At 2 a.m. in the morning on 19 December he fled the capital, heading down the Chumbi Valley with a substantial escort of his personal bodyguard.

Four decades earlier the 13th Dalai Lama had used the same route to escape Chinese troops. He had spent three years in exile in Darjeeling before the collapse of the Chinese Empire had allowed him to return.

Now, the 14th Dalai Lama, too, had to consider the prospect of exile in the face of a new Chinese army. But he was not ready to leave Tibet altogether. At Yatung, just short of the Sikkimese border, the party halted. The treasury, considered too valuable to leave within the grasp of the Chinese, was sent on across the Nathu La for safekeeping in Sikkim. It would remain there until 1959.[10]

The Dalai Lama and his advisers considered their next move.

-2-

On 14 December 1950, five days before the Dalai Lama fled Lhasa, Thondup's father, Sir Tashi, finally signed a new treaty formalising the arrangements between India and Sikkim. Given the worsening situation in Tibet, no one was under any illusions about the strategic rationale behind the terms. Sikkim's status as a protectorate of India was confirmed; Sikkim would 'enjoy autonomy in regard to its internal affairs' while the government of India would remain 'responsible for the defence and territorial integrity of Sikkim', with the right to station troops there too. The government of Sikkim was to have 'no dealings with any foreign power'.

Behind the scenes, however, the two signatories and other interested parties walked away with very different views on what the treaty meant for the future. The Government of India's External Affairs ministry was confident it had asserted its protectorate over Sikkim. Some in the Indian cabinet thought of it merely as an 'extended lease of life'. Sikkim's politicians, in the Sikkim State Congress, told their supporters that the 'demand to accede to India has in principle been accepted'.

Thondup viewed it entirely differently. He felt that he had successfully avoided being swallowed up by India and asserted Sikkim's distinct personality: it was not quite as good as Bhutan had achieved, but he felt that the very fact he had concluded a treaty meant that Sikkim's separate identity from the new Indian Republic had been recognised. However, he was conscious that something significant had changed. Writing to Rustomji in January 1951, he said:

Sikkim is still pulling on, but the good old happy days are gone. Although we have been able to save ourselves from merger etc., at present we are being led by the nose by the Indian Govt.

As the new arrangements bedded down, everyone recognised that the question of how Sikkim's government was going to be chosen was critical. For Thondup, the major unresolved issue remained how to protect the Buddhist heritage of his country and the interests of his own Bhutia-Lepcha community in the face of the majority Nepali population. He asked his friend and unofficial adviser, Nari Rustomji, for advice. Rustomji was wrestling with some of the same questions in Assam, so Thondup asked how the Assamese state differentiated between 'Assamese, Tribal and non-Assamese' and how 'domicile' was defined in regard to land acquisition. Rustomji, unwilling to become involved in this highly contentious issue, advised him to discuss the issue with Lall.

Lall recognised the depth of Thondup's concerns but had to perform a delicate balancing act. He knew that he had to ensure that the Nepali community also felt they had gained something. The compromise he devised was a convoluted system called the 'parity formula'. The Bhutia-Lepcha community (by now only 25 per cent of the population) was to have at least 50 per cent of the seats in elections reserved for them. The other 50 per cent of seats was reserved for the Nepali community (roughly 75 per cent of the electorate). For the Nepalis, it was an advance from the 33 per cent representation that they had been given under the earlier 'three secretaries' system, but it came nowhere near the fully representative government that the Nepali-dominated SSC were campaigning for. No one was entirely satisfied, but all parties agreed to work within the proposed new system. Reluctant compromises and half-hearted moves towards representative government would continue to plague communal relations throughout the next three decades.

From his desk in Gangtok, Thondup and his family wondered if he had won a hollow victory. 'Here in Sikkim things are not so good,' he wrote to Rustomji, 'and the Government of India is pretending that we rule while they rule through a Dewan.'[11]

But the Namgyal family would soon have other matters on their minds. They were about to get directly involved in the Tibetan struggle for survival.

Less than 30 miles away in Yatung, just over the Tibetan border, the Dalai Lama was approaching his 16th birthday. He was many miles from his capital Lhasa; his advisers told him that there was no realistic prospect of a return while Chinese troops remained in the city. Naturally, he continued to explore his options, including whether it would make more sense to head south to friendly Sikkim, to Bhutan or even to Kalimpong in northern India than to return to the Tibetan capital.

Meanwhile a new Tibetan delegation had arrived in Beijing to try and open negotiations directly with Chairman Mao. The man heading this delegation, Ngabo Ngawang Jigme, was more willing to consider the possibility of cooperation with the Chinese. In May 1951 news reached Yatung that Ngabo had been persuaded that it was in Tibet's interests to sign a new 17-Point Agreement, a document that essentially legitimised the Chinese occupation of Tibet, affixed with the seals of the Tibetan government (which many believe must have been forged).

The Dalai Lama and his entourage were astounded when they heard the Chinese broadcast reporting the agreement as the 'return of the Tibetan people to the big family of the Motherland – the People's Republic of China'.[12] They had not expected anything of the sort. As winter ended, the Dalai Lama cast around for signs of hope. One potential source of assistance lay in two telegrams that had arrived in Yatung during the spring. They were from the American Ambassador in Delhi, Loy Henderson. Henderson, a forthright man who was deeply distrustful of communism, had been watching the developing situation carefully. In his dialogue with Washington, he was now finding a consistently sympathetic ear when he raised the Tibetan issue. The increasingly fraught war in Korea had already highlighted the Asian dimension to the Cold War; Henderson urged Washington to see Mao's expansion westwards into Lhasa in the same light. Tibet was becoming a potential front in the proxy war against the Chinese, he told them, who in turn could now be viewed as an extension of the Soviet threat. It was as if Henderson had just put a Cold War gloss on the old Great Game that the British had played, this time seeing the necessity of holding back the encroaching Communist (Soviet) threat in the guise of the Chinese.

In May, when the news of the 17-Point Agreement legitimising the Chinese presence in Tibet reached him, Henderson took the bold decision to send a young CIA officer, Larry Dalley, to Kalimpong. The hill town was only a few miles from where the Dalai Lama was in Yatung. Dalley was told to make contact with the rebel Tibetan leaders who were gathering there and assess the situation. Meanwhile Henderson concocted an extraordinary plan to get the Dalai Lama out of Yatung and across the border: the explorer Heinrich Harrer (of *Seven Years in Tibet* fame) and a young Scottish adventurer, George Patterson, were to meet the Dalai Lama on the border and escort him into Bhutan initially, before whisking him to safety.[13]

But in Yatung the Dalai Lama was still not convinced that it was right to leave Tibet. The monks of the powerful major monasteries urged him to stay and to return to Lhasa. His presence was needed, they told him, to maintain morale in the rapidly changing situation. The Dalai Lama, still only 16, consulted the Tibetan Oracle. The answer was clear: he must stay in Tibet with his people. In late July he set off with a 900-mule caravan for Lhasa, arriving back in the capital on 17 August 1951. Henderson's bizarre exfiltration plan was scrapped.

On his arrival back in Lhasa, the Dalai Lama found a city changed irrevocably since his flight eight months earlier. The head of the Chinese delegation in the city was now an uncompromising party acolyte, Zhang Jingwu, who was of the opinion that, after Tibet, it was only a matter of time before Nepal, Sikkim and Bhutan were 'liberated'. He ordered the people of Lhasa to celebrate the Dalai Lama's return as a victory for common sense. Meanwhile he made a calculated effort to win over the Lhasa elite, enticing them with offers of roles in the corrupt Chinese administration. To win over the ordinary people, he set up free medical treatment and a bank, and offered free cinema shows; in November he ran a series of lavish parties to celebrate the invasion of the previous year.[14] All this was done with 'an ample supply of silver dollars', which, according to the Indian political officer, they 'squandered with the liberality of princes and the sleek abandon of rakes.'[15]

The Dalai Lama and the Tibetan leadership had little choice but to try and make the best of a difficult situation. Tibet's occupation was rapidly becoming a fait accompli, and there was little sign of outside support from either Britain or India. With Nehru focused on problems nearer to home (and persisting with his vision of a world where the giants of Asia worked together) and the UK government focused on an orderly withdrawal from its other imperial possessions, the Chinese occupation of Tibet did not merit much attention.

In America, however, interest in Tibet as a front in the Cold War, albeit a minor one, was now picking up in the offices of the CIA. Larry Dalley, the young officer who Henderson had sent to Kalimpong during the Dalai Lama's sojourn in Yatung, was based in the USA's Calcutta consulate. He had been tasked with collecting what intelligence he could on the events taking place in Tibet and the Chumbi Valley.[16] Dalley advised his superiors in the Calcutta consulate that there was one family that was superbly placed to help them understand the situation: the Namgyals, the rulers of Sikkim.

Dalley added that Sikkim's location, abutting the Tibetan Chumbi Valley to the east and with a mountainous border in the north, leading straight onto the main Tibetan plateau, was ideal for intelligence purposes. What was more, the Namgyals' ancient links with Tibet meant they could travel there freely. Best of all, Dalley reported, Thondup had two astonishingly beautiful sisters who were frequent visitors to Calcutta, where the US consulate was situated.

Thondup's two younger sisters could not have been more ideal as targets. By the early 1950s, they were both in their late twenties, and both married to high-ranking Tibetan officials. Their given names were Pema Tseuden and Pema Choki, but they were better known by the nicknames given them by an English governess employed in the Gangtok palace. She had found the Sikkimese words too much of a mouthful; instead, she gave them names that would stick for the rest of their lives: Coocoola and Kula.

Coocoola, the elder by 15 months, had already encountered the Americans as a teenager. In 1941 she had travelled up the Chumbi Valley to be married to a Tibetan nobleman. Thus she was in Lhasa in late 1942 when the OSS (the American intelligence service in the Second World War) sent two officers, Ilya Tolstoy and Brooke Dolan, on an extraordinary mission into Tibet to understand the lay of the land. The two men, preparing to present a gift from Roosevelt to the Dalai Lama, had realised they only had a plain box when they spotted the beautiful princess nearby. 'I came forward,' Coocoola later recalled, 'and donated the bright red ribbon in my hair.'

Few were able to resist Coocoola's beauty. Several years later, when the explorer Heinrich Harrer spent seven years in Lhasa, he found he could not stop himself gazing at her endlessly at social functions.

When I look back on the affection we had for each other it is the Tibetan words that most readily come to mind to describe my feelings. To fall in love is 'sem schor wa' and means 'to lose one's soul'; to describe a woman as one's darling the term 'Nying Dung' is used, which translates as 'to strike the heart'. In the case of Coocoola, both were accurate. She was very different to the other Tibetan girls. She had a delightfully attractive face and a lovely slim figure that was not hidden by several layers of thick clothing in traditional Tibetan style, but draped in close-fitting garments of colourful silk.[17]

Harrer was hidebound by her marriage ('any liaison remained unthinkable'), but in 1952 he had no hesitation in describing her as the most beautiful woman in the world, 'the stunning urbane archetype of a Himalayan princess'.[18]

Her younger sister Kula was hardly less striking. Fosco Maraini, the Italian traveller and author of *Secret Tibet*, fell in love with her 'delightfully frivolous' attitude while passing through Gangtok on the way to Lhasa. She wore 'elegant black leather French sandals, and her fingernails were painted red', he wrote. 'She knows about the west from books, but has never been outside Asia. At school she learned English stories and poems by heart (she went to school in Kalimpong) and now reads *Life*, *Vogue* and the *Reader's Digest*. She confused Colbert with Flaubert and Aristotle with Mephistopheles.' On a skiing trip up to the Nathu La, he watched with amazement as she transformed into a hardy, strong climber. 'Who would have suspected,' he wrote, 'there was so much strength and determination in her pearl and porcelain body?'[19]

The two sisters backed up their rare combination of beauty and toughness with a kindhearted nature that melted many European hearts.

It would become their trademark. When Maraini reached the first bungalow in Sikkim after the long trek down the Chumbi Valley, he

> found a letter from Pema Choki waiting for me with a basket of fruit; and a gramophone with several records of good music. What a delight! Who else would have thought of such a charming welcome? While I rested I listened to Brahms, Mozart, Scarlatti. It was like bathing in a fresh river after a long period of sweat and fatigue.[20]

By the summer of 1951 both sisters had gravitated into the CIA's orbit. Soon they were couriering notes destined for the Dalai Lama. A succession of CIA officers made themselves available for the 'discreet courtship' of the two sisters, arranging fortuitous meetings at the horse races in Calcutta and Darjeeling and accompanying them on trips into the high passes of Sikkim.

It was Coocoola, the elder sister, who became the more frequent of Dalley's contacts. She was deeply passionate about the Tibetan cause, even more so than her brother. She would become known later for her ability to both host and enjoy parties, with the best French wines being served in heavy decanters. But her position, her beauty and her love of the good life belied an adventurous and thrill-seeking nature. When travelling the trade route between Gyantse in Tibet and Gangtok, she always insisted on riding with a rifle slung across her shoulder and a revolver in her pocket to repel bandits.[21]

In 1951, during an early contact with Dalley in Calcutta, she brought down a Lee Enfield bullet as a demonstration of the old British ammunition that the Tibetans would need if they were to resist the Chinese occupation, along with a tin of the sweet tinned fruit in syrup that was favoured by Tibet's monasteries. Could, she wondered, a way be found to use the fruit tins to smuggle ammunition into the country? Dalley went as far as to bag up a tin and send it through the diplomatic channel to Washington; sadly, the ingenious scheme never saw the light of day. She was equally bold in her attempts to put pressure on the Americans to give their full support to Tibet's cause. After a visit to Lhasa in 1952, she brought an oral message from the Dalai Lama about the increasing food shortages in the city; he was hopeful, she said with a stern voice to her CIA contact, that when the time came the 'United States would give material aid and moral support'.

Thondup and the sisters were reportedly never on the payroll of the CIA. Thondup in particular was 'not the kind of person comfortable in dark alleys'.[22] But they were (according to John Turner, one of the Calcutta CIA officers involved) highly adept at offering 'tidbits of intelligence to try and influence US policy'.[23] Not surprisingly their activity came to the attention of the intelligence services of the newly independent India. B. N. Mullik, the new head, went so far as to visit Darjeeling in 1953 to assess just how deeply the Americans were involving themselves with the Namgyals and the region. Mullik had a difficult job: under the British, external intelligence had been run from London, meaning that the only intelligence infrastructure and experience in India in 1947 was internally focused. But Mullik was highly perceptive. He saw what others perhaps did not: with the Chinese establishing themselves in Tibet, Sikkim was rapidly becoming an international frontier-state between India and China. It was hardly a surprise, he said, that the small mountain kingdom had become a focal point for the Americans based in Delhi.

-4-

In Gangtok, Thondup's frustrations with the new power arrangements in Sikkim continued. The convoluted voting system designed to appease the Nepalis was bad enough, but things were even worse when it came to the day-to-day administration of Sikkim.

The theory was simple enough: under the 1950 treaty, defence, external affairs and communications were the responsibility of the Indian government; everything else was run internally from Gangtok. The Durbar (parliament) was headed by an Indian-appointed dewan. Thondup, as head of state (he was now to all intents and purposes the Chogyal, given his father's withdrawal from society), retained control over the police and finance; certain other areas – education, health, forests, for example – were 'transferred' to be dealt with by elected officials and the civil servants.

In practice, however, the system was labyrinthine in complexity. The Dewan, John Lall, on loan from India, had a house that was judiciously placed on the road between the old Residency on the hillside – where the Indian-appointed political officer was now based – and the Palace on the promontory. From the start, it was ambiguous whether Lall was an Indian official 'deputed' to Sikkim (and therefore reporting to the Indian political officer) or a Sikkimese official 'borrowed' from India, and therefore Thondup's man. Lall had no doubts: he felt his ultimate loyalties lay squarely with the Indian political officer and with New Delhi. This naturally irked Thondup, who wondered what powers he was actually left with; he 'bitterly resented even the hint of any suggestion, albeit unintended, that ultimate authority derived not from the ruler but from the Government of India through the Indian-loaned Dewan'.[24]

Lall also decided early on that, as there were no qualified administrators in Sikkim, Indians should be drafted in as an 'interim' measure. Not surprisingly these Indian officers formed their own little colony, huddling together against the cold weather and keeping themselves to themselves. Worse, they were paid higher salaries than the Sikkimese, 'as compensation for insecurity of service, and also to provide an incentive to them to uproot themselves from their existing billets to take up work in a remote country on an uncertain frontier'.[25] Thondup felt that his country was now being run by outsiders. His relations with the new Political Officer, Balraj Kapur, were also poor. The political officer, Thondup noted, was now viewed by the Sikkimese politicians as a supportive arbiter in the event of reaching an impasse with the Palace. It was a far cry from the days of the British, when he had thought of Sir Basil Gould as a 'friend, philosopher and guide'.

Thondup clung onto whatever he could to keep his idea of Sikkim alive. One source of support came right from the top – in the form of Pandit Nehru. In 1953 the Indian prime minister, who harboured an abiding love for the Himalayan states, and in particular for Sikkim, visited Gangtok with his daughter, who was already involved in politics, working tirelessly for her father and her husband, Feroze Gandhi, on behalf of the Congress Party. Despite his day-to-day troubles, Thondup showed off his country with considerable pride. It was the first visit by a prime minister of any country to Sikkim, which Thondup took to be another important step towards recognising its independent position. Sikkimese elections the following year, which passed off with little disturbance, increased the perception that the 1950 Indo-Sikkimese Treaty might, in fact, be the best thing for the country.

But Nehru was also operating on a bigger stage. As he persisted with his dream of a pan-Asian federation of nations, he moved ever closer to Mao and the new Chinese leadership. Some of the concessions he made were essentially pragmatic, but the outcomes were often at the expense of Sikkim's cousins in Tibet: in 1952, the Government of India agreed to downgrade their representation in Tibet to a consul-general, implicitly conceding that Tibet's foreign relations were controlled by China. Two years later Nehru agreed to withdraw the Indian military escort in the Chumbi Valley (that had been established by the British after the 1904 Younghusband mission into Tibet) and hand over the dak bungalows there. He also conceded control over the telegraph line (that the British had laid in the Chumbi Valley) to China. All of these minor concessions, Nehru believed, helped to improve Sino-Indian relations by removing awkward signs of India's colonial inheritance.

When Nehru and Zhou Enlai, China's Premier, signed the Panchsheel Treaty, the 'Five Principles of Peaceful Coexistence', in 1954, it ensured that India would never again intervene in Tibet. The following year Nehru arranged the Bandung Conference, which founded the 'Non-Aligned Movement', an attempt to create a powerblock rising above the factionalism of the Cold War. At the conference Nehru and Zhou Enlai publicly reaffirmed their commitment to the Panchsheel. This was, Nehru felt sure, a new era of cooperation in Asia.

The press were delighted. This was 'Hindi-Chini-bhai-bhai'*, a brotherhood of nations, a new model for the world. Nehru considered the partnership with the Chinese as a huge triumph. In the Indian parliament he laid out his views on the Panchsheel Treaty unequivocally:

> It is a matter of some importance to us, of course, as well as, I am sure to China, that these countries, which have now almost 1800 miles of frontier, should live in terms of peace and friendliness and should respect each other's sovereignty and integrity, should agree not to interfere with each other in any way, and not to commit aggression on each other . . .

---

* 'Hindi-Chini-bhai-bhai' (literally 'India China brother brother') became a popular press catchphrase.

But not everyone shared Nehru's optimism. The leader of the opposition painted a quite different picture of the agreement and its focus on Tibet:

Tibet is culturally more akin to India than it is to China, at least Communist China, which has repudiated all its own culture. I consider this [occupation of Tibet] as much colonial aggression on the part of China as any colonial aggression indulged in by western nations. . . In international politics when a buffer state is abolished by a peaceful nation, that nation is considered to have aggressive designs on its neighbours. It is also said that in the new map of China other border countries like Nepal, Sikkim, etc. figure. This gives us an idea of the aggressive designs of China. . .[26]

It was a very different view of the future of Asian relations – one that looked at the Himalayan states, including Sikkim, as vital Indian barriers, not as a 'Hindi-Chini-bhai-bhai' bridge, as Nehru liked to think.

In April 1954, it was Thondup's turn to go to Lhasa. His Tibetan wife, Sangey Deki, had already given birth to two boys, one in March 1952, another in April 1953; it was the Tibetan custom that a man should take his bride home to her parents after the birth of her first child. The journey also provided an opportunity for Thondup to see the Dalai Lama and to witness the Chinese occupation at first hand.

On his return, Thondup headed to the Calcutta consulate, where he debriefed CIA officer John Turner. Thondup had little good to say. On reaching Yatung after crossing the Nathu La, Thondup reported, he was accosted at the Chinese checkpost by drab and dour unfriendly soldiers, who demanded his papers as if he was nothing more than an ordinary citizen.[27] In Lhasa restrictions were placed on his movements; he was forbidden from photographing any government facilities and had found the whole city stuffed full of Chinese soldiers. Soaring prices were hitting the poorest in Lhasa hard. The Chinese had driven him out to the brand new Damshung airfield outside Lhasa and shown him a fresh stretch of road leading in to Kham, clear evidence that preparations were being made to make Tibet more accessible to Chinese troops. He had found the Dalai Lama, Thondup reported sadly to his CIA handler, 'unhappy but resigned to his fate'.

Thondup was right. The Dalai Lama and his advisers had now decided that their best option was to at least explore what an accommodation with China would look like. Shortly after Thondup's visit, the Tibetan leader left Lhasa for Peking to try to reach some kind of understanding with the Chinese over the status of Tibet. Initially the Dalai Lama was impressed with Chairman Mao in their meetings. Mao's charisma, he reported, 'inspired' him; the Dalai Lama was under no illusions that change and modernisation were required in Tibet, and Mao's insistence that this was a shared objective seemed to augur well for some level of cooperation. But over six months in Beijing their differences became clear, as did the underlying strategic rationale behind Mao's interest in Tibet. He realised that Mao saw Tibet as an answer to the need for mineral resources and that the Party had little respect for Tibetan culture. The single 'liberated' nation that Mao envisaged certainly encompassed Tibet.

The final straw came on the day before the Dalai Lama was due to leave Peking. Mao praised his 'scientific mind and revolutionary character'; the Dalai Lama was flattered. But then the communist leader lent over and added in a conspiratorial tone: 'Of course, religion is poison.'

The scales fell from the young Tibetan leader's eyes.

-5-

By the time Thondup returned from Lhasa to Sikkim in 1954, John Lall had come to the end of his term as dewan in Gangtok. Thondup and Lall had never seen eye to eye, and Thondup now persuaded the Indians that if arrangements were to work in the future, he should be the one to personally choose the dewan. The Indians agreed. Thondup's thoughts turned to his old friend from the Dehradun course, Nari Rustomji. 'Uncle Rusty' was just concluding a posting in Assam; a few phone calls and it was all arranged. Nari Rustomji arrived to take over as dewan in the second half of 1954.

Immediately the tenor in Gangtok changed. At last Thondup had an ally, someone who he felt understood Sikkim. Within weeks Rustomji submitted a report to the Government of India outlining what he saw as the looming problem left by his predecessor. Cognisant of the views expressed to him by the prince and his friends at every opportunity, he did not mince his words: 'I believe one of the main reasons on account of which the Dewan has been resented in Sikkim is that, in many ways, the appointee was considered to be acting more arbitrarily than ever did the Ruler himself.'[28] He then gave his prescription for enhancing relations between India and Sikkim:

> If people here could be convinced that India means to stand by the treaty and not merely to manoeuvre things towards the ultimate taking over of the state, the entire atmosphere would be altered and it would be possible to establish a firm and lasting confidence.[29]

The report won Rustomji allies among the Sikkimese 'palace set' in Gangtok. However efficient John Lall might have been, he had been dismissive of the social scene revolving around the Namgyals. Rustomji, it was clear, saw himself as Thondup's man, supporting the Sikkimese state, rather than an Indian stooge.

Now the Palace came alive once more. Princess Coocoola and her aristocratic Tibetan husband led the parties. A number of wealthy Tibetan families had settled in Sikkim, fleeing the increasing troubles in their homeland. The Tibetan women in particular were 'madly fond of western dancing . . . the champagne flowed as the revellers from distant Lhasa swirled to the Viennese waltz in the their dazzling, flowing brocades, the turquoise of their long, pendant ear-rings swinging and glittering with the lilt.'[30]

Meanwhile the strains of Beethoven could be heard from both Mintokgang (Rustomji's residence) and Tsuklakang (the hilltop on which the Palace stood).

Rustomji could not have been more different from the Indo-centric Lall. He adopted the Sikkimese *kho* on a daily basis*, even wearing it on occasion in Delhi; he worked with the Chogyal to devise a plan to promote Sikkim's culture and status; he brought in Thondup's Oxford-educated brother ('tall, dark and handsome, with hair like Senator Kennedy's; he wore a blue turtleneck sweater and a blue sports shirt hanging out, American style, over corduroy pants'[31]) to take a role as 'Sikkim Development Commissioner'. Thondup's mood lightened immediately.

---

* Perhaps akin to a top English civil servant deciding to wear a kilt every day while serving in the UK government's Scottish Office in Edinburgh

This was what he envisioned for the country – a plan for development, with a cadre of supporters to put it into action.

Together the two men submitted the first 'Seven Year Plan' for the economic development of Sikkim to the Indian Planning Commission, with a strategy for the 'expansion of educational and medical facilities, the construction and improvement of roads and bridges, and all the other social services expected of a modern welfare state'. Thondup persuaded Rustomji to include in the submission a project to construct an aerial ropeway to the Tibetan border.* This, he thought, would allow Sikkim to become more self-sufficient by replacing the old mule-caravan trade with a modern and efficient system. Although Rustomji knew this pet project would never be economically feasible, he helped win the argument with the Planning Commission. Thondup felt this was just what he wanted in a dewan: a champion for Sikkim's cause.[32]

In 1955, a new Indian Political Officer, Apa Pant, also arrived in Gangtok. Pant was from an established diplomatic family; he had been 'sitting in his office doing nothing, and doing it rather well', when someone had mentioned that the old political officer in Gangtok was ill. Overhearing that it involved 'not much work to do, a lot of riding and a wonderful house high up in the Himalayan foothills', Pant had been quick to volunteer. 'Miraculously,' Pant would write later, 'there opened up before me six and a half of the most glorious years of my life. It was as simple as that.'

Unlike Rustomji, Pant knew next to nothing about the Namgyals when he was appointed to the post in Gangtok. Tikki Kaul (a leading Indian bureaucrat) organised a party in New Delhi to introduce him to the Namgyals and Rustomji. 'This first encounter with the glamour, the polish and mystery of the ruling family of Sikkim,' Pant wrote, 'had me truly spellbound.' With a sharp eye, he soon noticed Thondup's complexities. The Prince was

> as if encased in thick armour plating, looking out on the world through small chinks that he would close down at the slightest sign of danger to his ego, his image of himself. I wondered what had made him so self-enclosed. Deep inside, I thought, he would be a very fine and capable person, if one could ever penetrate the aura of suspicion and self-defence.

---

* On the same principles as a ski-tow or chairlift.

His wife, Sangey Deki, was 'quite exquisite, like a delicate porcelain doll', but it was the Namgyal sisters, Coocoola and Kula, whose names he had heard 'whispered with sensuous mystery in Delhi's corridors of power', that intrigued him most: 'I could see what had captivated others in their soft, subtle gaiety, their gracious mannerisms and sophisticated patter. But why, I wondered, were they so sad behind all that glitter?'[33]

Pant would spend seven years in Gangtok, installed in the magnificent Residency on the hill. He saw himself as a quasi-ambassador for India in Sikkim, quite distinct from the hard-working administrative attitude of Thondup's Dewan, Rustomji.

Underneath the unusual triumvirate of Thondup, Rustomji and Pant, however, the day-to-day political administration was still hopelessly inadequate. American traveller John Sack passed through in the mid-1950s and wrote a brilliantly witty account of what he saw for *Playboy* magazine; the article would later be published in *Report from Practically Nowhere*, the story of his travels in 'thirteen no-account countries':

> Sikkim, in the Eastern Himalayas, is a democracy now. Its first election was in 1953, and its first law in 1955, but, in these few years, the alert Sikkimis have learned not only the outward forms of democracy but many of the refinements, subtleties, and secrets that are, to us in the civilized world, almost its very soul – parties, platforms, partisan strife, mudslinging, muck-racking, windbags, windfalls, major parties, minor parties, pull, plums, padded payrolls, stuffing, roughing, raucus caucuses, brass spittoons in smoke-filled rooms, bosses, losses, lobbies, gobbledegook, and gerryman-dering, among others.[34]

Later, as he tried to establish the distinction between the rival parties (the Sikkim State Congress and the National Party), he found himself

> none the wiser, [so] I went to the Sikkimi capitol and buttonholed the Chief Secretary, a sort of prime minister there, who said, 'On the whole the parties are identical,' but that I shouldn't noise it about. Down the hall, he suggested, I'd find the national chairmen of both, working in their office.
> 'In their offices?' I said.
> 'In their office,' he said, and while he went back to his papers, I hurried

down the hall and saw, indeed, that Mr Sonam Tsering, of the Nationalists, and Mr Kashiraj Pradhan, of the Congress, worked in the very same office, side by side.[35]

Neither did the issue of Nepali immigration avoid Sack's keen eye. 'The Nepalis,' he wrote, 'are immigrants, while the Bhotias, to their way of thinking, came over on the *Mayflower*.' It was a sharp observation of the growing tension in Sikkim between the two dominant ethnic groups. Thondup and the Buddhist minority in Sikkim could not shake their concern about the issue of Nepali immigration. Rustomji recalled that 'the Prince's aim was to call a halt to fresh immigration' while 'allaying the apprehension of the Lepchas and Bhutias that their culture was in danger of being eroded away.'[36]

For Thondup and the Palace faction, this was the major issue. He knew that there were old established Nepali families who were contributing considerably to the structure of Sikkimese society. He also knew that if he wanted to create a cohesive country, he would have to accept the immigration that had already taken place. But he was not willing to countenance further erosion of what he saw as Sikkim's core heritage. It frustrated him when Pant, a committed Hindu, gave the impression that Buddhism was in some way an offshoot of an overarching Hindu faith. To combat this, Thondup strongly supported Rustomji's plans for promoting a sense of Buddhist Sikkim, reinvigorating some of the old Sikkimese traditions and connections with Tibetan culture, setting up an Institute of Tibetology and generally promoting the country's strong links with Tibet, encouraging the preservation of precious Buddhist celebrations such as the colourful Pang Lhabsol.

Even if these initiatives were aimed at creating a clearer Sikkimese identity, they naturally created some unease in sections of the Nepali community.

-6-

In 1956, Thondup again found a reason to travel to Lhasa. This time, as President of the Indian Buddhist Society, he carried with him an invitation for the Dalai Lama to visit India for the Buddha Jayanti, the 2,500th anniversary celebrations of the Buddha's birth.

Again reports filtered back from Thondup to the US consulate in Calcutta. The news was worse than ever. Thondup, constantly accompanied by a 'Chinese guardian angel' found Lhasa 'one third . . . Chinese and it looks as if it will soon be half'.[37] The house-building programme was astonishing, he reported, with the city up to 50 per cent larger than it had been on his previous visit a year earlier. Heavy fighting was taking place in the east of Tibet as a rebellion in Kham drew the attention of more Chinese troops. It was all hearsay evidence, but the atrocities that he had witnessed provoked Thondup to suggest to his CIA contact in Calcutta that perhaps some Tibetans could be exfiltrated to Burma or Thailand, under the cover of religious training, so that they could receive instruction from American specialists in artillery and anti-aircraft techniques. It was a suggestion that would soon be acted upon in a slightly different form.[38]

Initially, the Chinese rejected Thondup's invitation for the Dalai Lama to attend the Buddha Jayanti in India.[39] Mao, carefully watching the challenges to Soviet power in Eastern Europe, had no intention of softening his stance on Tibet. But in October, when Nehru personally reiterated the invitation to Mao, it became impossible to refuse. Mao finally gave his assent in November.

As the Dalai Lama set off from Lhasa, the rumours of his impending visit spread through Gangtok. Not only was the Dalai Lama coming, but the Panchen Lama* was also travelling with him, along with a number of other high-ranking reincarnated lamas. Gangtok was alive with anticipation. Meanwhile the Tibetan party made its way across the plateau and down the Chumbi Valley. It was the same route the Dalai Lama had taken in 1950, but this time he was accompanied by an escort of Chinese soldiers. A few days later they crossed the Nathu La into Sikkim. A small group, including Thondup and the young C. D. Rai, now settled as a civil servant in the magistrate's department, met the party near the border.

---

* The 10th incarnation of the Panchen Lama was a point of dispute between the Chinese and the Tibetans. After the death of the 9th Panchen Lama in 1937, the Chinese nationalists declared that they had discovered the next incarnation, but he was never approved by the Lhasa government. Mao continued to support the same candidate, and the 17-Point Agreement was seen, in part, as being a legitimisation of the choice of candidate.

For Thondup, it was a moment of great religious and political importance. The party made its way on horseback to Karponang, a small village on the trade route, then by jeep and stationwagon to the outskirts of the capital, where the streets had by now started to fill with people. The last leg was made in convoy, led by Thondup's sky-blue Buick, through the crowds. Even in Gangtok, though, the Chinese control was unavoidable. A Tibetan flag fluttering from the Dalai Lama's car was swiftly removed by the Chinese minders.*

The group travelled on to Delhi, where the Dalai Lama met with Nehru in an attempt to convince him of the importance of the Tibetan struggle for self-determination. But in the background Chinese Premier Zhou Enlai was also shuttling back and forth to Delhi, creating further tensions. The Dalai Lama got little that was meaningful from Nehru: the Indian prime minister's sympathies lay with his partnership with the Chinese leader and not with the Tibetans. The Dalai Lama proceeded, downhearted, to Bodh Gaya for the Buddha's birthday celebrations at the end of the year.

In February, the Dalai Lama finally started to wend his way back to the border. But rather than heading straight back to Tibet he diverted to Kalimpong, the Indian hill town just south of Sikkim, which lay close to the southern tip of the Tibetan Chumbi Valley. It was a decision against the explicit wishes of Zhou, who warned him that the town was 'full of spies and reactionary elements'.⁴⁰

Zhou was absolutely right about Kalimpong's nefarious nature. Long before its role as one end of the wartime trading route to support the Chinese nationalists, the town had developed a rough, tough reputation. Located on a trading crossroads between Tibet, Bengal, Sikkim, Bhutan and even Nepal (trade was conducted through the Jelep La into the Chumbi Valley), Kalimpong had housed a vibrant trading community over many centuries, with thousands of semi-resident Tibetan muleteers.

---

* For Thondup's brother, George-la (considered 'highly sensitive'), the visit had a very different effect. He turned up at Rustomji's house in a 'state of acute emotional distress' due to what he called the 'impact on a highly sensitive mind of the accumulation of forces, or thought-currents, emanating from the unprecedented number of reincarnate lamas that had gathered together at Gangtok'. Like a 'bulb fused by an excess of electric charge', he was in need of rest and quiet. The remedy initially prescribed by the lamas was circumambulation, but he 'eventually proceeded abroad for treatment on more conventional lines'.

The reinvigoration of the trading route during the Second World War (when it was used to ferry gasoline via Tibet to China's nationalists) had poured money into the town.

By the mid-1950s Kalimpong had also started to attract an extraordinary assortment of characters. Adrian Conan Doyle, son of the Sherlock Holmes novelist Arthur, was one, seeking a 'spiritual reunion' with his late father; Prince Peter of Greece and Denmark, an anthropologist with a deep interest in polyandry (multiple husbands for a single wife), who was also a cousin of the British Queen's husband, Prince Philip, was another. Prince Peter and his white Russian wife Princess Irene were suspected of being spies. There were Afghan princesses, relatives of the deposed King of Burma, a Russian painter and mystic Svetoslav Roerich (who a former US Vice-President had once addressed as 'Dear Guru') and his wife, the Bengali actress Devika Rani, Christian missionaries, journalists and retired military officers. At the heart of Kalimpong's social scene was the Himalayan Hotel, run by the three elderly daughters of David Macdonald, the former Anglo-Sikkimese trade agent in Gyantse who had welcomed the 13th Dalai Lama on his flight in 1910, who was by now nearly 90 years old, 'a small wrinkled man beaming under his knitted cap'.[41]

The Dalai Lama knew full well that Kalimpong had also developed into a centre of espionage. His brother, Gyalo Thondup, had been hovering between Kalimpong and Darjeeling for a number of years. A few years senior to the Dalai Lama, Gyalo was the 'proverbial prodigal son . . . the only one of five male siblings not directed toward a monastic life'.[42] Before the arrival of the communists in 1950, Gyalo had been one of those developing good relations with Chiang Kai-shek and the Chinese nationalists in the hope of coming to a reasonable arrangement about an autonomous Tibet. After the arrival of the communists he had continued to move in diplomatic circles in Hong Kong and Washington during the early 1950s. By 1956 he was based mostly in Darjeeling, where he had settled and started a business. But his family connection meant that he had also become a natural focal point for links with the Khampa fighters congregating in Kalimpong and planning to return to give the Chinese a bloody nose.

Gyalo and two others formed the core of a new organisation, Jen Khen

Tsi Sum*, dedicated to fighting the occupation of Tibet from Kalimpong. Three others formed an outer circle. One of them was Sikkim's Princess Coocoola. During the summer of 1956, she had become the conduit for the group's connections with the US government. At first Gyalo, in his role as unofficial leader of this resistance in exile, sought practical support for the Khampa fighters from the Nationalist Chinese, now in control of Taiwan. He also sounded out B. N. Mullik, the head of the Indian intelligence services. Neither gave much hope of practical assistance.

When he approached the Americans, however, the response was quite different.

Gyalo came onto the radar of the CIA in the Calcutta consulate in late 1956. One of their officers, John Hoskins, was tasked with working out how to approach him. Hoskins discovered that Gyalo was a keen member of the Gymkhana Club, with a particular love of tennis – so much so that he was the local champion. The young CIA officer packed his racket and headed to Kalimpong, managing to arrange a doubles match partnering Gyalo. The contact had been made; shortly afterwards Gyalo and another of the Dalai Lama's brothers had headed to Delhi to be with the Tibetan leader during the Buddha Jayanti celebrations.

When the Dalai Lama and his brothers arrived back in Kalimpong in February, the discussions started in earnest. What was the best way to serve the people of Tibet? Should he return to Lhasa? Should he support the resistance movement? For the Dalai Lama, this nascent resistance threw up a particularly difficult problem. At still only 24 years old, he found himself in a quandary: the Buddhist faith that he led forbade the taking of life. After much discussion, it was decided in mid-February that he should return to Lhasa. There were few signs of support from Nehru; Mao meanwhile, in a calculated effort to encourage the Dalai Lama's return, was hinting that the hated reforms in Tibet might be postponed for six years.

In April 1957 the Dalai Lama headed to Gangtok, where he delayed for a month, staying along with his Chinese minders in the old Residency with Apa Pant, before returning, with a heavy heart, to Lhasa.

Discussions between the CIA and the Dalai Lama's brother, Gyalo, now

* An acronym of the three leaders' names.

suddenly took off. One of the members of the Dalai Lama's party (almost certainly unknown to the Tibetan leader) had carried a secret telegraphic book back to Lhasa; the other copy sat in Kalimpong, opening a line of secret communication.[43] The Americans immediately tabled a further proposal that a number of Khampa fighters should be smuggled out of India to be trained in guerrilla tactics and then airdropped back into Tibet. Even Princess Coocoola was involved in hurried discussions about drop zones and potential trainees. The idea of training a guerrilla force was readily accepted. Six of the best fighters were selected in early March and intensive planning started as to how to get them out of the country. The best option, Hoskins and the CIA decided, was to work with the Pakistanis, with whom the Americans had developed relations. The northern tip of East Pakistan (today's Bangladesh) snaked up to within less than 50 miles of Kalimpong. It was perfect for a clandestine exfiltration.

Late one night the six Khampas were driven across the border into Pakistan (with Gyalo at the wheel of the jeep), where they made their way through tea plantations and jungles and forded rivers before being met by another CIA officer waiting with hot tea and biscuits in a small bungalow. From there, a jeep took them to an old Second World War airfield, Kurmitola in Bangladesh, where a specialist unit of the US Air Force was waiting with a converted DC-6. After a short refuelling stop in Bangkok, they were taken to Okinawa in Japan, where they were met by another of the Dalai Lama's brothers, before proceeding to Saipan, a volcanic 'teardrop shaped island in the western Pacific' that was a US trust territory.[44]

The CIA involvement with Tibet was well and truly under way.

-7-

After the Buddha Jayanti, Thondup had returned to Gangtok. After a difficult period, he was finally finding some peace. He had been buoyed by the visit of the Dalai Lama and the Panchen Lama to Sikkim. The visit had inspired a sense of unity and reinforced ties between the Buddhists of Sikkim and Tibet. He was also pleased with the progress in the construction of the ropeway snaking up towards the Chumbi Valley, a project particularly close to his heart. For centuries traders had used the Jelep and the Nathu La passes into the valley to carry goods between Sikkim and Tibet. Tibetan muleteers would bring wool down from Lhasa, and return with goods from India. This trade had been a key reason for British interest in Sikkim in the nineteenth century. He was convinced that the ropeway could transform Sikkim's prospects.

Underneath the surface, however, both Rustomji and Pant noticed that Thondup's passion for Sikkim would occasionally overcome him. Pant supported all the prince's efforts but worried that his ego was sometimes preventing him from understanding the limits of what was achievable. He could see that Thondup firmly believed that his position in Sikkim was about far more than just worldly rule; he saw himself as a protector of the country's integrity, and of the Buddhist faith there. When the mountaineer George Evans approached the Palace in 1955 with a request to climb Khangchendzonga, it was with great reluctance that Thondup agreed to an ascent of the mountain. Among mountaineers, Evans and his climbers, George Band and Joe Brown, received praise for respecting the mountain, having stopped a few feet short of the summit. But Nari Rustomji (who was involved in the negotiations) tells a different story – that the Palace granted permission for the expedition to 'proceed only as far as necessary to ascertain whether or not there was an approach'. When the party claimed they had got within touching distance of the summit, Thondup was 'enraged, convinced that this was a deliberate breach, in spirit at least, of the solemn undertaking given by Evans'. Rustomji also noticed that Thondup's moods could quickly take a dark turn. In 1955, Thondup's brother George-la had challenged him: 'Why do you get so worked up about Sikkim? I give Sikkim twenty years at a modest guess, after which God only knows what.' A wounded Thondup had replied, 'If even my own family feel so little about the country, how can I expect more from my people? I might as well pack up and be done with it all.' That night he had swallowed 'a lot of pills', prompting an emergency call from Sangey Deki in the middle of the night.[45]

Despite these troubling outbursts, there was a sense within Sikkim in 1957 that things might be looking up. Rustomji had extended his tenure as dewan; Apa Pant was supportive. Thondup also now had a third child, a girl, and his wife Sangey Deki was once again pregnant.

Then, in June, tragedy struck. Sangey Deki was taken ill; within days she was dead. Thondup, 'broken in grief', withdrew inside himself for a number of months. Thondup's father Tashi, who had now lost a half-brother, a son and a (pregnant) daughter-in-law through untimely deaths, could only mutter that it must have been Sangey Deki's 'critical year'.

Rustomji looked for ways to distract Thondup. Together they galvanised their efforts to substantiate Sikkim's 'Seven Year Plan', mastering 'the tricks of salesmanship' to promote Sikkim's nascent enterprises, including a new fruit-canning factory with the slogan 'SIKKIM SUPREME', with marketing materials showing Khanchendzonga's pinnacles rising supremely aloft. Whisky from the new Sikkim distillery was named 'Snow Lion' and marketed as matching Scottish malts. More funds were found for the ropeway. The diversity of the projects supported (and their intended outcome) brought a biting satirical attack from the American John Sack, in the first of his articles in *Playboy* magazine after visiting Sikkim. He described a plethora of activity, including

> mills, wool presses, canneries, distilleries downstream, with coal, copper, graphite, gypsum rolling from the hillsides, and twice as many roads, and twice as many hospitals, and twice twice twice as many kids in school, taught, too, by teachers who went to school – a land of plenty, of happy people.

In 1957–8, two visits from Indian Prime Minster Pandit Nehru also cheered Thondup. The two men got on well. The Indian prime minister had a soft spot for the country; he admitted that he was considering retiring there, that he 'dreamed of passing the twilight of his life in a quiet retreat' in the country, where he 'could contemplate and record the essence of his life's experience'.

Nehru's first visit was to open the new Namgyal Institute of Tibetology, a project he fully supported in its aim to promote Sikkim's Himalayan status. The second visit in 1958 was en route to Bhutan. Again, he was accompanied by his daughter Indira, as he had been in 1953. To get to Bhutan, the small party, consisting of Chogyal Tashi, Thondup, Rustomji, Pant, Nehru and Indira, knew they would have to cross the Nathu La into the Tibetan Chumbi Valley. Despite the fact that Bhutan had already sent 20 bodyguards to protect the party, the Chinese insisted on sending a captain in the PLA and 50 further armed soldiers to escort them, citing rumours that Khampa rebels wished to stage a dramatic protest by kidnapping the Indian prime minister. Nehru, who 'could not have felt freer or more relaxed', laughed it all off; but it was an insight into the growing tensions in the region.

Sangey Deki's death, meanwhile, had another consequence: it gave Princess Coocoola a more prominent role in Sikkim's affairs. She too tried to distract the bereaved prince, becoming the consummate host, welcoming diplomats, travellers and businessmen into the palace and entertaining them with grace and style around an expansive table.* Many of the guests were well-to-do Tibetans, great numbers of whom continued to come down the Chumbi Valley and into Sikkim. Naturally, she also became more involved in political affairs, in particular with the continuing issue of immigration, a topic she was just as passionate about (if not more so) than her brother. When, in 1958, it was suggested that one of the seats in the parliament should be made available to 'any resident of fixed habitat', she raised the issue loudly with Rustomji, protesting that it could mean Indian traders would get representation in parliament. Her letter contained more than a hint of threat:

> Desperation can drive people, Uncle, and the Marwarees† being who they are, once they have the Sikkimese in economic bondage – what solution is there? What would you do as a Sikkimese? Would you try and combat one evil with yet another one? So many in the world today have been driven to it. Wouldn't you, with the interests of your heart, fight money with money?[46]

It was an issue for the Namgyals that just would not go away.

---

* One British civil servant, James Scott, recalled her serving the delicacy abalone, whispering into his ear that it was 'good for men's vigour'. The next morning, after a particularly long night drinking chang from bamboo cups, blond-haired Scott awoke sprawled on his bed to find the princess and her two young children at the end of the bed, with Coocoola saying, 'Look children! It's a Yeti!'

† A community of traders originally from Rajasthan, belonging to the trading caste of banias.

On his return to Lhasa in 1957, the Dalai Lama had found that Mao, far from postponing the pace of change in Tibet, had sped things up with a massive crackdown on dissent. Having promised to 'let a hundred flowers bloom, a hundred schools of thought contend' across Greater China, he had then performed a complete U-turn. In Tibet, as in the rest of China, the consequences were terrible. The Chinese ruthlessly suppressed the revolt in Kham, obliterating entire villages and holding public executions – including crucifixions – in an attempt to assert control.[47]

Meanwhile, on a small island in the West Pacific, the effort to train up the six Tibetan Khampas in CIA techniques was well under way. On arrival in the west Pacific island of Saipan where they were to receive their training, they found the place occupied by a variety of nationalities alongside their American trainers. Chinese nationalists, Koreans, Laotians, Vietnamese – all were being readied for the fight against the growing spread of communism. The Tibetans, like everyone else, were given new names that were easier on the tongue for the instructors (Bill, Dick, Tom, Walt, Lou, Sam) and started their training in an endless list of techniques to equip them for the task to come:

> Morse code, cut numbers, radio signal plans, the US-made RS-1 crystal operated radio transmitter and receiver, encoding and decoding using one-time pads, use of telecodes (Tibetan telecode was developed during the training), map and compass reading, small arms up to and including 60-mm mortar and 57-mm recoilless rifles, fragmentation and incendiary grenades, fire and movement tactics . . . offensive and defensive ambushes, an array of simple sabotage techniques, use of demolitions, Molotov cocktails, booby traps, unarmed and hand-to-hand combat, cross-country and night movement, observation, casing, authentication, elicitation, information collection, reports writing, tradecraft techniques, resistance organisations, sketching, preparation of drop zones, parachute ground training, simple psychological warfare techniques, first aid, simple disguise techniques, and physical fitness.[48]

It didn't take long for the Tibetans to become firm favourites with their CIA handlers. One, Roger McCarthy, recalled later that 'demolition was like "happy hour" . . . the bigger the bang and the more damage that the explosives achieved, the better! More than once we had to call in the base fire department to put out fires.'[49]

By October, the training was over; the men were considered ready to be flown to the American base in Japan's Okinawa for parachute training. Reserve chutes were considered unnecessary: they were to be dropped over land that rose to 14,000 feet above sea level, where the air was so thin that there was a risk that the smaller canopies would not even deploy. In place of the reserves, which would normally have been on their chests, the six men were given a small pack with 'some ammo, money (Tibetan, Nepali, and gold coins), emergency rations, compass, signal plans and crystals for radio operators, a knife, and a small flashlight'. They were also given a small cyanide ampoule, known as an L-tablet, carefully packed into a tiny box cushioned by sawdust.

In mid-October the first of the Khampas were flown back to Kurmitola airfield in East Pakistan and parachuted back into Tibet; a second infiltration took place in December. Once in Tibet the guerrilla-trained men buried their chutes and started to report back to their handlers on the situation, which had now deteriorated further. In January 1958, the Chinese committed eight PLA divisions and at least 150,000 men to Eastern Tibet alone. But the vastness of Tibet made it impossible to prevent the continued emergence of an organised opposition. In Lhoka, a town south of Lhasa, Gompo Tashi, a thickset Khampa, rallied 20,000 fighters under the banner of the Chushi Gangdrok, meaning 'Four Rivers Six Gorges', to represent the extraordinary landscape of Eastern Kham where the resistance to Chinese rule was strongest. In June, Tashi's Chushi Gangdrok was given an alternative name, the National Volunteer Defense Army. The old flag – a mythical snow lion against a blue background – was replaced by one of an altogether more military feel: crossed Tibetan swords on a yellow field. In the *Daily Mail*, correspondent Noel Barber, who had become embedded with the rebels, likened the story that he was finding to 'flicking over the pages of Dante's *Inferno*: monasteries bombed, monks shot at prayer, old Tibetans used as slaves'. Three days later he headlined an article 'Mao Sets His Sights on India', detailing what he called 'training schools for agents who infiltrate south, disguised as traders'.

There was little doubt that Gompo Tashi and his men were ready for a full-scale guerrilla conflict in the Kham region.

Tibet was by now considered important enough in Washington to have its own Task Force within the CIA's Far East Division. As they assessed the situation in mid-1958, it was clear that the infiltration of the first six CIA-trained guerrillas into Tibet had been only a limited success. Communications had regularly failed, and the training in the tropical environment of Saipan had been too removed from the conditions of Tibet to prove useful. The newly appointed head of the division, Desmond Fitzgerald, gave his approval for another exfiltration of trainees from Kalimpong. But this time, he told his team, the Tibetans would be taken to a more suitable location, one that would allow training in the kind of conditions they would encounter in Tibet: Camp Hale, in Colorado's Rocky Mountains.

Camp Hale was, like Saipan, a relic from the Second World War. But the environment could not have been more different. The camp had been set up in 1942 for training the 10th Mountain Division in 'skiing, rock climbing and cold weather survival skills'. Now it was to be resurrected for training Tibetans in guerrilla tactics. The aim of the training had now been stepped up a notch: rather than simply providing intelligence, the recruits were now to be trained to deploy more active resistance techniques. In fact, Camp Hale would not be ready for another six months; in the interim the next set of Tibetans – 'eighteen young recruits (average age, twenty-two) and three translators plus two older Khampas in their mid-forties' – were trained in a corner of the CIA's infamous training school, 'The Farm', in Virginia.[50]

Back in Tibet at the beginning of 1959 the Tibetans who had been parachuted back into their motherland in 1957 were busier than they had ever been. CIA-sponsored operations were now making regular airdrops of arms, supplies – and cash – into pre-designated dropzones in remote areas of the country, sending as many as three C-130 aeroplanes over at a time.* But the sheer volume of the Chinese presence – and its superior

---

* Initially the airdrops consisted of the old British-made Lee-Enfield rifles and ammunition, because that was what the Tibetan army had used and was familiar with. Over time the Tibetan resistance migrated to American-made weapons.

coordination – was beginning to have a drastic effect across the country, and in particular in Lhasa. The capital, for so long the focal point for the country, was increasingly under the firm grip of the Chinese. And it was in Lhasa that things were about to come to boiling point.

There had been an indication in early February 1959 that the Chinese might be preparing to make a move against the Dalai Lama. Radio Peking had announced that the Tibetan leader 'had made plans to visit the Chinese capital'. In fact, the Dalai Lama had made no such plans.

On 5 March, the Chinese commander in Lhasa, General Tan, made his move. At the time, the Dalai Lama was in the Jokhang, the central religious building, which constituted the heart of the city, preparing for the tough final examinations of his monastic training. Two Chinese officers entered unannounced and demanded to be given a date when the Tibetan leader could attend 'a theatrical show' in the Chinese army camp. The Dalai Lama's advisers were immediately struck by the emphasis that General Tan seemed to be laying on fixing an early date. Under pressure and against the advice of his closest officials, the Dalai Lama gave a date of 10 March.

On the streets of the city, the rumour mill went into overdrive. Many feared that it was a plot to kidnap the Dalai Lama. The ordinary people of Lhasa piled onto the streets, surrounding the Norbulingka, the Dalai Lama's summer palace, where he had returned after passing his examinations with flying colours. Suddenly it was the people who were in control: even if the Dalai Lama had wanted to make the 10 March appointment, he would not have been able to.

That same day a Tibetan who had been working with the Chinese was killed as he tried to make it through the crowd from the Norbulingka to talk with General Tan, raising tensions further. Later, in an attempt to start discussions with the Chinese, a Tibetan delegation managed to make it through to the Chinese camp. There they found a furious General Tan, who demanded that they gain control of the crowd. The delegation returned to the palace and explained the situation to a powerless Dalai Lama. Outside the palace the people – not just Lhasans, but Khams and Amdoans too – had now set up their own 'Freedom Committee'. Slogans started appearing daubed on walls, saying, 'Chinese return to China!', 'Tibet belongs to Tibet!' and 'We will wipe out the Chinese!'

In the Dekyi Lingka next door, the British Resident's old bastion, the Indian consul radioed Delhi about the rapid escalation in the violence. But Nehru dismissed him, telling the consul to stick to his own business and 'not get entangled'. A day or two later, British journalist George Patterson – who was based in Kalimpong and had direct access to news in Lhasa – wrote a full account of what had happened. Nehru dismissed him as 'an absurdist'.

The Chinese and the Dalai Lama watched from their respective positions for five days as pockets of violence and confrontation sprang up across the city. The Chinese were reluctant to intervene; the Dalai Lama and his advisers were powerless to do so. There was also a split of opinion among the Tibetan leadership – what should the Dalai Lama do? He was desperate to prevent a massacre and wanted to stay with his people, but those close to him urged him to flee while he could.

Everything changed on 17 March, when a shell exploded inside the grounds of the Dalai Lama's palace. With a potential threat to his life, he and his advisers agreed there was now no option but to flee. Together they hastily constructed an escape plan that minimised the chances of being caught. That night, as a sandstorm whipped through Lhasa, the Dalai Lama slung a rifle across his shoulder and was smuggled out of the palace and headed across the Kyi Chu river that ran across the edge of the city. On the southern side of the river he was met by a group of Khampa warriors. Any hesitation that the Dalai Lama had in supporting their violent cause was put to one side as he mounted a horse for the long ride south towards India.

Over the next week the violence in Lhasa spiralled out of control. There were fierce pitched battles and shelling of all the major buildings. The Chinese were still unaware that the Dalai Lama had escaped. The destruction was on a major scale – some estimated the Tibetan dead and wounded at more than 15,000.[51] In Delhi Nehru spoke of the situation in Tibet as 'a clash of minds rather than a clash of arms'.

By 25 March, the Dalai Lama and his party had reached the safety of a small monastery, where they met two of the CIA-trained guerrillas. A message was sent back to Washington by radio. At that point the members of the CIA's Tibet Task Force were the only ones with a general fix on where the Dalai Lama was. Aware that the Chumbi Valley would be the expected route and would be packed with Chinese soldiers, his advisers had instead chosen a route through the Tawang Valley, on the other side of Bhutan in India's north-east. As they made their way towards the Indian border, the question of exile became the main topic of discussion. Given Nehru's pronouncements and his continued belief in Asian unity, there was some doubt as to how he would react. It took pressure via the Americans to extract a confirmation from the Indians that the Tibetan leader was welcome.

Just two weeks after leaving Lhasa, the Dalai Lama finally crossed the border into India, near Tawang, to the east of Bhutan. Mikel Dukham, author of *Buddha's Warriors*, captured the final moments:

> Late in the afternoon of March 31, the Dalai Lama, significantly weakened by his ordeal, rode into a clearing with tall bamboo gates up ahead. He dismounted his dzo [mule]. Gurkha soldiers offered him khatas*. With Phala by his side, the Dalai Lama put on a brave smile and walked through the proscenium of exile. The ruler was twenty-three years old.[52]

Just under two decades after he had been brought to Lhasa as a four year old, the Dalai Lama, 'a God turned refugee', stepped out of Tibet, almost certainly for the last time.[53]

It would take a few months for Nehru and India to fully comprehend the ramifications of the Dalai Lama's flight to India. The Indian prime minister's dreams of pan-Asian unity were in tatters. Thousands of Tibetans followed the Dalai Lama out of the country and into India, most accompanying him to Mussoorie and then on to McLeod Ganj, an old British hill station that would eventually become the seat of the Tibetan Government-in-Exile.

The impact on Sikkim was just as substantial. On a practical level, streams of Tibetan refugees started pouring into the country. Nari Rustomji, who would soon leave Sikkim, recalled that not everyone welcomed them. 'Many in Sikkim had not forgotten the air of cultural arrogance assumed by the Tibetans in the past towards their remote and

---

* Also known as khadas, a white silk scarf offered as greeting in Buddhist custom.

"backward" brethren, and decided it was now their turn to swing the lead.' Thondup's mother, a Tibetan by birth, and Coocoola, married to a Tibetan, led the efforts to attend to the needs of the refugees, finding land and employment where they could and helping them to establish a new life.

There was another curious consequence arising from events in Tibet: suddenly Sikkim became newsworthy. In January, *Time* magazine included a page-length feature on 'little Sikkim, the size of Delaware', a country that they said had 'managed to preserve its identity over the centuries'. The author portrayed Sikkim as a mystical land, mocking 65-year-old Tashi who, he wrote, spent all day painting and praying: 'Recently he had a "vision" of the Abominable Snowman, put him on a canvas as a skinny, jet-black creature with a red face, carrying a naked pink lady across the peaks of the Himalayas.' Thondup, the article went on, was 'the real power' in 'the battle against "evil outside influences"', alongside 'buoyant N. K. Rustomji'.

'What happens in Tibet,' the article concluded with some prophetic power, 'has always echoed in Sikkim.'[54]

By the summer of 1959 Thondup was weary, feeling the loss of his wife, the strain of the refugee crisis and the pressures of bringing up three children under the age of ten. The influx of Tibetans had only multiplied the political complexities he was facing. The most recent proposal from the politicians in Sikkim was to increase the number of seats in the council yet further, again diluting the Bhutia-Lepcha community. With his ally Rustomji leaving after five years in Sikkim, Thondup knew he would also have to deal with a new dewan.

He found himself increasingly focused on the simple pleasures – the walks around Gangtok, and the regular trips he made to Darjeeling, where his two sons were thriving at school.

It was on one such trip in the summer of 1959 that he met a 19-year-old American woman who would have a considerable bearing on the events of the next 15 years.

Hope Cooke was about to arrive in Sikkim.

CHAPTER THREE

Where There's Hope

1959–65

-1-

One evening in the summer of 1959, Thondup pulled up outside the Windamere Hotel in Darjeeling in his Mercedes, walked into the lounge and ordered his usual evening drink. The Windamere, a throwback to the colonial era, was fast becoming an iconic establishment in the hill town. Thondup often dropped in after visiting his children in the local boarding school. He always knew that he would find friends who would allow him to relax and forget his troubles.

On this particular evening, his eye was drawn to a pretty young girl in the corner of the room. She was dressed in an Austrian dirndl, the kind of aproned dress that would soon become famous as a result of the film *The Sound of Music*. Within minutes he had established from his friends that she was American, a student, on holiday in India, and that she had been at the Windamere for a few days.

The two soon found themselves ensconsed in deep conversation.

From the moment Thondup and Hope Cooke met, there was a strong attraction. He was a widower, with three young children, 36 years old, endearingly shy and with a slight stammer. She was an adventurous, naive, nervy 19-year-old on the trip of a lifetime. 'My friends tell me I was travelling on a pink cloud, yet I did not recognise fate when I first met it,' she wrote a few years later.

It must have made a most unusual site: Hope in her dirndl, Thondup in 'a cream-coloured Bakku, his national dress, high-collared, ankle length, long-sleeved, and folded back tightly around the waist with a crimson sash.'[1] To Hope, this man, 'tall and straight . . . his face, its skin drawn smooth across high cheekbones, looked lightly sunburned', was 'truly, truly handsome'; he, intrigued by the unusual sight of a pretty young American girl in Darjeeling, felt the attraction too.

At that first meeting they talked for some time about 'ballet and Oriental religions', the young American hanging on Thondup's every word. Over the next few days they met a number of times. 'I found it exciting just to sit and, mostly, listen to him talk,' she wrote in a magazine article a few years later.

In one conversation Hope recalled a particularly 'skilful dissection of United States foreign policy in Southeast Asia', also noticing how Thondup was taken up with the plight of the Tibetan refugees pouring over the border into makeshift camps. He told the teenage girl 'painful stories', providing his own historical context:

> You must understand. Back in the fifties when I tried to help Tibet, the only time they could be helped, your government let me down. Some pipsqueak in the Calcutta consulate told me 'Your Highness, you must realise that we with all our resources and intelligence have a clearer view of what should be done than you ever could.' We had everything lined up – pilots, supplies. All we needed was a few planes. A few planes. Now they're helping. They're helping this Johnny-come-lately crowd of Tibetan politicians – and what happens? The weapons all fall into Chinese hands and more Tibetans are killed. It had to be earlier. Now it's certain death to encourage the Tibetans to fight rearguard. Certain death.[2]

Hope listened, spellbound.

If fate had already thrust Thondup into his position as heir-apparent in Sikkim (through his elder brother's fatal crash in Peshawar in December 1941), it was another fateful crash on the other side of the world just two weeks later that had shaped Hope Cooke's life.

On 4 January 1942 Hope Cooke's mother, a free-spirited 25-year-old, had taken off for a solo flight from an airfield in Nevada. When a search party eventually found her plane in the snowy desert – with an empty fuel tank – there was no avoiding the obvious conclusion: she had set off with no intention of returning. She left behind two daughters. The younger was Hope Cooke, only 18 months old.

Thondup's life had been drastically altered by his brother's crash; within a fortnight, the course of Hope's had also been changed irrevocably.

The extraordinary circumstances of her upbringing had eventually led to the bid for freedom that had taken her to Darjeeling. By the time of Hope's mother's death, she was already under the guardianship of her wealthy maternal grandparents, shipping company president Winchester Noyes and his wife. Hope's father, John Cooke, had been a handsome flight instructor at Roosevelt Airfield in Long Island; by the time Hope's mother met him, she had already been married and divorced once. Possessed by a desire to fly, she had signed up for courses at the school and fallen in love. It was not a match that Hope's mother's parents had approved of – John Cooke was Irish and from a 'fairly poor' background. The couple had moved around the States without apparent purpose, living in Long Island and Los Angeles before settling briefly in San Francisco, where Hope was born in 1940. At the time of her death, Hope's mother was suing for her second divorce. John Cooke was long gone.

So, from before the age of two, Hope – and Harriet, her half-sister from her mother's first marriage – lived with their grandparents in New York.[3] Installed in a separate apartment across the corridor on smart 62nd Street between Park and Madison Avenues, Hope and her half-sister fell under the influence of their strong-willed grandmother. A series of governesses looked after them and escorted them to the local school and to summer breaks in either Long Island or Maine. Hope later wrote that even in these early years she 'rebelled against the stuffiness and smugness' at Miss Madeira's, the New York school she attended. When she needed an escape, she would turn to a letter her mother had written from Nevada about her love of flying: 'It seemed to me as if the stars and sky had some powerful pull on my mother – that she had been caught between the gravitational spheres of earth and a galaxy where she remained spinning in space.'[4]

In 1956, shortly before her 16th birthday, Hope's grandparents died within weeks of each other; overnight the two girls became wards of their maternal Aunt Mary and her husband, Selden Chapin. Chapin was a career diplomat, highly respected in US Foreign Service circles; before the war he had held posts in North Africa and China (where the couple had married), he had worked with de Gaulle during the war, and had been serving in Hungary when the Iron Curtain descended. By 1956 he was US ambassador in Iran, newly 'liberated' by an American-sponsored coup that installed the Shah. The important posting was a recognition of both his status within the US Foreign Service and his reputation as a 'rather well-known anti-communist'.

That summer Hope and Harriet flew to Iran for the summer holidays from their Virginia boarding school. Iran's capital Tehran was a whirl of excitement. A sparkling expatriate social scene had sprung up, much of it centring around the tennis court of the US embassy. For the first time in her life, Hope 'had a really true feeling of being part of a family'. As the summer came to an end she pleaded in vain not to be sent back to school in Virginia.

In the summer of 1957 she returned to Tehran. Again she implored her uncle and aunt not to send her back to Virginia. This time her new guardians agreed and Hope was enrolled in the community high school in Tehran. Suddenly she had the freedom to make 'slightly radical' new friends, sparking a sense of her own identity for the first time. She became intoxicated by the sounds, smells and sights of the Shah's Iran, dressing in a *shador* as a disguise on trips into the bazaar, or heading up into the Elburz Mountains with a young colleague of her uncle's. Her mind fizzed with the possibilities of 'the East'. She was 'intellectually and emotionally captivated by Central Asia'.

In the spring of 1958 she jumped at the chance to accompany her aunt on a short holiday to India. As they toured through Delhi, Agra and the holy city of Varanasi the breathless 17-year-old fell in love with everything she saw. 'India! My heart explodes,' she wrote in her autobiography, trying to capture how she felt visiting the subcontinent for the first time. But she returned feeling frustrated from touring with her 55-year-old aunt. 'I suspected even then that I would have enjoyed the out-of-the-way places much more,' she wrote in a 1963 magazine article. 'Before I returned to Tehran, I was planning – no, scheming – how to get back to see the entire subcontinent.'

Back in Tehran that summer she came out as a debutante: 'Though I was not, at least in my own estimation, a debutanty type . . . on my eighteenth birthday, Aunt Mary and Uncle Selden gave a dance at the Embassy, at which Princess Shahnaz, the Shah of Iran's daughter, and I shared the honours. It was an extremely glamorous party . . .'[5]

That autumn she returned to study at Sarah Lawrence College, a liberal arts school in Westchester County, New York. Soon she had established strong friendships with a group of bright and intelligent girls, finding herself 'spun around by the intellectual possibilities' on offer, enrolling in history classes and taking every opportunity to incorporate Asia into her studies. Outside college she became increasingly bohemian, 'testing my boundaries or lack of them'.

By the spring of 1959 she was desperate to return to India, the youthful country run by Nehru, 'the beautiful visionary with a dreamy smile'. A college-led trip to the USSR provided an opportunity. A friend helped her draft a fictitious itinerary for a trip through India, complete with an imaginary accompanying group. Her aunt and uncle bought it. After a month in the USSR, she flew on to Nehru's India, finding it (in contrast to the USSR) 'aflame with ideas as well as national spirit'.

Within a week she was on an adventure through the country. In New York, the two girls had searched through brochures for suitable hotels that would please Hope's aunt. They chose one in Darjeeling – the Windamere – partly because its name was 'the most Englishy hotel we'd found in the brochures', and partly because 'the name sounded wonderfully romantic'.

'It seemed,' she wrote four years later, 'just the place to get the real feel of the East.'

Meeting Thondup would turn out to be a defining moment in Hope Cooke's life. But after their first encounter in late summer 1959, she had to return to college for the autumn semester at Sarah Lawrence, satisfied only with relaying the news of her Asian adventures to her college friends.

Hope and Thondup would not see or talk to each other for another two years, but the young American could not get the Sikkimese prince and the impression he had made on her out of her mind:

[His] rueful, droll manner, his obvious integrity, and his extraordinary, handsome looks: intelligent dark eyes, smooth bronze skin, sloping cheek-bones, and sensual mouth. I imagine him in the countryside up the river by a pool of light. By chance, on the several occasions when we'd looked up across the Tista River to the foothills in Sikkim, the sun, as it tends to do during the monsoon in the Himalayas, had broken into a yellow burst.[6]

If it was a crush for the young American, it was a serious one.

-2-

Thondup, too, had enjoyed meeting Hope. But thoughts of the young American in the dirndl soon faded as he returned to Gangtok, where he found there were other more pressing matters to deal with.

With the flight of the Dalai Lama into India, the international commu-nity had to face up to the fact that the Chinese were de facto in full control of Tibet. Since Sikkim lay on the only feasible overland trading route between Chinese-occupied Tibet and India, its geopolitical importance became more glaringly obvious than ever.

For the Indians in particular, any idea that Tibet acted as some sort of buffer between the main body of India and China disappeared once and for all. The impact on foreign-policy thinking was immediate. The ideal-istic impulse behind the 'Hindi-Chini-Bhai-Bhai' slogan was mocked by a belligerent press as 'Hindi-Chini-Bye-Bye'. There was now no question that Sikkim, Bhutan and Nepal directly touched the Chinese communist empire. And it was Sikkim, with its historic links with Tibet and its active trading passes between Gangtok and Lhasa, that the Indians feared was the weakest point on the new border. Almost immediately, Indian troops started to pour into the tiny Himalayan state, taking over an area in the lower reaches of Gangtok and manning the pass into the Chumbi Valley.

Thondup watched the rapid influx of Indian troops with mixed feelings. As an honorary Lt-Colonel in the Indian Army, he knew the set-up well and found the officer class convivial company. He was also well aware that under the terms of the 1950 treaty – which gave India the responsibility for Sikkim's external affairs – there was precious little he could do about it; his country was vulnerable without Indian support. But there was no escaping the fact that the troops' presence changed the atmosphere in Gangtok. Between 1939 and 1959 the town had retained the 'fairy tale' feel that Fosco Maraini had commented on when he'd travelled through in the 1940s.

The arrival of the Indian Army base changed that irrevocably.

One person who could not help but notice the influx was Martha Hamilton, a tall, spirited, single 28-year-old Scottish missionary teacher who had just taken over as headmistress of the Paljor Namgyal Girls' School in Gangtok. Martha had first come to India in 1955 to fulfil a promise to her grandfather, Lord Maclay (a shipping magnate and key member of Lloyd George's cabinet in the First World War). Maclay had lost two sons in the war, one of whom (Eben) had sent a letter to his father days before his death, saying he wanted to be a medical missionary in India. Martha promised her grandfather she would follow in Eben's footsteps. With no medical training, she instead found an educational posting with the Church of Scotland in 1955, and persuaded the church to limit her posting to two years rather than the normal 30-year commitment. On a short visit to Sikkim in 1957, near the end of her posting, she had met both Tashi ('a dear old man, dressed in a beautiful silk brocade') and Rustomji ('the real ruler of Sikkim, a Parsee and a delightful person'). She had fallen in love with the place immediately. When the opportunity to return to Sikkim at the head of the school arose in 1959, she jumped at the chance.

The school, set up in 1942 in memory of Thondup's elder brother, stood directly over the burgeoning army base. Hamilton, a self-assured woman with an incisive sense of humour who had come to the region to fulfil a pledge to her grandfather, would remain in Gangtok for the next six years. As a European and the school's headmistress she had an unusually high level of access to the Palace. Each week she wrote a letter home to her parents, providing a remarkable perspective on events. In September, she observed:

The army below the school has been increased in size and we have an endless sound of bagpipes as the General of the Eastern Command is here and the troops are practising for his guard of honour. 'The Skye Boat Song' is being murdered daily till we nearly sent a note of protest. He leaves tomorrow and I hope they now will stop.

On Boxing Day 1959, Hamilton was given an unusual opportunity ('the Christmas party probably helped' she admitted in her letter) to venture up to the Nathu La pass, leading into Tibet. Escorted by Indian soldiers, she gazed across the Chubi Valley to the holy mountain Chomolhari, 'a great white cone perfect against the blue sky'. But looking down from the windswept border on the heights of the Nathu La she sensed she was being watched: 'The Chinese checkpoint is quite far down the other side of the pass and not a soldier or anyone else could be seen though no doubt our arrival was noted by their binoculars.'

Hamilton was well aware that, with the Chinese occupation of Tibet completed in 1959, Sikkim's border had once more taken on an international dimension. By the time she came to Sikkim she had already spent two years in Kalimpong, the Indian hill town just to the south of Sikkim, where the Tibetan rebels had plotted and schemed. She had become accustomed to the Western journalists tripping over each other to dramatise the events of the Dalai Lama's escape, concluding, probably correctly, that 'most of the news reports were made up in the local hotel'.

In Gangtok she saw a quite different side of the situation: the urgent refugee problem. It was quite clear to Hamilton that Princess Coocoola, Thondup's sister, had taken control of the issue. The strong historic ties between Sikkim and Tibet meant that there were family members who were affected by events. Coocoola in particular, married to a Tibetan nobleman, felt a personal responsibility to help the large numbers of refugees who were now piling into the state.

Hamilton noticed something else about Coocoola: following the death of her brother's first wife, she had now taken on the role of being Thondup's partner at official functions. Coocoola and her sister Kula had been determined that palace life should not suffer; between them they had ensured that Sikkim's social life had continued. Rock and roll had reached Sikkim, and Martha Hamilton's ability to dance – and teach others how to dance – to the new music meant she quickly became a part of this social set, invited to parties at both the palace and the Residency, the home of the Indian political officer. She noticed at one such party in the Residency Library that it was Thondup ('a terrible flirt') who was the centre of attention for many giggling young girls in Sikkim: 'As soon as HH* entered all the young girls seized huge philosophic tomes from the shelves and studiously looked at them.'

Meanwhile Coocoola worked night and day on behalf of the refugees from a small office in the palace.† Martha Hamilton brought the scale of the project to life in one of her letters home:

We went with the Kumari‡ down to the Refugee Camp for which we collected money from our concert. It was very interesting – also pathetic. There is just no room to put them so they are all on the floor with what belongings they managed to bring out with them. Incredible number of children considering they had to cross passes of 12,000 and 14,000 feet and they had practically no clothing on arrival. It is supposed to be a transit camp but so many of them are sick when they come from the plains where conditions are pretty grim that it is about impossible to move them all on. The really sick are put into hospital and the less desperate lie and shake with malaria on the floor. They are delighted to be in Sikkim and there are those of course who prefer to be a little sick rather than go off to build some road in the north of Sikkim. Two days later the Kumari came again and took some of the girls down and distributed the sweaters they had made. I hope my photos will come out well, for some of the children were marvellous, with their new sweaters being positively heaved over their poor ears as they were a bit small.

*

Nehru and his Indian government were also faced with the question of what to do with the Tibetan exiles, and how to react to the new de facto position of Chinese control in Tibet.

After his flight in 1959, the Dalai Lama had little choice but to make

---

* Martha Hamilton often referred to Thondup as 'HH', or His Highness.
† In June 1959 Coocoola wrote to Colonel Bailey, the old Political Officer (who she had known as a child and with whom she maintained a close friendship), while in the midst of 'another packed-to-overflowing day . . . I've ensconsed myself in Thondup's office tonight and sit on his carpet with a sheet of his letter paper laid on a file that's balanced on my knees and write to you.'
‡ Commonly used term for Coocoola, as consort to Thondup.

the argument for full Tibetan independence. The Indian leader, however, continued to believe that a compromise based on Tibetan autonomy could be possible. When the two men met in the hill station of Mussoorie in April 1959, their aims were already diverging. By June 1959 the young Tibetan had decided to take things into his own hands, with a speech seeking a return to the position before the disputed 17-Point Agreement of 1951, when Tibet had enjoyed and exercised 'all rights of sovereignty whether internal or external'.[7]

The British prevaricated even more than the Indians. The Foreign Office, if 'forced to declare itself', one mandarin said, 'would have to go along with Nehru's position'; but 'on balance it would be far better if the Asians took the lead', said another.

In October 1959, the Tibetans finally persuaded Ireland and Malaya to sponsor a UN debate on the Chinese aggression in Tibet. Still the British refused to commit to a position. The British representative at the debate was told 'to make clear their abhorrence of the Tibetan situation' but (with strange logic) 'to avoid as far as possible influencing other votes'.[8] In the final vote, Britain abstained. It was enough to make Hugh Richardson, the man who had served as the last British resident in Tibet under Sir Basil Gould, 'profoundly ashamed' that his own government had 'sold the Tibetans down the river'.

The one country that the Tibetans did find willing to help, at least behind the scenes, was the USA. Although they had also been taken by surprise by events, the Americans encouraged the rebellion taking place in Kham, and reinforced the CIA-backed efforts to stimulate the resistance in Tibet; one group within the government called it a 'windfall for the US', offering opportunities to strike a blow for freedom.[9] The American charge d'affaires in Delhi, Winthrop G. Brown, was told to make sure the Dalai Lama was aware of American support and to tell him that 'the US remained "strongly" opposed to Communist China's admission to the UN' (which would have consolidated the communists' control over China).* The American media also took up the Tibetan cause – a picture of the Dalai Lama with the headline 'THE ESCAPE THAT ROCKED THE REDS' filled *Time* magazine's front cover for 20 April 1959.

---

* The Chinese seat at the UN was, at this time, held by the Chinese nationalists in Taiwan.

Tangible signs of American support came in the form of the CIA's continued links with the exiled Tibetan freedom fighters. When Gompo Tashi, a senior figure within the Tibetan Resistance movement Chushi Gangdrok, arrived in Darjeeling as Tibet fell, he was greeted at the Agency's safehouse by CIA officer Robert McCarthy with two bottles of Scotch and two cartons of Marlboros. In Camp Hale, Colorado, meanwhile, gnarled CIA agents continued to train young Tibetans to fight a guerrilla war. There, the Tibetans took a particular liking to the latest Hollywood Westerns: *Viva Zapata!*, *Walk East on Beacon*, *Rogers' Rangers* and *Merrill's Marauders* among others. *Cheyenne*, starring Clint Walker, was a particular favourite; some of the Tibetan trainees even started to imitate Walker's swagger through the post-Civil War Wild West in preparation for their reinsertion to their homeland.

But the practicalities of the situation in Tibet meant that airdrops were becoming less and less feasible. In May 1960, the shooting down of a US U2 spy plane over Soviet Russia led to the suspension of all flights over communist countries. A new plan was needed – one that would give the thousands of Tibetans living in and around Sikkim a more permanent base from which to strike a blow in aid of recovering their homeland. The Americans – with Indian support – would soon choose a base on the Nepal–Tibet border to fulfil that purpose: the Mustang Valley.

-3-

While the Americans had been planning support for clandestine operations into Tibet, Thondup had been faced with a more local issue: the rise of a new political movement in Sikkim – and the emergence of a new leader, Kazi Lhendup Dorji.

Frustrated by the byzantine electoral system, a group of politicans formed a new party in September 1959 – the Sikkim National Congress – out of the ashes of the two parties that had contested the previous system in the 1950s. Soon this new party was being led by Dorji, a diminutive local landowner who came from an old Sikkimese Lepcha family, the Khangsarpas.

The Khangsarpas and the Namgyals had not seen eye to eye for many years. The Lepchas were considered the indigineous people of Sikkim; they had been in Sikkim before the Namgyals and their Bhutia kinsmen arrived in the country from Tibet. Although there had been some natural tensions, the Namgyals had reduced these by assimilating the Lepchas into the hierarchy of the kingdom they had established.

In the 1890s, however, Claude White (the first British Political Officer) encouraged widescale Nepali immigration; the Namgyals objected, fearing dilution of their Buddhist heritage by the incomers. Since Dorji's Lepcha uncles were more welcoming of the Nepali labour (and more tolerant of their Hindu beliefs), the British had rewarded them with land and favours, while constraining the Namgyals' power for the first two decades of the twentieth century.

By 1918, the British were seeking to develop links with Tibet, and the Namgyals became more useful again. Now Tashi Namgyal was given his full powers back by the British. There was an immediate impact on the Khangsarpas, who the Namgyals had not allowed to retain the same status to which they had become accustomed. For Dorji – who would become known simply as 'the Kazi' – the impact had been personal. Trained as a Buddhist monk as a young man, he had become head of the prestigious monastery at Rumtek. But when Thondup Namgyal came of age, Dorji was set aside. It was something that he would resent for the rest of his life.

Dorji, therefore, held very different views from Thondup Namgyal as to the future of the country. His family's strong connection with the Nepali immigrants in south-west Sikkim (in Chakung, where his family's estates were) led him to champion their cause. He was convinced that a fairer voting system, which did not discriminate against Sikkim's Nepali population, was essential and he was entirely willing to work with the new Sikkimese Nepali political class to achieve this.* Dorji was also one of those certain that the future of Sikkim lay in closer ties with India.

During the late 1940s and early 1950s, Dorji was just another of the

---

* The parity voting system set up in 1951 (see chapter 2) had, in fact, become even more convoluted. But the basic principle remained the same: the Bhutia-Lepcha community (by now only 25 per cent of the population) had at least 50 per cent of seats reserved for them in elections, with only 50 per cent reserved for the Nepali population (75 per cent of the electorate).

young politicians trying in vain to navigate the convoluted power structures in Sikkim. But in 1957, Dorji, like Thondup, met a woman in Delhi
who entirely changed his political career.

By the time Dorji met Elisa-Maria Langford-Rae she was, like him,
already in her fifties. She had also been through two marriages. Born
into an ordinary family in Edinburgh, Scotland, she was a woman with
an infinite capacity for reinvention. After a period in Belgium, she had
emigrated to Burma with her first husband, an Anglo-Burmese man,
Frank Langford-Rae, in the 1920s, where, she would later claim, she
had been a close acquaintance of Eric Blair, who found fame as George
Orwell. When that marriage collapsed, she had a short marriage to Dr
Khan, a Muslim, but by the early 1950s she was single again and in the
Indian capital.

In Delhi, Langford-Rae became a teacher, first as a private tutor to the
son of an important Nepali prince, and then teaching French at a school
run by Christian brothers. Tall and statuesque and with a strong sense
of social justice, she soon built up a reputation for moving in diplomatic
and political circles, preferring the company of the socialists to that of
the ruling Congress Party. No one doubted her intelligence, although few
were able to pin down the exact details of her past. It was while in Delhi
that she began to actively encourage a sense of mystery about her background – a mystery that would attend her for the rest of her life. To some,
she claimed her uncle was a Field-Marshal Mannerheim, the founder of
modern Finland; to others, that she had connections with Belgian royalty.
Very few knew that before arriving in Burma she had been Ethel Maud
Shirran, daughter of a Colour sergeant in the Black Watch.[10]

It was through a party held by a Nepali political contact that the
mercurial Elisa-Maria met Kazi Lhendup Dorji. Soon, an unlikely late-
life romance developed. By late 1957, Langford-Rae had arrived in
Kalimpong. With remarkable haste, Dorji moved his then wife out of his
house in Kalimpong, and Langford-Rae moved in. (She would later claim
the family of Dorji's first wife made an attempt on her life to avenge this
insult.)

With marriage to the Kazi, Langford-Rae entered a new phase of her
remarkable life. Soon she had adopted the title of Kazini of Chakung. The

more she learnt about the situation in Sikkim, the more she recognised a new cause that she could associate herself with: her husband's struggle to move Sikkim away from what she saw as its colonial hangover (a feudal mini-state run by a king from a minority community with strong links to the Tibetans) towards becoming a functioning state with closer links with India.

The newly styled Kazini fitted in perfectly to the exotic community in Kalimpong, with its assortment of spies, adventurers, socialites and other weird and wonderful characters described in the previous chapter. It was a place where, in the words of one UK newspaper, 'innocence is a guise, not a virtue'. Chinese Premier Zhou Enlai believed the town to be 'full of spies and reactionary elements'.[11] Nehru had been forced to admit in 1959 that the town was indeed 'a nest of spies' and contained more intelligence agents than any other profession.

By 1959, when the Kazi started his new political party, the Sikkim National Congress, the Kazini was already well established in Kalimpong, where she was known for her witty, amusing articles (often satirising Sikkim's unique situation), written on a typewriter in the back room of the house, in support of her husband's political aims.

All she needed now was a female counterpart upon whom she could focus her venom.

-4-

After meeting Thondup in 1959, Hope Cooke returned to America and her studies at Sarah Lawrence College in New York, determined to find out more about Sikkim. That year she took a paper in 'Cultural Frontiers of China'; the following summer of 1960 she strongly considered an immediate return to Darjeeling to find Thondup again, but instead went to see her uncle Selden and aunt Mary, now posted to Lima, Peru. But all the time it was 'the Prince' and Sikkim that were on her mind:

> There was somewhere inside me the conviction that I would return to Darjeeling and that I would know instinctively when the time was right to do so. I cannot explain why I was so sure of this nor what I expected. It

was just there – a deep, unflinching feeling of which I was constantly aware. I was equally aware of the Prince's existence, certainly, but I did not hear from him. Nor did I write to him; it didn't seem the thing to do.[12]

Finally, in the summer of 1961, she flew to India and booked back into the Windamere Hotel. She had no idea how long she was going to spend in Darjeeling – but she was now determined 'to find out . . . whether I was egging on fate or whether fate was dogging me'. She recalled later:

> I do not know how the Prince found out that I was back at the Windamere Hotel. This time I was sipping tea alone and unesthetically munching a cookie when he entered the chintz-curtained parlor. I looked up, startled, and could think of nothing to say. Through the silence, I could hear myself chewing with embarrassing loudness. My teeth kept thudding in what sounded like a deafening 'boom-boom.'
>
> The Prince, an honorary officer in a Gurkha regiment, had come from Gangtok to attend a military affair. He invited me to a dance that evening at the private Gymkhana Club. He was in a gay mood that night . . . He murmured that someday we would be waltzing together in Vienna.[13]

During that first night of dancing Thondup asked Hope if she would consider marrying him. The young American, still a few days short of her 21st birthday, was bowled over. It was not quite a marriage proposal – but it was close.

Within days Thondup had whisked her up to Gangtok. Hope immediately fell in love with the palace. The centrepiece of the building was now an annexe-type extension, 'a cheerful, white-walled room with a curved bay window and a fireplace . . . furnished in a simple Sikkimese style. A continuous divan, made of a double-layer of almost rock-hard, coral-colour cushions, rings the walls. Small, brightly lacquered tables face the divan at intervals.' In this room she sat and ate with the court of Sikkimese and Tibetan noblemen, many of them with perfect English, whose 'weather-beaten faces made quite a contrast against their earrings – a turquoise stud in the right ear and as a symbol of their standing as prosperous citizens, a much fancier, long pendant in the left'. To Hope, they looked like 'dashing pirates'. After dinner, the Prince brought out his record collection, playing Brahms' Hungarian Dances and Bach's Brandenburg Concertos as the court danced the night away.

She was only in Gangtok for six days, but it was enough to convince her that Sikkim was her destiny. She had stayed in the Royal Apartments; the romance of it all made her feel like she had entered some kind of fairy tale. But even during this short stay there were signs of some of the difficulties to come; at one party, she met the Crown Prince's sister, Princess Coocoola. Their first encounter did not go according to plan. When Hope recalled the story in her autobiography nearly 30 years later, she painted a vivid picture of royal life at the time:

Maharaj Kumar's [Thondup's] family is being quite warm to me . . . Even his sister Coocoola is being sweet, although sometimes I get the feeling she is just being kind to me for her brother's sake, that she too thinks I'm a beatnik eccentric, possibly an adventurer. I'm in awe of her for several reasons; first of all she is so strikingly beautiful and sophisticated that often I feel boorish. I had a disaster at the palace the very first time I went there. People had been drinking a lot. (People drink too much here – sycophants are always pushing drinks at Maharaj Kumar – 'Just one more, Prince, just one more!') Many toasts in my honor. Maharaj Kumar's brother drinking champagne out of my scruffy shoe. Anyway as I don't drink as a rule, I threw up in the hall as M. K. was getting out of the car to take me back to the guesthouse. Threw up! Can you believe it? And there was no one to apologize or explain to. I lay awake for hours in agony thinking of what I'd say the next morning. When I did meet Coocoola the next day, I shuffled out an apology. 'Er, er, Your Highness,' I blurted out, 'I'm very sorry about last night.' She took my hand, and, gazing straight in my eyes, said in this silky voice, 'Oh, that's all right, Hope La. You must treat this house as if it were your own.' I didn't know what to say – 'I don't throw up in my house, only in others'?' It was mortifying. I couldn't take my hand back.[14]

Despite Coocoola's silky smooth reassurances, it was not an auspicious start.

For Thondup, a critical part of the attraction was the relationship that Hope struck up with his children from the moment she met them. Yangchen, the youngest, was only five years old. When Hope left Gangtok to return to

Darjeeling at the end of the week, Thondup sent Yangchen and her nanny with her, making Hope guardian to his daughter and putting her and the nanny up in the room next to Hope. It was a remarkably bold move.

Hope would stay in Darjeeling for seven months in all, struggling into a suit of British tweed to go and collect Yangchen at the end of each day, as she tried to fit in with the smarter end of the Darjeeling set of ex-patriates who had 'stayed on' after independence.*

She lived for Thondup's visits, listening awestruck as he talked of his plans for Sikkim. He was open, too, about the problems he faced, in particular from the Kazi and his wife in Kalimpong. He told her how the Kazini was writing articles wrongly portraying the situation in Sikkim as one of conflict between Thondup and his Nepali subjects. He laughingly told her that the Kazini had even described him as 'the Lumumba of Sikkim' and 'a most despotic, miscreant ruler' who physically persecuted the Nepalis.[15]

For Hope, the drama of the opposition to this handsome prince only made her adore him more. 'It's his foreground I love, his immediacy . . . It's so extraordinary what this man can do. Sikkim is a flower of his care,' she wrote. When the time came to return to Sarah Lawrence College, she 'simply could not go. I felt that I just couldn't, and soon afterward, the Prince and I became engaged.'[16]

He proposed at the Gymkhana Club, where they had first met. Thondup 'was like Peter Pan with the lost boys. I felt like Wendy.'[17]

The engagement became a political issue as soon as it was announced. Earlier in the year, Thondup had introduced legislation entitled the 'Sikkim Subjects Regulations' aimed at clarifying who was and was not a Sikkim subject, restricting future Nepali immigration and making a further statement about Sikkim's separate identity. The legislation also stressed that marriages between Bhutia-Lepchas and Nepali could undermine

---

* Hope would later write: 'When my husband was asked why he had fallen in love with me, he said, "Well, besides the fact that Hope is a beautiful woman, I fell in love with her because she is so quiet. And I loved her, because she seemed to love my children so much. In choosing a wife, I had to take into consideration that she would have to be content to live in Gangtok. I couldn't have a wife who wanted to go to the theater or opera every evening, because there is no theater or opera in Gangtok and—" I stopped him short and laughed. "You're making me out a cultural bankrupt!"' (*McCall's Magazine*, September 1963)

the solidarity of minorities. It was necessary, the regulations implied, to adhere to customary practice in order to ensure the survival of Sikkim's fragile identity. By marrying an American, as Nari Rustomji put it, he 'laid himself open to the charge of acting against his own widely proclaimed principles'. The Buddhist monastic community agreed, and laid down a condition for the marriage: if Hope was to marry Thondup, she must give up her American citizenship (something she did eventually do).

It was clear that the announcement of Thondup's engagement to Hope Cooke was ill timed, to say the least. It gave the Kazini ammunition for her articles printed in the newspapers in Kalimpong; meanwhile it alienated elements of the Bhutia-Lepcha constituency, who felt that a marriage within the community would have sent a more appropriate message.

Hope, who had returned to America after becoming engaged to complete the final year of her university course, noticed that more sinister stories were emerging in the newspapers in the US and in India:

> The *New York Times* notice said 'Miss Hope Cooke, who has been in Darjeeling studying typing . . .' No wonder people think I'm a CIA agent . . . Worse than the gossipy whore rumours are the political allegations. Although the CIA cover joke concerning my typing is funny, it isn't completely a joke. Some people here would do anything to unseat the Maharaj Kumar politically – and if he goes, so does Sikkim. I love Maharaj Kumar and Sikkim too much to jeopardize them. I can just see them using me as a wedge to help destroy his rule. It's a squeeze from all sides.[18]

If that was her view in 1961 (although the memoir was written with the benefit of hindsight in 1980, it is penned in an engaging present tense) it was remarkably prescient. Sikkim was about to be slowly squeezed.

-5-

Hope Cooke had entered Thondup's life at a critical juncture. His father, in his late sixties, was still theoretically the Chogyal, but in reality it was the younger man who had taken over in all but name: it was Thondup who was setting his mind towards the future of Sikkim, representing the country at an increasing number of conferences and events in a bid to further emphasise Sikkim's independent status. He was under no illusions that he needed Indian support to defend his borders, but he feared the potential 'Indianisation' of Sikkim's administration. During the 1950s he had become used to avuncular support and advice from his old friend Rustomji; the man who replaced him, Baleshwar Prasad, was not cut from the same cloth at all – he was much more in the mould of the new Indian bureaucracy, with no hint of the colonial past.

To emphasise Sikkim's separate identity, he approached Delhi with a plan for Sikkimese soldiers to play a role in the defence effort, proposing that Sikkim should form an indigenous 'Sikkim Militia'. Nehru initially approved the idea in principle, but in Sikkim, the Kazi, who was starting to organise a nascent political opposition, was implacably opposed to the idea.

Thondup considered the Kazi and his cronies a troublesome minority. In a letter to Rustomji, he wrote of his distrust of the Sikkim National Congress, the Kazi's party:

> They seem to be following the popular communist tactics of trying to make people believe they have a grievance and that they are martyrs with the object of breaking down the established system and social order. At the same time they are making out that Sikkim is on the verge of revolt and the Chinese are about to invade it.[19]

When Thondup refused to give the Kazi a position on the Executive Council in 1960 (despite his new party being the second largest party on the council), the Kazi immediately took a delegation to Delhi to convey all his grievances (there had also been arrests and suspensions of some of the Sikkimese politicians) to Prime Minister Nehru. Nehru promptly shelved the idea of the militia, although a few years later Thondup would gain approval for an increase in the size of the Sikkim Guards.

In fact, the attitude of many Indian politicians to Sikkim was changing. Nehru, somewhat chastened by the collapse of his dreams of a pan-Asian federation with the Chinese, was now coming under political pressure to tighten up security across the entire northern frontier of India. The ambiguity that had been left by the British in terms of the border with Tibet was no longer acceptable to Nehru's increasingly hawkish advisers.

The strategic importance of all three Himalayan states – Sikkim, Bhutan and Nepal – was becoming all too apparent. Sikkim, as the smallest, was the most vulnerable of all.

Despite the opposition to the formation of a Sikkim Militia, Thondup was confident that as long as Nehru was in power, India would respect Sikkim's position as an independent Buddhist monarchy. But he also recognised that there were some in India who saw Sikkim's independence as a weak defensive link in the Himalayan chain and were advocating change, even incorporation. In that context, he was very conscious of the need for Sikkim to have friends outside the immediate realm of the Indian subcontinent. No harm, he felt, could come from his marriage into Hope Cooke's family, with its distinguished American diplomatic connections.

So, in December 1961, he flew off to a Buddhist world conference in Cambodia and then on to Rome's Flora Hotel, where he was to meet his future in-laws, Selden Chapin, now retired from the US Foreign Service with a heart condition, and various other Foreign Service colleagues of Chapin's. Despite Thondup being more than an hour late for a Christmas Day lunch at Alfredo's Restaurant, he charmed the assembled guests; for Uncle Selden, the fact that 'he holds his own in every way – even in drinking martinis' was quite enough evidence of his suitability.[20]

If winning over his future in-laws was simple, convincing the monastic community in Sikkim of the virtue of the marriage proved to be more of a challenge. After a meeting of the Bhutia-Lepcha monastic community, it was declared that the following year was to be 'a black year' and therefore the marriage must be postponed.

Somewhat unsettled, Cooke returned once again to New York to continue her studies.

Hope concluded her university course in New York at the end of the spring term of 1962. She had not enjoyed the intercontinental nature of the relationship, developing a deep belief that her new fiancé was still involved with other women.* When he flew to New York to reassure her,

---

* In her autobiography, Hope makes clear that there was a specific relationship between Thondup and an American socialite that survived well into their engagement, and possibly beyond. (*Palm Beach Daily News*, 16 April 1981)

she was convinced that he had arranged the itinerary so that he could spend time with another woman in Paris on the way. Whether this was in her imagination or not hardly mattered.

For the rest of the year, the couple entered what she later called a 'kaleidoscopic' period of travel back and forth between New York and Sikkim. In the summer of 1962 she returned to Sikkim for a visit, along with a friend. At a party held at the palace, Martha Hamilton, now well settled into Gangtok life, watched as Hope demonstrated the latest trends and crazes from the USA:

> We were asked to the palace. It was a party for Miss Hope Cooke and the younger officers – very few and great fun. They were teaching me to do the twist (at which Kumar and Kumari are very good) so I borrowed the record when I left at 12 (they all stayed till 2) . . . Kumari rang to say she'd bought it for me in Calcutta so I now have my daily exercise in the late evening doing the twist.[21]

But while Hope Cooke, Thondup and Coocoola twisted the night away, the tensions between India and China were about to reach fever pitch.

-6-

The Dalai Lama's flight to India had changed the relationship between India and China irrevocably. For India, and Nehru in particular, it was a wake-up call. The Himalayan states – Sikkim, Bhutan and Nepal – all took on a new, more prominent role for Indian foreign policy-makers. Dealing with fully independent Nepal was a matter of diplomacy, but Sikkim and Bhutan were different. A Border Roads Organisation (BRO) was set up to make the two countries more accessible. Nehru also reiterated that India was the 'only competent authority' to deal with Bhutan's – and by inference Sikkim's – external relations.

China's occupation of Tibet had also increased the USA's interest in Himalayan politics. In Camp Hale, the reopened high-altitude training school for Tibetans in the Colorado mountains, there had been a subtle change in the programme. English lessons became mandatory and there was even an attempt to use Plato's dialogues to instil a greater under-standing of the value of political freedom in the young men.[22] (It all had a faint echo of an earlier experiment in 1913, when the British had taken four Tibetan teenagers to Rugby School 'to produce a type of man, fitted for some kind of useful public service in Tibet, who will be united to England by ties of affection and esteem'.)

The airdrops, of course, were both expensive and, after the U2 incident, increasingly impractical. The USA needed another solution. In late 1960 the Dalai Lama's brother Gyalo Thondup (now a primary liaison with the resistance fighters and the growing numbers of refugees) proposed a new approach. Nestling up against the Tibetan border in the north of Nepal, not more than 100 miles from Sikkim, lay the small kingdom of Mustang. Gyalo Thondup and Gompo Tashi were convinced that it was the perfect base for operations.[23] President Kennedy's administration was quick to back the idea.

As word emerged of the new base, Tibetan refugees in Sikkim started to flood south to Darjeeling, from where they could proceed across the Nepali border to Mustang. It was another echo from the past: more than 120 years earlier Thondup's great-grandfather had been faced with an exodus of his Lepcha subjects to Darjeeling in search of economic pros-perity. Now the Tibetan refugees (who had become a valuable and cheap source of labour, working as gangs on Indian road projects) were treading the same path for different reasons.

In March 1961, Kennedy secretly sanctioned an initial drop of 29,000 lbs of arms and ammunition over the valley. Not everyone was in favour: it was not until two weeks after the drop that J. K. Galbraith, the newly appointed American Ambassador to India, was briefed on the wider Mustang operation. Galbraith 'took an instant dislike for the whole thing', which he called a 'particularly insane exercise'.[24] He was particularly wary of the potential negative effect on the USA's relationship with the Indian government, which had not initially been informed. But Kennedy was insistent that support for the Mustang project must continue. He had seen 'no evidence that Mao was relaxing his hostility to the US' and saw it as a great example of the kind of unconventional warfare that could be developed as an alternative to a nuclear stand-off.[25] Kennedy did, however, put a requirement on the project that Indian approval should be sought for the supply drops. (The CIA interpreted this in its loosest form, taking it to mean that they merely had to make sure there was no explicit Indian opposition.) Galbraith's opposition eased a little when a raiding party operating out of Mustang managed to capture 1,600 classified documents intact from a pouch carried by a Chinese patrol. The documents revealed some of the weaknesses in the Chinese control in Tibet, and in particular the low morale of many of the PLA soldiers serving there. It gave impetus for a second major arms drop in December, which included a helpful colour catalogue of the weaponry that the Mustang project might want to choose from.

The Chinese were well aware of – and concerned by – the newly established Tibetan rebel base in Mustang, but for them it was only part of a wider picture of rising tensions across the Himalayas. There were specific problems in two highly contested areas. One was Tawang, to the east of Bhutan, which had been the subject of the convoluted partial agreements made by Sir Henry McMahon in 1913–14, and had also been brought up in discussions about supply routes during the Second World War. The other was a vast barren tract of land, where China, India and Pakistan meet, known as the Aksai Chin. The latter was of such limited strategic interest to the Indians that it was not until the completion of a two-year Chinese road-building project in 1957 that the area had come to the attention of the Indian government – via notices in the Chinese press.[26] For the Chinese, the Aksai Chin held significantly more strategic import, providing a potential solution to the endless problem of how to supply and resupply the troops in Tibet (from the outer reaches of Western China).

The problem was that the British, prior to their departure in 1947, had sometimes found fuzzy borders to their advantage. The Indians were initially less concerned with this ambiguity than Chinese Premier Zhou Enlai; the latter sought to settle both issues in 1960 with a proposal to recognise the nebulous McMahon Line in the Tawang region (which the Chinese argued they had never officially agreed in 1914) in exchange for recognition of China's claim to the Aksai Chin.* But the ageing Nehru

---

* The McMahon Line defined the southern border of Tibet, agreed in the Simla Convention of 1914. It was notoriously ill-defined (the markers used a thick red pencil to draw it, covering many kilometres in width) and had been contentious for more than half a century.

was now under considerable pressure to stand up to the Chinese after their actions in Tibet. He refused their offer.

Instead, an increasingly confident India moved onto the front foot, deploying what they called a 'Forward Policy' (ironically the same name given to the policy adopted by Younghusband and his successors in 1904) during the second half of 1961 and the first half of 1962. In an article entitled 'The Himalayas: Struggle for the Roof of the World', *Time* magazine reported an Indian as saying: 'Tibet is the palm of the hand, and the Chinese have it. Now they want the five fingers without which the palm is useless.' The five fingers were identified as Ladakh, Nepal, Sikkim, Bhutan and the North-East Frontier Agency (NEFA). 'To the Chinese, all five stick out like sore thumbs,' the article said, mixing metaphors.

The Indian Forward Policy involved establishing military outposts to the north of existing Chinese positions, particularly in the Aksai Chin region. At first, China did not respond, being faced with monumental challenges elsewhere. Internally the country was recovering from the disaster of the Great Leap Forward: on its eastern seaboard there was still the possibility that Taiwan might become the base for an attack on the mainland; and in Laos, a proxy conflict with the United States was just getting under way. But by the middle of 1962, Mao and Zhou decided it was time to act. During the 1950s Mao had characterised the era of Hindi-Chini-Bhai-Bhai as one of 'armed coexistence' in the border areas with India. But India's Forward Policy, Mao now argued, had put paid to that idea. Not only were the Indians occupying the strategically important Aksai Chin, they were also actively challenging China's interpretation of the McMahon Line in Tawang.

By the autumn of 1962, both sides began to prepare for war. The main conflict developed in Tawang. The Indians occupied a position just inside territory that the Chinese claimed. The Chinese responded by taking dominant positions around it. On 9 September, the Indians countered with an attempt to evict the Chinese. In the high altitudes and unforgiving terrain neither side had much chance of success. But for the Indian commander, General Kaul, it was now a matter of pride. Reinforcements were called in and an attack was planned for October.

By now the numbers of well-trained Chinese troops, battle-hardened from Tibet, had increased substantially. A tense stand-off resulted, but when a rumour reached Beijing that the Indians were planning a more direct assault than previously (the Forward Policy had thus far been concerned with outflanking and encircling rather than confrontation), the Chinese leadership decided to discuss the matter with its counterparts in Moscow.

Involving the Kremlin was a calculated escalation. Although relations between the USSR and China were characterised more by competition than cooperation, events on the other side of the world – where the Cuban Missile Crisis was rapidly developing – were rapidly shifting the pieces on the international chessboard.

On 13–14 October, Khrushchev gave Peking his tacit approval, stating that he 'understood' the need for China to take appropriate counter-measures. With the necessary geopolitical support in place, the Chinese troops took swift and decisive action, launching military strikes in both sectors on 20 October 1962 and thus turning the Indian Forward Policy backwards at great speed.

The timing gave conspiracy theorists in search of an anti-communist plot a field day. On the other side of the world, US President John F. Kennedy had just detected – and was in the midst of dealing with – the Soviet deployment of missiles in Cuba, one of the most serious crises of the Cold War. Having failed dismally with his planned invasion of the Bay of Pigs the previous year, the president could not afford another climb-down and made it clear that he saw Cuba as a completely unacceptable front line between the communist and capitalist spheres of orbit.

It was just as he faced up to the greatest crisis of his presidency right on his doorstep that the Chinese were making their incursions into the disputed regions in the Himalayas. The American president had to perform a double act. As he confronted Khrushchev over Cuba, he also dispatched an American aircraft carrier to the Bay of Bengal.[27] It was not inconceivable that the long-awaited confrontation between democratic America and the world's communist powers could now open on not one but two fronts.

After 13 days of high drama, the Cuban crisis was resolved when the Russians backed down from the brink of Armageddon by withdrawing from Cuba on 28 October 1962. In the Himalayas, however, the Chinese were not in the habit of being denied what they wanted. Their aim was nothing less than to see the Indian Forward Policy, which they felt had been designed to antagonise them, in tatters. Despite an Indian counterattack on Nehru's birthday, 14 November, the Chinese continued to push forward. After 31 days the 'war' was all but over. By 21 November neither side was willing to admit defeat, but it was undoubtedly the Chinese that were in the stronger position. It was they who felt confident enough to declare a unilateral ceasefire and, in early December, to withdraw from the disputed areas, saying they had achieved their policy objectives of securing borders in Aksai Chin in the west.

Kennedy's aircraft carrier, therefore, turned tail no sooner than it had arrived. But with the Russian threat contained in Cuba, the Americans sought to increase their influence in the Asian sphere in late 1962. Within days of the Chinese withdrawal from Tawang, a 'KC-135 jet tanker converted for passenger use' had set off for New Delhi stuffed with yet more CIA agents.[28] Despite Nehru's continued misgivings, he accepted $120 million of aid from the Americans to resupply the Indian military.

The worldwide arms race to equip less developed countries was well under way. Within a year, the Soviets would also be supplying MIG fighters to the Indians.

Just as the Tawang crisis was developing in September 1962, Thondup had flown with Hope Cooke to New York after her summer break. All too aware of the possible impact of a Sino-Indian conflict on Sikkim, he wanted to 'see the UN in action' and to explore what it would take to achieve international recognition. When the UN was set up in 1945, Nepal had been recognised with a seat, but Bhutan and Sikkim had not, leaving both countries without the international protection afforded to others.

By early October Thondup had returned to Sikkim, leaving Hope alone in New York. From her apartment, she read the front-page news reports with some concern, terrified by the 'tiny *New York Times* border map [which] showed Sikkim hardly a hairbreadth away from the clashes in NEFA'.

In fact, there had never been any serious threat to the Sikkimese section of the border from the Chinese side. The reason was a curious one: the Chinese maintained that both Sikkim and Bhutan were actually independent states and that there was no special relationship between India and Sikkim or Bhutan. A military attack would have challenged this logic. But, even if there was no physical threat, there was no let-up on the threatening rhetoric: Beijing now talked of Sikkim, Bhutan, Darjeeling and Kalimpong as 'fingers on the hand of China' and complained bitterly of the spies in all four being 'lice in China's clothing'.[29]

For the Indian Army and the growing political class, Sikkim had now taken on an even greater importance. They were on the lookout for any hint of pro-Chinese leanings in the Himalayan border states. Some even suggested that Crown Prince Thondup had been suspiciously slow to declare a state of emergency in Sikkim in the run-up to the crisis. Once he did so, Martha Hamilton's recollection was of a rapid and significant build-up of Indian troops. In a letter home just before the major Chinese offensives, she wrote that:

> I really hadn't thought about the Chinese attacks worrying anyone as when I went to the district they were very minor. It was not till I returned that I found the army pouring in and nothing but war furore on every side.[30]

The army had arrived in numbers to honour its commitment to safeguard the Sikkimese nation as embodied in the 1950 agreement. As is often the way with military deployments, they would never really leave.

-7-

Towards the end of 1962 and in the shadow of the Sino-Indian conflict, the build-up to the royal wedding started in earnest.

Once the powerful Buddhist priests had accepted that there was little they could do to prevent the wedding taking place, they identified an auspicious date for the nuptials in late March 1963. While Gangtok mobilised its scant resources for the expected influx of dignitaries, the newspapers in America had a field day. The press corps were eager for a re-run of Grace Kelly's famous wedding in Monaco: *Time* declared that Hope was 'the first American girl to wed royalty since the daughter of a former Philadelphia bricklayer married Monaco's Prince Rainier in 1956'.

Alternately portrayed as a 'Cinderella orphan' and a 'New York debutante', she became a source of great fascination for the press, even in the pages of the fashionable *Paris Match*. It was deemed irrelevant that – with her slightly strained, earnest looks – she neither resembled nor wanted to resemble the effortlessly beautiful actress. This was the period when the American Dream reached its apogee, when reveries almost became reality. The marriage of an all-American girl into a secretive Buddhist kingdom had all the ingredients of great copy.

In fact, as all this was going on Hope Cooke was in New York – and was increasingly frazzled. As if the geopolitical tensions weren't enough, she still harboured suspicions about her future husband's infidelities. It hardly mattered whether they were real or imagined.

Meanwhile attempts to trace her genealogy for the ceremonies turned up 'lowly' origins (her father's 'Irishness' led to her realising she was 'not entirely top drawer'), which only increased her feelings of social vulnerability. During a Christmas visit to Sikkim she found Princess Coocoola 'increasingly haughty . . . going on about the unsuitability, the rawness of people who have no roots, no background'. Things got even worse when she contracted a dose of hepatitis, with the wedding only weeks away. Thondup flew to New York to be by her side; when she confessed her fears about his commitment, she was furious that he responded by having a 'physical attack' with 'drenching sweat, constant tremors, fevers and chill by turn'. She felt as if he was trying to trump her own illness, even though she knew that it was a flare-up of the malaria he'd caught as a child. Three days later, when he left for Gangtok to cope with the 'intricate logistics' of the wedding, she felt bitterly alone once more in New York.

None of that, of course, was known to the American press, who, as the day of the wedding approached, tripped over each other to write the most effusive words about the romance of the improbable love match. *National Geographic* ran a 31-page feature on Sikkim in March 1963, cataloguing the mystical and beautiful sides of the land. The author, Desmond Doig, was a former Ghurkha officer who had stayed on with a Calcutta newspaper. As he toured the country with Thondup, he recalled sitting

with the Crown Prince, watching a storm approach. 'That's hail,' he remarked, pointing to the swollen bruise-blue belly of an advancing cloud bank. Sure enough, hail soon ricocheted off the tin roof of the palace and bounced like table-tennis balls on the lawn. As suddenly as the cloudburst came it passed, climbing over the valleys to the Northern ranges.

The Crown Prince watched its direction. 'Good,' he said at last. 'It missed my cardamoms.' For a moment the country's next ruler was no more than a Lepcha farmer. Then he called for champagne.[31]

It was a telling image of the contrasts and contradictions in the Chogyal's life, and just the sort of thing that aggravated the brooding Kazini of Chakung. As the palace sent out invitations across the world, the Kazini mulled over the events about to take place in the garden of her husband's political ambitions. She had refused to renounce her British passport and become a 'Sikkim Subject' under Thondup's new regulations; she and the Kazi had therefore settled in Kalimpong instead of in Sikkim, but all her venomous energy was squarely focused on the country's situation. She came under suspicion for meddling when in early 1963 an article appeared in a UK newspaper with the headline, 'Sikkim Crown Prince's Wedding Opposed'. The article bore all the hallmarks of the Kazini, reporting that the Sikkim National Congress was 'feeling aggrieved and apprehensive', and describing the marriage as 'against the best traditions and customs of Sikkim, a small state in the Himalayas. [The party] declares that it was incorrect to say that the marriage had the approval of the people of Sikkim.'

Hope Cooke finally flew back to India with the wedding only a week away. Accompanied by her aunt Mary, she carried no less than 26 suitcases and 12 umbrellas and parasols. On a stopover in Karachi she changed effortlessly from her Western frock into long Sikkimese clothing, a pale-yellow blouse and a tea-colour robe brocaded with chrysanthemums. 'Never again will I wear a Western Gown!' she declared in a magazine article a few months later. She was determined to shed her American background and start a new life, including becoming a Sikkimese citizen because 'dual citizenships, permitted in many countries but often abused as profit-making conveniences, are forbidden in my new country'.

Despite the Kazini's efforts there was genuine excitement and anticipation across Sikkim at Hope Cooke's arrival and the forthcoming wedding: at the border Hope was greeted by the bagpipe band playing 'The Skye

Boat Song'. (Presumably this Sikkimese band had not 'murdered' the song in the way that Martha Hamilton had heard in December 1959.) As she made her way back up to Gangtok she could see Kalimpong from the jeep. She noticed a glow of fires in the distance, convinced for a moment that it was the demonstration that the Kazini was rumoured to have arranged. The police commissioner travelling with her tried his best to reassure her that they were part of the celebrations.

In Gangtok, the reception from Coocoola confused her even further:

> Sometimes she is overwhelmingly kind and generous. Sometimes as well as being obviously cruel (she introduced Grace [who Hope suspected of having an affair with Thondup] to the Maharaj Kumar) I think she is practicing downright voodoo on me, or at least on my relationship with her brother . . .[32]

For Hope, the highly charged atmosphere was almost too much. She chose her wedding day as the first time to try out a half pill of Valium that one of the guests offered her to control her nerves.

On the wedding day itself it was the understated opulence of the event that made the biggest impression on Martha Hamilton:

> The maharaja was sitting on his throne in gorgeous gold brocade, ambassadors all down one side and Sikkim officials the other and general guests elsewhere. It was all very Sikkimese. The bridegroom arrived and Dewan and then the bride looking really lovely with, thank heaven, her hair done properly for once . . .

The Polish hairdresser, imported from Calcutta for the wedding, spent a considerable time lacquering Hope's hair into a 'boxlike shape' while Coocoola fussed over the wraparound Lepcha dress that had been chosen for the bride. *Time* fawned over the 'frost-white brocade silk mokey, held in at the waist by a gold belt, from which hung a small dagger'. Hope, 'feeling that a pageant was in progress and I was merely a spectator', tried to embrace the Sikkimese customs. She pressed a small piece of dough into her hand, designed to ward off evil spirits, and recalled the double rainbow that she had seen the first time she had arrived at the palace nearly two years earlier, a deeply auspicious omen, according to Buddhist beliefs.

Two Buddhist lamas led her to the chapel to 'a fanfare of trumpeting, 10 ft-long Himalayan horns, braying conch shells, and booming bass drums', where Hope sat on a throne slightly lower than that of Thondup, who in turn was seated lower than his father, Tashi. For the marriage itself, a red-robed lama invoked the blessings of Sikkim's deities, while the couple exchanged 12-foot-long white silk scarves, hanging them around each other's neck to seal the marriage contract.

Once the simple ceremony was complete, the guests repaired to a 'great sapphire-blue-and-white sharmian tent, at least two stories high', built on the palace lawn and surrounded by white Tibetan prayer flags on tall bamboo poles, while the palace fluttered with red, white and green pennants. The ambassadors of nine nations attended, among them John Kenneth Galbraith, the economist who Kennedy had appointed as US ambassador in Delhi. Hope Cooke's uncle, Selden Chapin, who was unable to travel to the wedding due to a heart condition, had asked Galbraith to act as witness to the wedding on his behalf.

But it was the appearance of Coocoola that made the greatest impression on Martha Hamilton: 'Most dramatic prostration to the floor by Coo Coo la in a gold lamé dress. People were alternately fascinated and repelled . . .'[33]

Coocoola had planned this fashion statement carefully – before the wedding she had reportedly written to all the guests asking them not to wear gold. A large gaggle of press photographers caught the moment as they struggled gamely on against odds that were rumoured to be outwith their control: 'quite a few of the professionals had trouble with their cameras – lamas voodoo was the professional opinion.'[34]

The Kazini, meanwhile, attended the wedding parties dressed all in black.* In one of the more extraordinary stories from what was a bizarre

---

* The Kazini never failed to make an impression. Indian journalist Sunanda Datta-Ray later described the effect she had as she entered a room: 'A stately woman with honey blonde hair drawn into a tight bun swept into the room, long skirts rustling about her ankles. "I am the Kazini of Chakung," she announced. Her face was a thick smooth white, resembling the chalk masks of Japanese Kabuki dancers. On it arched a pair of thin blue-black eyebrows and the scarlet gash of a painted mouth. Her long lashes were stiff with kohl. Only the eyes were real, glittering like live coals.'

event, a poem was posted under the door of each member of the international press corps.[35] Hope Cooke was in no doubt that the Kazini, who was taking 'every opportunity to talk down Sikkim to reporters'[36], was responsible for the verse and it's vicious satire directed towards her:

> I am Hope, the New York Lepcha,
> Oh, yes I really am
> Though I'm marrying a Shamgyal
> Don't think I'm just a sham.

Chorus of Lepchas (after partaking of marriage chang)

> She's Hope the Yankee Lepcha
> Oh, yes she really is
> Despite her Bowery accent
> And her pure Caucasian phiz.

> She's Hope, the Kumarani,
> Our unfed children weep;
> But ten lakhs* for a wedding
> Is really very cheap.[37]

The evening festivities reflected the diversity of the guest list. During the meal, one overzealous American evangelist distributed stacks of Christian tracts with an anti-Buddhist picture on the front, even giving one to the bride. Meanwhile the Maharaja of Jaipur, still one of the richest men in India, had 'true to legend, brought with him his own cases of champagne'. Later, Ambassador Galbraith twisted the night away with Coocoola, while the band (from the former Portuguese colony of Goa, recently annexed by India) played Dixie music.[38] Galbraith recalled rather wistfully that while the 'dancing was good fun' his arthritic hip was what got 'generous attention from the press'.[39] Later, 'mountain tribesmen in blue pajama-like clothes danced in the streets'.

The extraordinary clash of cultures at the wedding put Sikkim well and

---

* A lakh is the equivalent of 100,000 rupees.

truly under the spotlight of the world's press.* Later in 1963 *National Geographic* ran a further feature, this time with colour pictures from the event. But it was *Time* magazine that caught the culture clash best in an article entitled 'Where There's Hope' a week after the wedding:

> Guests in top hats and cutaways mingled with others in fur-flapped caps and knee-length yakskin boots last week outside the tiny Buddhist chapel in Sikkim's dollhouse Himalayan capital of Gangtok. Wedding parcels from Tiffany's were piled side by side with bundled gifts of rank-smelling tiger and leopard skins. Over 28,146 ft Mount Kanchenjunga, the world's third highest mountain and Sikkim's 'protecting deity,' hung a blue haze. It was an 'auspicious sign,' said Gangtok astrologers. [. . .] Outside the chapel door was the only distinctively American touch in the $60,000 Buddhist rite – a mat on which was written in English, 'Good Luck.' [. . .] Mixing happily with the celebrators, Hope settled into her new role with aplomb. When a pigtailed Sikkimese girl asked for her autograph, the new crown princess signed without a moment's hesitation: 'Hope Namgyal.'[40]

Like it or not, with Thondup's marriage to Hope Cooke, Sikkim had been put well and truly under the spotlight.

-8-

In the midst of the two weeks of festivities, news arrived that Hope's uncle Selden had died of a heart attack. The couple rushed down to Calcutta to catch a flight to Washington. Before they left India, Hope formally renounced her US citizenship to qualify for an 'Indian Protected Person' passport under which residents of Sikkim travelled. It was a move that would have major complications only ten years later.

Back in Gangtok in May, despite what she herself called a continuing

---

* The couple received an extraordinary list of wedding gifts: a Steuben glass punch bowl from the US ambassador, an autographed photograph from Pope John XXIII and many gifts in 'exquisite silver' from the Dalai Lama, as well as a number of specially bound volumes containing poems by Hope's favourite authors: Dylan Thomas, T. S. Eliot, Villon and Wallace Stevens.

'obsession with [her husband's] infidelities', Hope Cooke discovered she was pregnant. It was a self-confessed bid to 'make some kind of statement of femaleness'. But despite – or perhaps because of – the pregnancy she was struck by a deep loneliness: 'Upstairs in my room I listen to Joan Baez records all day and cry. I know how the Sikkimese got their eyes – little damn Mongolian eyes; they damn well cried all the time.'[41]

In September, less than six months after the wedding, the elderly Chogyal Tashi contracted cancer. If nothing else, it provided a distraction for the young couple's challenging relationship – a focus beyond them-selves. As it became increasingly clear that he would die, Hope Cooke, Coocoola and Thondup flew between London and Calcutta, seeking the best treatment possible. As Tashi neared the end of his life in November 1963, the USA was plunged into a crisis when Kennedy was shot. Sikkim was so isolated that Martha Hamilton initially missed the news: 'How appalling about Kennedy – my wireless is broken so I didn't hear till late . . .'

In December, Chogyal Tashi Namgyal lost his fight with cancer. After nearly 50 years on the throne of Sikkim, his death marked the beginning of a new era for the country. Thousands of villagers turned out to follow the funeral procession. But the death, far from uniting the couple in grief, brought tensions back into the Palace. With her record player banned during the traditional 49 days of Buddhist mourning, Hope had to sit with her ear to the machine, playing her music softly while her husband wandered the house muttering, 'Poor Sikkim! What will happen now?'

Thondup's concerns were exacerbated by the arrival of a film crew from CBS, arranged by India's External Affairs ministry to show off India's defence efforts. In response, he and Hope arranged for another crew from NBC to film a 'scenic beauty cum social development' documentary, soon reported in the 'People' section of *Time* magazine. 'One of the most important things to know for any girl hoping to become a princess is how to conduct a TV tour,' they wrote. 'Grace Kelly led the way in Monaco, and now the US's only other princess in a ruling family is doing it too. NBC is traveling to the Indian Himalayan protectorate of Sikkim to be shown up and down and all around by Hope Cooke, 22.' Hope, now several months pregnant, knew she was the real 'news peg'. But even as she gave an interview in a room carefully arranged with 'typically Sikkimese' objects and walked the crew through 'our small shabby house à la Jackie Kennedy', she could hear the 'BOOM, BOOM, BOOM' of the Indian artillery blasting away, as they created new roads up to the Sikkim–Tibet border.

At Christmas the tensions boiled over when Coocoola sent a Christmas tree down to the NBC crew. 'It's a time for mourning!' Thondup shouted at her. 'You want everyone to know that you are making a Christmas party for a bunch of foreigners?'[42]

As one scion of the Namgyal dynasty passed, Hope Cooke gave birth to another. For Hope, it was another possibility, another chance at integrating with this society that she still felt destiny pulling her towards. As she looked at her new baby she recalled her husband's 'Gauguin-handsome face' and told herself, 'This baby is going to belong, really belong to these people, and through him I will belong too.'[43]

Thondup and the Palace, conscious of the increasing presence of the Indian military, also saw an opportunity to capitalise on the birth and create a renaissance in national identity within the state after his father's death. One obvious way of doing this was to emphasise the importance of Sikkim's own tiny military force. Delhi had abandoned support for his attempts to raise a militia, but he had won agreement to double the size of the Sikkim Guards shortly before the 1962 war. The Guards, originally intended for ceremonial duties only, claimed origins from the thirteenth century. Although only a token gesture, it was one that aggravated those, such as the Kazi, who were adamant that Sikkim did not need such impractical symbols.

An even more thorny issue was the language used to describe the royal family. Sir Tashi had been far more interested in his meditation and improving his painting technique than in stoking any confrontation with either the British or the new Indian government over titles. So he had been perfectly content to use the Indian term 'Maharaja' that the British had brought with them when they concluded the very first treaty with the Sikkimese. For the new Indian government, too, the term had fitted their perspective: 'Maharaja' – or 'Great King' – was very firmly an Indo-Aryan term, rooting Sikkim firmly in the Indian orbit.

Thondup, on the other hand, while appreciating the reality of the

Indian protection afforded to his country (especially since the events of 1962), felt a need to continually assert the fact that Sikkim tended towards independence rather than assimilation into the Indian state. He had watched neighbouring Bhutan – where his cousin Jigme Dorji held the hereditary prime ministerial post – carefully build up its deck of playing cards in the game of poker being played with the Indian government. Why not Sikkim too? He was also convinced that the Indians, perhaps seeking to check his credentials, had been spying on him during a visit to the Himalayan Mountaineering Institute in Darjeeling. It made him even more determined to assert Sikkim's rights.

The question of nomenclature presented an opportunity to change – or at least to challenge – the status quo. Thondup informed Delhi that he and Hope wished to use the ancient Sikkimese titles Chogyal and Gyalmo rather than Indian terms such as 'Maharaja' and 'Maharani'.

The Indian government, however, was in no mood for any change that might signal a weakening of their resolve in the Himalayas. Nehru's administration had been seriously shaken by the Sino-Indian conflict of 1962 and Indian newspapers were delighting in painting the Chinese as evil aggressors. China's attack had been 'dastardly', the 'theory of coexistence had been exposed and the real face of the devil, a wolf in sheep's clothing' had been unmasked. Nehru himself came under attack for having been an idealist and a pacifist, too trusting of the 'wily enemy'.[44]

Neither had the tensions between the two countries dissipated with the ceasefire. In January 1963 the focus moved right onto the Sikkimese frontier, as Beijing accused the Indian government of putting up pillboxes on the Chinese side of the Nathu La. India naturally refuted the allegations as 'preposterous and baseless'. But the war of words rumbled on and Tashi's death created another diplomatic incident. When Liu Shaoqi, Vice-Chairman of the Chinese Communist Party, sent a message expressing his condolences directly to Thondup, it was considered a major affront. Nehru's response was an indication of just how seriously he was taking the issue:

The government of China has in contravention of normal diplomatic courtesies in its relations with the government of India, addressed a telegram from Chairman Liu Shao Chi directly to the Maharaja of Sikkim, on the

5th of December, 1963, instead of forwarding it to this government for onward transmission. The government of China is well aware that the external relations of Sikkim are entirely the responsibility of the government of India and that any communication, either formal or informal from the government of China to the government of Sikkim or its ruler, should be channelled through the Indian government. The procedure adopted by the Chinese government is, therefore, entirely unacceptable to the Indian government and they trust that in future all communications pertaining to Sikkim will be addressed to the government of India only.[45]

In early 1964 there were reports of further incursions, this time into Sikkim. They happened across both the Jelep La and the Nathu La into the Chumbi Valley, and on the northern border by the Kongra La, the area where a similar lack of border definition had so frustrated Sikkim's first Political Officer, Claude White, more than 70 years earlier. Tensions were further raised when Thondup's cousin and friend Jigme Dorji, the Prime Minister of Bhutan, was assassinated in an attempted palace coup. For Thondup, it was a bitter blow – and a warning of sorts. Only a few weeks earlier Jigme had told Thondup that he felt 'he'd done enough for the country' and that he 'really wanted to get out of harness'. The night before he was killed he had slept on the floor, afraid that his life was under threat. Hope had to hold Thondup all night as he lay awake, shaking. Understandably the atmosphere in the region tightened further.

Within the context of all these events, it is perhaps understandable that the Indians viewed the request for a change in the titles used by Thondup and his new American wife (with diplomatic family connections) with some suspicion.

-9-

The Sino-Indian conflict of 1962 had also radically shifted Indian thinking about its defences in the Himalayas. Before 1959, it had fallen to the intelligence chief B. N. Mullik to establish a series of informal checkpoints along the border staffed by Tibetan speakers; after 1962, the northern border became a military as well as an intelligence priority. Proposals for new mountain divisions were put forward in Delhi, and a road-building programme was put in place to enable the rapid deployment of troops in the event of war. Over the next decade the regular Indian Army doubled in size to 750,000.

There was also a major change in the Indian attitude towards the Tibetan community-in-exile and the operations taking place out of the kingdom of Mustang in northern Nepal. The tacit acceptance of US supply flights before September 1962 was replaced by a much higher level of cooperation with the CIA in 1963, now that the Chinese were more clearly a joint 'enemy'. Working with the Dalai Lama's brother Gyalo Thondup, Mullik helped to coordinate the creation of a new force comprised of Tibetan fighters. The 'Special Frontier Force' would be based and trained in India. As cover, the new regiment – Tibetan apart from a few senior officers – was named the 12th Gurkha Rifles. Major General Uban, a tough Sikh who had commanded the Indian 22 Mountain Regiment in the Second World War, was recruited to run the new outfit, which would later come to be known as Establishment 22. The Tibetans viewed it as another step on the way to a return to their homeland; the Americans saw the whole exercise as an opportunity to further strengthen their ties with the Indian government. By March 1963 Indians were being trained in the US; in September a joint centre was set up in Delhi to direct the despatch of CIA-trained operatives overland into Tibet.[46]

The Indian intelligence service also underwent a significant development. For arcane reasons dating back to the handover from British rule, India had inherited an intelligence service that was firmly focused on domestic threats. Now, with a real and present external threat, the Indians took steps towards creating their own external intelligence service. In 1963 R. N. Kao, a 'Kashmiri with piercing eyes and razor sharp mind',[47] was chosen to head up what was initially called the 'Aviation Research Centre' (ARC) within the Indian Intelligence Directorate-General. The extent of Kao's focus on the Chinese threat made quite an impression on his American counterparts: one CIA officer remembered driving back from Kathmandu to India with Kao while he recounted the technical specs of each bridge they crossed, providing an assessment of their ability to support the heaviest tank in the Chinese inventory.[48]

From a base in Orissa province, Kao oversaw the creation of ARC, including 'two large receivers and transmitters [that] were hooked up to special antennas to maintain regular, encrypted radio contact with Tibetan insurgent forces'. The CIA, too, were involved in providing radio equipment for the Tibetan teams on the ground in the Himalayas, including, by the spring of 1964, one in Gangtok.[49]

By coincidence, Thondup Namgyal had also just acquired his own new radio set. During 1964 an American, Gus Browning, had passed through Sikkim. Browning, an amateur radio maniac,* was obsessed with introducing radio to 'countries that had never been heard of before' and transmitting from far-flung countries. In September 1963, after successfully activating a set in Bhutan, he turned up in Gangtok. It did not take much persuasion to get Thondup interested, and Browning had soon arranged for Sikkim to have its own 'country' code of AC3. Thondup naturally welcomed this as further recognition of the status of Sikkim. In early 1964, Thondup ordered a complete Collins-S-Line radio system and started transmitting under the callsign AC3PT.†

The radio set provided a distraction from the events of 1964, which had been particularly difficult. His father had died just before the start of the year; his cousin Jigme was assassinated in April, only a month after the birth of a son to his new American wife, who was herself attracting the attention of the world's press, not all of it welcome.

Then, on 27 May, Pandit Nehru died.

Nehru had been a hugely important supporter of Sikkim. He had always regarded the place with fondness, and had talked about Sikkim as the one place that he would like to retire. His love for the land, combined with his idealism, had persuaded him to agree to the 1950 settlement. He had been a good personal friend to Thondup too, willing to listen whenever the young prince came to Delhi with a grievance. On the day of his death he had been about to open talks with Thondup and his representatives on Sikkim's future relations with India.

Thondup's reaction on hearing the news was to break down in tears. It was a personal blow, felt particularly keenly due to the mentoring

---

* Part of a remarkable group of adventurous travellers known as the DXpeditioners, or DXers. There is no substantive evidence of a link with the CIA.

† Eleven years later, this radio would be put to good use (see chapter 10).

relationship the two had developed. Thondup and Hope attended the funeral, which drew more than two million mourners to the banks of the Jumna river, where Rajiv, the eldest grandson, rose to light the funeral pyre.[50] Afterwards, in their room in the Raj Bhavan, the potential wider significance for Sikkim seemed to hit Thondup. As he sat on his bed, he stared into the darkness.

'I don't know' he said, 'what's for Sikkim now.'[51]

Nehru's ashes arrived in Sikkim a month later as part of a tour round India and were greeted with genuine affection. Thondup was not the only one to have formed a close bond with Nehru – he had been a much-loved leader throughout the region.

The succession of events had hit Thondup hard, but they had also been challenging for his wife, still not 25 years old. By August, Martha Hamilton reported with some concern that 'Hope needs a break I think.' And that's what Hope planned. Along with Thondup and the new baby, she set off for New York to honour the Sikkimese tradition of returning a baby to its mother's birthplace within a year of its birth.

Unsurprisingly their progress through America was the focus of intense media scrutiny. Hope and Thondup were now a bona fide celebrity couple, with a press relationship to match. Their lives had become a regular feature of the *Time* magazine 'People' section. 'They travel in separate planes for "Precautionary reasons",' an article said on their arrival in the States, fawning over the royal family with American connections.

> The Maharani in native gown and raw silk cloak, was first to land in New York last month with her six-month-old son, Prince Palden, and Crown Prince Tenzing. The mysterious Occident is what the Maharajah digs, however, and so does his other son, Prince Topgyal Wangchuk, 11. One of the boy's dearest possessions, beamed Pa when they touched down the next day, is a wild west gun and holster.

Meanwhile everyone who had been at the wedding – and quite a few who hadn't – clamoured to entertain the intriguing couple. It was enough to leave the vulnerable Hope feeling 'oppressed', 'exhausted' and 'eaten alive'. In her autobiography she recalled the media hype:

Articles on us, as one friend says teasingly, have run the gamut from 'Princess Hope's Dilemma: Should I Raise My Children by Astrology or Doctor Spock?' to 'My Thirty Favorite Ways of Preparing Yak' to 'How will I Tell My Children About the Communist Chinese in Tibet?' Thank God in Sikkim I just get the *Herald Tribune*, which Clover [a friend] has subscribed to for us, and don't have to read or be around when others read the things written about us. The stuff written is not vicious, simply banal, but its effect on me here is paralysing. We are owned by strangers.[52]

Nehru's death in 1964 left India bereft. Since long before independence, there had always been strong and undisputed leadership of the Congress Party (and thus of India), bringing a sense of stability to the country. The death of the architect of Independence left a hole at the top of the party and of the state. Nehru's daughter, Indira Gandhi, had been shadowing her father for years, travelling with him as he toured the country. In 1958, when they visited Sikkim and Bhutan together, she and her father had travelled by horseback through the Chumbi Valley to get from Gangtok to the Bhutanese capital, Thimpu. In Delhi, she had become an important part of his informal decision-making forum.

But Indira Gandhi would have to bide her time. On Nehru's death, it was Lal Bahadur Shastri who took up the reins of power in India's capital. One of his early diplomatic duties was to attend a meeting of the nonaligned movement (so carefully crafted by Nehru and others) in Cairo in October 1964. With the break-up of imperial power across the globe well under way, the conference took on a more polarised feel than ever. Radicals from Indonesia, Ghana, and Algeria – who argued strongly for the struggle against what President Sukarno of Indonesia called the 'Old Established forces' – were lined up against the Indian-led moderate viewpoints, arguing that peace and abolishing war (in particular nuclear war) was a primary objective.

From the sidelines of the conference Beijing criticised Shastri's moderate line. The *Peking Review* noted that the Indian prime minister had 'made no mention at all of fighting imperialism, the common enemy of the people of Asia, Africa, and Latin America.'[53] 'Protectorate' relationships, such as India had in Sikkim, some even muttered, made India look imperialist themselves.

-10-

In Sikkim, after the return of Thondup and Hope from the USA, the preparations for the coronation started in earnest. The designated year of mourning after Tashi's death had passed.

During the past two decades, many Sikkimese had studied in India or further overseas, bringing skills and knowledge back to their country and creating a strong and active group of bureaucrats to help build the country's infrastructure. The advent of the coronation brought everyone together, as Hope Cooke noticed. 'From high and low, everyone is doing some kind of work for the upcoming festivities. Carpeting, tenting, music rehearsing – everyone is contributing.'[54]

Lama artists spent days painting the roof of the coronation room a golden yellow, the Sikkim Guards practised their drills for hours on the palace lawn, hairdressers were brought up from Calcutta, 'waiters, cooks, sweepers, drivers, guards, caretakers, the police and officials saw that nothing was misplaced'.[55] The best tailors in Sikkim worked on beautiful robes for the royal couple; the inside of the palace was redecorated to impress 'Mrs Gandhi, who's staying with us'.[56] Nothing was spared to show Sikkim to the world's press.

The Government of India watched these preparations carefully. The tensions along the border with China were by no means resolved, and they felt they had to tread carefully when it came to Sikkim's position as a protectorate of India. Some felt the significance of the event should be downplayed. At times this ambivalence slipped out, as Martha Hamilton noted:

India House London has put its foot in it as usual. Reported in the papers here that they had told the wife of the *Sunday Times* Editor not to bother going to the Coronation as Sikkim affairs were of no importance at all. They may think it, but not the best moment to say it so forcibly.

The Indian government also consciously delayed giving official approval of the use of the ancient titles Chogyal and Gyalmo (essentially King and Queen), only removing its silent objection shortly before the ceremony. The switch to the new titles was clearly an important one for the Sikkimese ruler and his advisers – only two weeks before the coronation Martha Hamilton noted in her letter home: 'We're all trained to Chogyal and Gyalmo now as Govt of India has at last accepted their titles.' Nari Rustomji, now an adviser to the King of Bhutan, worried about the confused Indian approach. While a strong supporter of Thondup and of Sikkim, he was also a realist. He harped back to pre-1947 days – the British, he thought, would never have allowed this kind of situation to develop, where 'it was the Prince, not the Indian Political Officer, who was the centre of attention'.[57]

The coronation was, if anything, 'conducted in an even ampler style than the wedding'.* The newspapers found ever more ways to romanticise Sikkim. 'Americans are well aware that Monaco is touched by Grace,' an editorial in the *Washington Post* read, 'now Sikkim is radiant with Hope.' Messages from Queen Elizabeth II, and from Dean Rusk, the US Secretary of State, were proudly displayed in official programmes. *Time* magazine once again caught the sharp contrasts:

Last week excitement galore gripped the populace as chic photographers, starchy diplomats and perfumed post-debs from abroad suddenly inundated the charming little capital of Gangtok. Hope Cooke (Sarah Lawrence, '63) . . . wore a pearl chaplet, a red bhakku over a white silk gown, and high-heeled shoes for the occasion. Her vast hazel eyes downcast, she whispered "Thank you, thank you" as a parade of lamas and top-hatted guests pressed forward to present the royal couple with cards marked with mystic symbols and heaps of white scarves for good luck.

With that, corks popped from champagne bottles, and turbaned bandsmen struck up tunes from *My Fair Lady* as lissome American girls, friends of the Queen flown in for the occasion, joined young Sikkkimese aristocrats in dancing. Even the King and Queen did the twist and a quartet

---

* The succession of events held over two days was something of a challenge for all the guests: Martha Hamilton wore no less than five different dresses to the various functions.

of Sikkimese Beatles shrilled their Himalayan version of "I Want to Hold your Hand"...[58]

As the new Chogyal, Thondup knew that his accession speech was just as important as the celebrations and summoned Rustomji from Bhutan to help prepare it. Rustomji was concerned to see that 'rather more importance was attached to the seating of guests from abroad than to important dignitaries from Sikkim itself'.[59] He also noticed that Hope was beginning to relish 'playing Queen... gifted with a sense of the theatrical'. She now had, he wrote, 'for backdrop the snow-capped peaks of Sikkim's guardian mountain deity, Kanchenjungha, for plot the diplomatic manoeuvrings over Sikkim's identity and the Prince's role in a democratic set-up, and for audience the world itself.'

Despite any reservations he may have had, Rustomji helped prepare a speech for the Chogyal that was remembered by all who heard it. The representatives of the Government of India – Indira Gandhi, then Minister for Information and Broadcasting, and Mrs Lakshmi Menon, the Minister of State for External Affairs* – must have been aware of the calculations involved in the new Chogyal's carefully crafted words:

> We recall with profound affection the memory of Jawaharlal Nehru, a true and steadfast friend of Sikkim, and we have confidence that the Government of India will continue to hold out to us the hand of friendship. Our good neighbours, Bhutan and Nepal, are also much in our thoughts today and we shall continue to cherish their friendship... Ours is a small country, but we have pride in our institutions, our way of life and cultural heritage. It is for this that we are resolved to maintain our national identity and so direct our affairs that our land may develop according to its own natural genius.[60]

The talk of 'national identity' and 'our country' (and the referral to the words 'natural genius' that C. D. Rai recalled used by Nehru himself) raised the eyebrows of the Mrs Gandhi and Menon. Mrs Menon replied in kind, saying that 'India has had long and historic bonds with Sikkim which,' she pointedly remarked, 'go far beyond the terms which Your Highness's late distinguished father concluded with India.'

---

* Mrs Lakshmi Menon was the official representative – Mrs Gandhi attended in a personal capacity.

The event acted as a national unifier for those living in Sikkim. 'It might well be regarded,' Rustomji wrote later, 'as the Prince's Finest Hour.' The editors of the glossy booklet that was produced to celebrate the event worked hard to portray the pride of the people. The 'national flag of Sikkim' was proudly presented as the opening picture on the first page; a picture of Thondup's uncle, Sidkeong Namgyal, in 1906 at Oxford drew a link with the British rule in the country; sections on the history and the religions of the country celebrated the distinct nature of the Bhutia-Lepcha inheritance.

But the Nepali majority in the country still received scant recognition in the pictures and text. It was a further sign of the inability of the Chogyal to fully accept that the ethnic make-up of his country had changed. The pressure for fair representation of the Nepalis may have been momentarily suppressed in the heady celebrations of Sikkim's wider identity, but it was an issue that was not going away.

It would come back to haunt the Namgyals only a decade later.

Among the congratulatory messages that the new royal couple received was another one from the Chinese government. It was a deliberate affront to the Indian demand for communications to be conducted via the Indian External Affairs Ministry, and a further escalation of tensions between the two countries.

The press were never afraid to link these tensions to Sikkim. When Thondup gave an interview to a reporter from the *New York Times* in 1964 about the relations with China, the headline had read 'Sikkim Ruler Hails Red Chinese Ties'. The US was being sucked into Asian politics via the Vietnam War and the spectre of the expansion of Chinese influence was not a hard one to conjure up.

Meanwhile, in the post-1962-conflict atmosphere, some in India questioned Hope Cooke's motives for being in Sikkim. Years later Indian journalist Satyendra Shukla, in his account entitled *Sikkim: The Story of Integration**, wrote about the rumours surrounding Hope Cooke's presence:

---

* Compare and contrast with the title of Datta-Ray's account: *Smash and Grab: The Annexation of Sikkim*

What a coincidence that Sikkim was the most-talked about subject on the international chess-board then, with rival armies of India and China facing each other on the Sikkim–Tibet border. In certain quarters it was openly suggested that Cook [*sic*] was a CIA plant and was sent there to fish out information of logistic and diplomatic importance and to send the same to her masters. Her duties perhaps also included to wean the Maharajkumar – who was shortly to be the new Maharaja – away from India and help as far as possible the establishment of an Independent state, where US might build up some sort of defence structures against China. This also suited India at that time because India was also opposed to China. But perhaps even then India would not have entertained any proposal for the Independent Sikkim. [. . .] The US had been looking for some days to find a foothold on Indian soil since it started its world-wide programme to contain communism, just after World War II.[61]

The rumours about Hope Cooke were contrived. But Shukla was undoubtedly right about one thing – the patchwork of alliances and enmities surrounding and within Sikkim had the characteristics of a fiendishly complex multi-player game of chess.

Things were about to get even more complicated by events on India's western border with Pakistan.

-11-

In 1947, the problems of the Himalayan nations' continued existence had paled into insignificance when compared to the challenge of creating an entirely new country, Pakistan. It was a state that almost by definition was set up in opposition to and competition with India. A sense of rivalry had not taken long to surface: the messy question of Kashmir had been one of the first items on the newly formed United Nations' agenda in its early years.

The rivalry soon infected diplomacy too, with both countries competing for favours from more established countries during the 1950s. Both developed open relations with the USA, and both were quick to recognise the People's Republic of China. The Pakistani leadership in particular recognised the importance of strong relations with China. In 1956, it tried to enlist Chinese support for its position over Kashmir. Zhou Enlai refused,[62] but the approach was an indication of the importance the Pakistanis laid on having the ear of the Chinese.

In 1959, at the time of the Chinese suppression of the Lhasa Uprising and the flight of the Dalai Lama, a new leader, General Ayub Khan, assumed control of Pakistan in a military coup d'etat. Khan was a pragmatist. Seeing the growing tensions between India and China, he made an early offer to the Indian government to resolve the Kashmir issue once and for all, proposing that in return Pakistan and India would work together to defend the subcontinent against 'external powers', i.e. China. For a brief moment there was the prospect of Indo-Pakistani cooperation; but Nehru, under pressure to show India's strength, brushed Ayub Khan's offer aside, just as he had when Zhou proposed to resolve the India–China border dispute around the same time. Instead, Nehru had authorised the Forward Policy that contributed to the 1962 Sino-Indian war.

India's unconvincing military display in the 1962 conflict gave the Pakistanis fresh hope that their neighbour might be vulnerable diplomatically – or even militarily – over Kashmir. The Pakistanis also felt aggrieved at the sudden increase in military aid flowing to India from the US. What, the Pakistanis asked themselves, had been the point in supporting the US during the 1950s in the battle against communism if the Americans were willing to turn on a sixpence and provide military support for the Indians? It was a reasonable question.

After 1962, therefore, as India and Pakistan both embarked on significant armaments programmes, the pieces on the board started to arrange themselves into a quite different configuration. China, already involved in a shadowy proxy conflict with the US in Vietnam*, sensed an opportunity – or perhaps even a diplomatic necessity – to align itself with Pakistan against India. Suddenly there was a real basis for Sino-Pakistani cooperation, tacit or otherwise.

By 1965, Pakistan's relationship with China had deepened significantly. As the preparations for the Sikkimese coronation took place in Gangtok

---

* The second such proxy conflict, after the Korean War of the early 1950s.

in March 1965, Mao and Ayub Khan met in Beijing. Chairman Mao's view was clear. 'Pakistan and China [can] trust each other,' Mao said, 'as neither has the intention of pulling the rug [out from] under the feet of the other.'[63] As Ayub Khan left Beijing, Mao reportedly told the Pakistani general that there was now no doubt that the Chinese would side with the Pakistanis, not with the Indians, in the event of any future conflict.

Zulfikar Ali Bhutto, Ayub's aggressive Foreign Minister, spotted an opportunity. Within a couple of months he had persuaded Ayub to activate a plan that he had been developing for some time. Under the codename 'Operation Gibraltar', it involved encouraging an anti-Indian uprising by infiltrating Indian Kashmir and creating an 'urban insurrection' in Srinagar.[64]

The language that the Pakistani press used to characterise the conflict was very carefully chosen. By calling the struggle in Kashmir one of 'national liberation', a link was drawn with North Vietnam's efforts to 'liberate' South Vietnam. This allowed some Chinese Communist Party editorials to also draw this link, tarring the Government of India with the brush of imperialism. In June 1965, the CCP-controlled Hong Kong paper *Da Gong Bao* crowed that 'the crest of the anti-imperialist revolutionary struggles in Asia, Africa and Latin America is rising to a new high . . . US imperialism is being battered everywhere.'[65]

There was, they said, a need to 'strengthen their unity, and support and help each other in their common struggle against imperialism, colonialism, and neo-colonialism' in the wake of an 'unprecedented upsurge of the national liberation movement in Asia and Africa'. There was no doubt that things were changing across Asia. While tensions in Kashmir intensified, America moved its first combat troops into Vietnam. This was the year that America's military presence in Vietnam went from 23,500 'military advisers' to nearly 200,000 total troop strength.

While the Chinese, with the proxy war against the US in Vietnam intensifying, did not wish to encourage direct conflict between Pakistan and India, there was no doubt that they were lining up behind the former – while the Americans were backing the latter.

Meanwhile in Sikkim, the rising tensions in the region made the Indian government even more cautious about the Chogyal's continued desire for increased autonomy in Sikkim.

Trouble occurred on a post-coronation visit to Delhi, when Thondup annoyed one of the army officers sent to escort him by insisting on the Sikkimese flag flying on the official car alongside the Indian one.[66] There were other signs of the growing assertion of Sikkimese national identity, in particular the growth of the term 'Tibeto-Burman' to describe the basis of Sikkimese nationality and language. It was a clear attempt to reinforce the idea of separateness from India. It also allowed the Sikkimese Nepali immigrants to claim a more 'culturally Buddhist' heritage than that given them by Indo-Aryan theorists in India.[67]

Sometimes the tensions were all too obvious to the people of Sikkim. In 1965 the political officer was so concerned at the increasing prominence of the expanded Sikkim Guard and its ostentatious use in Palace ceremonies that he boycotted the Guard's annual presentation and advised other Indians against attending the ceremony too.[68]

All this posturing even made dinner parties in Gangtok problematic – Martha Hamilton recalled in a letter home: 'I'm thinking of having two parties, one for HH and one for PO* and India lot. Definitely better in separate parties.'[69] The increasing tensions had other implications too: when Princess Coocoola tried to use the normal channels to apply for a visa to visit outside the country, the Indian government at first refused to give her foreign exchange. (They later relented.)[70] To complicate matters further, in Kalimpong the Kazini was slowly mustering support for the anti-Chogyal (though not yet pro-Indian) elements in the country, with her clever publicity on behalf of the Sikkim National Congress party.

For India, these internal problems in Sikkim seemed minor compared to the grave challenges arising on the border with Pakistan – but the two were about to become linked.

The Pakistanis launched the first strikes through the Rann of Kutch in the south and in Kashmir in early August. The Indians responded by taking strategic high positions above the Kashmir valley a few days later. Critically, the Chinese immediately came out 'firmly supporting Pakistan's just action in hitting back at armed Indian provocations'. But the Indians were not deterred and on 6 September launched major counter-punch offensives into Pakistani Punjab.

---

* HH is Thondup; PO is Indian political officer.

While the conflict progressed along the Indo-Pakistani border, the stakes were raised significantly when news came through that the Chinese had moved troops to the Sikkim border. Indian defence experts realised that if the Chinese were to launch an attack through Sikkim they would be forced into a two-front war, the nightmare scenario for any general.

In Sikkim the uncertainty was starting to bite. In a letter home to her parents on 13 September, Martha Hamilton warily noted all the signs of impending war:

> Slightly uncertain news these days and it is virtually impossible to disen-tangle facts from propaganda so I try to get the BBC but it keeps getting buzzed by China. The battery has now gone down so I listened to the news on a friend's radio via the telephone! I told the chowk to get a new battery but he got involved in paying the bills so I'll have to wait till tomorrow. The Chogyal and Gyalmo went off to Calcutta today and we all sat from 2–3.30 waiting to see them off – fearful waste of an afternoon, but I don't think they knew we were there. One of Haldipur's [the Dewan's] efforts probably to give them a nice send-off. Special prayers said by the lamas today for their journey – certainly Bagdogra our airport was attacked two days ago* and paratroops fairly near. Goodness knows.

Within a week, things had deteriorated significantly. As the fighting in the Punjab increased, Beijing raised the stakes in the Chumbi Valley on 17 September. The Chinese issued a strongly worded ultimatum to the Indians that accused them of planning further 'aggression' on the China–Sikkim border: 'The Chinese government now demands that the Indian government dismantle all its military works for aggression on the Chinese side of the China–Sikkim boundary . . . Otherwise the Indian government must bear full responsibility for all the grave consequences arising therefrom.'

The Indians were now facing the very real possibility that they would have divisions tied up in Sikkim, reducing their efficacy in the conflict with Pakistan.

Martha Hamilton recorded the tensions in Gangtok, as well as the

---

* A rumoured rather than actual attack.

portent-laden viewpoint of the local Buddhist monks on 18 September, the day after the ultimatum had been issued. Her letter evokes some of the plucky spirit and humour employed during an earlier threat on 1940 London:

I'm an air raid warden (!!!) for this area because I have car and phone, and now have 11 helpers, all men, for the area. Somewhat hilarious if it weren't for the real possibility this time that something could happen, much more so than 1962 when the Chinese kept saying they had no quarrel with the Sikkim boundary. News tonight they are moving troops nearer the Gangtok border – we presume they mean Sikkim border. No black out here yet – very cheering to see blazing lights after the murk of Darjeeling.

We cut up bandages out of sheets with great energy this afternoon and the chowk is making splints. Trenches are to be dug I think in the compound so don't worry mum about the Garden arrangements – the whole place is holes. HH came back from Calcutta today – drove his best Mercedes through all that muck on the road. No wonder he goes through them at such a rate. I hope the advance to the border is only a move in the game but if the worst happens I have my car and this time I have filled it with petrol . . . Did I tell you I took Nicky [her white dog] for a walk by a small pond in the Palace garden while waiting for HH to come and that evening a branch fell by the pond – both I'm told holy and it was a v bad omen and huge pujas were done. Hence Chinese ultimatum came as no surprise as Buddhists waiting for bad omen to take effect! . . . BBC the same – moving troops nearer the border. By the time this reaches you situation will be v different.[71]

Hope Cooke was in London as the crisis broke. She had flown to Britain to take her stepchildren back to their schools – the boys to Harrow; Yangchen, the girl, to a school just outside London. But even on the flight she could not escape the delicate politics of the situation; she discovered that the Secretary-General of the UN, U Thant, was on the plane with her. Given that she had met Thant before, she took her chance, approaching him to plead Sikkim's case, but due to a 'tablet' that she had taken for the flight found herself incapable of taking advantage of the situation:

Now is the chance to express to him our anxieties that Sikkim might get caught in the power plays going on. Being himself from a small country, he is sympathetic. What a piece of luck that he's on the plane! He himself is saying it – I think. He is saying that Sikkim might be in danger from her protectors – I hear him foggily, I can't focus, my tongue is thick and won't form any words. He looks at me kindly and says I need to rest. I've messed up this chance; we could never approach him officially if we needed to explain any predicament. At London airport the children have trouble waking me.[72]

Nari Rustomji, too, was doing his best to help. He made a broadcast on All-India Radio in an effort to ensure the Indian public were aware of the gravity of the situation, and where Sikkim actually was. Rustomji, keenly aware of the concerns that some in Delhi had about Sikkim's ruler, had written a carefully worded statement for Thondup, to which he referred in the broadcast. 'What really matters,' Rustomji said on the radio, pleading for the people of India to respect Sikkim's independent identity,

> is not how *I* should like to see Sikkim or what I or anyone else think about the Chinese ultimatum, what matters is the feelings regarding these issues of the people of Sikkim themselves. Sikkim's ruler did not waste time in announcing, in terms that were unmistakeably clear, that his people would resist to the last man any aggression into their country, and while indicating his satisfaction with the arrangements made for the protection of his country, expressed his confidence that, should the need arise, his people would be proud and happy to lay down their lives in Sikkim's defence. Self respect is not the prerogative of only large countries, and Sikkim has sufficient pride in the legacy of her past and her institutions to make a determined stand for their preservation.

Rustomji left no one in any doubt as to his support not only for Sikkim but also for its ruler, a man he called a 'genius' in the same broadcast.

In mid-September Coocoola, who was in Ireland at the time, realised that Hope would be facing the press in London. She immediately flew to join her sister-in-law, sensing an opportunity to reinforce Sikkim's unique identity. 'We've got to stop the Indians from taking advantage of this,' she told Hope. 'Already in their official reports about the situation they're calling Sikkim an area of India and talking about the border being the Indo-China border. The nerve. We've got to remind people of Sikkim's identity before it gets lost. They're doing it deliberately – they know this is the perfect chance.'[73]

Coocoola drew on her friend David Astor (editor of *The Observer*) for advice for Hope on how to act as a spokesperson; Hope, despite the fact that her 'legs are trembling both from thinking about Palden at home [the Chogyal and her one-year-old son Palden were still in Sikkim] and from fear of the press itself', tried to make light of the situation, telling the press that 'reports about the border are usually dramatised and things on the whole are calm in Sikkim'.

In fact, the tensions were ratcheting up. On 18 September, the Chinese, recognising the impossibility of the demands they had made to remove all border posts within 48 hours, extended the deadline by two further days, thereby prolonging the stand-off. By now China had 60,000 troops in the Tibet Military Region, and 'fifty five hundred positioned for quick commitment to combat in Sikkim'.[74]

For the next week, Gangtok was a mass of confused tension and efforts to prepare for the possibility of attack. While the town prepared for the worst, Thondup took the unprecedented step of creating a consultative committee of those considered 'Class 1 Officers' in Sikkim, which included Martha Hamilton in her capacity as head of the school. Journalists flooded north, eager to see some action. Martha Hamilton's letter home on 25 September caught the high drama of the week, and her own (sometimes comic) response to being caught in the limelight:

My dear mummy and daddy

What a week! Since last Sunday I have scarcely sat down till now. I wonder if you saw anything in the papers or on ITV and what it was like. Pretty poor I imagine as I wasn't honestly in a fit state to cope adequately or think clearly. I can't imagine what tales reach England.

Last Sunday morning HH held a meeting of Heads of Department on the Palace lawn. Rather vague and woolly statements about roads and fire hydrants and trenches and protecting glass – quite sure Chinese not coming but prepare for worst. Black Out etc. So all off to church then to hostel to fix up black out and strip the windows across and across and make an air raid shelter in the kitchen. My warden list arrived – I had eight others with me so divided out the area which was huge. The . . . warden and I sallied forth to do our area – humping up and down stairs – flights of steps – over muddy fields telling people who'd never heard of black out. No time to black out own house so just sat in the dark to phone and wash etc.

Monday school as usual and the girls had a marvellous time cutting up newspaper and covering the entire school with gum. Ghastly sticky mess everywhere . . . Tuesday was digging day and trenches for 200 is no joke. First I chose out the ground and luckily we had two or three enormous natural drains which had been run dry to build quarters and the whole primary fitted into them but had to dig them deeper. The first television man, Indian, arrived that day and took pictures of children carting enormous sacks full of wood shavings to line their trench. The High school dug in the Primary Gardens and each vied with the others to make a better trench . . . By 2.30 all were ready and when the siren blew at 3.30 they all shot out and the entire school was battened down into trenches within exactly two minutes sitting crouched with hands over ears. I ran round them all – endlessly up and down and hundreds of leeches but all were very safe and I really felt much happier. At night there was a surprise warning which many thought was an actual raid – the hostel shot down to the shelter like rabbits but were very quiet . . .

Wednesday reporters began to arrive by the score. To me came Harper of the *Express*, Claire Hollingworth (Defence correspondent of *Guardian*) and an American Assoc Press. Looked at trenches and took pictures of children jumping in. All v nice so asked them to dinner on Thursday after Nathu La trip. Class tests as usual and beginning of preparations for English debate and more first aid. Went to prayer meeting – surprisingly sparse attendance – and popped in to the hotel on road back to see if reporters were there. Had had lunch with Claire etc and heard news of ceasefire but Chinese still moving up on Nathu La so thought they might have more news in the evening. Three more reporters, *Newsweek* with French name B--- and Dean Bayliss of NBC television and Agence France with huge moustache . . .

By Thursday trench drill was beginning to pall with staff but *Newsweek* and BBC arrived so out again. Coffee first and NBC then photographed me blowing whistle leading children then fearful interview. Weather v damp – hair frightful, real mis looking. And no clothes to wear as dhobi* not back for 2 weeks. Not a single dress clean or even shirt! And no time or water to wash. No water all week. Not a single drop. It really was the last final straw. I was half dead because hadn't slept well as it was end of ultimatum and many thought with the usual underhand methods of the Chinese they would attack. Had slept about 3am only to be woken by the phone at 6.15am. – the executive councillor to say 'Miss Hamilton, I haven't received the receipt for the money given to the artist who painted the backdrop for the coronation.' You can imagine what I felt but I merely told him coldly that since he had paid the money in person to the artist I presumed he had collected the receipt.

At nine o'clock a car arrived and out leapt 4 journalists. Tra La. Luckily with the black out they didn't see my astonishment but I murmured something about a note – oh but we told them to make it clear we were coming (i.e. *Guardian* and *Express*) and we hope you don't mind but we've brought Stephen Coulter of *Sunday Times* and Guy Race of *Telegraph*. I was delighted as all food was ready and Claire (*Guardian*) I know thought she ought to come to me as a European though actually she was out on her feet . . . *Sunday Times* I liked tho he is v unpopular here for writing such anti-Indian articles. Harper of *Express* also v nice – after he left a cable arrived for him 'send pics of Martha immediately'!! . . . all v critical of Indian press arrangements and lies and hold-ups – frustrations fantastic they say and hence v anti-Indian articles appear. Obviously not only for this reason but plays a large part. Press here v v anti British. Personally I don't blame them. I think Mr W† made a big mistake in his statement re crossing the line.

Friday last day of school . . . I hung on to the hostel girls – heard Betty had let hers go to Kalimpong. They had escape routes all worked out – we didn't have time honestly and there is only one road anyway . . . At 11 had a ring that ITV were coming and come they did and *Observer* and Assoc Press. Incredible lads – v young, bouncing with energy and great fun. . . . In afternoon took beginning of debate in English on 'In times of crisis a student's duty is to stay at school and not join the forces.' Girls did v well though I had spent ages on Wednesday jockeying them into it and on need

* Indian word for a person who washes clothes.
† Harold Wilson, British Prime Minister.

for morale etc. In end girls v thrilled to be on TV . . . end of blackout. Joy. Rapture.

Although the ITN piece was never broadcast in full, it is still possible to access it today. Against footage of Indian troops trudging up to the Nathu La with pack ponies, the journalist solemnly announced that the pass through Sikkim had now become 'another potential starting point for a Third World War'.

'The team had been warned to expect machine gun fire,' he added, 'but found the Chinese to be more interested in an exchange of camera shots.'*

Martha Hamilton was interviewed against a magnificent backdrop of Himalayan mountains, talking of her life in the region. But the footage of Thondup was perhaps the most revealing. The king was first shown on a visit to the front in his Indian Army uniform (he had been promoted to honorary Major-General at the time of the coronation), accompanied by the political officer, whose presence, the voiceover pointed out, 'underlines that Sikkim's future lies partly in Indian hands'. In a further interview outside the palace, Thondup disguised his stutter carefully while answering all the questions with great precision. Something in his eyes tells of the need he felt to be careful with the press, and to emphasise Sikkim's separate status. When asked what he thought the Chinese were trying to achieve, he replied in his clipped English accent,

> One's really not quite sure what they were trying to do. . . we do not believe that they meant actually Big Business because apart from the troops they had in this part of the world, they are of course dependent on the USSR for oil, so I don't think they meant an all-out war, so one assumes that it was really to tie down Indian troops in this part of the world from maybe going across Pakistan side.

On the day after China had issued their extended ultimatum, the UN Security Council demanded that India and Pakistan accept a ceasefire by the morning of 22 September. The revised deadline from China therefore fizzled out. The crisis had been averted. After delaying to the last possible

---

* One of the more ridiculous accusations from the Chinese was that India had stolen '59 of their yaks'. The whereabouts of the yaks was never determined.

moment, Pakistan agreed to the Security Council's demand for the cease-fire. India had 'feared a two-front war'. Comments from G. W. Choudhury, the director of research for Pakistan's foreign office from 1967 to 1969, suggest they had been right to. Choudhury was sure that 'China was prepared in September 1965 to initiate operations in the Himalayas to reduce Indian military pressure on Pakistan – if Pakistan requested this aid.' Choudhury also reported a conversation where Mao told General Ayub that 'if there is nuclear war, it is Peking and not Rawalpindi that will be a target'.[75]

It had apparently been a close-run thing. As the tension subsided, Hope Cooke flew on to New York to try and gain further publicity for what had happened in Sikkim, managing to get a spot on the Walter Cronkite broadcast. But with the peace talks between India and Pakistan still top of the agenda, the news that 'tensions in Sikkim had abated was really non-news'.

Within a couple of weeks Hope Cooke was back in Gangtok. As usual, Martha Hamilton reported back to her parents, a little disappointed at Hope's rushed welcome. But the letter was of significance for another reason – there was an ominous change in her tone. This time she kept it short and to the point. There was one sure sign in her final sentence that the Indians now viewed matters in Sikkim as of more than just local importance:

Hope is just back from England – 'oh yes I saw you on TV and in 3 newspapers in the evening'. And that was all the comment. I gather she had a happy time in the Hilton avoiding the press and trying to put across the Sikkim image.

Nuff said. I think they are opening letters.

CHAPTER FOUR

A Fragile State

1965–70

-1-

Twenty-five-year-old Hope Cooke arrived back in Gangtok happy after the press conferences she had conducted in London on her husband's behalf during the crisis of 1965. Despite her youth, she had felt 'good and mature' in front of the microphones. She was pleased to have played her part in representing Sikkim's cause; it boosted her confidence when she realised that 'Chogyal is proud of me . . . He knew I wouldn't get panicky.'[1]

Soon, however, a sense of loneliness returned. As Thondup's children from his first marriage (Tenzing (13), Wangchuk (12) and Yangchen (9) – all closer to her in age than her husband) drifted back to school, she was left feeling isolated. Martha Hamilton, who Hope had counted as a friend, left too in early 1966, to support her father after her mother's unexpected death. Alone in Gangtok, Hope found that all too frequently 'boredom wraps me in a sad net'.[2]

She was still also unable to trust Thondup not to slip back into his infidelities. The rumour that one of her husband's former lovers might be returning to the palace on a social visit left her 'gut pulled into a tight skein of jealousy and anger'. She found it hard, too, to accept the frequent presence in the palace of her sister-in-law Coocoola, whom she believed resented her. This paranoia, justified or not, developed to such an extent that she became 'so scared of her I take Valium before I see her. "Ma belle-soeur," I write [to a friend], "continues to be a little bit difficult."'[3]

Even writing letters to her friends in New York, which had become such a cherished lifeline of unrestricted freedom of expression, became problematic, curtailed by the crude censorship that Martha Hamilton had also noticed in late 1965:

> I can't write what is really on my mind; all the letters are opened (as if by police dogs – the flaps are jaggedly torn, reglued with heavy paste that sticks the letter to the envelope) by the Indians. 'So kind of you to rewrap my letter,' Alice [a friend] writes in a postscript to the censors.[4]

Despite these challenges and her loneliness, she was starting to feel a strong connection to Sikkim, in particular through her son Palden, now nearly two years old. For the first time in her life, Hope Cooke felt like she had found somewhere she really belonged. 'I've stopped being floaty, boundless, unattached,' she wrote. 'Perhaps it's because I've borne a child that I feel rooted, earthbound. And I love it.'[5] Her new child gave her a personal sense of identity; she hoped it might also strengthen her relationship with Thondup.

Desperate to become part of Sikkim's future, she built on this newfound sense of belonging by beginning a series of initiatives to give philosophical, cultural and historical underpinnings to the country's assertion of its own identity. She helped produce a glossy commemorative booklet on the coronation; she gave support to the development of local cottage industries to demonstrate Sikkimese handicrafts; she chaired a major project to develop school books focused on bringing Sikkimese history and culture into the classroom.

It was her influence, too, that helped turn the Namgyal 'palace' into not only a home but also a place to entertain and welcome visiting dignitaries from the USA and beyond who came up to see the sun set over Kangchendzonga's five magnificent peaks. The self-styled 'Queen' of Sikkim gave the inside of the building a makeover, ordering new soft furnishings that lent the home an international feel for the first time. Great care was taken to ensure that there were symbols of Sikkim's individuality and Buddhist heritage. One reporter recalled arriving at the palace through 'bright-red-and-blue gates, ornately covered with dragons' heads, past bright Chinese-style sentry boxes, from which Guards clad in bright-red felt jackets, striped kilts and straw hats step out to salute'.[6]

For Thondup, now 42 years old, these Sikkim Guards on the gate in their unique ceremonial attire were the ultimate symbol of Sikkim's separate identity. He was proud of them and of what they represented. In 1961 he had tried to argue for the creation of a militia in Sikkim in case of 'internal disturbances', but questions in India's parliament about the wisdom of such an independent force in a protectorate had scotched those plans. Instead, Thondup had settled for a doubling of his Sikkim Guards to two companies. It was still less than 200 men, led by a commanding officer from the regular Indian army, but for Thondup the Guards served a purpose. One company served on ceremonial duties; the other assisted the Indian Army in border defence. The very existence of his own Guards made him feel more secure.

But in reality the Sikkim Guards were mere window-dressing. Large numbers of Indian Army infantry and artillery (two divisions, about 2,000 men) were now all but permanently stationed in Sikkim – and there were vast reserves ready to be moved to the border if there were further murmurs of trouble from the Chinese.

Thondup realised it would have been churlish to complain about the presence of the Indian Army in Sikkim. He was under no illusions about Sikkim's security – he knew that Sikkim needed the protection of India (guaranteed under the provisions of the 1950 treaty between Sikkim and India) and he wanted that protection to continue. As an Honorary Major-General in the 8th Gurkha Regiment of the Indian Army, he also found the commanding officers posted to Gangtok invariably convivial company and good for a 'peg' of whisky or two. But he was far less comfortable with the two other main provisions of the 1950 treaty – namely that India was responsible for Sikkim's external relations and for its communications. Nor was he a fan of the continued presence of the political officer and of the dewan, the prime minister who had the delegated power – in theory from

Thondup, in practice from Delhi – to run the state. For Thondup, these were symbols of Sikkim's emasculation, a slight on the proud history of his country.

By 1966 he was convinced that something had to change. He decided it was time to demonstrate that Sikkim had an identity all of its own. At the very least, he realised, that would mean a change in the treaty between India and Sikkim.

The opportunity to raise the question of treaty renegotiation arose with an unexpected change in Indian political leadership.

On the final day of talks at the Indo-Pakistani peace conference (hosted by the Soviets) in Tashkent in January 1966, Prime Minister Shastri keeled over and died of a heart attack. Coming only weeks after the conclusion of 1965, the death thrust India into political turmoil. Rumours of foul play only intensified the atmosphere of crisis.

One person towered head and shoulders above those jostling to replace Shastri. Indira Gandhi had ducked the opportunity to replace her father, Jawaharlal Nehru, on his death in 1964, but two years later there was no question that she was the leading candidate. Some said she was the only person in India worthy of the job. Her perceived bravery during the Pakistan war – as Minister of Information and Broadcasting she had been in Kashmir at the time of the Pakistani incursion and had refused to leave – had led the press to hail her as 'the only man in a cabinet of women'.[7] The ruling Congress Party quickly shuffled her in as prime minister. For the world's press, her anointment as India's saviour was a sensation. 'Troubled India in a Woman's Hands' announced the 28 January 1966 cover of *Time*, alongside a flattering portrait, days after she had been sworn in.

Thondup already knew Indira Gandhi well. She had visited Sikkim with her father twice, and had attended his coronation the previous year. She was only a few years older than him, and he had always found her agreeable company. He felt confident that she would continue with her father's affectionate and understanding attitude towards Sikkim. But Thondup was also astute enough to recognise that the weakness of her political position (as a new, unproven prime minister facing major economic challenges) created a window of opportunity for him to argue his case for a revision to the treaty.

Buoyed by an article in the respected Calcutta magazine, *The Statesman*, calling the Indo-Sikkim treaty a 'hopelessly outdated straitjacket', Thondup briefed the Indian press on his views on treaty revision.[8] Carefully acknowledging 'India's vital interests in Sikkim' (to ensure no one could accuse him of pro-Chinese sympathies), he reminded the press that the appointment of a dewan from Delhi had only ever been intended as temporary and that if 'a properly qualified person from Sikkim' should become available, that person should be given the post.[9]

Thondup was confident that most people in Gangtok supported his call for a rethink of arrangements – the dominance of Indians in the administration had not gone unnoticed and was resented by many in the Sikkim civil service. He was therefore not overly unconcerned when the Kazi (prompted by the Kazini, who by now had become the unofficial press officer for the Kazi and the Sikkim National Congress that he led) publicly opposed the idea of treaty revision from his base in Kalimpong, calling it 'ill-timed' and suggesting that it would not benefit the people.[10]

Thondup was satisfied that he had achieved what he wanted: he had floated the idea in the press. Discussions soon commenced with the Ministry of External Affairs in the Indian government. He was also hopeful that once his friend Indira had settled in as prime minister she would respond positively.

But it was his wife's involvement with the Institute of Tibetology, and an article that she wrote in its obscure academic journal, the *Bulletin of Tibetology*, that brought the question of Sikkim directly onto the desk of Indira Gandhi – and created a minor political storm.

-2-

Gangtok's Institute of Tibetology had been established in 1950 to promote the academic study of Tibet-related subjects. The timing of its formation, coming so shortly after the Chinese invasion, was not accidental. The Dalai Lama had laid the foundation stone of the building in the late 1950s and by the mid-1960s, despite persistent rumours that it was being used as a training centre for the CIA*, the institute was developing a reputation for scholarly work on Tibetan and Himalayan Buddhist history and thought.

Hope's intellectual curiosity was stimulated by the institute. In 1966, she decided to write something for its magazine. The article bore the innocuous title, 'The Sikkimese theory of landholding and the Darjeeling Grant', but the contents were political dynamite. In it, she chose to question the legitimacy of the grant of Darjeeling District to the British East India Company in 1835, suggesting that Darjeeling had only ever been *leased* to the British by the Sikkimese, and inferring that, since all land in Sikkim belonged to the royal family, there was a legitimate (albeit theoretical) argument that Darjeeling should be returned to Sikkim.

Even if, as Hope says in her autobiography, her article was intended only to 'mildly provoke, pique really, but in a scholarly way', it was hopelessly naive. To the Indian press still with their tails up after the 1965 war, it appeared that she had questioned the legitimacy of Indian ownership of Darjeeling; that was bordering on the inflammatory, a clear challenge to the territorial integrity of India. Headlines such as 'CIA Agent on Borrowed Plumage' and 'American Trojan Mare in Gangtok' appeared within days.[11]

Soon the article ended up on Mrs Gandhi's desk. She knew Hope Cooke – they had met at least twice before, the first time shortly after the royal marriage in 1963 over dinner with Nehru in Delhi, the second time at the coronation. But, for Indira, the timing of the article could not have been worse. India's economic problems had forced a massive devaluation of the rupee only weeks before the article appeared. She had also faced intense criticism over a visit to the USA, where she had asked, cap-in-hand, for aid; President Johnson had been charmed – he promised three million tons of food and $9 million, saying that he wanted to ensure that 'no harm comes to this girl' – and was appreciative when she issued a statement saying that she 'understood America's agony over Vietnam'.[12] But in Delhi such toadying to the Americans was not appreciated. Against this background

---

* This was probably another 'grey area' for the CIA. Although there is no evidence that the institute was directly involved with the Agency, Ken Conboy in his book *The CIA in Tibet* mentions one of the CIA officers involved with the Tibetan project at the time as having taken English lessons there.

of anti-Americanism, the article by Hope Cooke – who some genuinely believed was a CIA plant in the Himalayas – only served to complicate matters.

Under questioning in the Indian parliament Mrs Gandhi tried to brush the issue aside, assuring MPs that 'there has been no demand from any responsible quarter in Sikkim laying claim over the Darjeeling district'.[13] The barbed use of the phrase 'any responsible quarter' was meant as a clear message to Gangtok about Hope's naivety.

In Gangtok, Thondup also felt it necessary to distance himself from his wife, putting out a haughty statement: 'My government is quite competent to handle any matter concerning the rights and well-being of my country and my people . . . without resorting to the assistance of an academic body like the Namgyal Institute or its bulletin.'[14]

It had been an irritating episode for Indira Gandhi, albeit a minor one. She faced a far bigger challenge consolidating her political position, as she prepared for an election in March 1967.

Nevertheless, Hope's article had not done Sikkim any favours.

The outraged reaction of some in the Indian Congress Party to Hope's article was part of a strategy to push Indira Gandhi to prove her credentials as a strong politician and to distance herself from the USA. Still relatively weak, Indira could not have resisted this pressure even if she had wanted to. On 1 July 1966, she therefore issued a strong statement condemning the American bombing in Vietnam. The impact was immediate: Johnson was furious, and relations with the USA cooled almost overnight.

A knock-on effect of this was felt by the Tibetan resistance fighters in Mustang on the Nepal–Tibet border, who noticed a distinct change in tone in terms of the support they were getting from both the Americans and the Indians. For months the Americans had been trying to extricate themselves from the Mustang project by getting the Indians to take a greater lead in the organisation of the supply flights. Now they all but demanded it.

But Indian priorities were changing, too. China's control in Tibet was now total. And with the retiral of intelligence chief Mullik – the one man who had tacitly supported the Americans' Tibet projects – the Tibetans were left isolated and without a champion in India or in the USA.

Within a year, the Americans' Special Center in the Hauz Khas area of Delhi had put infiltrations into Tibet on hold and started to wind down military support for the Tibetan operation in Mustang. The Special Frontier Force continued to attract Tibetan recruits but the short-lived resistance movement funded by the Americans and operating out of India was all but over.

For the Indians, too, supporting the return of Tibetans to their homeland was no longer a primary concern. Instead their focus shifted to preventing the possibility of Chinese incursions into the Himalaya, and infiltration into India itself. As a result, Sikkim was in the spotlight more than ever as a strategic pillar in India's northern defences.

In the middle of 1966, Martha Hamilton returned briefly to Sikkim to hand over her duties to her successor. During her six years in Sikkim she had fallen deeply in love with the country. It was a wrench to leave. Back in Scotland she had found herself 'looking up at every plane wishing I was on it'.

Even on this visit Thondup teased her by trying to persuade her to break her rule of 'not drinking East of Suez' – but she held firm. In recognition of her contribution to Sikkim, he awarded her the Pema Dorji medal, one of a series of medals made in Spinks of London; she was the first – and only – European to receive one.

While in Sikkim, Martha passed the baton to Ishbel Ritchie as the new headmistress of the Paljor Namgyal Girls' School. Ritchie was also a Scot, but from a different background. Where Martha had sought out the adventure of missionary work for the joy of teaching and to fulfil a pledge to her wealthy grandfather, Ishbel felt more of a calling and a sense of Christian mission.

In a few important respects, however, the two were alike. Just as Martha had written frequently to her parents, Ishbel wrote home every week to her mother in Scotland. And while Ishbel was perhaps more dedicated to the Church and less intimate with the Palace than Martha had been, she shared her predecessor's humour and keen eye for detail.

One of her first visits to the palace, on Christmas Eve 1966, coincided with an important visit from the Secretary for External Affairs in the Government of India, a tall Kashmiri called Tikki Kaul. Thondup had known Kaul since the early 1950s and saw him as a powerful friend in Delhi. He had invited the Indian to Gangtok in the hope of enlisting his support for the cause of treaty revision.

Ishbel Ritchie found the evening relaxed but impressive, the kind of dinner for which the Palace would become known. Guests included the American consul-general, the political officer and the dewan. Hope had already become adept at getting the best supplies sent up to Gangtok by whatever means she could, and Ishbel, while feeling 'a trifle out of place', marvelled at the range of food – 'caviar, mild gorgonzola, Christmas cake, and Egg Nog.'*

The strange menu worked; in February 1967 Thondup secured a vital concession from Kaul: that the border between Sikkim and India should be demarcated as an international line. For Thondup it was a step in the right direction. It seemed that he was well on the way to achieving his goal of treaty revision.

But, despite some minor successes such as the international border-line agreement, Thondup faced one major problem: without a democratic political system, he could not claim any real legitimacy to speak for his country. He tried to laugh off the invective from the typewriter of the Kazini in Kalimpong, which suggested that Thondup and Hope were the last vestiges of a crumbling feudal monarchy – but he knew her well-crafted articles hit the mark for those of a 'leftist' disposition. Both Thondup and Hope did their best to make the case for the existing system. When Indian journalist Ved Mehta interviewed the pair, Hope made a point of referring to the Kazi as the 'Al Capone of Sikkim', while Thondup defended his laissez-faire approach. 'Now there is no popular agitation for merging with India,' he told Mehta in 1966. 'I think the reason . . . is that the Sikkimese like my government. My friends in the Indian government are always telling me that monarchy is on its way out, that I have to change my government, and I'm always saying to them that people will like monarchy as long as monarchy continues to be useful.'

---

* On another occasion, Indian-born journalist Ved Mehta (during a visit to Gangtok) recalled Hope's plea: 'When you get back to America, please, please, please, send me some Sara Lee frozen cheesecake. If you send it on a plane that has a freezer, we'll have the cheesecakes bailed out in Calcutta.'

In early 1967, elections were held in Sikkim, testing the existing system again. The Kazi and his SNC party were quite clear in their message to the electorate: getting democracy in Sikkim was far more important than Thondup's attempts to fiddle around with the treaty with India. The SNC message hit home, particularly with the young Nepali electorate. Despite the imbalanced voting system, designed to favour the Bhutia-Lepcha community, the SNC won enough seats to justify the Kazi's inclusion in the appointed Executive Council that served as an advisory board to the Chogyal and the Durbar (parliament). Here was an opportunity for Thondup to try and build a consensus, to bring Lhendup Dorji into the fold. Instead he deliberately snubbed him, appointing a rival contender for the leadership of the SNC to the Executive Council instead. The Kazini was livid, frustrated that her husband had been sidelined so publicly. But there was little she could do – except write more articles.

Thondup pressed ahead with creating an environment to reinforce his claim that Sikkim had a distinct international identity. One key move was to set up a seemingly innocuous committee in Gangtok, called the Study Forum, to 'advise the Darbar on specific matters relating to the national interests of the Kingdom'.[15] Consisting of a group of 'intellectuals' in Sikkim, the Study Forum stood clearly for revision of the treaty to enhance Sikkim's credential as a 'separate' nation (a position diametrically opposed to that of the Kazi).

The Study Forum's members were always searching for further symbols that would help demonstrate that Sikkim's identity was separate from that of India. As a model they had Bhutan (Sikkim's near neighbour geographically and culturally, which was seeking revision of its own treaty with Delhi) and Nepal (whose independent status had never really been in doubt). The Study Forum advocated that Sikkim should follow Bhutan's lead and join the Colombo Plan (seen as a natural step on the way to UN recognition), should begin to print its own stamps and earn foreign exchange (both of which Bhutan did successfully), and retain control of the Inner Line Permit system that required visitors to Sikkim to register for a permit.

In the search for symbols of nationhood, none were considered too small – in 1966 the Asia Society in New York was persuaded to establish a 'Sikkim Council'; in 1967 Princess Coocoola arranged for two Sikkimese women to represent Sikkim at the 'Associated Country Women of the World' conference, displaying a collection of items to represent their country, including the national flag and a number of other artefacts which stressed the Bhutia-Lepcha roots of the nation. In 1968 two Sikkimese artisans flew to Peru to represent the country in a World Craft Council meeting.[16]

Few of the Study Forum's big ideas came to fruition; but for those like the Kazi and Kazini, opposed to Thondup's plans for greater autonomy, it became a symbol of all that was wrong in Sikkim – an unrepresentative group, predominantly Bhutia-Lepcha, with a misplaced loyalty to an outdated feudal system.

Clear divisions were emerging in Sikkim.

-3-

In March 1967, Indira Gandhi went to the polls across India for the first time. The results were a huge setback. Since independence in 1947, the Indian Congress Party had never failed to win less than 60 per cent of the vote. Now, with Indira at the helm, the party was reduced to just over 40 per cent of the seats and was forced into a minority government. In London, the *Times* called the election result a personal 'slap in the face' for the Indian prime minister.[17]

Things were particularly bad in West Bengal, the Indian state to Sikkim's south, where Congress lost power for the first time to a communist-dominated coalition. Worse, the communists themselves in West Bengal were starting to splinter, reflecting the global split between Chairman Mao's revolutionary vision and the more moderate communism of the Soviet Union. The Maoists coalesced around the hills near Naxalbari, a small town in the narrow chicken-neck of land in the north of the state that ran between the northern tip of East Pakistan and Sikkim. Delhi considered it a major threat, particularly when Radio Peking announced provocatively that the Naxalbari rebellion was 'the front paw of the revolutionary armed struggle launched by the Indian people under the guidance of Mao Tse-Tung's teachings'.[18] In the Indian capital the liberal journal *Thought* worried that 'these pro-Peking Reds would "fan out from Naxalbari to link up with their cells in Bengal, till they come right into the heart of Calcutta. Behind them will be the Chinese army menacing the Himalayan border."'[19]

The writer scarcely needed to mention that if the Chinese were to consider invasion, the easiest route would be straight through Sikkim.

Thondup, well aware of Delhi's grave concerns about the threat from the Chinese, picked this moment to pile on more pressure for treaty revision, which he tried to portray as the only viable way forward. He also calculated that Mrs Gandhi might seek to resolve matters quickly, given the trouble in the north of neighbouring West Bengal. In May 1967, he held another press conference, telling journalists that while he recognised the Indian government had 'more important things on their hands than we have'[20], he sought changes to the treaty at 'the convenience of the Government of India' and through 'discussions'.[21]

The Indian press reacted with predictable outrage at Thondup's statements: change could only bring problems, they said. Both publicly and privately Thondup expressed surprise at the negative reaction – he remarked to one journalist that it seemed to him that Sikkim had 'been pushed around too much by not only Indian officials, but also by others who see even in our simplest statements a deep and sinister meaning'.[22] He complained to Rustomji that 'the Press Trust of India has taken it into its head to run me down'. In the *Sikkim Herald*, a Sikkim government publication, they went even further, saying that if India did not open up discussions over the Indo-Sikkim treaty, it was in danger of stepping 'into the shoes of British imperialism'.

The following month, Sikkim's Executive Council (the body from which the Kazi had been conveniently excluded) issued a 'historic joint statement', again requesting immediate talks on treaty revision, and highlighting what they saw as economic grievances. The closure of both Sikkim–Tibet passes in the aftermath of the 1962 war, they said, had caused loss of Sikkim's traditional trading revenue; and excise duty (collected by India) was crippling the Sikkimese economy.

Then, to compound Delhi's worries about the Chinese threat, there were fierce clashes between Indian and Chinese troops at the Nathu La in September 1967, after the Chinese dismantled a stretch of barbed wire laid by Indian soldiers.* *Time* reported that 'for four days gunfire and cannonades echoed through the thin Himalayan air'.† In the febrile atmosphere of Delhi, some MPs had no hesitation in making a link between the clashes and the emergence of the Study Forum, which one called 'a sinister group on the very lines of the Red Guards in China with the help and aid of Chinese funds', adding that 'this organisation has started very strong anti-Indian propaganda in Sikkim and neighbouring border areas'. *National Geographic's* description of Sikkim as 'the weakest buckle in the Himalayan belt' was beginning to sound uncannily accurate to many in India.

Whether Indira Gandhi liked it or not, Sikkim was right back at the top of her agenda. She decided that the issue had to be addressed – one way or the other. In March 1968 she sent her deputy, Morarji Desai, to Gangtok for discussions. Desai was a particular man, fussy about his food to the extent that he sent a long list of requirements to Gangtok before his arrival, detailing what he could and could not eat.‡ But he was also, Thondup felt, 'a good man, an honest man of principle'.[23] During their meeting, Thondup won over Desai by raising the question of excise duty, which went straight to the heart of the question of Sikkim's status. It seemed ridiculous, Thondup argued, that India was giving government aid to Sikkim with one hand, then taking the money away by collecting excise duty on the other. Why not simplify matters and take the problem off Indian hands altogether? Desai was persuaded. The Indian deputy prime minster returned to Delhi to argue Sikkim's case – that the state was indeed a separate entity and, as such, the excise duty should be returned.

When Indira Gandhi herself came to Gangtok for further discussions accompanied by her daughter-in-law, Sonia, and Tikki Kaul, it seemed that Thondup might be on his way to genuine talks on a revised treaty. In

---

* It was an uncanny echo of events seven decades earlier when the first British Political Officer, Claude White, erected pillars on the same spot only to have them torn down by the Tibetans.

† The exact extent of the subsequent confrontation has never been fully clarified by either side, but there were certainly some casualties.

‡ Desai also believed that drinking his own urine cured his piles, something that he explained in 1978 (when he was prime minister) to a bemused Dan Rather and the American nation on *CBS 60 Minutes*: urine therapy was, he believed, the 'perfect' medical solution for the millions of Indians unable to afford medical treatment.

meetings and over dinners at the palace, Thondup outlined his vision of a future where responsibility for defence remained in Indian hands, but external affairs and communications were returned to Sikkim. In private, Hope Cooke later recalled, Mrs Gandhi (who was 'a delightful guest – unassuming, appreciative') seemed to 'respect Sikkim's otherness from India and to be pro-Sikkim'.[24]

For a brief moment, it seemed that Thondup was winning the argument and that greater independence was within reach. But some comments from Tikki Kaul towards the end of the dinner seriously alarmed him. Perhaps, Kaul suggested, 'Indians from hilly Garwhal and Kumaon* should be settled in the Lachen and Lachung valleys'[25] in the north of Sikkim. To Thondup this was anathema. From his point of view, the Bhutia-Lepcha community had already been slowly marginalised by nearly a century of Nepali immigration. There was also already huge resentment that the administration was entirely dominated by Indians. Thondup had even proposed halting further immigration from India altogether in 1965. Besides, the proposed areas in the north of Sikkim around these two valleys were 'reserved', holy areas with access restricted even for Sikkimese. The whole suggestion seemed incongruous with the rest of the discussions.

Something had subtly changed. Just before Mrs Gandhi and Tikki Kaul left Gangtok, she told the Chogyal and his Executive Councillors that the timing was not right – she was not yet out of the woods politically and needed to be more secure before contemplating anything so radical as treaty revision. Thondup was disappointed. There had been very warm words, with both sides praising each other and talking of the importance of the relationship between India and Sikkim, and a promise of a ceremonial visit from the Indian president in 1970; but he wondered if Mrs Gandhi was merely playing for time.

One Indian official would later refer to Indira Gandhi's 1968 visit as 'the high point of Indo-Sikkimese cordiality'.[26] He was right: from here, it was all downhill.

It was a provocative newspaper article, and the subsequent actions of a group of schoolchildren, that proved the turning point.

---

* To the south and west of Nepal.

During the 1950s and 1960s, a number of independent newspapers had sprung up in Sikkim. Among them was a fortnightly, titled *Sikkim*. The editor, Kaiser Bahadur Thapa, was an unapologetic proponent of independence – *Sikkim* took as its masthead the famously patriotic epigram 'Dulce et decorum est pro patria mori'. During the 1960s the paper had carefully and pointedly catalogued all the former colonial territories that had changed over one by one to independence, particularly in Africa. In the wake of Mrs Gandhi's visit, the fortnightly *Sikkim* took an even more aggressive stance. On 6 August 1968, only a few weeks after Indira had left Gangtok, a leader in the newspaper thundered:

> Revision of the 1950 treaty there must be, and in keeping with our present-day trend, not only should our treaty be revised but it should also be registered with the United Nations Organisation. If our rights are not given to us gracefully, we are prepared to get it anyhow. But in doing so let us hope that we will not be driven to the extreme so that we are compelled to repeat the underground Naga story.[27]

The reference to the disturbances in Nagaland was particularly incendiary. For months the tribal Nagas had been fighting for their independence on the extreme eastern frontier between India and Burma.

A few days later, on 15 August, Indian Independence Day, a group of schoolchildren walked through the streets of Gangtok carrying banners that reflected the growing sense of frustration felt by some in Gangtok. 'INDIANS GET OUT OF SIKKIM' read one; 'WE ARE A BUFFER NOT A DUFFER' read another; 'WE WANT INDEPENDENCE' proclaimed a third.[28]

In the Delhi parliament, MPs fired questions at Mrs Gandhi about the existence of a 'Quit Sikkim' movement, echoing the 'Quit India' movement that had raged across the subcontinent during the 1940s in protest at British imperial rule. She dismissed the whole issue as a 'minor demonstration' but pointedly added that officials had 'taken up the matter strongly with the Chogyal of Sikkim'. In Gangtok the Indian political officer ensured that those involved were forced to publicly denounce the incident.

The whole affair of the schoolchildren and their banners was a storm in a teacup. But it had an effect on the attitude of the Indian government. Any intentions they had of supporting treaty revision and discussing greater independence on Thondup's terms were disappearing fast. Towards the end of the year, Tikki Kaul returned to Gangtok. This time his message was quite clear: until such incidents stopped, Thondup could forget his fond hopes of Indian support for UN membership, or Indian support for inclusion in other international bodies.

-4-

In February 1968, a few months before Indira Gandhi's visit, Hope Cooke gave birth to her second child, a girl. Between them the royal couple now had five children. Despite the pressures that her husband was under, life for Hope at last seemed to be settling into some kind of routine. She loved the sense of being part of a home, a family. She missed the elder three when they were away at boarding school, but in the summers, when Coocoola's family of five also gathered in Gangtok, she revelled in the atmosphere, putting her differences with her sister-in-law to one side. The palace would 'explode with children', with picnics, large family meals and board games at night.

Both Thondup and Hope had always appreciated that Hope's American nationality brought with it the potential for press coverage for Sikkim, which could help to build up the idea of the country as a separate entity. It had never been hard to get journalists interested in their story – the glamour of the marriage and coronation aside, the *New York Times*, the *Washington Post*, the *New Yorker* and others were always eager for copy about the American 'Queen' in a faraway Himalayan land. Hope's well-heeled and intelligent friends, too, helped get the message out in all kinds of outlets. *National Geographic* ran features; *McCall's* (a popular glossy in the 1960s) ran a piece by Hope herself. Other friends such as Alice Kandell, who wrote about Sikkim in *Redbook* magazine, were only too happy to help. 'We played up the smallness, the fragility of our nation-building effort,' wrote Hope later, 'while clinging to a truculent notion that we would prevail because of our righteousness.' Perhaps to portray some of this fragility her voice had dissolved into a whisper, almost as if she believed her own fragility would somehow communicate Sikkim's vulnerability.*

In Gangtok, too, the international nature of their marriage, combined with the fact that English was almost a first language for Thondup as much as it was for Hope, brought a solid stream of foreign visitors. Some were Hope's friends, some were acquaintances, many had diplomatic connections – and not all were complimentary about the couple's increasingly anti-Indian stance. William Andreas Brown, a US Foreign Service officer in the embassy in New Delhi (who would go on to become ambassador to Thailand), recalled that in the late 1960s Hope 'was always sarcastically knifing the Indians in our presence'; Raymond Hare, US Assistant Secretary of State for Near Eastern Affairs from 1965 to 1966, remembered Hope and Thondup as 'a strange couple. He was very outgoing, liked a good time, and he drank with gusto. His wife, the American girl, used to sit with her head bowed and her hands folded like she thought a demure little Nepali should, I guess. It was a bit ludicrous.' Another American diplomat, Anthony Quainton, recalled that Hope 'had quite a following in the United States and constantly stirred up American domestic opinion about the plight of the Sikkimese under India'.[29] Sometimes the conversation would take bizarre turns. When General Westmoreland, who was a key player in the Vietnam conflict, visited, he recollected that 'the leader of the opposition party urged me to initiate steps for the United States to take over protectorate responsibilities of his country from India; so absurd was the request that I may have been abrupt in my reply'.[30]

By 1969, the couple were also travelling to New York and London twice a year. Tenzing was now at school in Harrow in London and, despite a small number of close friends in Sikkim, Hope's social circle was still deeply embedded in New York. London also presented the opportunity to stock up on luxury foods for transportation back to the palace in Gangtok. There was a wider implication behind these overseas visits, too.

---

* Geoge Griffin, at the US Consulate in Calcutta, recalled that Hope 'had learned a tradition that says one may not speak loudly in the presence of the king, so she whispered. I couldn't hear her very well, and had the worst time trying to figure out what she was talking about. It was made worse by the fact that she would whisper behind her hand.'

Hope and Thondup knew that membership of international bodies was critical as a sign of international status; by meeting diplomats and politicians around the world, they felt they were building support for Sikkim's international status.

This globetrotting and nation-building did not go down well with everyone back in India and Sikkim. In New Delhi, some suggested that just holding overseas press conferences could be interpreted as 'external relations', one of the three activities specifically assigned to India in the 1950 treaty. In Kalimpong, the Kazini too continued to make comparisons between the extravagance of the royal couple's lifestyle and that of the average (Nepali) worker in Sikkim, mocking the coverage that Hope and Thondup got in the US. It was easy to lampoon articles such as the one that appeared in *Time* magazine in 1969, entitled 'Sikkim: A Queen Revisited', describing the lifestyle of 'America's only working queen'.

The article gave details of Hope's daily routine: rising at 8 a.m., breakfasting on 'tea and fruit', browsing the 'foreign newspapers and magazines' until her secretary arrived for four hours of 'writing letters, devising menus and supervising the palaces 15 servants'. After social work and perhaps 'a set of tennis' in the afternoon, evenings were 'usually filled with official functions, or private parties', Hope 'confiding' to the magazine that she liked 'a Scotch and soda before dinner – or "even after dinner".'

In the reports of progress made in Sikkim since the coronation (an increase in literacy rates from 25 per cent to 40 per cent, quadrupling the number of children in school, average per-capita income of $100 – up a third), there was no mention of the continued heavy reliance on Indian aid. Instead, the focus was on the export-led revival of 'Sikkim's long-dormant cottage industry', the evidence of which was two 'chic Manhattan stores' that carried 'deep-pile rugs and silver jewellery painstakingly made by native craftsmen'.

The final section, entitled 'No Great Splendour', portrayed Hope as having found peace and happiness in the simplicity of Sikkim.

> At home, she dresses informally in the *kho*, the traditional Sikkimese costume, which is an ankle-length jumper that wraps around the waist and is worn over a blouse of contrasting color – cotton or wool for the daytime

and silk in the evening. She uses cosmetics only occasionally and does her own hair – though she admits that she is encouraging a romance between a Sikkimese youth and a Calcutta hairdresser in the hope of importing the kingdom's first coiffeuse. She describes her home as 'a poorish palace but a palace.' It is a 64-year-old, two-story white stucco building with five bedrooms and a tin roof. In Gangtok, the family gets around in a white Mercedes convertible. On foreign trips, however, they make a point of flying economy class and often stay with friends. 'It's no great Oriental splendor we live in,' Hope observes.

The Gyalmo and Chogyal travel in the West for about two months a year, which helps to overcome any surge of homesickness, but Hope admits that she sometimes misses 'cheese, the Sunday *New York Times* and the sea.' Still, those are hardly important. Hope says: 'My happiest times are right here in Sikkim. Being a queen is nice because it gives you a whole fabric, a structure, and because there is so much we need to do. I feel accepted, very comfortable, very inspired and completely happy.'[31]

If articles such as this were intended to advance the cause of Sikkim's drive for independence, they were almost certainly counterproductive. It was public opinion in India – and inside Sikkim itself – that Hope and Thondup needed to convince of the rightness of their cause, not in America.

Despite what she had told *Time* magazine, Hope was not happy in every area of her life. She believed her husband capable of more affairs. In London she sometimes found herself 'so jealous I don't dare let him leave without me'.[32]

Back in Sikkim the reality of her emotional isolation sometimes plunged her into a depression. However much she pretended to be satisfied with the role of Sikkimese wife and mother, she needed more than that. She felt intellectually isolated too, writing that finding a 'book of substance' among the shelves of Agatha Christie in the palace library was a challenge.

Her relationship with Coocoola also continued to deteriorate. She found herself questioning her sister-in-law's continual presence in the palace, convinced that from the moment she had arrived in Sikkim

Coocoola had 'thought I'd disappear fairly soon and is in a fury that I haven't'.

To assuage the feelings of loneliness, she spent an increasing amount of time in Thatongchen, at the school that had been developed as a model for education in the state. There she formed a close friendship with a young Sikkimese student at the school, Norbu, who taught her the basics of the Lepcha language and helped her to understand the folklore of Sikkim: 'Sometimes we just sit listening to records – Cat Stevens, James Taylor, Judy Collins. Occasionally he plays a flute he made himself from bamboo . . .'[33]

Her relationship with Thondup, never simple, was also coming under pressure. One evening, when Thondup decided to stay up late playing mah-jongg with friends, she deliberately turned her music up to its highest volume. Thondup stormed upstairs and threw her record player, which he knew she regarded as her 'lifeline', out of the window in a rage. She lashed a kick out at him in response. At 2 a.m. Thondup called his friend Karma Topden, often the fixer in such situations, who calmed the situation, getting treatment for Hope's damaged foot.

In a post-mortem the following morning, Topden, also married to a Western woman, gently reminded Thondup that both their wives might have every reason to feel lonely.

'You think I'm not lonely, too?' Thondup flashed back.

-5-

In May 1969, six months after Tikki Kaul had warned him that the chances of an independent Sikkim were rapidly receding, Thondup had a more positive meeting with India's External Affairs Minister, Dinesh Singh. Singh made encouraging noises about a status for Sikkim something similar to Monaco. It was an interesting analogy – Monaco, a principality, had a 'special relationship' with France whereby the latter was responsible for its defence only, but also agreed to pursue policies in their mutual interest. But by now Thondup was fixated on something more akin to complete independence. Monaco, Thondup pointed out, had only 'observer' status at the UN, countering Singh's informal suggestion by comparing Sikkim to Luxembourg, the landlocked European state of similar size to Sikkim.

Thondup was making a subtle point, and one that was not lost on Singh: far from having only 'observer' status, Luxembourg had been a founder member of the UN from 1946. He was setting his sights higher than Monaco.

While articles about the royal couple were appearing in the world's press and Thondup was having esoteric arguments about which European country Sikkim resembled, the Indian Political Officer in Gangtok, N. B. Menon, was noticing a distinct change in mood in the capital. He was also tired.

When he had taken up the post in 1967, Menon had made a speech invoking the spirit of former British Political Officers Sir Charles Bell and Colonel Bailey. From the magnificent Residency that the first Political Officer, Claude White, had so deliberately built to look down over the palace and the rest of Gangtok, it had seemed natural to link the pre-1947 past to the happy post-coronation glow in Sikkim. But over the next three years Menon's gentle paternalism had ebbed away amid anti-Indian demonstrations and the Sikkim Study Forum's increasingly belligerent calls for treaty revision.

In early 1970 Menon watched wearily as elections in Sikkim heightened the divisions between the pro-palace contingent, who demanded greater autonomy for Sikkim, and the growing political movement coalescing around the disenfranchised Nepali minority, led by the Kazi's SNC. When the political system, still heavily biased in favour of the Bhutia-Lepcha constituency, left the pro-palace National Party as the largest party, the Kazini ridiculed the result as yet another example of why the political system had to change. She mocked the National Party for their anti-Indian stance, suggesting that a withdrawal of Indian armed forces would be an open invitation for the Chinese to walk into Sikkim. The Study Forum (seen by some as allied to the National Party) responded by criticising the SNC for failing to raise its voice against 'Indian Imperialism'.

Menon was disappointed by these continuing tensions. He was, therefore, greatly relieved when bad weather forced the cancellation of the proposed visit by the President of India, V. V. Giri, in 1970. He had heard rumours that the president might have been welcomed by a 'black flag' demonstration and banners demanding that India leave Sikkim, and even that the Chogyal might not have welcome the president's visit. He had no desire to be caught up in that kind of political dilemma.[34]

In May 1970, an exhausted Menon left Gangtok for the last time in a car bedecked in flowers. In his final speech, he spoke to the Indian business community about the need for accepting change.

The problem was that no one really knew what kind of change, if any, would satisfy the increasingly divided communities within Sikkim.

The Indian President, V. V. Giri, had been in neighbouring Bhutan when he cancelled the visit to Gangtok. The warm relations between India and Bhutan could not have been more different from the tense relationship between India and Sikkim. Bhutan's leaders had been assiduous in staying close to the Indians and making Delhi feel comfortable with their desire for greater autonomy. Bhutan also had the advantage of a looser relationship with India. The Indo-Bhutanese treaty had been negotiated in 1949, a few months before the first Chinese incursions into Tibet; crucially, Sikkim's had been negotiated more than a year later, when the political environment looked quite different. But the Bhutanese had also been careful to avoid developing a confrontational relationship with India. They saw the Indian president's 1970 visit as another step on the road towards that ultimate goal of UN membership, something that they were ruthlessly focused on. Bhutan's co-operative approach was a far cry from the casual belligerence displayed towards India by the Palace in Gangtok and bodies such as Sikkim's Study Forum.

In London's Foreign Office, they were also staying abreast of developments in Sikkim and Bhutan.[35] Despite Britain's steady withdrawal from empire in the post-war period, the Foreign and Commonwealth Office maintained an active interest in all the former colonial possessions. Sikkim and Bhutan, with their interesting 'esoteric complications', were no exception.

In July 1970 an FCO official was asked to express an opinion on whether the UK could support the Bhutanese application to join the

UN. In general the FCO was careful about expressing support for new nation applications, but the FCO considered Bhutan's case to be a good one. The question had arisen after an informal approach by Apa Pant, the former Political Officer to Sikkim and Bhutan in the late 1950s, and now the Indian High Commissioner in London. But when Pant suggested that 'he thought in due course there would have to be similar developments in Sikkim', the FCO baulked at the prospect. The Sikkim treaty, they concluded, would not only be inconsistent with UN membership, it would also be inconsistent with 'most specialised agencies' that recognised sovereign status.

Not that the Foreign Office was dropping support for Sikkim completely. The British imperial connection still counted for something. In June 1970, a note from H. C. Easterling, the admissions tutor at Trinity College, Cambridge, arrived on the desk of Sir Denis Greenhill, the Permanent Under Secretary at the FCO.* Easterling had become aware that Prince Tenzing, the eldest of Thondup's children at Harrow, wanted to attend Cambridge. 'By our normal academic standards,' he wrote, 'he is not a very promising candidate, but we might be able to stretch a point if asked to do so by the FCO.'

Greenhill, perhaps consulting his files and recalling that an earlier British government had had no hesitation in 'stretching a point' in 1907, when a former Chogyal, Sidkeong, had attended Oxford University, wrote back:

> I am most grateful to you for consulting me in your letter of 2 June about the possible admission to your college of the Crown Prince Tenzing Namgyal, the son of the Chogyal of Sikkim. I have no hesitation in saying that I consider it important that the Prince should be able to complete his education at Cambridge. Sikkim's geographical position on the Indo-Chinese border gives it considerable political significance, and it is therefore in our interests not only to meet the wishes of the present Chogyal with regard to the education of his son but, more important, also to enable the future

---

* In 1971 Greenhill became famous as the PUS instructed by Foreign Secretary Sir Alec Douglas-Home to inform the Soviet embassy in London that 90 Russian diplomats and officials were to be expelled for spying.

Chogyal to benefit from all the good influences which would be brought to bear on him at your college. I therefore very much hope that, despite the heavy pressure for admission you must face, you will find it possible to make a place available for the Crown Prince. I know the boy's parents quite well. Thank you for consulting me.

Some things, it was clear, had not changed.

In August 1970, Delhi sent a new political officer to Sikkim.

Forty-two-year-old K. Shankar Bajpai was one of a new breed of young up-and-coming diplomats in the Indian Foreign Service – sharp, polished and urbane, and with impeccable credentials. His father, Sir Girija Bajpai, had served as Indian agent-general to the USA in the 1940s before becoming a leading foreign policy adviser to Nehru as secretary-general of the Ministry of External Affairs after independence; K. Shankar Bajpai's own education had been in Washington and then at Merton College, Oxford. Joining the Indian Foreign Service had been a foregone conclusion. By the time he was appointed to Gangtok he had already made his mark, first in two prestigious postings in Pakistan at the height of the tensions there and then for three years as the Indian consul-general in the USA.

Bajpai knew that Tikki Kaul, who had handpicked him for the job in Gangtok, was committed to revising India's relations with Bhutan and was also keen to resolve the question of the future of Sikkim. But it did not take Bajpai long to assess that there were critical differences between the situations in the two countries. For a start, the military presence in Sikkim was far greater than that in Bhutan. There were the best part of two divisions of the Indian Army stationed in Sikkim. Then there was the administration – almost entirely peopled by Indians, far more so than Bhutan.

He also thought that Delhi was underestimating another important factor in the problem in Sikkim. The geography of the area was particularly sensitive. To the south in Darjeeling, the strong and vibrant Nepali community was increasingly identifying with its ethnic cousins – both in Nepal itself and in Sikkim. A change in the status of Sikkim, Bajpai mused, might be an encouragement to the formation of a Gurkha or Nepali state

across the Himalayas, encompassing Sikkim, Kalimpong and Darjeeling.*
Trouble in the chicken-neck of the Sikiguri corridor – the area where the
Maoist Naxalites had their base and which included both Kalimpong and
Darjeeling – could even cut the north-east states off from the rest of the
country. The Naxalite terror campaign had already spread beyond West
Bengal, reaching as far as Calcutta, where the insurgent Maoists and the
state government were engaged in murderous combat. Although there
were no signs yet that the Naxalite violence was spreading to Sikkim, the
potential for a spread of Maoism in the region sent shivers up the spines
of the politicians in Delhi.

Gangtok, Bajpai realised, was quite a posting.

With his suave and sophisticated manner, Bajpai was soon invited
to the palace. His intelligence and intellect immediately struck a chord
with Hope Cooke; they had the US in common (his last posting had
been in San Francisco) and were soon exchanging gramophone records.†
But right from the outset, Bajpai noticed that Thondup seemed uncom-
fortable with him. He wondered idly if this might be because the
Namgyal family was less comfortable with the idea of an Indian holding
the post of political officer than they had been with a British person
doing so.

Bajpai also observed how effective Thondup and Hope's partnership
appeared. While Thondup was the 'driving force' behind the demands for
treaty revision, he could see that it was Hope that brought a vital 'intellectual cast to his ambition'. Bajpai recognised the marital tensions, but
he also observed the importance of Hope's American connection, which
gave Thondup a feeling of international context for Sikkim, a place in the
world for his country.

One thing Bajpai was certain of was that life in the palace was in danger
of becoming a caricature of itself. He could sense that something needed
to change. He knew from his time in San Francisco that the royal couple's
life was hardly jetset in the way that the Kazini tried to paint it, but he
realised that there were plenty of people in Sikkim who saw Thondup and

---

* While this was not a major concern in the 1970s, it was a prescient identification of a
problem that has continued to dog the region since.

† The exchanges did not always work; in an interview with Bajpai, he noted 'Hope was very
fond of the pop-singers of the day . . . I was more into classical music.'

Hope as unnecessarily extravagant, with their cars and their twice yearly foreign flights. Delhi needed to make up its mind about what it was going to do with Sikkim before it was made up for it.

But, for Delhi, events in East Pakistan were about to become all-consuming – events that would eventually have a significant bearing on Sikkim's fate.

CHAPTER FIVE

The Bigger Picture

1970–3

-1-

After the wake-up call of the 1967 election result, Mrs Gandhi had slowly strengthened her grip on power across India. In doing so, she had demonstrated her remarkable ability to connect with Indian voters; but her direct and occasionally autocratic manner in parliament had also split the Congress Party. Not everyone believed that Indira was the right person to lead the party forward. Pro- and anti- Indira factions emerged; by 1969, Congress was split wide open into two distinct groups: Congress (R) comprising Indira's supporters; and Congress (O), those opposed to her.*

In early 1971 she called a snap election to resolve matters. Events soon turned ugly. Congress (O) and the other opposition parties campaigned on a slogan of 'Indira Hatao' (Remove Indira). Indira and her Congress (R) supporters retorted with a slogan that suggested she was above the personality game: 'Garibi Hatao' (Remove Poverty). It was a characteristically populist move and generated the political support she needed.[1] In February 1971, she swept back into power in the 'biggest democratic poll in history: 150 million people voted in 520 constituencies'.[2]

For five years Indira Gandhi had operated without a clear mandate from the Indian people. Now that she finally had one, she intended to use it. Almost immediately an opportunity arose to consolidate her electoral victory: the rapidly worsening situation in East Pakistan.

---

* Congress (Requisition) and Congress (Organisation).

The geographically divided state of Pakistan was one of the oddest and most contentious legacies left by the British after 1947. In an effort to deal with the competing demands of the two largest religious communities – the Hindus and the Muslims – two separate homelands for the Muslims had been created: West Pakistan (now Pakistan) nudging up against Afghanistan, and East Pakistan (now Bangladesh). Despite the fact that these two geographical territories were separated by a vast swathe of India, in 1947 they had been formed into a single unitary state.

The new East Pakistan – which lay directly below Sikkim, across a narrow band of Indian land – had been created by splitting the ancient state of Bengal. Despite the fact that this was an idea that had been tried by Lord Curzon in 1905 but rejected as unworkable only six years later, the imperial bureaucrats had decided to try again in 1947, seeing a partition of Bengal as the only feasible answer to increasingly violent communal strife. West Bengal, predominantly Hindu, remained a part of India; East Bengal, which was overwhelmingly Muslim, became East Pakistan.* It was an exceedingly odd geographical solution, which meant that over-night the East Bengalis became East Pakistanis. Worse, they were yoked together with West Pakistan – a remote and completely unknown land to most of them – on the basis of little more than religious affiliation.

Two decades of political instability followed. The 1965 Indo-Pakistani war only served to accentuate the lack of any geographical coherence; the conflict – fought over the border between India and West Pakistan – barely touched East Pakistan, whose reluctance to get involved in the war was resented by their western counterparts.

In December 1970, Pakistan (both East and West) finally held its first elections based on full adult suffrage. The results reflected the geographical split. There were completely separate but equally strong majorities in the two split halves of Pakistan: the greater population in East Pakistan meant the Awami League, dominant there, had an overall majority in terms of both votes and seats; West Pakistan, therefore, faced, for the first time, the prospect of a Bengali prime minister for all Pakistan. It was a recipe for further trouble.

The Pakistani President Yahya Khan (who had replaced Ayub Khan

---

* For the jute industry (in which my grandfather was employed), the impact was particularly deleterious, with the mills of West Bengal separated from the jute fields of East Pakistan.

two years previously in yet another military coup) refused to acknowledge the election result. A non-cooperation movement in East Pakistan quickly turned into an active challenge to the government forces, which were mainly from West Pakistan. Yahya Khan cracked down fiercely on the dissent. Soon India's neighbouring West Bengal became a de facto base for the liberation movement.

Indira Gandhi immediately recognised the importance of these events: the questions they raised about the territorial integrity of West Bengal, and the opportunity they provided for her to further consolidate her position, both in West Bengal (where the Congress had lost badly in 1967) and across India. She was also very aware, like others, of the potential threat that instability in the region might have on the narrow chicken-neck of land between East Pakistan and Sikkim that linked the main part of India to its volatile north-eastern states. The creation of this 'Siliguri corridor' (named after the largest town in the area) had become far more politically sensitive after the invasion of Tibet by the People's Republic of China in 1950. If things got out of hand, there was a risk that the Chinese could break through the Chumbi Valley and link up with a sympathetic East Pakistan – or indeed with the Maoist rebels who had congregated around the town of Naxalbari – cutting off the fertile plains of Assam. The turmoil in 1971 raised all this as a possible scenario in Indira Gandhi's mind – one with devastating consequences.[3]

In March, the Indian parliament therefore passed a resolution expressing 'profound sympathy and solidarity with the people of East Bengal for a democratic way of life'. The use of 'East Bengal' rather than 'East Pakistan' to describe the territory in question was particularly loaded. The following month a provisional government of Bangladesh (Nation of Bengal) was established in exile in Calcutta, the capital of West Bengal.

Six years after the 1965 Indo-Pakistani war, India and Pakistan were once again on the brink of conflict, one that could drag in the Chinese – and therefore spread into the Himalayas.

Naturally, this raised the profile of Sikkim.

The events in East Pakistan were not happening in isolation. Across Asia 1971 was a critical year, not least in the fiendish complexity of the shifting alignments of the big powers with interests in the region – the USA, China, India and the USSR.

The Americans had never forgiven Indira Gandhi for denouncing the Vietnam War after accepting American aid in 1966. Indira's slow drift to the left had only worsened matters. By 1970, President Nixon and his National Security Adviser, Kissinger, had decided that, given strengthening relations between the USSR and India, it made strategic sense to start secret talks with the Chinese, aimed at forming a working relationship that would help the USA to maintain stability in Asia. Hints at what was going on emerged in April 1971 when two US table-tennis players received and accepted a last-minute invitation to participate in a tournament in China; this infamous 'ping-pong diplomacy' was, in fact, the culmination of months of backstage negotiations by Kissinger and Nixon. A few months later the US lifted the trade embargo on China, a further public symbol of the rapid thaw in US–China relations.

Against this background, Henry Kissinger passed through Delhi, supposedly as part of an 'extended tour of Asia'. In fact, he was heading to China to prepare the ground for further détente with Mao. If Indira had any doubts that a shift was taking place, they disappeared in a meeting with Kissinger in the Indian capital: Kissinger made it clear that the US would not be prepared to side with India in a war over East Pakistan.

Partly in response (and partly to get her hands on Soviet armaments) Indira signed a Friendship Treaty with the Soviet Union in August. The Soviets had been wooing her for some time, but the treaty was a major strategic coup, the latest step in what Oleg Kalugin, a retired major-general in the KGB, described as 'a model of KGB infiltration of a Third World government.' New Delhi was made into a 'main residency' for the Soviet intelligence arm, which now had 'scores of sources throughout the Indian Government – in intelligence, counterintelligence, the Defence and Foreign Ministries, and the police'.[4]

If anything, the Indo-Soviet Treaty increased the pace of US–Chinese rapprochement. The biggest change of all came in October 1971, when the People's Republic of China finally took its seat at the United Nations. Since the formation of the United Nations in 1945 it had been Chiang Kai-shek's nationalists in Taiwan (the only viable government at the time) who had held the Chinese seat at the UN, including a permanent seat on the UN Security Council. Mao had always seen this as an injustice; now the Americans – who for years had resisted Mao's calls for a UN seat – had switched their allegiance overnight.*

Indira Gandhi was understandably furious. India had always felt slighted by not having a permanent seat on the UN Security Council; now the Americans had secretly negotiated to give the seat instead to the Chinese – who she perceived as an aggressive neighbour.

Within the course of a few months, the geopolitical alignment in Asia had changed radically. Although not explicit yet, the lines were becoming clearer: if the USA were siding with China, Indira would happily side with the USSR.

Meanwhile, as the repression continued in East Pakistan, the refugee crisis worsened: up to 150,000 people were flooding across the border to West Bengal each day. The cost of supporting such an influx only exacerbated India's financial crisis. Under intense pressure, Indira embarked on a major tour of the Western world to try and galvanise international opinion that something had to be done.

She reached Washington in early November to meet with Nixon and Kissinger. The meeting was a disaster. America was knee-deep in the quagmire of the Vietnam War; for the president and his national security advisor, Indira's actions in East Pakistan just complicated matters further. Besides, Nixon liked to do diplomacy on personality. He had formed a strong personal relationship with the straight-talking President Yahya in Pakistan, but he took an instant dislike to Indira Gandhi. 'Nixon's comments after meetings with her were not always printable,' Kissinger would later write, adding that the two 'were not intended by fate to be personally congenial. Her assumption of almost hereditary moral superiority and her moody silences brought out all of Nixon's latent insecurities.'[5] Kissinger himself later referred to her as a 'bitch'. Indira left empty-handed.

As the situation in East Pakistan deteriorated, the Pakistani Air Force made pre-emptive strikes against Indian forces in West Bengal

---

* During the 1960s the Communist International had brought an annual resolution at the UN, organised and led by Albania's Enver Hoxha, to recognise the PRC as the rightful representative of the Chinese people. Every year the US had successfully mobilised the UN to block it.

on 3 December. On 5 December Mrs Gandhi struck back – hard. In Washington, Nixon denounced the Indian 'aggression'; nine years after the USS *Enterprise* had been sent to the Bay of Bengal by Kennedy in support of the Indians during the Sino-Indian conflict, Nixon ordered the same ship back into the area at the head of a task force – this time to send a message to Indira Gandhi. With Russian ships in the area, it looked for a brief moment as if the conflict could take on a wider international dimension. But in a short, sharp one-sided war, Indian firepower (to which West Pakistan had no answer) quickly forced a ceasefire. East Pakistan was removed from the map; in its place Bangladesh – 'Free Bengal' – emerged, a brand new nation. Just as it had in 1962, the USS *Enterprise* turned tail and left.

Indira Gandhi walked taller than ever.

India's involvement in what would become known as Bangladesh's Liberation War had taken a sizeable military effort. The Indian Air Force had provided the main thrust of the attack from bases in West Bengal, supported by Indian Army soldiers on the ground, who benefitted from the local knowledge of the infamous Mukti Bahini, the East Pakistan resistance movement. But in the far eastern side of India, in the state of Mizoram, it was not Indians but Tibetans – including some of those who had fled through Sikkim in the years after 1959 – who had fought for the liberation of Bangladesh.

It was nearly a decade since the Special Frontier Force (also known as Establishment 22) had been formed from Tibetan exiles during the days of closer US–Indian cooperation. As US support for Tibetan independence had evaporated,* General Uban Singh, maverick Sikh commander, had fought hard to keep the force alive. While Singh found work for his Tibetan force busy patrolling in Ladakh and NEFA (and occasionally conducting covert incursions back into Tibet), the group steadily expanded, recruiting Gurkhas as well as Tibetans, and by 1971 numbered over 3,000.

---

* The CIA did continue support of sorts, which included enlisting Kellogg Company to develop a special version of the Tibetan tsampa (a kind of hardened porridge) loaded with special nutrients and vitamins that could be packed into small packages and air-dropped, if necessary, to Tibetan fighters.

When the trouble in East Pakistan started in 1971, Singh immediately proposed that his highly trained (and under utilised) guerrilla force should also be used in the conflict. The Tibetans were initially reluctant, pointing out that the SFF had been formed to support the cause of Tibetan independence; they failed to see what the remote East Pakistani war had to do with them. The matter was referred to the Tibetan government-in-exile in Dharamsala, the town in Himachal Pradesh that had become the home of the unofficial Tibetan government-in-exile. Wary of offending their hosts, the Tibetan leaders quietly approved the mission.

So, in October 1971, well over 2,000 troops, most of them Tibetans, were airlifted from the SFF base in Chakrata (north of Delhi) into remote Mizoram province, the narrow strip of Indian land that snaked down to the east of Bangladesh. Facing the fierce heat of the jungle and equipped with Bulgarian AK47s to allow deniability, the Tibetans advanced through the Chittagong hill tracts into East Pakistan, tying down elements of the elite Pakistan Special Services Group who had amassed on the other side of the border. Enduring terrible deprivations, they fought their way bravely through the jungle.* General Uban Singh, their commander, remembers them as 'unstoppable'.

By the time the ceasefire was declared the Tibetans had reached Chittagong, looking out over the Bay of Bengal. Their reputation in the Indian Army was secured; but it had come at a high cost. The Tibetans had lost 49 men; another 160 had been injured.

It was ironic, some of the Tibetan survivors pointed out, that after struggling for their own cause for so long their compatriots 'had paid with their lives for the birth of a nation not their own'.[6]

India's military had also received support from another source: India's new external intelligence services, the Research and Analysis Wing – known as RAW – formed in 1968.

---

* Ratu Ngawang, who had been a bodyguard to the Dalai Lama on his 1959 flight from Tibet, fought with the SFF in Chittagong. I interviewed him in the Tibetan colony in Delhi in 2012. He recalled watching colleagues die 'not for our cause, not for our independence'. The experience was 'terrible'. Carrying 35 kilos in poorly designed rucksacks through thick jungle, the Tibetans developed terrible sores; to treat them they scrubbed them till they bled, and then used weapon oil to clean them before dressing them with weapon cleaning cloths.

Rameshwar Kao, the tall Kashmiri with piercing eyes who had run the Aviation Research Centre with the Americans in 1963, had long advocated a specialised external intelligence agency in India. After the 1965 conflict with Pakistan, Kao pulled together plans for a formalised split of the Indian Intelligence Bureau (IB) to accommodate a new organisation focused solely on external intelligence. With Indira's backing, he formed the RAW on 21 September 1968, with a ready-made staff – 250 colleagues from the China and Pakistan desks in the IB were immediately transferred into his new organisation.[7]

Bangladesh was RAW's first serious deployment on the ground, running agents, gathering intelligence and working with the leaders of East Pakistan's resistance movement. They exceeded expectations. The war of 1971 cemented Indira's loyalty to and support of the new intelligence chief and his outfit, who (in inner circles) rapidly became known as Indira's 'Kaoboys'. They would play an important role in Sikkim in the coming years.

The Chinese reaction to the events of December 1971 was strangely muted compared to 1965. But they did use their new seat on the UN Security Council to make a specific point about Tibet. India, with Soviet support, had used the pretext of national liberation in the war over East Pakistan; one of their justifications for invading East Pakistan was that the refugees who had poured into India from East Pakistan needed to be returned to their legitimate homeland. For the Chinese, this set a very dangerous precedent, as the new PRC Ambassador to the UN, Qiao Guanghua, made clear:

> The Indian ruling circle . . . some time ago forcibly coerced several tens of thousands of the inhabitants of China's Tibet into going to India [to] set up a so-called government-in-exile headed by the Chinese traitor Dalai Lama. To agree that the Indian Government is justified to use the so-called refugee question as a pretext for invading Pakistan is tantamount to agreeing that the Indian Government will be justified in using the question of the so-called 'Tibetan refugees' as a pretext for invading China.[8]

Indira Gandhi had been worried that Sikkim and the Chumbi Valley represented a route for the Chinese to cut off the Siliguri Corridor. The

Chinese thought Sikkim and the Chumbi Valley represented the route that the Indians might take into Tibet.

The Bangladesh war had, if anything, increased the geopolitical importance of Sikkim.

-2-

At the height of the tensions in late November 1971, Hope Cooke and Thondup were nowhere near Sikkim. While Indira Gandhi and Richard Nixon had their fateful meeting in Washington, the Sikkimese royal couple were to be found further up the US East Coast, running a fashion show in one of New York's finest high-end department stores, Bergdorf Goodman. The owners, who were friends of friends of Hope, agreed to display and sell the collection (designed by Hope and the royal tailor in Gangtok) and put on other events around the show.

Ever since her arrival in Sikkim a decade earlier, Hope had been struck by the beauty of the handicrafts in the country. She was certain that, if presented in the right way, they could find an international audience. During the summer of 1971 she worked with designers to combine some of the elements of Sikkimese dress with the latest New York fashions, so that they could put on a show, the kind that would attract the attention of the cream of fashionable New York society.

For a week in November 1971, Sikkim took over the shop windows of Bergdorf Goodman and a stretch of Fifth Avenue:

> There were not only Sikkimese things in their windows but they had coordinated their efforts with those of their neighbours Van Cleef & Arpels and Delman, both of which filled their windows with Sikkimese art. On the night of the opening, Sikkimese flags flew on both sides of Fifth Avenue from Fifty-seventh to Fifty-eighth streets [the heart of Manhattan]. The next day there was another fashion show, in the ballroom of the Colony Club, and the following day the clothes were shown in the guest-of-honour spot by the Pan Pacific Association at the Waldorf. Our final and most satisfying success – as the space was big enough to show the fashions to full advantage – was the jam-packed show in the Smithsonian's Red Hall in Washington.[9]

The show was a success, but underneath all the glamour there was a lack of clarity as to what it was all for. As Hope herself later wrote, the whole thing

> had the earmarks of a fund-raising event – and yet we never asked for money. That would have been very un-Sikkimese. What did we want? The answer was simple and not so simple. Often we didn't dare define it ourselves, let alone to the people we were mutely appealing to. We wanted people to have Sikkim in their consciousness. If, God help us, something happened, we wouldn't be quite so alone.[10]

It was an ill-defined aim, more style than substance, as the *Washington Post* hinted:

> His majesty [...] looked calm throughout the pre-show confusion ... In place of Sikkimese boots, he was wearing gray wool socks and black Gucci shoes. Some of the guests got the idea that the clothes had been taken off the backs of natives in the Himalayas, and maybe some had. But they were mixed in with exotic evening gear, replete with zippers, leotards and Isotoner body suits which caused a little puzzlement among serious students of historical costume.[11]

Reports in US newspapers at the time, painting a picture of Sikkim as a fragile Himalayan state in need of support, unsurprisingly irritated Indira Gandhi. India was supposed to be responsible for Sikkim's external relations; although the fashion show was not officially a diplomatic event, Hope and Thondup used it ceaselessly to promote the idea of Sikkim as 'a country'.

But it was the constant reference to the Chogyal as 'His Majesty' in the US newspapers that irked Indira most. After 1950, when the Indian government had agreed that Sikkim and Bhutan should not be merged into India or Pakistan along with the other Indian Princely States, only the King of Bhutan had been addressed as 'Your Majesty' by the Indian government: the Sikkimese Chogyal had continued to be addressed with the less honorific 'Your Highness'. This was deliberate: from the Indian point of view, it made a distinction between the status of Bhutan (whose sovereignty India had all but recognised in the 1949 treaty) and Sikkim (which they considered to be a protectorate and therefore of a lesser status). By ostentatiously using the more prestigious term, Thondup and Hope Cooke were highlighting what they saw as their equal status with Bhutan.

Indira was well aware of why they were doing it: that year she had helped Bhutan gain its place in the UN, alongside the PRC and a quartet of Middle Eastern states – Bahrain, Oman, Qatar and the UAE. For the Bhutanese, UN membership was a reward for years of patient diplomacy, but it left Sikkim as the only country in the region without UN recognition, showing up the latter's continued status as a protectorate of India. A few months earlier an amendment to the Indian constitution, forced through by Indira Gandhi, had further highlighted the idiosyncrasies surrounding Sikkim's constitutional status. In introducing radical legislation to abolish the privy purses of the Princely States across India, she had reduced the former rulers of the Princely States to virtually nought by removing 'their revenues and their titles in this brave new world of post-imperial egalitarianism'.[12] But Sikkim and the Namgyals escaped the legislation. As a 'protectorate', Sikkim had never been considered a typical Princely State. This raised a tricky question: if Sikkim was not to be considered a Princely State, and it wasn't a constituent part of India, what exactly was it?

Thondup and Hope arrived back in Sikkim in early 1972, confident that they had boosted the country's international profile with their fashion show. But almost immediately Thondup was faced with signs of an increased demand for political change from Sikkim's aspiring politicians. Some were driven by a genuine desire to see democracy flourish; others resented being second-class citizens behind a coterie of unelected palace favourites from aristocratic families. Worse, they felt they got less respect than the representatives of the Indian Army in Sikkim. Grievances sometimes seemed petty: the Executive Councillors were not allowed flags on their cars while Indian Army officers were. When events were held in Gangtok, this meant that the Executive Councillors had to walk, being passed by cars carrying Indian Army officers.

But it was the SNC party and its leading couple, the Kazi and Kazini, who were most active in their opposition. The Kazi had finally been appointed as an Executive Councillor after the 1970 elections. Towards the end of January 1972 an anonymous article appeared in the *Sikkim Bulletin* highlighting the growing divisions. Entitled 'Sikkim at the Crossroads', the author fired a broadside at the Chogyal, accusing him of absolutism and warning 'there can be no king without a people'. Perhaps most significantly the article ended by making a comparison to the time of the Russian Revolution, saying

> And to those who persist in seeking their own petty, personal benefits, who will neither listen to the voice of wisdom or decency, who will not read the writing on the wall, for those whose pastime is a desultory indulgence in barley-water diplomacy, Kerensky's words to the Duma in 1917 are pregnant with meaning: 'If you will not listen to the voice of warning, you will find yourself face to face with facts not warnings.'

To those in the know, the article, with its reference to the Russian Revolution, bore all the hallmarks of the Kazini and the coterie of radical and adventurous young men – almost all Nepali – who were now frequent visitors to her home in Kalimpong. Prime among them was Nar Bahadur Khatiawara, who she and the Kazi had adopted. Khatiawara, just turned 20, would become the president of the Youth Congress in Sikkim, with a passion for oratory matched only by his willingness to fight for what he believed. The Kazini had immediately recognised that Khatiawara was just what she needed – some fight and fire.*

Thondup knew that he had to respond. He summoned the Kazi to the palace and asked him to explain the article. The Kazi apologised profusely, claiming the article had been published against his advice, but the damage had been done. The article was on everybody's lips. Thondup stripped the Kazi of his position as an Executive Councillor.

Thondup had now become so bound up in the belief that the treaty with India needed to be revised that his own identity was starting to merge with that of his country. He took attacks on Sikkim and the system

---

* In an interview with Khatiawara in 2011, he proudly claimed co-authorship of the article. Neither had he lost his rhetorical touch, as he demonstrated with his own view on the events of the 1970s: 'If you shut the door on a cat and chase it around the room, it will eventually turn on you.'

of government as personal attacks on him and his family. There were growing signs that it was also having an effect on his marriage.

Hope was now 32. Thondup was a year away from turning 50. In February, Ishbel Ritchie noticed the impact of the age gap: 'Here we tend to regard the Gyalmo as the one who is always ready to take part in the dances organised by the young folks etc. and the Chogyal who puts in an appearance (not always) but is not terribly interested, or should I say not terribly keen on dancing.'

In fact, there was a more serious problem developing. Bitterly frustrated by the lack of progress he was making on clarifying Sikkim's future, and perhaps feeling slightly upstaged by his wife's efforts in New York, Thondup had started drinking more heavily than usual. In April, the FCO in London received a request for help with alcoholism. Sir Alec Douglas-Home, then a junior minister, picked it up and sent it on to the Treasury medical adviser, who recommended specific treatment:

> [His] royal patient should come to the Liver Unit at King's College Hospital, which is under Dr Roger Williams who specialises in the treatment and care of alcoholics. Whilst at King's College Hospital, psychiatric treatment can be arranged with the help of Dr Griffith Edwards of the Medical Research Council who is also attached to the Maudsley Hospital where he undertakes research into the problems of alcoholism. Dr Lorriman confirms that this would be the best arrangement as there are few clinics taking alcoholic patients and many charlatans offering speedy cure.[13]

The pressure was beginning to tell on Thondup.

-3-

In the aftermath of the Bangladesh war, Indira Gandhi's personal popularity across India reached cult levels. In the parliament 'she was praised as a new Durga', the Hindu warrior goddess, and likened to Shakti, the manifestation of female energy and power. Even the foreign press viewed her in grandiose terms, as the new 'Empress of India'.[14] In March fresh elections took place in 13 states across the country. As one opposition leader ruefully remarked, 'while the opposition had put up 2,700 separate candidates, the ruling party had in effect fielded the same person in every constituency – Indira Gandhi'.[15] She captured 70 per cent of the seats contested.

But victory in West Bengal, to the south of Sikkim, had required manipulation and coercion. The state had been in a political mess for nearly five years, with factional wars within the Communist Party causing endless problems. In West Bengal more than anywhere else, the splits in the Communist Party had become evident: first a group had broken away from the Communist Party of India (CPI), accusing them of straying from the Marxist-Leninist line. The new grouping, the Communist Party of India (Marxist) – or CPM – had emerged as the main alternative to Congress in West Bengal. But within the CPM splits had also emerged, mirroring the increasingly antagonistic split between the different interpretations of communism in China and Russia. Naxalbari, near the state's hill towns of Kalimpong and Darjeeling (and within a stone's throw of the Chumbi Valley and Chinese-occupied Tibet) had become the base for those who supported Mao's violent interpretation of class struggle. By 1970 and 1971 Naxalite influence had reached Calcutta, creating a violent and dark political atmosphere in the city. The CPM fought to disassociate themselves from the breakaway Naxalites; the Congress tried to tar the CPM and the terrorists with the same brush. Governance, such as it existed at all, had been through a series of weak coalitions and a period of centrally imposed 'president's rule'. Delhi found the existence of the openly Maoist rebels particularly troubling.

Re-establishing Congress control in the state elections of 1972 was, therefore, a priority for both the local Bangla Congress and the national Congress Party; to make sure of victory, Bangla Congress employed a 'mixture of terror, intimidation and fraud' at the ballot box. 'There was "mass-scale rigging" ... as one activist recalled, *goondas* paid by the Congress told voters assembled outside polling stations that they might as well go home, since they had already cast all the registered votes.'[16]

More than ever before, underhand tactics became almost an accepted part of the democratic process in West Bengal.

High up in the Gangtok Residency (now renamed India House), Political Officer Bajpai observed the deepening divisions in West Bengal carefully.

The rigged Congress victory had taken care of the immediate problem of CPM political power, but in the north of the state, the politically disenfranchised Nepalis had naturally allied with the leftist factions. Thus far the Nepali majority in Sikkim had shown less leftist tendencies but, with frequent interchange across the border, that could change quickly. Bajpai reiterated to Delhi that it might not take much for the volatile political atmosphere in West Bengal to spread to Sikkim, particularly given the problems in the Palace. He continued to advocate that something needed to change.

Everyone in Delhi understood the logic: since Bhutan's accession to the UN, the antiquated constitutional status of Sikkim stood out as a painful reminder of the pre-independence past. Indira Gandhi, in particular, was hurt by accusations that India's relationship with Sikkim smacked of outdated colonialism. But the practical implications of *loosening* India's grip on Sikkim were not quite so attractive. As things stood, Delhi retained almost total control over the political agenda in Sikkim. On the one hand, agreeing to Thondup's call for greater autonomy under his own leadership raised the spectre of a weak independent state at the mercy of the Chinese in Tibet; some even rumoured darkly that Thondup was sympathising with the Chinese. On the other hand, democratisation leading to political power for the Nepali majority raised the possibility of an unpredictable Gorkhaland movement (based in Darjeeling, calling for an independent Nepali state in North Bengal, and suspected of allegiance with the Chinese) causing further instability.

The status quo – or something like it – definitely had its attractions.

In March 1972, Indira sent Tikki Kaul back up to Sikkim to take the political temperature. It was Kaul's first visit to Sikkim for a while. At a dinner in the palace, Kaul was shocked by the greatly increased vehemence of opinion against India's continued presence in Sikkim among those who represented political opinion in Sikkim. Ishbel Ritchie, who was also invited to the dinner, recalled, 'The chief interest of the evening was the (verbal) attack launched on the chief guest by some of the Councillors – the circle round them in the middle of the big "durbar room" got bigger & bigger!'

There were other signs of growing anti-Indian sentiment. When the head of the Indian Air Force visited later in the month, there 'were considerably less in attendance than usual'. A few weeks later the new brigadier in charge of the Indian Army contingent in Sikkim was 'furious' when he was kept waiting for two hours for dinner because other guests (from the political elite) had 'been at another cocktail party'.

Palace life had indeed taken on an increasingly frenetic pace, led, like a female Pan, by Hope Cooke. Late one evening Ritchie received unexpected visitors at her small bungalow down the hill from the palace grounds:

> Yesterday evening after I'd gone to bed, about 11.30pm, there was the most terrific hullaballoo outside – drums & cymbals & flute etc. – & I thought we'd acquired a drunk wedding band. This lot ended up on my doorstep however and when I went to see (in my dressing-gown and bare feet with hair standing up on end) I found some of my most distinguished friends on the doorstep – there's a slightly nightmarish quality, though, when one expects to confront either a crowd of drunk strangers or some of one's more disreputable acquaintances and finds one is confronted with Mr Chopra* banging cymbals, and on further investigation, the Gyalmo bashing a big drum.

During the first half of 1972, Thondup continued to surround himself with symbols intended to assert Sikkim's separate identity from India which, with the opposition to his rule largely coming from the Nepali population, had the effect of making the Palace appear more and more biased towards his own Bhutia-Lepcha community. Sir Terence Garvey, Britain's High Commissioner in Delhi, visited Sikkim around this time. Garvey, a highly experienced diplomat who had already served in Peking and would go on to serve as ambassador in Moscow, had little doubt about what was happening:

> Thondup is, I should guess, resolved to retain control of his country's affairs in the hands of the ethnic minority and oligarchy from which he springs. In this task he relies less on the inchoate departments of state than upon

---

* I. S. Chopra was the (Indian-appointed) Principal Administrative Officer (previously known as Dewan) at this time. His close relationship with those in the Palace faction was a contributing factor to his removal from the post later in 1972.

his Private Secretaries, two black-gowned white-cuffed characters called Densapa and Topden, who might have been taken straight from 16th century Florence.[17]

Densapa was the 42-year-old scion of an important noble family in Sikkim and a source of wise advice, but it was Karma Topden, still in his twenties, who had become a really close friend. Bright, able and good-humoured, Topden had studied economics at Manchester University after which he had attended a short police training course at a Detective College in provincial England. On his return, Thondup had asked him to set up an intelligence service for Sikkim. By 1972 Topden had become a confidant for Thondup, always staying to the end at the palace parties, when the two men could swap stories on how to cope with their respective foreign wives (Topden too had married a foreigner, from England).

This small court became a discussion forum for Thondup, but he knew that ultimately the weight of responsibility lay on his shoulders alone. During his visits to Delhi for discussions with Kaul and others about treaty revision he found that things had changed greatly since the issue had first been seriously discussed five years earlier. Then, Indira's government had been politically weak; she had played for time, cognisant of the risk of losing Thondup's support. Now, in the aftermath of the Bangladesh war, her government and her faction within the Congress Party were stronger than they had ever been.

There was no doubt that Indira wanted to change the treaty – she was embarrassed by the neo-colonial nature of the term 'protectorate' – but her proposals were now far more politically astute. In the middle of the year Kaul proposed a revised treaty wording which, while acknowledging Sikkim's right to 'autonomy in regard to its internal affairs', talked of Sikkim's 'permanent association' with India.

The proposal rang alarm bells in Thondup's head. The terminology seemed to allow little room for Sikkim's individual identity. He consulted Sir Humphrey Waldock, an eminent international lawyer in the UK, to clarify the legal implications of the proposal. Waldock confirmed that 'permanent association' as written in the document that Kaul had proposed would indeed emasculate Sikkim. Worse, once accepted, there would be no easy way back. The term 'protectorate' might be aggravating, but at least it had some form of legal basis; 'permanent association' was a vague and undefined term. Agreeing to the bald statement that 'Sikkim shall be in permanent association with India' might later be seen as meaning that Sikkim would have given up the ability to call itself an independent nation. He told Thondup to revert to Kaul, proposing a wording that expressed it as 'Sikkim *in full sovereign rights* enters into a permanent association with the Government of India.' But when Thondup approached Kaul with the new wording, he met a brick wall. India could never agree to the phrase 'in full sovereign rights'.

It was a stalemate.

Around the same time Inder Chopra, who had been serving in Gangtok as the Indian-appointed Dewan (now referred to by the Tibetan title of 'Sidlon'), was recalled to Delhi. Chopra's appointment had not been a success; he was affable enough but had never really been on top of his brief. Instead of making a new appointment (Delhi realised by now that whoever they chose was likely to antagonise a section of the population), Thondup managed to argue that he himself should take over the responsibilities as Sidlon. It was an outrageous suggestion – concentrating all political power in Thondup's hands. But India surprisingly put up no objection, perhaps calculating that such an arrangement might make Thondup aware of the challenges he faced.

The decision left only two men with any real political power in Sikkim: Thondup and K. Shankar Bajpai.

Since the publication of the article 'Sikkim at the Crossroads', the Kazi and Kazini had been lying lower than usual, spending the summer in Europe. But by October they were back in Kalimpong. The Kazi knew that, given he had been indicted after the article's publication, the only way he could participate in the elections planned for late 1972 was if he issued a written apology to back up the verbal one he had given earlier in the year. Both he and the young firebrand Khatiawara offered their 'unqualified apologies'.

The unusual threesome was back in the game.

As the rains ended in the autumn of 1972, Tikki Kaul made another attempt to persuade Thondup to accept the appellation of 'permanent association' for Sikkim. He offered a timetable with milestones to show that India intended to maintain Sikkim's identity – India could offer Sikkim control over the postal system, the telegraph system; Kaul even held out the prospect of sponsored accession to some of the international bodies that Bhutan had joined during its march to UN membership. Analogies were made to Puerto Rico, Panama. But Thondup was now utterly convinced by his legal friends in London that this was a trick and that he was being asked to sign away his country with no safeguards. He proposed any number of alternatives intended to ensure that legally Sikkim's 'separate' identity was maintained, even arguing that if Sikkim were recognised in the UN, India's power would increase because Sikkim would always vote with India. All his suggestions were turned down.

Indian intransigence further convinced Thondup that there was another agenda at play. His relations with Indira Gandhi, which had always been cordial, had all but disappeared into a morass of platitudes. Karma Topden was also bringing him reports that there was 'evidence of an Indian intelligence plot to cause widespread disturbances in Sikkim with the help of some Sikkimese Nepalis and [the] Kazi and Kazini in Kalimpong'.

According to Hope, Thondup even went as far as informing one of Henry Kissinger's younger team members that he feared a plot against him was being formed in Sikkim.[18]

Kaul and Delhi dismissed these vague accusations as fantasy. The Government of India was now resolute: the Chogyal must accept their offer of 'permanent association'.

-4-

In October, Sir Terence Garvey, Britain's High Commissioner in Delhi, visited Sikkim for a second time. His confidential report back to Alec Douglas-Home in London (now Foreign Secretary in Edward Heath's Government) highlighted the extreme difficulties that Thondup now faced.

On arrival in Gangtok, Garvey was whisked up to the Nathu La by his Indian escort. As they neared the top of the pass, where Chinese troops lined the other side, the Indians swiftly removed the Union Jack pennant on the jeep. It tickled Garvey that 'for all I know the Chinese may have taken the pale-faced visitors for Russians'. But what struck him most was the proximity of the Chinese Army: 'Indian and Chinese troops face one another divided by a no-man's-land not much wider than a cricket pitch . . . in a mountain wilderness at 14,420 feet.'* It was this military and geopolitical reality that suffused Garvey's report. 'If Sikkim today is more than a geographical expression, the causes are mainly accidental,' he opined, due solely to the Chumbi Valley being 'the least impossible route to Lhasa'.

Staying with Political Officer Bajpai in the Gangtok Residency, he started to witness something of palace life – and how Bajpai interacted with it. Nothing he saw gave him much confidence in Sikkim's future prospects:

> The palace . . . is not an entirely happy ship. There is the silly business of the title. The ruler dislikes being called Highness (his due as a Maharaja) aspiring to be a Majesty like his cousin of Bhutan. Since the Indians will not have it, he is called nothing, being addressed simply as 'Chogyal' (in the vocative). To this is added resentment, which members of the court are keen to make known, that Sikkim should be in an inferior position to Bhutan, now a sovereign state and a member of the United Nations.

The whole business, Garvey noted, was taking an immense toll on Thondup:

> The Chogyal is too intelligent to be a mere musical comedy princeling and periodically feels futile. When the sense of futility envelops him he seeks anodyne in the bottle, which, combined with an awkward retroflex sniff, gives him a somewhat blurred and absent manner. He was reckoned when we were there to be moving back on to the hard stuff after a relatively dry period.

Garvey's views on Hope Cooke (referred to as the Gyalmo), and the Palace scene were equally morose:

---

* They were close enough for Garvey to note that 'the Chinese People's Army, in their soft caps and padded jackets, looked much the same as when I last saw them on leaving China in 1965'. After retreating a short way from the front, Garvey lunched with the 1/2 Punjabi Regiment, celebrating the 211th anniversary of their raising.

The present Gyalmo ... assorts oddly with the Tibetan ladies of court and, perhaps wishing to banish any taint of transatlantic stridency, has adopted a tone of voice which verges on the inaudible. I should guess that the strains of sustaining this synthetic personality may tell on her with the passage of time. Though she now makes a rather dim impression (she has three subjects – education, handicrafts and gardens) I can conceive of her proving a bit of a nuisance later on in the I suppose not unlikely, event of her ending up as Queen stepmother. Whether by the Gyalmo's contrivance, or through her husband's wish to gratify her, guests drawn from Western café society are invited, or invite themselves, in large numbers to Gangtok. Ten such (six from France, two from the United States and two from Britain) were staying at the palace during our visit. They are naturally receptive to anti-Indian tittle-tattle, which no doubt offers some relief to the Royal Family but is unlikely to endear them or their hosts to the Government of India.*

His conclusion, no doubt influenced by his host Bajpai, was imbued with a pessimistic realism:

It would be rash, on two days' acquaintance, to predict Sikkim's eventual disposal. China, the ravisher of Tibet and the suppressor of the Khampa revolt, offers no pole of counter-attraction and geography is heavily on India's side. Moreover the requirements of defence must, in the absence of a fundamental change in Sino-Indian relations, oblige India to ensure that Sikkim's territory is at India's disposal. It would be much tidier if Sikkim became part of India, adding one more to the growing number of tribal Himalayan states, but it would probably not be easy at this late stage, in the absence of some external or internal convulsion, to bring this about. And the example of neighbouring Bhutan, now enjoying a form of pseudo-independence as a member of the United Nations has, I should judge, made absorption appreciably more difficult. As noted, parity of

---

* How far the FCO's attitudes to Hope Cooke were driven by general British attitudes towards Americans is a moot point. Another official wrote an equally dismissive description of her a couple of months later: 'the Gyalmo, in spite of her affectations, has all the do-gooder intensity of the well-born American female and has devoted herself to securing a sensible education for her step-children'.

treatment with Bhutan has become an aspiration and if it were adopted by the Nepali majority as a platform for popular enfranchisement the Indian Government might not find it easy in the longer run to stand in the way. For the Indians, the abiding requirement is the maintenance of their military position and any eventual political arrangements will have to conform to this. The only prediction which one can with reasonable certainty make is that the Chogyal and his successors will have to make some pretty radical adjustments if they are to stay in business.

There were many in India who shared Garvey's analysis that time was running out for the Namgyal dynasty – and that it 'would be much tidier if Sikkim were part of India'. Thondup, however, was most assuredly not among them. He refused to give up hope. He knew that Sikkim needed some sort of relationship with India, but was equally adamant that Sikkim must maintain its separate status.

In late 1972, he made another attempt to break the logjam with Tikki Kaul and to put the kingdom on a new footing. He would accept India's 'permanent association' draft, but only if a rider were added explicitly acknowledging that the countries were 'separate' and stating that the association between the two countries would be 'within the framework of the purposes and principles of the United Nations'. Kaul refused; accepting the request would have been tantamount to accepting that Sikkim was a separate nation and that was now far from Delhi's mind.

Towards the end of November, Thondup tried again, travelling to Darjeeling to meet with Mrs Gandhi and plead his case. He told her he was certain that the intelligence bureau in Calcutta was planning something, possibly independently of Delhi's knowledge. Supporting the Nepali cause, he told her, would be tantamount to 'playing with fire'. If the Kazi and his supporters were able to win in Sikkim, he warned, it would only make it easier for the Darjeeling Nepalis to call for autonomy and bring the prospect of a 'Greater Nepal' stretching across the Himalayas that much closer.[19] Mrs Gandhi did not need much convincing of the challenge that Darjeeling posed: she had to be helicoptered out of Darjeeling because of Nepali demonstrators shouting 'randi Gandhi' ['prostitute Gandhi']. Nevertheless she told Thondup she had no intention of changing her government's position on Sikkim. Thondup returned to Gangtok muttering that the Indian government were in danger of forgetting who their real friends in the region were.[20]

But at the very moment that her husband was in Darjeeling meeting with Mrs Gandhi, Hope was putting on a play at Thatongchen school that indicated a different attitude to the relationship with the Indians. The subject matter, Ishbel Ritchie recalled, was 'a theme of mankind as puppets and centuries of oppression and final liberation . . . (the Gyalmo, as always there, was the leading inspiration)'. The choice of such an obvious political analogy was just one example of what Tikki Kaul would later call the 'pin-pricks to India on matters big and small'; others, mostly initiated by Hope, were intended as practical jokes. On one occasion a pack of mules appeared on the lawn of Bajpai's residence; on another invitations were sent out to guests for a non-existent party at India House.

Bajpai found it hard to laugh.

In December, as the political parties in Sikkim prepared for the elections planned for early 1973, Thondup, Hope and the five children left Sikkim for their annual trip to London and New York. In London, the news that Yangchen, Thondup's daughter from his first marriage, had an incurable kidney disease only added to the intense pressures on their relationship. After spending Christmas in New York, Thondup returned to Sikkim. Hope, back in the city that was closest to a place she could call home, somehow found the time to start a brief affair with an old friend.

On the way home, in Zurich airport, she felt torn between two cultures more than ever before. She did not know where to turn.

CHAPTER SIX

A Raw Deal

1973

-1-

Thondup hoped 1973 would offer the chance of a new start – for Sikkim
and for himself. In April he would turn 50; he hoped the occasion might
provide another chance for a celebration of the country to which his life
had been dedicated.

But by the end of January, he was faced with further political problems sparked by the elections in Sikkim. As the results were counted, it
became clear that the pro-Palace National Party might win a majority.
Buoyed by the possibility of electoral success, the National Party leader
made a deliberately provocative statement, accusing the Kazi of seeking
Sikkim's 'disintegration'. Confident of a National Party electoral mandate,
he also sent a message to the Indians, saying he hoped Sikkim could 'feel
confident that the Government of India will not lag behind in fulfilling
the ambitions of our people in enabling us to enjoy the status like that of
Nepal and Bhutan'.

Immediately the Kazi's SNC and a new party, Janata Congress (more
nakedly pro-Nepali), responded, alleging that the presiding officer had
rigged the election in favour of the National Party. The allegation veiled
the underlying problem: that the voting system was weighted in favour of
the Bhutia-Lepchas and therefore against the Nepalis. When the results
were announced, the National Party emerged triumphant, with 11 out of

18 seats, most of which were from those reserved for the Bhutia-Lepcha community, emphasising the communal divisions.[1]

While the politicians flung accusations and counter-accusations around, Thondup continued with the preparations to mark his 50th year. Ishbel Ritchie, the headmistress of the Paljor Namgyal Girls' School, was one of those co-opted onto a 'birthday committee' set up to plan the events. She sensed immediately that there were tensions: the first committee meeting was, she wrote to her mother, 'a rather haphazard affair, with a good half of the potential attenders absent'. Against a backdrop of 'various agitations – of varying degrees of belligerence', she was surprised that the Chogyal was 'planning to have 2 days of events instead of one – there is to be some kind of pageant and cultural show'.

While Thondup was planning his latest effort to promote his homeland's separate identity, he had no idea that Sikkim was cropping up in the latest summit meeting between Henry Kissinger and Zhou Enlai, now Premier of the State Council in China. In February 1973, a year after Nixon's groundbreaking visit to meet Mao, Kissinger was back in Peking for an extraordinarily wide-ranging foreign policy discussion with Zhou. The pair galloped through Western Europe and the Middle East before the subject turned to India, touching on the Himalayas and the recent addition of Bhutan to the ranks of the UN.[2]

Bhutan's accession was a curious anomaly, Kissinger pointed out. Since India retained control of their foreign relations, he suggested it was reasonable to assume that they also controlled the Bhutanese vote; Zhou agreed, musing that India's relationship with Bhutan's UN membership was not much different from the Soviet Union's relationship with Ukraine's: when the UN was created in 1945 Stalin had successfully gained three seats – one for the Soviet Union and one each for the Ukraine and Byelorussia, both Soviet states for whose defence the USSR was responsible.

But it was the discussion on Sikkim itself that provoked the most interesting comment from Zhou: Sikkim, he suggested, might be considered as India's 'Byelorussia'. It was an analogy that Kissinger got immediately – and it had nothing to do with the UN. Kissinger realised that Zhou was drawing a skilful comparison between India's recent policy of migration of

Indians into Sikkim with Stalin's policy of 'Sovietisation' in Byelorussia, designed to scotch any signs of Western influence.

As the two diplomats chuckled conspiratorially, they swapped other anecdotes about the Himalayan region. Hope Cooke, Kissinger admitted to Zhou, had become something of a nuisance. 'She keeps using her prayer beads and sifting her beads all the time,' he told Zhou. 'She has become more Buddhist than the population. She makes me so nervous I always avoid seeing her.' Zhou responded with his own story – this time of the period when Nehru and he were building bridges between their two countries:

> PM Chou*: In 1957 on my way back to China from the Soviet Union and Poland I also stopped in India. The scene then was different – another story. Nehru invited me to a tea party in his garden and among the guests were people in costume. There were two Tibetan lamas, and there suddenly appeared a female lama. Do you know who she was?
>
> Dr Kissinger: Madame Binh?†
>
> PM Chou: Madame Gandhi. [laughter] She was dressed up entirely in Tibetan costume. That was something that Nehru was capable of doing. I am not among those that go in for memoir-writing.
>
> Dr Kissinger: It is a pity.
>
> PM Chou: So perhaps we can ask you to write it in your memoirs since you have it now in your minutes. [laughter][3]

Relations between the Chinese and the Americans had never been better.

Although Mrs Gandhi was blissfully unaware that Kissinger and Zhou were chuckling over her sartorial choices, she was all too cognisant of their strengthening relationship, and deeply distrustful of both countries' intentions towards India. Her distrust only served to increase her sensitivity to any developments in the Himalayas.

A key dynamic was the relationship between Delhi and Washington. The events of 1971 – the US rapprochement with China, the Indo-Soviet

---

* Zhou Enlai
† The Vietnamese communist leader.

treaty and US criticism of Indian action during the war which formed Bangladesh – had all contributed to a deepening *froideur* between the two countries. She had never liked Nixon, and had little sympathy for him when the Watergate crisis broke in early 1973. An article she had written in the August 1972 edition of *Foreign Affairs* had not helped matters either. The article was a clear attack on American foreign policy in Asia, and towards India in particular. After an historical analysis in which she noted with 'grave concern' that 'US policy as it developed impinged seriously on our national interests', she got into her stride. 'It is necessary,' she lectured, 'to take note of the dispatch of the warship *Enterprise* to support a ruthless military dictatorship [in Pakistan] and to intimidate a democracy, and the extraordinary similarity of the attitudes adopted by the United States and China. Imagine our feelings.'

The appeal for emotional – rather than rational – sympathy had become a hallmark of Indira's increasingly personal leadership style.

Her sense of persecution only increased when America partially lifted a long-standing embargo on arms sales to South Asia.* The announcement infuriated Mrs Gandhi and her ministers – the policy change clearly favoured Pakistan (who had convinced the Americans that they needed arms) over India. India's antipathy to Pakistan was perhaps the only thing that trumped the poor relationship with the US. In the Indian parliament the foreign minister expressed his 'utmost concern', saying that the decision would 'once again pose a grave threat to India's security'.[4]

It also gave the larger-than-life Pakistani President, Zulfikar Ali Bhutto, an opportunity to have a dig at Indira Gandhi – and to paint her, not him, as the one posing the threat to peace in South Asia. Pakistan 'did not wish to get into an arms race with India'[5], he told the press pompously, arguing that the country's small size relative to India meant that it would reach an 'arms saturation point' sooner rather than later. The situation for India, however, he added mischievously, was different 'in that India was a larger country, had pretensions of being a dominant power, and had other areas to "look after" such as Bhutan, Sikkim and now East Pakistan'. A few weeks later Bhutto even suggested privately to Kissinger that in order to maintain South Asian stability the US should 'better its relations' with Sri

---

* The term 'South Asia' refers to India, Pakistan, Nepal, Sikkim, Bhutan, Bangladesh and Sri Lanka.

Lanka and other peripheral states – including 'the Indian protectorates of Bhutan and Sikkim'.

While Sikkim was being discussed in speeches from and private conversations between world leaders in early 1973, Thondup was swearing in the new council of elected politicians in the Royal Chapel on 8 March. For a moment it seemed as if the disputes between the factions in Sikkim might have dissolved. At a lunch afterwards, Ishbel Ritchie reported the Chogyal to be 'on good form, teasing as ever'.

But for those who sought democratic change – and for the young Nepali radicals, led by the Kazi and Kazini's adopted son, Nar Bahadur Khatiawara – the February election result had become a rallying call. They were now determined to push for reform to Sikkim's political system.

Bajpai found it astonishing that Thondup did not seem to appreciate the clamour for some kind of democratic change around him. Even the pro-Palace National Party was now muttering openly about the antiquated 'appointment' system that vested all the power in the Chogyal. Bajpai also thought Thondup's continued talk of treaty revision genuinely out of touch. It ignored the geopolitical realities – Sikkim needed India, not the other way round, as Thondup seemed to be suggesting. More importantly, *Thondup himself* needed India. Bajpai was open with Thondup as to his views: if the Indian government were no longer in Sikkim as protector, he told Thondup, the Palace would be much more vulnerable to the growing clamour for political change.[6] He also warned the Chogyal to be careful: Indira Gandhi, he pointed out, was not the same woman since her triumph in Bangladesh.[7]

Bajpai also tried to be as frank as he could with Delhi. The challenge lay, he told them, in where India would stand if trouble started. He knew full well that there was a substantial Indian intelligence presence both in Sikkim and in the north part of West Bengal around Darjeeling and Kalimpong – and that they were in contact with the opposition parties in Sikkim. He also shared Delhi's view that a supportive Chogyal gave some stability in the region, but what frustrated him was Delhi's inability to commit to a firm position.

Bajpai had two main routes into the core Indian bureaucracy. The first was via the new Foreign Secretary, Kewal Singh, who had replaced Tikki

Kaul (now in Washington as Indian Ambassador). Bajpai and Singh knew each other well – they had worked together in Pakistan in the run-up to the 1965 conflict, after which Singh had been so impressed that he had then demanded that Bajpai be transferred to the Ministry of External Affairs. Bajpai liked Kewal Singh's quietly determined approach to diplomacy.

But Bajpai also had another important contact in Delhi: R. N. Kao, the head of the Indian external intelligence service, the Research & Analysis Wing, known as RAW.

Kao, notoriously close to Indira Gandhi, had been watching the situation carefully for some time. Unwilling to take any chances, he had already deployed his intelligence agents on the ground during early 1973 in northern Bengal and the south of Sikkim to provide encouragement to the anti-Chogyal forces and to 'build up their organisation and make their weight felt in the politics of Sikkim'. P. N. Dhar, Indira Ghandi's Principal Secretary, confirmed RAW's active involvement in his memoirs published in 2000: 'Under Kao's overall guidance, the RAW team helped the pro-democracy leaders build up their organisation and make their weight felt in the politics of Sikkim. This process had started several months before the storm broke in April 1973.'[8]

In Sikkim, Thondup had no idea about RAW's involvement – but he could see that trouble was brewing.

The first signs appeared on 20 March when two of the six appointed 'Executive Councillors' did not turn up to be sworn in at a separate ceremony. Both were from the Kazi's SNC. Hearing that one of them was in Kalimpong, Thondup sent his intelligence chief, Karma Topden, to investigate. Topden reported that the councillor was locked in a room in the Kazi and Kazini's house, guarded by some of Khatiawara's young thugs. A couple of days later, both Kazi and Khatiawara held rallies near the border with Sikkim, where the distinction between the movement for change in Sikkim and the Gorkhaland movement in Darjeeling and Kalimpong blurred. The new opposition party, Janata Congress, also sought to whip up Nepali anxieties.

Thondup knew that something needed to be done to deal with the rapidly deteriorating situation. The problem was that the popular support for Kazi and Khatiawara in the south of Sikkim and beyond made them

1. (*left*) The author's grandfather in the Himalayas, c. 1928

2. (*below*) Crown Prince Thondup Namgyal (second from left) with his two sisters Princess Kula (fourth from left) and Princess Coocoola (second from right), his mother, Maharani Kunzang Dechhen Tshomo (centre) and other members of Sikkim's Royal family, c. 1940s. Taken on the slope of the Maharani's residence, known today as 'Mintokgang', the residence of the Chief Minister of Sikkim (Photographer: Yap Tse Ten Tashi. Collection of Tenzin C. Tashi. From the original collection of late Chum Renchin D. Rechung)

3. (*right*) Princess Pema Tsedeun Namgyal (Princess Coocoola) on her wedding day at the Tsuklakhang Royal chapel in October 1941. She smiles at her paternal aunt, Rani Choeni Dorji, sister of Chogyal Tashi Namgyal, who married Raja Dorji of Bhutan. (Photographer: Yap Tse Ten Tashi. Henry Baker Collection, Namgyal Institute of Tibetology)

4. (*below*) The Dalai Lama, with the Panchen Lama behind (both on horseback) coming down from Natu La Pass, 1956, on the way to the Buddha Jayanti. The Sikkim flag is in the background (Collection of late Martha Steedman/Patrick Hamilton)

5. Crown Prince Thondup Namgyal (far right) with Nari Rustomji, Dewan of Sikkim 1954–9 (second from right), Maharani Kunzang Dechhen Tshomo, Thondup's mother (second from left) and Nari Rustomji's mother, late 1950s (Collection of Tenzin C. Tashi from the original collection of Sem T.O. Tashi)

6. Hope Cooke, Crown Prince Thondup Namgyal, Martha Hamilton (left to right) outside PNG Girls' school, c. 1963 (Collection of late Martha Steedman/Patrick Hamilton)

7. Children from the Paljor Namgyal Girls' School, digging trenches against the Chinese threat, October 1965 (Collection of late Martha Steedman/Patrick Hamilton)

8. A Chinese soldier gesticulates at Lt-Col. Rai Singh of 2 Grenadiers, Indian Army, during the tense stand-off at the Nathu La in 1967 (Collection of Brig. Rai Singh, courtesy of Squadron Leader Rana T.S. Chhina (Retd))

9. (*left*) Hope Cooke (Gyalmo) and Chogyal Thondup Namgyal, studio photograph, late 1960s (Collection of Tenzin C. Tashi from the original collection of Sem T.O. Tashi)

10. (*below*) Hope Cooke (Gyalmo) dancing, watched by Chogyal Thondup Namgyal, c. late 1960s (Collection of Sem T.O. Tashi)

11. Jawaharlal Nehru and his daughter Indira Gandhi with the Kennedys (at a dinner in Prime Minister of India Nehru's honour in Washington), 7 November 1961 (Photographer: Abbie Rowe. White House Photographs, John F. Kennedy Presidential Library and Museum, Boston)

THE AUTUMN COLLECTION !

12. Cartoon from the *Hindustan Times*, mocking Indira Gandhi, around the time of the vote to make Sikkim an 'Associate State', September 1974 (Courtesy of *Hindustan Times*)

THE PALACE,
GANGTOK,
SIKKIM.

19th. July, 1974.

My dear Martha,

Thank you for your kind letter which has remained
unanswered so long. We have been through a thoroughly bad eighteen
months. What the External Affairs have done is despicable and
shameful. When the whole of Gangtok from the Chief Secretary to
Chaprassi from drivers to school children went on a peaceful
demonstration they were tear gassed etc. Whilst other demonstrators
were stopped by the CRP counter-demonstrators mostly hired and Border
roads coolies were allowed to come into Gangtok on a rampage. People
were openly beaten up and some officers and their wives as also M.B
Basnett, President of the National Party, was made to carry Congress flag

13. Letter (extract) from Chogyal Thondup Namgyal, to Martha Hamilton, date 19 July
1974 (Collection of late Martha Steedman/Patrick Hamilton)

14. The Kazi and the Kazini outside the Raj Bhawan with first governor of Sikkim,
BB Lal, c. late 1970s. *Left to right*: The Kazi, HH the 16th Karmapa Lama, BB Lal,
The Kazini (Collection of Sem T.O. Tashi)

15. (*above*) The Kazi and the Kazini, c. mid 1970s (G.N Khangsarpa collection, courtesy of Namgyal Institute of Tibetology)

16. (*right*) Beleaguered monarch – Thondup Namgyal, c. 1981 (Photographer: Yap Paljor Dorji Tashi. Collection of Tenzin C. Tashi from the original collection of Sem T.O. Tashi)

1. (*left*) Crown Prince Thondup Namgyal, Chogyal Sir Tashi Namgyal with Apa Pant (Sikkim's political officer), outside Royal Chapel, early 1960s (Collection of late Martha Steedman/ Patrick Hamilton)

2. (*below*) Crown Prince Thondup Namgyal and family, including first wife, Sangey Deki, c. 1956 (*Left to right*: Princess Coocoola (in Tibetan hat), Sir Tashi Namgyal, George Namgyal, Sangey Deki (Thondup's first wife), Apa Pant, Tenzing Namgyal (face obscured) and Crown Prince Thondup Namgyal (Collection of late Martha Steedman/Patrick Hamilton)

3. (*right*) Hope Cooke and Crown Prince Thondup Namgyal, newly married, 1963 (Collection of late Martha Steedman/ Patrick Hamilton)

4. (*below*) Hope Cooke at the Royal Wedding, March 1963, with her step-children Wongchuk Namgyal, Yangchen Namgyal, Tenzing Namgyal (Collection of late Martha Steedman/ Patrick Hamilton)

5. Coronation ceremony of Chogyal Thondup Namgyal and Hope Cooke (Gyalmo), Gangtok, Sikkim, April 1965 (Library of Congress, Prints & Photographs Division. Dr Alice S. Kandell Collection of Sikkim Photographs [LC-DIG-ppmsca-30216])

6. Chogyal Thondup Namgyal on throne at his coronation, April 1965. (Library of Congress, Prints & Photographs Division. Dr Alice S. Kandell Collection of Sikkim Photographs [LC-DIG-ppmsca-30219])

7. (*right*) Chogyal Thondup Namgyal, late 1960s (Library of Congress, Prints & Photographs Division. Dr Alice S. Kandell Collection of Sikkim Photographs [LC-DIG-ppmsca-30179])

8. (*below*) Chinese and Indian border emplacements at the Natu La Pass after tensions flared between India and China, late 1960s (Collection of late Martha Steedman/ Patrick Hamilton)

9. Mt Chomolhari from Natu La Pass, late 1960s (Collection of late Martha Steedman/ Patrick Hamilton)

10. Chogyal Thondup Namgyal, Hope Cooke (Gyalmo), with their children Hope Leezum and Palden, seated on cloth on the ground, c. 1971 (Library of Congress, Prints & Photographs Division. Dr Alice S. Kandell Collection of Sikkim Photographs [LC-DIG-ppmsca-30801])

11. Chogyal Thondup Namgyal and Hope Cooke (Gyalmo) with their daughter Hope Leezum watching birthday celebrations in Gangtok, April 1971 (Library of Congress, Prints & Photographs Division. Dr Alice S. Kandell Collection of Sikkim Photographs [LC-DIG-ppmsca-30171])

12. Sikkim Guards parading in Gangtok, c. 1960s (Collection of late Martha Steedman/ Patrick Hamilton)

13. Princess Coocoola and Martha Hamilton at Sports Ground, 1964. (Note Sikkim flag in left of picture) (Collection of late Martha Steedman/Patrick Hamilton)

14. Chogyal Thondup Namgyal and Hope Cooke (Gyalmo) with members of the court on palace lawns, Gangtok, April 1971 (Library of Congress, Prints & Photographs Division. Dr Alice S. Kandell Collection of Sikkim Photographs [LC-DIG-ppmsca-30164])

15. Indira Gandhi outside Namgyal Institute of Tibetology, early 1980s
(Collection of Namgyal Institute of Tibetology)

16. Children from Paljor Namgyal Girls School looking after Khadas domated at funeral of
Thondup Namgyal, February 1982 (Collection of Ishbel Ritchie)

virtually untouchable. Instead, in order to demonstrate that he was in control, the leader of the Janata Congress, Krishna Chandra Pradhan, was arrested for 'fomenting communal strife'. The arrest backfired. On 28 March, the day of the Executive Council's inauguration, a large crowd assembled near the palace in Gangtok to protest at the arrest. Sensing that this was his moment, the Kazi handed the Chogyal a note after the inauguration demanding three specific actions: the release of Krishna Chandra Pradhan; a commitment to the principle of one man, one vote; and a fully democratic administration.

As the crowd swelled near the palace, Thondup realised he was in an impossible position: the previous August he had effectively appointed himself as Sikkim's dewan (prime minister) in an effort to simplify the administration and reduce Indian influence. Now he had to live with the consequence: there was no place other than the palace where popular grievances could be taken. Anxious to calm the situation, Thondup spoke to the crowd at length, astutely choosing to address them in Nepali. He explained that Pradhan had been arrested under the auspices of the legal system and that he had no mandate to unilaterally alter the laws of Sikkim. Neither, he told them, did he have any power to make changes to the system of government. That too would have to come from within; in other words, the people would have to persuade the councillors to request change. Although strictly correct, it was somewhat disingenuous – there was little chance of the recently elected National Party backing the idea of one man, one vote in the knowledge that it would sound their death knell. Nevertheless, Thondup's words had an effect, calming at least some of the Gangtok crowd, many of whom – despite everything – still had respect for the institution of the Chogyal.

But as the crowd thinned a little, two determined young Nepali men stayed on. They announced that they would remain – on hunger strike – until the protestors' key demands were met.

As the two young men made their dramatic protest, reports started to flood in to the palace of trouble in other areas of Sikkim, particularly to the south and west, where the border with West Bengal was extremely porous.

Hope felt conflicted: she had always made a point of supporting young

Nepalis in Sikkim, in an effort to create the kind of tolerant, multi-ethnic state that she believed the country could be. Now she had to watch as her husband tried to defend the indefensible – a political system where the Nepalis, more than 75 per cent of the population, were marginalised. Worse still, she knew one of the hunger strikers well. As Thondup wrestled with what to do, someone suggested that Hope should attempt to break the hunger strike by going out with food for him. Thondup forbade it, snapping at Hope that she was the one who had 'built up' the hunger strikers by 'making such a fuss' over them in the palace.

Over the next three days, the situation worsened. Protestors started to pour into Gangtok. Many of them were obviously from outside Sikkim. Rumours circulated that the protests were suspiciously well coordinated.* Meanwhile the two opposition parties, the SNC and the Janata Congress, put aside their differences and formed a Joint Action Committee (JAC), immediately demanding reforms by 4 April, the Chogyal's birthday.

The date of the ultimatum was chosen carefully as a potent symbol of the privilege they were looking to end.

In fact, the hunger strike was half-hearted, fizzling out only a few days after it started: by 1 April, the two men had sloped hungrily away to the hospital. But on the streets the protest intensified; a mob, estimated in the thousands, 'armed with kukris and lathis',† was now hovering near the junction just below the bazaar.

That evening, Thondup and Hope went up to dinner with Bajpai and his wife at India House (the former British Residency), accompanied by Thondup's sons, Crown Princes Tenzing and Wongchuk, both now in their early twenties. Everyone knew that trouble was now highly likely – and that there were Indian intelligence agents involved – but Bajpai and Thondup were now operating in a strange hinterland of innuendo and oblique references. Bajpai had been reading Harold Nicholson's *Congress of Vienna* (which Hope had lent to him) and made references to the conflict between Talleyrand and Napoleon, as the younger and more

---

* B. B. Gurung, one of the leaders of the agitation, admitted in 2014 that the agitators were well aware of the support they had from behind the scenes from RAW.
† A lathi is a long wooden stick used by the authorities across India; a kukri is a Nepalese knife, similar to a machete.

powerful man outgrew the advice of the old statesman. Later, Bajpai, perhaps recalling his days at Oxford in the 1940s and hoping to compete against Tenzing (now at Cambridge), brought out four tankards. While the crowd gathered below them in the bazaar, Bajpai, Thondup and his two sons downed pints of ale. It was as if Bajpai wanted to make sure this particular evening provided memories. Soon the party were dancing, Bajpai grabbing Hope's wrist and declaring that they would dance 'the last tango in Gangtok'.

Despite herself, Hope found herself caught up in the moment, 'enjoying the almost sexual energy of his high'.[9]

Bajpai's sudden display of unbridled hedonism was understandable: over the past few weeks Delhi had finally agreed that if Thondup was unable to accept that it was Indian support that was maintaining the status quo in Sikkim, then something had to be done to bring the Chogyal to his senses. 'Having served as a seawall between the Chogyal and popular urges,' Bajpai would say later, 'we thought he should see just what would happen without our protective help.'[10]

The Kazi and the JAC were now fully aware of the implicit support that they had for their cause, and the strong position that it put them in. Even the release of the imprisoned Krishna Chandra Pradhan on the 2nd was not enough to stop the steady flow of demonstrators, some paid, congregating below the bazaar in Gangtok. The local Sikkim police force commander pleaded with Thondup to invoke a section of the criminal procedure code that would ban the assembly of more than five persons, which Thondup finally agreed to do on the 3rd.

Some of the elected councillors, desperate to avoid a violent confrontation, therefore sought a meeting with the JAC. On the same day as the criminal procedure code was implemented, a group from the JAC, including the Kazi, met with representatives from the Palace – led by Jigdal Densapa, Thondup's right-hand man – seeking to thrash out a last-minute compromise. By the evening, it seemed that they had reached an agreement: Densapa indicated that he could get Thondup to agree to the one man, one vote principle; he also acknowledged that a new constitution was required.

But at the last moment the Kazi left the room, saying he had to confirm the SNC's position. Within minutes he had returned to tell the confused group that the deal was off. Who had he called? Khatiawara? The Kazini? Bajpai? Whoever it was, none of those assembled were in any doubt about what was likely to happen next.

-2-

Hope Cooke woke with a start at 7 a.m. on 4 April, the day of her husband's birthday celebrations. It took a few moments to realise that what she was hearing was shots down below in the bazaar. A few minutes later, Karma Topden, Thondup's intelligence chief, rushed breathlessly into the bedroom. In the bazaar below the palace, members of the small Sikkim police force in Gangtok – locally staffed and loyal to the Sikkim administration – were desperately trying to maintain order in the face of a crowd of 'five or six thousand demonstrators'. Pelted with bottles and stones, the police had used tear gas and lathi charges to repel the protestors and prevent them from ascending to the palace, he added. They had already been forced to use live fire, injuring two protestors.

It had started.

Thondup got dressed, determined to act as if nothing was going on, going down to his sitting room, where he sat for the traditional receiving of silk scarves, Hope by his side. Later in the morning, with the sound of the demonstrators rising from below, he put on his gold coronation robe and advanced down to the Royal Chapel, where Karma Topden, looking slightly shaken, read the traditional birthday message to the group of those who might be considered the extended court. Bajpai was there too, waiting expectantly for Thondup to request Indian support to protect himself from the mob below.

But Thondup received constant updates from runners who would come in to whisper in his ear, telling him that the protestors were now under control. He was determined to carry on. He could see no other way – accepting Indian support would, he feared, lead to his country's downfall. The only solution was to play out the battle of nerves. He allowed the organisers of his birthday celebrations to cancel the afternoon sporting events but refused to countenance a cancellation of the birthday dinner in the palace grounds that evening.

With the streets of Gangtok still tense, less than half the normal number turned up for the dinner. It was a bizarre occasion. Bajpai, despite still awaiting a request for intervention from Thondup, brought Fred Vreeland and his wife, American friends from his time in San Francisco, to the dinner: Vreeland was a staffer in the US Foreign Service. Hope made a beeline for Vreeland, remembering that his mother, Diana, was the American editor of *Vogue* who had helped out with the fashion show the previous year. But in the heightened atmosphere she suddenly panicked that if Bajpai saw her, he might conclude that she was planning something with the Americans and hurried on to the next conversation.

That night, at around 11 p.m., after all the guests had left, the scale of the problems in south Sikkim emerged. The commissioner of police came to the palace, pleading with Thondup to do something. Without Indian support, he warned, the police were in danger of being overrun. Karma Topden, too, brought reports of more trouble in southern Sikkim, where police stations had been looted. Still desperate not to have to request Indian intervention, Thondup beckoned the Sikkim Guards into the room; Hope watched anxiously as Tenzing and his friends pulled out the guns, kept in cupboards under the stairs for years in case the family needed protection. As she retired for the night, she had every right to be paranoid: 'We go to bed. Chogyal's loaded gun is on the mantelpiece next to Clover's* little statue and the painting of the Buddha.'[11]

Thondup woke the next day determined that, despite his son's exuberance, he would avoid fighting violence with violence at all costs. A man of deeply held Buddhist principles, he had been distressed when he heard that the police – *his* police – had opened fire on the crowd the previous day.

But events were now outside his control. An incident later that day gave the leaders of the agitation ample opportunity to paint the Namgyal family as an oppressive force. Tenzing and three friends decided to leave the palace compound in a jeep to assess the situation. Nothing untoward

---

* Clover was an American friend.

happened on the two-hour journey to Singtam, a junction town towards the south of the state, but on their return they were stopped at a hastily assembled road block by a group of youths from the Joint Action Committee. Panicking, one of Tenzing's companions shot his pistol into the air.

Suddenly the JAC had the evidence they needed. The Kazi and the others headed to the Residency to make a dramatic plea to Mrs Gandhi, asking her to 'intervene quickly and fully before we are massacred'.[12]

Within hours, the plea was conveyed to the press. With access to information about Sikkim being carefully controlled from Delhi, there was little reason for the eager journalists to believe anything but the Indian government line – that India might have to intervene to 'save Sikkim'.

Delhi now moved fast. Avtar Singh, a senior secretary in the External Affairs Ministry who had also been Sikkim's political officer in the early 1960s, was sent to Gangtok to assist Bajpai in persuading Thondup that his only option was to request Indian assistance. On the 6th, Mrs Gandhi met with another Singh – Kewal, her Foreign Secretary – and other members of her inner circle to decide on the next steps.* P. N. Dhar, one of those present in the meeting with Mrs Gandhi, later wrote an account of the meeting:

> Kewal Singh and I met the Prime Minister on 6 April to brief her on the situation and seek her instructions. Kewal was surprised to find that she had already made up her mind before listening to what he had to say. He guessed that the leaders of the anti-Chogyal movement had kept her informed through RAW. She was brief, and told us she would accept the Chogyal's request for help as soon as it came. Since she was leaving for Lucknow the next morning, a meeting of the political affairs committee of the cabinet was convened the same afternoon so that the decision could be endorsed in anticipation.[13]

*

In Gangtok, it was down to Bajpai and Avtar Singh to ensure that such a request came – and quickly. But they were finding that harder than expected.

---

* 'There seemed to be a lot of Singhs floating around,' Princess Coocoola later commented to the journalist Sunanda Datta-Ray. (Datta-Ray, *Smash and Grab*, p. 307)

The protestors' spirits were flagging. Now gathered in their thousands in the sports stadium, the Indian Central Reserve Police (CRP) distributed food, which had the effect of ensuring that they did not disperse back to their villages in despondency. Meanwhile Thondup still resolutely refused to bow to pressure and ask for Indian assistance. Time and again Bajpai presented the latest draft of a request for Thondup to sign. Time and again Thondup found reasons to object, determined that he should not have to concede any more than he absolutely had to in line with the 1950 treaty. But the noose was tightening. When *Time* magazine spoke to Tenzing for an interview, the young prince was adamant about what was happening. In an article entitled 'Alarum in Cloudland', *Time* reported that Tenzing had made 'a series of oblique references to "the element outside us that has been causing problems . . . we have several times been approached by the political officer to hand over all power to the government of—"'[14] at which point, *Time* reported, 'the line went briefly dead'. There was no doubting the inference – communication between Gangtok and the outside world was being closely monitored.

For Hope, life in the palace felt almost surreal as she watched her husband and his eldest son searching for a response to events. 'About thirty kids, all of them known to me, are out with Tenzing on the front lawn, practising firing on the front lawn against the embankment that leads to the upper lawn,' she wrote. 'Often when I am indoors and the trouble starts, I play Eric Andersen, guitarist and folk singer, really loudly on the new record player I've brought back from America,' she confessed. As news of Picasso's death and the breaking of the Watergate scandal in the US filtered through, she found herself identifying with President Nixon's 'encirclement'. She was now 'living on consommé, bananas, Valium, and cigarettes . . . I lie in bed stoned most of the day and grimly continue to read. Durrell's *Alexandria Quartet*, Balzac's *Pere Goriot*, Male's *Gothic Image*, anthologies of poetry.'[15]

By the 7th, Thondup was wilting under the pressure. It was becoming more and more difficult to ignore the continuing protests. News that Khatiawara had 'collected another mob in Kalimpong' and was bearing down on Singtam piled more pressure on the beleaguered ruler. The previous day he had reluctantly accepted limited Indian CRP assistance to protect threatened police stations across the south of his country. But he was still desperate to avoid asking the Indians to take complete control. He had been fighting all his life for the idea of an independent Sikkim and feared that any further Indian involvement would be irreversible. He cast around among his advisers for options, even asking if a merger with Nepal might be preferable to being 'stuck into the dominant welter of India'.[16] But he was a lone voice. Around him, almost everyone had resigned themselves to the inevitability of the situation. The small Sikkim Guards force was struggling to fulfil any meaningful role; the head of police was pleading with Hope to get her husband to see sense.

On 8 April, Thondup, worn down by sleepless nights, finally gave in.

Realising he had been outplayed, he signed Bajpai's document, formally requesting the Indian government to assume control in his country.

The Kazi and the JAC immediately suspended the agitation.

As Thondup signed away his powers in the palace, Ishbel Ritchie sat down to write her weekly letter to her mother from her house above the stadium. She had watched the week's events with some dismay and realised she would have to trick the censors with her Scots if she were to get the message through.

'At the moment there is a large and somewhat noisy crowd parked on the stadium below us,' she wrote:

> They've been there since yesterday evening, after having taken a long procession up the main road and along to the palace and then down through the market. We don't know how long they'll remain although we're hoping they may go today.
>
> Although I've heard the BBC overseas service news of course, I don't know what you've been hearing at home. If it's anything similar I'd advise a few pinches of salt – unfortunately it's a bit hirpling* – if you see what I mean.
>
> (You'll realise I've to ca' canny – gin this arrives there'll have been a wheen of keeking een).'†

---

* Translation from Scots: 'hirple' means to hobble, or walk unevenly.

† Translation from Scots: 'You'll realise I have to be careful – before this letter reaches you, there will have been a few people looking at it.'

Four days earlier, she and a colleague from the school had been preparing excitedly for Thondup's 50th birthday celebrations in the knowledge that she was to be awarded the Pema Dorji medal, a symbol that she had finally matched the efforts of her predecessor Martha Hamilton. Now, she told her mother, 'I've a feeling those are honours we'll never receive.'

She chose her words carefully as she wrote of what had happened over the next few days.

> There were some intimations of trouble building last weekend and on the 4th . . . a fair degree of long-term planning was obvious – maybe not entirely indigenous. There're all sorts of accusations being hurled around – many the pot calling the kettle black – and it's difficult to see anyone the gainer in the long run. In the meantime, day-to-day life continues tho' the high heid yins swither and there's nae official darg.* The army are adopting a non-meddle role and so far supplies aren't moving. We're going to run short if they don't soon. (Petrol is short already and I was caught short with an empty tank).
>
> We've just been made very anxious about how things will shape now.
>
> This is v obviously a watershed and things will not be the same again here.

She was right.

In Delhi, Kewal Singh, the Foreign Secretary, received the news of Thondup's request with relief. He immediately took charge of the situation, pulling together his best team to execute the next steps, working 'round the clock without respite'. The Indian Army units stationed throughout Sikkim took control of the administration of the country.

More importantly, now that the Indian government had an official request from Thondup for assistance, Singh needed a bureaucrat who could run Sikkim during what was sure to be an exceptionally tricky period. Bajpai was out of the question – he was a diplomat, not an administrator, and in any case it would have sent entirely the wrong message to the Sikkimese people: the political officer was too obviously India's

---

* Translation from Scots: 'those in control aren't sure what to do, and no government officials are working'.

representative in Sikkim. What was needed was someone who could fulfil something akin to the old role of dewan – albeit this time reporting to Delhi, not the Chogyal.

The man he decided upon was B. S. Das, who he considered to combine a high level of administrative ability with the political antenna of a diplomat. Better still, Das had spent four years in Bhutan as a sort of envoy (including during the time when Bhutan had acceded to the UN); he also therefore already knew Bajpai.

As soon as he received the call from Singh on the 8th, Das was whisked to the Indian Foreign Office for a briefing. What he found astonished him:

Never before had I seen the Foreign Secretary's office converted into an operations room. Long messages on situation reports were pouring in every half an hour, with the Foreign Secretary, Kewal Singh, dictating replies after replies to a team of stenographers. The desk officers dealing with Sikkim were walking in and out, seeking and taking instructions every hour. Kewal Singh looked as cool and composed as ever in his immaculate dress.[17]

Over two days, Das was given clear instructions. Naturally it was imperative, he was told, that 'Indian interests were to be fully protected, with Delhi having an overriding say in Sikkim's administration'. All support was to be given to the anti-Chogyal movement; Das later recalled that he was told 'to ensure that all my actions had the support of the political leaders; thus giving a legitimacy to all our moves. The feudal character of the existing system, and the people's revolt against it, were to be highlighted constantly.' The Foreign Secretary made it absolutely clear that 'if the Chogyal did not concede their demands, Delhi was prepared for a showdown.'[18]

When Avtar Singh, the External Affairs secretary who had once been political officer in Gangtok, returned from Gangtok on the 9th, his advice to Das was unequivocal: 'Do not allow the Chogyal to get on top again. We will never have a second opportunity like this. 1949 should not be repeated.'[19]

When Das arrived in Gangtok on the 10th, he was embarrassed to be greeted like some sort of conquering hero. A car took him straight to the Residency, where he related to Bajpai the instructions he had been given by Kewal Singh: to support the anti-Chogyal forces and, if necessary, push matters to a conclusion, even if it required a final showdown with the Chogyal's supporters.

Bajpai was apoplectic. For the past four days he had been operating under the impression that he was merely to 'go on building support for the agitation and maintain its tempo'; if he had been told from the start that Delhi was willing to provoke a confrontation from which the Chogyal's opponents would emerge the victors, he told Das, 'the matter would have been resolved to Delhi's satisfaction on the 4th itself'.[20] Now there was an added problem: the demonstrators – having expected the Chogyal to give in earlier – were tired and ready to go home after nearly a week of demonstrating. It would not be an easy job to get them back into the mood to protest. Das could only sympathise.

The following day, Das started to piece together the complex picture that confronted him. He soon identified the key power-brokers who he had to deal with: 'Kazi, the father figure of Sikkimese politics, Kazini, the brains trust, and Narbahadur [Khatiawara], the young firebrand with great organisational capacity, were the trio who dominated the scene throughout the agitation.' He also quickly surmised that the personal animosity between the Kazi and the Chogyal – and indeed between the Kazini and Hope Cooke (who, he noted, spoke so quietly that 'one had to beg her pardon several times before one understood her') – were important factors in the way things had developed over the previous decade, and could prove critical in the coming months.

That day he also met Thondup for the first time. He found him in a belligerent mood. Angry and disillusioned, the Chogyal also left the newly appointed bureaucrat in no doubt as to the scale of the task. Das later reported the tirade that he received from Thondup:

Mr Das, Sikkim is not Goa that the Government of India has sent you to take over as Chief administrator. We have our separate identity and

Indo-Sikkimese relations are governed by a Treaty. The so-called 'popular leaders' are nothing but a bunch of scoundrels propped up by outside forces. If my Police had not been disarmed and dishonoured by the Indian Army, I would have exposed each and every one of them. I shall never forgive the Indian Army for this.'[21]

Against this challenging background, Das and Bajpai 'chalked out [their] plan of action'.

It was something of a baptism of fire for Das: within 48 hours of arriving in Gangtok news reached him that a mob of Bhutias, loyal to the Chogyal, had begun descending on Gangtok. Fearing that he might have a bloodbath on his hands, foreign visitors were banned from Sikkim altogether. Bajpai told Pat Moynihan, the new US Ambassador in Delhi, that this was due to 'Indian concern over possible Chinese reaction'. Moynihan did not entirely believe him, cabling Washington, 'I am dubious of the alleged concern over the Chinese. It seems more likely that the Indians didn't want any foreigners around should Indian troops have had to open fire on local crowds.'[22]

In fact, a confrontation was only avoided by feeding both the Bhutias and the Nepali protestors, and providing free bus travel for them to return to their homes. Apart from Khatiawara – and possibly the Kazi – no one, Das noted with some surprise, seemed to have 'the will power to sustain a prolonged profile of confrontation'.

Bajpai and Das were therefore somewhat relieved when a call came in that Kewal Singh himself would be arriving in Sikkim on the 15th.

The plan, no more than a week old, was about to change.

While Bajpai and Das had been following their orders to increase the pressure on the Chogyal in Gangtok, Kewal Singh and the Indian government had been carefully monitoring the domestic and international reaction to what they had done.

While the press at home had generally parroted the government line, there were enough dissenters to concern Singh. More worrying still was an unexpected intervention from Coocoola, in Hong Kong on a 'week-long shopping trip' when her brother finally asked the Indian government to intervene. The princess immediately went on the offensive. While she 'stopped short of charging Mrs Gandhi with complicity', she made very significant accusations. She told the press that India had financed the opposition; that many of the 'rebels' had come from outside Sikkim; and that she was sure that the disturbances in Sikkim had been 'caused by "low-level Indian intelligence agents"', although she felt that 'Delhi was not aware of the activities of these agents from the Subsidiary Intelligence Bureau.'[23] On the Chinese mainland the Xinhua news agency* also reacted, charging that India's intervention was both political and military, and said it stemmed from the 'unequal treaty' in 1950.

In London, too, supporters of the Chogyal tried to raise a voice of concern. Denys Rhodes, a relative by marriage of Queen Elizabeth II and the appointed guardian of Thondup's children in the UK, approached the British Foreign Office accompanied by a firm of solicitors, Macfarlanes (who acted as trustees for the Namgyal children). Rhodes charged that 'the Indians had long been looking for a reason to intervene' and told the Foreign Office official that he was prepared to take the matter to the United Nations. The sniffy Foreign Office official, dismissing their 'somewhat romantic view of their connection with the Sikkimese royal family and the idealist faith, common amongst lawyers, in the power of written communications',[24] managed to convince them to hold their fire; but Rhodes' sentiment was shared by others in Britain who, in the post-colonial world, felt it was their duty to support the underdog.

The matter had not escaped the attention of the Americans either. Questioned in Washington, a press officer gave a low-key response, making clear that the US felt 'no compulsion to express an American view where American interests are so tangential'; pressed on the fact that the 'Queen is an American citizen', the press officer responded that the US 'may have some consular interests but none other'. But the new Ambassador in Delhi, Pat Moynihan, took a keener interest and was trying hard to stay on top of events in Sikkim. Moynihan had been posted to Delhi to try and repair relations between the US and India; he was, therefore, assiduous in seeking the truth behind what he knew to be an effective government press machine.[25] In a typically detailed analysis, he said he had the impression the Indian government was 'not averse' to the demonstrations, although

---

* Also known as the New China News Agency.

stopped short of an outright accusation of complicity. The 'dilemma' for the Indians, he continued, lay in the 'ironic fact that chastened Chogyal will be easier to deal with than aggressive Nepali youth' whose militant demands 'may soon produce a situation which is less easily controlled by the Government of India'.[26]

Inevitably, news of the American and British interest in events filtered through to the Indian Foreign Ministry. Combined with Coocoola's accusations and some adverse reaction in Delhi itself, they were enough to cause Mrs Gandhi and Kewal Singh pause for thought.

But it was the US ambassador in Kathmandu, Carol Laise, who reported the most interesting piece of intelligence. One informed diplomat told her that he thought India would not 'swallow' Sikkim without a 'green light' from the Soviets.[27]

Whether from Soviet pressure or not, Singh made the decision that Indian action in Sikkim needed to have, at the very least, a sheen of legitimacy.

When Singh arrived in Gangtok on 15 April, the Indian government's approach changed overnight, from 'aggressiveness to conciliation'.[28] There was a certain amount of relief from Bajpai and Das. In Ishbel Ritchie's words, it had been a 'gey orra'* few days. 'I was glad to hear on the radio last Monday evening that things were returning to normal,' she wrote sarcastically. 'You could have fooled me.' Advising her mother to have her 'interlineal glasses handy' (to read between the lines), she referred to the 'stadium-based entertainment' that had lasted the whole week.

Kewal Singh's arrival meant that all thoughts of encouraging or even tolerating confrontation evaporated. Neither Das nor Bajpai was ever made fully aware of why the approach had changed; but Das put two and two together when Kewal Singh told him that Mrs Gandhi had been unhappy with the 'unusual publicity' her actions had attracted, confirming Das's 'suspicion that some foreign governments friendly to India cautioned against hasty steps'.[29] It seems likely that this was the USSR cautioning against unleashing a democracy that might not turn out to be as supportive of Indian policy as expected.[30]

---

* Translation from Scots: 'very odd'.

Singh's new approach was simple: instead of supporting the democratic forces of change, India would assume all important powers within Sikkim. These powers would be transferred to an Indian chief executive who, it was planned, 'would virtually rule the State at Delhi's behest'. Thondup, meanwhile, would be maintained as Chogyal; this would be merely as a constitutional monarch – a figurehead – but allowing him to retain his position would deflect any serious criticism of the Indian actions.

Now that the decision had been taken that India herself would assume such complete control, the effect was immediate: the police were reinstated in their duties in Gangtok, administrative offices were reopened, order was restored albeit with a heavy Indian presence on the streets in the form of the Central Reserve Police.

Das had some concerns about the new approach, particularly the reception he knew it would get from those who had cheered his arrival as a liberator in Gangtok only one week earlier. He knew that if Delhi effectively tried to assume the powers that the Chogyal had formerly occupied, it risked the possibility that Delhi would be in 'direct confrontation with the political parties we were supporting'. Further, the demands of the protestors for genuine democratic reform would not be met.

To counteract the possibility of serious opposition from the leaders of the agitation, they were, as Das put it, 'assured, in unusually large doses, of Delhi's full support to their demands for a democratic set-up'. In other words, money was dispensed with a largesse hitherto unknown in the Himalayan state. Bags full of cash were parcelled out to influential people in order to win their acquiescence to the new state of affairs.* Some found it easy to adjust to the new realities. The Kazi was one of them. He had never hidden his belief that closer ties with India were necessary, and he was quickly identified as the key to maintaining Indian control in Sikkim.

As soon as Singh started discussions with Thondup, the Sikkimese ruler saw 'a ray of hope in the position being restored to the status quo ante with minor changes'. He railed at Delhi for instigating 'those hooligans' to cause trouble and insisted that Kazi, the Kazini and Khatiawara were 'communists and consequently a danger to both Sikkim and India'.

---

* A number of people in Sikkim were open about witnessing this when I talked to them in 2009; understandably none were willing to go on the record.

He had warned Indira Gandhi that something like this might happen, he reminded Singh, adding that he would do everything in his power to ensure Sikkim would retain its distinct identity.

There was no doubt that Das would be the man in charge and would be answerable only to Delhi in the new set-up. But to retain Thondup's support, Singh conceded two vital points: first, that a form of parity voting might be allowed to continue, and second, that the institution of the Chogyal would be protected. A bemused Das pointed out that, given these concessions were directly opposed to the main demands of the agitators, the agreement changed nothing of substance in Sikkim – apart from making Delhi (in other words, Das himself) the focal point for any discontent within the state, rather than the Chogyal. Nevertheless, a secret bilateral agreement was signed between Singh and the Chogyal on 23 April to this effect.

As Singh left for Delhi to get final approval, he asked Das and Bajpai to finesse the proposal with the elected leaders, primarily the Kazi. It quickly became apparent to Das that for the agreement to work at all, at least a semblance of authority would need to be given to the politicians. He relayed his view back to Singh. Thus when Foreign Secretary Singh returned in early May he carried with him a somewhat different agreement to the one he had signed with Thondup. The new agreement – which was to be tripartite (that is, signed by Singh, the Chogyal and representatives of the politicians) – passed some (admittedly limited) powers to the politicians; made clear that one man, one vote was to be instituted; and, crucially, did not include the precious guarantees about the Chogyal's position.

Thondup blew up at Singh, who tried to mollify him by saying that the new revised agreement was for 'Public Relations' purposes only; the agreement that really counted, Singh reassured Thondup, was the bipartite one signed on 23 April. Thondup begrudgingly accepted Singh's smooth reassurances but asked Singh to reaffirm that the 1950 treaty still ruled all arrangements between Sikkim and India. Singh, knowing that his plan needed an acquiescent Chogyal, agreed to give him such a commitment.

The tripartite agreement that was finally signed on 8 May 1973 was therefore a complete fudge, acceptable to everyone within the confines of their own narrow interpretation: Delhi was confident that it had fully protected its interests in Sikkim; Thondup, although he had not enjoyed the whole proceedings, was reassured that the agreement that really mattered was the one signed in secret on 23 April that allowed him to retain his position; the Kazi was convinced that he and the other politicians had inherited the mantle of power in Sikkim, albeit under Indian protection.

At the signing ceremony, the underlying tensions could not be hidden away. The timing – 9 p.m. – was not ideal for Thondup, who had started drinking again. Das recalled him turning up

> full of liquor already and surcharged with emotions; he accused the leaders of betrayal and sell-out to India. Sikkim and her people would never forgive them for their treachery. They were not worthy of being called Sikkimese having sold their country. None uttered a word, as if they were under his spell.[31]

The reference to 'betrayal' was deliberate: the term *'desh bechoa'* (sellers of the country) was one that would, over the coming years, become a hauntingly familiar one, levelled at the Kazi and his supporters. But for now the *Himalayan Observer*'s headline – 'Sikkimese Magna Carta: Kazi, Father of Democracy in Sikkim' – suggested a new dawn.

In reality India had assumed a position remarkably similar to that held by the British in the pre-1947 days – with a political officer, K. Shankar Bajpai, in the Residency and a highly powerful Indian-appointed dewan, B. S. Das, running the show.

To give the semblance of modernity, Das was to be given the official title of 'chief executive'. But even he was left in little doubt as to the bizarre imperial echo of the new arrangements: 'I was greeted by the Chogyal the next day with the words "Welcome Mr. Das, our new Chogyal." It summed up the agreement.'[32]

-4-

On 25 April, during the tense negotiations over the future of the country, Hope and Thondup had somehow found the time to send a congratulatory birthday telegram to the British consulate in Calcutta for onward transmission to Queen Elizabeth II. 'We thought it rather remarkable this year,' the consulate wrote in a dry covering note as they forwarded the telegram to London, 'in view of all the other events competing for their attention.'[33]

Attending to royal protocol, however, could not mask the bitter truth that life in the palace had changed irrevocably. After the 8 May Agreement, both Thondup and Hope sunk into morose moods. Thondup knew that his power had been irreversibly reduced; all Hope wanted was to be in New York with her new lover. The Indian authorities no longer tried to hide the fact that they were opening mail; Hope became paranoid that references to her New York lover in earlier letters might be used against her.[34]

By late May, once Das and the Indians had established a good measure of control across the state, the siege mentality lifted a little. At a palace dinner, Ishbel Ritchie noticed a welcome 'return to a little lightheartedness'. Thondup, she wrote to her mother, was 'in one of his teasing moods, saying outrageous things because he knows I haven't a comeback', though she added that he was 'on the whole much affected – naturally – by what has been going on and tends to be gloomy and rather backward-looking'.

That summer, life took on a slightly surreal feel. Thondup took up baking; Hope started knitting, 'something I haven't done since kindergarten'. Searching desperately for things that would keep spirits light and take Thondup's mind off the reality of his changed circumstances, she organised a play at the palace. Every week a small group – including Ishbel Ritchie – would meet in the palace to rehearse *The Enchanted* by French playwright Jean Giraudoux.* Proud Coocoola watched from the sidelines, complaining bitterly that the palace was becoming a mockery, reduced to play-acting by a woman of whom she had never approved.

The play would never see the light of day, a casualty of fast-moving

---

* The summary of the plot may provide some clues as to why Hope chose this particular play. From a 1950 edition, published by Samuel French: 'STORY OF THE PLAY: It is the biography of a critical moment in the life of a young girl – the moment when she turns from girlhood to womanhood. In this moment, Isabel's belief in the life of the spirit is so strong that it is sufficient to evoke a real phantom, and even to threaten this world with a spiritual revolution. But where the Inspector, who represents the powers of Government and Science, is powerless against Isabel, the Eligible Young Man succeeds, and for Isabel, as for all young girls, the adventure of love proves more attractive than the adventure of death.'

events. During May and June, a series of articles appeared in *Newsweek* impugning her character. Hope had become used to attacks on her character in the Indian press, but when she saw what the American press was now writing about her, she was horrified. Former US Ambassador J. K. Galbraith wrote to the magazine in her defence, but the final straw broke when a feature article appeared in early July. The earlier effusive and fawning reports of her time in Sikkim were replaced by something altogether darker. This time *Newsweek* described her as a 'Himalayan Marie Antoinette'. Where *Time* had lauded her efforts to develop the country, she now stood accused of rewriting history 'to establish the kingdom's validity as a sovereign land'.

It was the personal assault that hurt the most. She was mocked for her 'Jackie Kennedy whisper' and her 'burbling letters back home', which had suggested 'a story-book land where orchids grew like weeds, oranges were the sweetest in the world, and everybody lived happily ever after'. Sikkim's story was, the article went on, 'the classic tragedy of a dull man pushed along by a scheming ambitious woman'; it had been 'her influence, many Sikkimese believe, that launched Namgyal on the pursuit of the trappings and appurtenances of monarchy.' Four years earlier, *Time* had written of her modest spending habits; now *Newsweek* drew a link between her lifestyle and the troubles. 'While the pretensions and the required kowtowing were hard enough to swallow,' they wrote,

> Sikkimese refugees said the royal family's profligate spending in a land of poverty was a bitter pill indeed. The Chogyal and Hope seemed to be dashing off to Europe or the United States almost constantly. On each return, the palace-controlled *Sikkim Herald* would make a big thing of announcing just which kings and queens had entertained the Sikkimese rulers – a not very subtle attempt to imply parity between the royal houses of Europe and the rustic court of Gangtok. 'We are a poor people,' a Sikkimese journalist told me, 'but we are not fools, and we know how much money it takes to travel like that.'

The royal couple had been 'playing with fire,' living 'a life of imitation royalty' with Hope 'obsessed with the desire to be a *real* queen – of an independent nation'. Now, the closing paragraph hinted, there was no way back.

'It was so stupid and ridiculous,' a Sikkimese politician said. 'It did not need to have happened this way. But they kept flaunting this monarchy thing until it blew up in their faces.' The explosion left Hope's delusions of grandeur shattered and the future of the ruling house of Gangtok very much in question. 'How long,' a prominent Sikkimese asked me last week, 'can we go on putting up with this sort of mediocrity?'

It was a crushing blow for a delicate personality. With few pushing her to stay, she calculated it was time to go. Thondup had no desire to stand in her way. For reasons of political sensitivity, the departure date was delayed until after Indian Independence Day, 15 August. 'I drag myself toward this date with bleeding hands and knees,' she wrote.

When the day came, Hope found it impossible not to notice the irony as the band played the Indian national anthem and an Indian flag was triumphantly unfurled during the morning's celebrations.

In the afternoon, accompanied by her children, Hope Cooke left Sikkim for the last time.

CHAPTER SEVEN

We Also Want Our Place in the Sun

1973–4

-1-

Thondup's marriage to Hope had been disintegrating for some time, but her departure for New York, along with the younger children, left a gaping hole in Thondup's life. 'I think the Chogyal is missing the Gyalmo and the children quite a bit,' Ishbel Ritchie wrote after a dinner in the palace later in the month, 'although these days he has v much less business to occupy his attention anyway.' Not only had his wife left him; he had also been deprived of his life's passion, the thing that he felt was his solemn duty – the administration and protection of Sikkim.

There were other worrying developments. Karma Topden, the Sikkimese Head of Intelligence for so long, and a close friend, had been wooed away by the new Indian authorities with the offer of a job in Calcutta heading up the Sikkim Trading Corporation. Meanwhile the *Hindustan Standard* reported that the Kazi was seeking the 'externment (from Sikkim) of all Tibetan refugees', including Thondup's sister, Princess Coocoola, who acted as president of the Refugee Resettlement Board. It was clear that the Kazi was determined to destroy the edifice of the Namgyal dynasty, bit by bit.

Despite these threats to his and his family's position, the reality was that Thondup remained – officially – Chogyal of Sikkim. The tripartite agreement of 8 May 1973 had not simplified things. Under international pressure, the Indians had backed off pushing through with their original plan to topple Thondup. They had failed to heed Avtar Singh's warning not to miss the opportunity to settle matters that should have been concluded in 1949 once and for all. That failure left Thondup's position in Sikkim entirely unclear, and gave him fresh hope that he could somehow still manage to rescue a level of independence from India for his country.

The US Embassy, however, was certain that Thondup's days were numbered. They could not see how he would find a way back from the emasculation of the tripartite agreement. In the summer of 1973, one of their officers made a dry assessment of the avenues now open to Thondup:

> It remains to be seen how the Chogyal will accommodate himself to his now permanent position of virtual impotence (which radicals within Sikkim will almost certainly try to intensify and emphasise in the near future). His options are few: to abdicate, to leave the country and spend most of his time elsewhere while not formally abdicating, to play out his role of "constitutional monarch" in good faith, or to attempt to organize clandestine opposition from among loyal members of the Lepcha or Bhutia community. At this point, prospects for the long-term survival of the Royal House do not look good.[1]

In early August 1973, just before Hope left, Thondup gave a good indication of the route he intended to go down when he decided to reach out to King Birendra in Nepal. Educated at Eton and Harvard, Birendra was 27 and had succeeded his father the previous year. Like Thondup, he faced a difficult set of political challenges.

Nepal's independent status had never been in doubt in 1947 when India won its independence from Britain. The country had a strong, war-like past and had coexisted with the Empire as an equal, never a subordinate. It was also three times the size of Bhutan – and 20 times the size of tiny Sikkim. But since 1947 Nepal's relationship with India had been just as testy as Sikkim's. Birendra's father had introduced democracy in the late 1950s, but had promptly banned political parties in 1960, when the experiment had turned out to be not quite what he had expected. Nehru had not been impressed. The Indians had always felt an affinity with the Nepali people, and Nehru felt that the return to autocracy was a backward step. It also troubled both Nehru and his daughter Indira that the Nepali ruling family continued to cultivate as strong a relationship with the Tibetans and the Chinese as with the Indian government. During the 1960s, India had sought to maintain some leverage over events in Nepal by turning a blind eye to the Nepal Congress Party (the main opposition to the royal family) using India as its base.

At around the same time the Americans had also begun to take an increased interest in Nepal. During the 1950s the US had appointed a single ambassador for both India and Nepal, but in 1960 they appointed a dedicated ambassador to the Nepali kingdom. The Indians had been wary of this move, particularly in light of the monarchy's avowed position as a 'bridge' between India and Chinese Tibet. By the early 1970s, as the US–China rapprochement took root, the Indians were keeping a very close eye on the US relationship with Nepal.

For his part, Birendra attached 'great importance' to the US presence in the region, particularly during a period of uncertainty in South Asian relations. In May 1973, he told the retiring US Ambassador, Carol Laise, that he was convinced the Indians were 'seeking dominance in Nepal'. Birendra's foreign affairs adviser also told Laise he was certain the Government of India had deliberately introduced the agitators at the time of the trouble in Sikkim in April. Worse, he was sure they were '"lower echelon" adherents in India of the banned Nepali Congress Party'. Given that the NCP were opposed to Birendra's rule, this troubled Birendra and his advisers greatly.

All of this meant that there was some natural affinity between the Sikkimese and the Nepali monarchies, united by what they both perceived as the threat of increased Indian involvement in their own affairs. In the wake of the events of April 1973 (and given the possibility that the two kingdoms might be facing similar threats), Thondup sought to open up communications with Birendra in August. The man he chose to do so was the most trusted of his Sikkim Guards, Lieutenant Sonam Yongda.*

Yongda was in his early thirties. From an early age, his life had been bound up with that of the Chogyal. As a boy he had been selected for preferment, taken out of his local school and educated at St Joseph's

---

* The monk I met at Pemayangtse in 2009 (see Introduction).

College in Darjeeling. His father was an important figure in Pemayangtse, the monastery in the west of Sikkim; Yongda himself had undergone training as a monk, identified early on as exceptionally bright. In his late twenties, he had been sent to the military academy in Dehradun, a town north of Delhi, to train as an officer for the Sikkim Guards, which he joined when he returned to Sikkim in 1971. He had been out of Sikkim on another military training course at the time of the disturbances in April 1973, but on his return had soon become one of Thondup's closest confidants, a sort of aide-de-camp who could help with Thondup's religious duties as well as act as a bodyguard. As a scion of one of the leading families in Sikkim, he shared Thondup's deep and abiding belief in the legitimacy of the unusual theocratic state, and felt strongly that Sikkim must maintain its identity distinct from India. He was also not afraid of saying so.

The official purpose of Yongda's visit to Nepal was for Yangchen (Thondup's daughter, who travelled with Yongda) to spend time with the daughter of the British Ambassador, Terence O'Brien, but it did not take long for O'Brien to realise that Yongda was on a mission. The monk-soldier, he wrote back to London, was 'certainly no diplomat', causing the perplexed O'Brien considerable trouble, as he recorded in a slightly farcical memo:

Within five minutes Yongda had breathed such venomously anti-Indian sentiments that I thought it prudent to find him a bed in the Snowview Hotel nearby. As I rather expected, he has taken the opportunity to pursue various Sikkimese interests (undoubtedly on instruction) rather than to trail around with Princess Yangchen. His first request was that he should use my telephone to ring up Prince Tenzing, at Cambridge, and tell him that he was needed back in Gangtok, since his father had now ceased to exercise any power at all. I had no wish to have his call traced back to my number by the Indians and told him that it might be better if he rang from elsewhere. Subsequently I discovered that Lt Yongda had had two lengthy discussions with the Foreign Secretary, General Khatri, no doubt to give him the Sikkimese story and possibly to use the Nepalese wireless link to summon Prince Tenzing back to Sikkim.[2]

Nothing significant came from Yongda's efforts, but the very act of making contact with Nepal was an astute political move by Thondup. Birendra looked like an excellent ally: someone who was as determined as Thondup himself to assert his independent status, and who had excellent contacts with the wider diplomatic world. Thondup also knew that events in Sikkim had only served to emphasise the strategic worth – and vulnerability – of the whole Himalayan belt. The rapprochement with Nepal also came at a time when relations with Bhutan had deteriorated – Thondup had been slightly put out when Bhutan's royal family, which included his own relatives, had managed to secure UN membership in 1971, when Sikkim had not. As a result he began to see as much value in an association with Birendra and the royal family of Nepal as with his cousins in Bhutan.

Thondup's shift towards Nepal did not escape the notice of the Indians. From their point of view, Nepal's continued insistence on maintaining strong relations with China was troubling. The development in recent years of two additional border routes from Tibet into Nepal had particularly spooked them – if China were to gain traction in Nepal, it opened up the possibility of a Chinese threat to India's Gangetic Plain. The American interest in Nepal only increased Indian anxieties, given their links with China.

In fact, the American approach to the whole of Asia was undergoing a fundamental shift following the withdrawal of the last combat soldiers from Vietnam, which had taken place just as Thondup had come under siege in his palace in Gangtok. The US, led by the Ambassador in New Delhi, Pat Moynihan, was well aware of the delicate balancing act that they had to play across the region.

In an effort to help his counterparts in the countries bordering India to understand the position in India and more widely in South Asia, US Ambassador Moynihan sent out a long note entitled 'India and its smaller neighbours' to embassies and consulates in the region in late August.* 'All the smaller neighbors suspect India really wants hegemony, and

---

* In his autobiography, William Saxbe, US Ambassador after Moynihan (Feb. 1975 – Nov. 1976), says that 'New Delhi was a communications center for much of Asia, clear up into the Mediterranean – top secret operations.'

indeed it may,' he wrote. As a result, he foresaw a battle for influence in the countries on India's periphery, all of whom were seeking reassurance from either the US, or from one of the other two major world powers: the USSR and (increasingly) China. The US had no choice but to engage with India's smaller neighbours (if nothing else to keep the Soviets out), but Moynihan recognised that such strengthened relations would almost certainly worry the Indian government:

> While we can argue that such relations help India by reducing the super-sensitivity and increasing the economic viability of its neighbors, they also decrease Indian leverage over these countries. This is an ambiguity we must live with. We have made clear that we are not going to give India a veto over our relations with these countries. The most we can do is to try to avoid creating unnecessary suspicions, and to set the Indians straight swiftly and frankly if they begin acting as though we are poaching on their turf.[3]

Moynihan felt it was essential to control what he saw as India's 'hegemonic' tendencies in South Asia. He saw, for instance, Birendra's assertion that Nepal was 'not part of the subcontinent; it is that part of Asia which touches both China and India' as admirably pragmatic – and as good a way as any of maintaining stability in the region.

Such analysis struck a chord with Nixon and Kissinger, who continued to favour the largest of India's 'smaller neighbours', Pakistan, over India. Nixon had struck up an excellent relationship with Pakistan's Zulfikar Ali Bhutto, just as he had with Yahya Khan. His relations with Indira Gandhi, on the other hand, had never recovered from the terrible meeting in Washington in 1971. Nixon was unable to divorce personality from politics – and he had always like Bhutto. He therefore naturally lent towards Pakistan and away from India (a country with which, he told Bhutto with unconcealed distaste when they met in September 1973, the American liberal establishment was conducting a 'love affair'). Bhutto lapped it up, happily putting Sikkim in a box with Pakistan, China, Burma and Nepal as countries that had 'suffered' at the hands of India. 'Living in peace with India does not mean Indian hegemony in South Asia,' he told President Nixon.*

From Thondup's point of view, it would do Sikkim's chances of survival no harm if it were to be seen as firmly in the 'anti-hegemonist' camp.

-2-

While Sikkim was being tossed about casually in discussions between the leaders of the USA and Pakistan, Thondup went to Delhi for talks with Indira Gandhi. Given the pressures she was under, he felt confident he might be able to salvage something from the ashes of the disturbances in April and the subsequent 8 May Agreement.

The year had not gone as planned for the Indian prime minister. Her government was besieged by problems: the monsoon had failed for the second time in two years, bringing another poor harvest; she was under political pressure over the appointment of a political ally as Chief Justice to the Supreme Court; she was also facing accusations that her fast-living son Sanjay's Maruti Suzuki car project was propped up only by shady deals and cheap government loans. Territorially, too, she felt under pressure. Sikkim was far less pressing than the two major genuinely separatist headaches on her northern periphery: Kashmir and Nagaland. Nevertheless, perhaps thinking of her father's fondness for Sikkim, she squeezed a meeting with Thondup into her busy schedule.

For Thondup, the meeting held great significance. The very fact that it was he and not the Kazi who was meeting Mrs Gandhi also bolstered his own standing and felt like a triumph. After the events of April, he despised the Kazi more than ever. More importantly he still had faith

---

* As an indication of how important a role Pakistan and India played in Cold War thinking in this period, in the same Washington meeting Kissinger admitted that during the 1971 war he had 'told the PRC [People's Republic of China] that if they came into the [Bangladesh] war in support of Pakistan, and if they were attacked, they would have our full support'. He had also told 'Brezhnev that we would consider an attack on Pakistan in any form as inconsistent with the detente between us'. Nixon then added that he had also told Brezhnev that he considered 'Soviet aid to India as one way the Soviets commit aggression through using third countries'. (Memorandum of conversation, 18 Sept. 1973, available online at us.gov)

in the goodwill of the Indian prime minister, who he had known since childhood. He felt sure she would continue to listen to his pleas on behalf of his people.

In preparation for the meeting, he checked legal opinion on Sikkim's situation and his own position. A crucial strength, the lawyers told him, was the existence of the 1950 treaty. A treaty by definition could only be between the leaders of two sovereign nations. Both parties would need to agree to any renegotiation. He should portray the 8 May Agreement as a 'working arrangement' only, the lawyers advised him, designed to restore order after the disturbances and allow for fresh elections. When they met, Thondup therefore emphasised to Mrs Gandhi that his main aim was to maintain some protection for the Bhutia-Lepchas in the planned elections. Mrs Gandhi listened patiently, consumed by thoughts of the many other problems she faced across India. Sikkim was not high on her agenda.

After the meeting ended, Thondup held a press conference to high-light the fact that he had met with Mrs Gandhi. He was trying to be constructive, he told the waiting journalists, and wanted to correct some of the wilder rumours doing the rounds in the newspapers. He had 'faith and trust in India'; criticism that he had been 'looking more to the West and the US than to India' for guidance was 'absolute nonsense'. As for the agitation in April, he said it had not been 'inspired by China or Nepal', as some irresponsible newspapers had suggested. But neither had it been a 'spontaneous' uprising. Instead it had been 'Communist Party of India (Marxist) and other demonstrators . . . from Darjeeling and Kalimpong that had caused the trouble'. It was clever politics – painting himself as the India-friendly bulwark against the Naxalites and their associated supporters.

But it was in response to press articles making dark suggestions about his recently departed wife's role in Sikkim that he was most vehement: Thondup told journalists that 'the Gyalmo [Hope Cooke] had not been involved in politics; her departure was not prompted by political consid-erations or family misunderstandings; and he planned to join her in New York at Christmas'.[4]

On the specifics of the future relations between India and Sikkim, he stuck rigidly to his lawyers' advice. The 8 May Agreement, he told the press, must not be allowed to supersede the bilateral 1950 treaty, 'which continued to govern the relations between India and Sikkim'. The vital thing was to protect Sikkim's diversity. To that end, he would work with India's chief election commissioner to 'reconcile the one-man one-vote principle of the May 8 Agreement and the "parity" of different ethnic groups'.

All this was carefully minuted in a cable from a US embassy diplomat, who thought Thondup's press conference to be a Machiavellian Indian ploy. They suspected that 'the Chogyal's trip and the publicity the Indians permitted him [were] further evidence of the Government of India's desire to preserve his figurehead status in Sikkim'. Nevertheless, they concluded, there was little doubt that 'the Government of India will remain in effective authority in Sikkim'.[5]

For Thondup the idea of ceding even greater political control to India in return for preserving his own position would have been a deal with the devil.

He was now more determined than ever to assert Sikkim's right to independent political control within Sikkim, and was convinced that could only be achieved with preservation of the monarchy in Sikkim.

When Thondup returned to Gangtok, he found Chief Executive B. S. Das trying his best to cope with the fallout of the 8 May Agreement. Das knew it was completely deficient; he also knew that Thondup did not believe in the validity of the agreement. Worst of all he realised that the new politicians, who had never exercised real power before, were largely incompetent and deeply faction-driven. As a result he found himself effectively running a 'one-man' administration.[6]

Das's main task was to arrange for elections, which involved getting all parties to agree on a format. It was an extremely delicate task, balancing the different interests in Sikkim and seeking concessions from all sides. He persuaded Thondup to concede that the election commissioner would not be Sikkimese; instead, oversight of the election would be in the hands of 'a senior officer from India who would function directly under the chief election commissioner'. Meanwhile he won a major concession from the Kazi and the politicians: that the parity formula should continue, with 15 seats reserved for candidates from the Bhutia-Lepcha ethnic group and

15 for those of Sikkimese Nepali origin. (There were also two additional seats: one to represent the monks of Sikkim, and one for the so-called 'scheduled castes'.)

While Das put in place these arrangements, Thondup began to take a more active approach to saving the country.* Hope's return to New York had resulted in Princess Coocoola resuming a more prominent role in her brother's life, becoming his principal adviser. Frustrated by what she saw as her brother's lack of appetite for the coming electoral fight, Coocoola sought to reinvigorate the campaign for Sikkim's independence. In Delhi she redecorated Sikkim House (the residence that the Namgyals maintained there). It soon became 'the most impressive building in the whole diplomatic enclave', Ishbel Ritchie reported after visiting it. 'This is Sikkim's "embassy" to all intents and purposes I suppose.' Meanwhile, in an effort to revitalise the flagging National Party, Coocoola's daughter Sodenla set up a youth wing called the Sikkim Youth Pioneers, whose members quickly gained a reputation for aggressive campaigning for a return to the status quo ante.

With the elections set for April, Thondup flew to the States for Christmas 1973 to see his children. It was not an easy trip. He and Hope had never fully agreed how long she would be in New York. As Thondup prepared to leave in the early part of 1974, he realised for the first time that she would never come back.

Thondup returned to Gangtok alone, in time for a muted celebration of his 51st birthday. A few days later, with the Sikkim elections only days away, he gave an interview to the *New York Times*. The headline betrayed his mood: 'Ruler of Sikkim, Alone in Palace, Broods and Waits'. He denied rumours of a divorce or separation as 'loose talk' and 'wishful thinking', and railed against those who had portrayed him as 'anti-Indian'. The Indian Foreign Ministry (who he blamed for the portrayal) had been 'led up the garden path . . . I was dubbed as an autocrat and a wicked person,' he said with feeling, asserting that he had a 'special relationship' with the people of Sikkim and challenging anyone to 'bring up specific instances

* In early December Ishbel Ritchie found herself rather disappointed at having enjoyed a dinner at the palace but returning home in time to do the ironing. 'With the Gyalmo away and the Chogyal not drinking, things seem to be getting more and more speedy,' she wrote.

of my wickedness'. He gave an impassioned plea for understanding of his position, taking his critics head on:

> What choice has Sikkim but to live under the protection of India? The only choice is China, but any practical-minded person will know that is not in the interest of Sikkim. All that I said and wanted was that India be the big brother and Sikkim the little brother. You give us love and support, which we will reciprocate. Under your protection we will become strong, economically viable, which will be a good thing for you. After all, we also want our place in the sun.[7]

The elections took place in late April. The result was a complete disaster for Thondup and the Palace. A few months before the election, the Kazi's SNC had formed an astute alliance with the Janata Congress, the other main party with a strong appeal to the Sikkimese Nepali vote. The combined effectiveness of the new party (Sikkim Congress), along with the new delineation of constituencies decided by the Indian election commissioner, gave the Kazi a huge advantage. Meanwhile the emergence of the hard-line Sikkim Youth Pioneers had hopelessly split the Palace faction and the National Party. At the last minute Thondup formed a new political party – the People's Democratic Party – in an effort to galvanise the anti-Kazi vote. All that did was split the natural pro-Chogyal vote even further. The Kazi swept to victory in 31 out of 32 seats in the elections. There were some murmurs that the scale of the victory seemed suspect,* but no one was under any illusion that the Kazi was now firmly in the ascendant. Thondup's world, it seemed, was falling apart.

With such an overwhelming democratic mandate, the Kazi was triumphant. The Kazini was no less elated. She had spent the best part of two decades chipping away at what she saw as the crumbling edifice of the Namgyal dynasty by firing out anti-Chogyal articles from their home base in Kalimpong.

---

* P. N. Dhar, Principal Secretary to Indira Gandhi from 1973 to 1977, dealt with this election somewhat ambiguously in his book *Indira Gandhi, the 'Emergency' and Indian Democracy*, stating that 'there was no interference whatsoever from outside – unless the efforts of RAW to boost the morale of Congress leaders is considered interference'.

Now, in the late spring of 1974, as Sikkim's flower gardens started to bloom, the Kazini was finally the first lady of Sikkim.

-3-

Neither the Kazi nor the Kazini were under any illusions that the election result meant the game was over. It had certainly reduced the Chogyal's claim to any political role; but the 8 May Agreement of the previous year still had force, and there was no doubt that under that document the Chogyal retained considerable – if largely theoretical – power. The Kazi was determined that this must change.

For Das and Bajpai, too, the election result meant a change in policy. It had been quite clear during the polling that Delhi was firmly behind the Kazi. Now that the result had been so overwhelmingly in his favour, the Kazi was even more closely aligned with his Indian masters. P. N. Dhar, Indira Gandhi's principal secretary, was quite clear on where Das and Bajpai must stand. It was, he said, 'no longer possible for Delhi to stay neutral between the Chogyal, whose ambition was to remain the focal point of power, and the Kazi, who represented the popular will'.[8]

The Kazi, meanwhile, was determined to make a strong statement that things had changed – and that he had the full support of Delhi. The date set for the swearing-in of the Assembly, 10 May, provided the first opportunity. For decades, the tradition had been for the Chogyal to swear in Assembly members. Now the Kazi announced that he would not accept being sworn in by the Chogyal – he would only accept being sworn in by B. S. Das himself.

Thondup was furious. He knew he was being sidelined, but there was little he could do. After the ignominy of seeing his role usurped by Das, he was at least allowed to give an 'inauguration address'. Thondup, in what Das later acknowledged was 'an exercise in self-control in spite of his bitterness', pointedly stressed the importance of Sikkim's continued separate identity to the newly elected members. 'We should . . . bear in mind that the future of our country and the survival of our Sikkimese identity rests on the level of our wisdom, maturity and performance. So long as we fail to fathom these basic essentials,' he added with implicit criticism of the Kazi and the new Assembly, 'our efforts will have been meaningless.'

The Kazi, now in his seventies, was riled by the public suggestion that he lacked maturity. More determined than ever to show that he was in control, he ordered his Assembly members to boycott the reception that the Chogyal was giving after the inauguration at the Tsuklakhang Palace. Ishbel Ritchie, as head teacher of the school, was one of those waiting at the palace all afternoon. She could sense the anger on both sides – the whole thing was 'pandemonium', she wrote, and an 'incredible display of bad manners'.

Such trivialities were just for show. It was on the following day – the first official session of the new elected Assembly – that it became clear just how far the Kazi was prepared to go in order to reduce Thondup's power to naught. After an introductory speech from Das, the diminutive Kazi rose to his feet. Determined to demonstrate the break with the past, he ignored the tradition of giving thanks to the Chogyal (who was conspicuously absent); instead, he fired a shot across the bows of his long-time foe, warning that 'those who fail to adjust themselves to the change of time and circumstance will have perforce to face stark reality in all its consequences'.

He then reeled off no less than 15 'resolutions', almost certainly prepared with the help and encouragement of Das and his assistants. Some directly contradicted the 8 May Agreement, which had prohibited the Assembly discussing the future of the Chogyal: the third resolution stated that the functions and role of Thondup in the future could 'not be more than those of a constitutional head of the Government of Sikkim'.

That much Thondup had expected and would have been willing to at least discuss; but when he reviewed the full list of resolutions later, there was one in particular that alarmed him more than any other. It stated that the Assembly should resolve to draw up a constitution, and to take immediate steps 'for Sikkim's participation in the political and economic institutions of India'. To do this, the Kazi insisted, a constitutional adviser from India should be sent to Sikkim immediately. Publicly, he talked of the necessity of such a step to bring democracy and economic progress; privately, he had concluded that it was the only way to get rid of Thondup once and for all. With almost total control of an Assembly of politicians still basking in the glory of a first election victory, the Kazi's resolutions were quickly passed.[9]

Thondup was aghast. He knew that the Kazi was determined he should go but he was convinced that, with the new resolutions, the Assembly were sleepwalking into sacrificing any identity that Sikkim retained. An Indian constitutional adviser would be bound to propose closer union.

He jumped on a plane from Bagdogra airport (near Siliguri) to Delhi at once to meet with Foreign Minister Swaran Singh, Foreign Secretary Kewal Singh and Mrs Gandhi. He told them that not only had the Kazi broken the 8 May Agreement's specific article preventing the Assembly from discussing the future of the Namgyal family, but also, by raising the issue of Sikkim's relations with India, the Assembly had raised a matter covered by the 1950 treaty. Such issues, by definition, could only be negotiated between the parties to the treaty; given that he was still Chogyal and therefore head of state, this was a role that he argued fell to him alone.

If a constitutional adviser was to come to Gangtok, Thondup suggested three specific conditions: that Sikkimese participation in the government be maximised; that Sikkim's separate juridical identity should be recognised; and (he was willing to concede this much) that India's legitimate security and other interests should be protected. Mrs Gandhi listened, nodded and smiled* but committed to nothing. Thondup noticed that she seemed distracted. On the second day of his visit to Delhi, it became clear why.

On 18 May 1974, India became a nuclear power with the explosion of a test device in a remote corner of the Rajasthani desert, not far from the border with Pakistan.

International reaction to the Indian nuclear test was initially stunned silence. No one had any indication that it had been about to occur; in fact, information about the plans was so tightly controlled that even

---

* Ambassador Moynihan writes of the way Mrs Gandhi used to 'nod, smile' without responding directly to questions in 1973–4, leading to many pleasant but totally unproductive meetings with her in this period. (see Weisman, *Daniel Patrick Moynihan*, p. 310)

Swaran Singh had only been informed of the test 48 hours before it took place. The Pakistanis expressed their deep concern; the Chinese – who had conducted a test of their own a decade earlier – were also taken by surprise.

American Ambassador Moynihan immediately cautioned against over-reaction. Keen to protect the progress in his rapprochement with elements of the Indian government, he downplayed the significance of the test, noting drily 'any government seeking to reinstate a measure of national progress in an otherwise dismal situation might be expected to consider such a step.'[10]

Moynihan was right: domestically the test was a masterstroke, providing a distraction from the continuing economic and political problems Indira Gandhi was facing. For two months, she had been coming under intense pressure from Jayaprakash (JP) Narayan, a charismatic politician from India's Bihar province, who was calling for 'total revolution' to fight against Mrs Gandhi's 'corruption and misgovernment and blackmarketeering, profiteering and hoarding'. With the nuclear test dominating the headlines, Narayan's sniping was forgotten for a brief moment, replaced by 'an unmistakeable air of excitement' and pride in Delhi at what had taken place.[11]

When Thondup heard the codename for the test – 'Smiling Buddha' – he must have wondered if someone, somewhere was sending some kind of subliminal message. His own good humour was rapidly disappearing. He was now worried that Mrs Gandhi's non-committal attitude was evidence that she no longer cared about Sikkim's future as a separate nation. During the next two days, he snatched some further time with her. She listened again to his views, but – now emboldened by the political success of the nuclear test – told him haughtily she could not halt the progress of 'democracy'. She advised him that his best course of action was to wait for the report from the Indian Constitutional Adviser, the eminent jurist G. R. Rajagopaul. Thondup had little choice but to reluctantly agree. He returned to Sikkim.

By mid-June, a mere three weeks after being given the job of creating the constitution, Rajagopaul's recommendations were complete. Thondup could not help but be suspicious of the astonishing speed. Even B. S. Das, when he saw them, commented on 'the anomalies and unworkability of the provisions', which he realised made Delhi's 'direct involvement in every matter inevitable'.[12] But he knew it was his job to see things through. Delhi made clear that it was time to resolve what was becoming an increasingly messy situation.

On 12 June, Thondup returned to Delhi, expecting to meet with the relevant authorities to discuss Rajagopaul's recommendations. But instead of recommendations to consider, he was presented with something closer to a fait accompli – a fully formed 'draft constitution' to comment on. He immediately sought a meeting with Mrs Gandhi. When he was told that she was too busy for a face-to-face meeting, he fired off a letter to her on the 15th, asking for ten days to consider his position on what, in his view, constituted (to all intents and purposes) a renegotiation of a treaty between two nations. He returned to Gangtok the next day, believing he had bought himself some time.

The gist of the proposed 'draft constitution' quickly reached Gangtok. It was soon obvious that it was not only Thondup who had grave concerns. Two of the young Sikkim Congress leaders were worried by the lack of clarity in the document. A number of points in the document also seemed to propose a greatly enhanced role for India. It was certain that a lot of power was to be vested in the Indian chief executive, Das. Further, any disputes between the chief executive and the Assembly or the Chogyal were to be referred to Delhi. Another clause made provisions for the head of the Assembly to be called 'chief minister' rather than 'prime minister'. The distinction was not lost on anyone: 'chief minister' was the term used for states within the Indian Union.

Gangtok was small – news travelled fast. People inside and outside the Assembly began to appreciate the major implications behind the proposals. What they had expected from Rajagopaul's work was a framework for a democratic Sikkim, not a proposal for integration with India. Suddenly there was a groundswell of people demanding that the head of the Assembly be called 'prime minister' in recognition of the 'separate and distinct identity of Sikkim', and that India's role in Sikkim should be explicitly limited.

There was now substantial public disquiet at the proposed constitution.

Things deteriorated rapidly when Das declared on the 18th that the Assembly would meet two days later. The next day demonstrators started to appear on the streets of Gangtok. But this time, unlike the previous April, when the demonstrators had been predominantly Nepalis from outside brought into the capital by the Indian government, the crowd contained representatives from all the communities in Sikkim – Bhutia, Lepcha and Nepali. They were united by their opposition to the speed of the planned constitutional changes. The scale of the opposition became even more apparent when more than 2,500 civil servants walked out on strike, bringing Gangtok to a virtual standstill.

But there was an urgency about events that caught almost everyone off guard. Everything came to a head on the 20th. Das had planned a rushed Assembly session for 12.45 p.m. A substantial group of Gangtok's citizens were now convinced that something was afoot and climbed the hill to the Assembly building, surrounding it to prevent the Assembly members from entering. Das needed to regain control. The army were on hand, but he knew that involving them would be incendiary. He ordered the Central Reserve Police (CRP) – armed with lathis – to restore order with force, but the demonstrators stood firm. When a violent fight broke out between protestors and the CRP, Das authorised them to use tear gas to bring the situation under control. The main bazaar in Gangtok, a normally quiet place, was in chaos – the hospital later reported treating more than 100 people with injuries.[13]

By that evening, however, the action had had the desired effect. The streets were still tense – but quiet. Shortly after 9.30 p.m. the elected politicians were ferried to the Assembly building in army vehicles. What followed was an extraordinary session – as short as it was farcical. With Das presiding, the Assembly members started a discussion of the draft bill. The Kazi, despite being 'considerably shaken up' by the events earlier in the day, began the session. Since the discussion was in English and more than half of the Assembly members (including the Kazi) 'were not at all conversant with that language', the debate was virtually non-existent. Four members, none of whom could understand what was being presented to them, proposed eight amendments. All were seconded – but none would find their way into the document that would be agreed a few days later. The session closed hurriedly with the reading of two further resolutions 'fully' endorsing 'the proposals of the Constitutional Advisor' and asking that they should be implemented in 'the shortest possible time'. Both were passed unanimously.[14]

Many of the members would later complain that the atmosphere was heavily pressurised. Khatiawara* reported it was 'over in less than sixteen minutes'.[15]

Das had fulfilled his brief: the resolution had moved integration with India another step closer.

In Delhi, the British and American embassies scrabbled around for information about what had happened. Although reports that there had been disturbances in Gangtok had leaked out, foreign reporters had been carefully excluded from Sikkim, and access for Indian journalists was severely restricted. The press corps relied for their information on the heavily government-controlled Press Trust of India.

One person who could not be controlled, however, was Crown Prince Tenzing, still a student in England. On 23 June, the *Sunday Observer* ran an interview with him on their front page. Tenzing told the paper he had spoken to his father, who had told him 'all roads to Sikkim are blocked and communications with the outside world controlled', adding that 'if it is a choice of being a protectorate of India and being absorbed, we obviously want to be a protectorate'. An Indian government spokesman in London quickly dismissed the article as 'highly mischievous'.[16]

From her house below the bazaar, Ishbel Ritchie's letters were also getting past the censors – albeit slowly. When she wrote to her mother on the 23rd, the strike was already four days old and showed no signs of abating. An 'amazing cross-section of all the educated population of Gangtok ... have been made suspicious by the curiously hurried and devious way in which it has been introduced in the end. There is a most hamfisted air – if one can have such a thing – about the whole proceedings.'

---

* The young firebrand who had been involved with coordinating the events outside Sikkim in April 1973 had won a seat in the Assembly by forging records on the voters' roll to show that he was 25 years old and could therefore stand as a candidate. Having fallen out with the Kazi and Kazini, he campaigned as an independent candidate; but once elected the Kazi had little option but to allow him to rejoin the Sikkim Congress.

In Delhi, the American embassy could have done with Ishbel Ritchie's insights. With serious doubts about the press reporting, they made assiduous attempts to find out more about the situation. N. B. Menon, one of the joint secretaries at the Ministry of External Affairs, opened up to one of the embassy officers. Any problems, Menon told him, were solely down to the Chogyal and his 'refusal to accept his legislative responsibilities' by assenting to the bill endorsed by the Assembly on the 20th. The Government of India was perfectly within its rights to 'simply declare the Assembly bill as enacted' and was only refraining from doing so for the Chogyal's benefit. 'We suspect,' concluded the US embassy officer, that 'the Government of India anticipates a new wave of popular uproar on behalf of the constitution in the wake of which either the Chogyal will concede defeat or the Government of India can invoke the pressures of democracy and override the Chogyal'.[17]

Which is exactly what happened.

During the demonstrations on the 20th, Thondup had been powerless, confined to the palace 'for his own safety'. Initially Bajpai had reassured him that 'if he did not agree with the resolution to be passed by the Assembly he could inform the Government of India and the Assembly of changes he desired and the Government of India would consider the matter'. But on the 23rd, after three days of demonstrations (and the appearance of Tenzing's article in London), Bajpai told Thondup that the situation had changed. 'It has now become necessary for you to give your assent,' he wrote bluntly from India House. There was, he implied, no alternative. It was time to stop 'this nonsense'.[18]

Thondup gave Bajpai and Das a sharp reminder that he had said he would take ten days to consider the bill, and those ten days were not yet expired. He also reminded both men of the three conditions he had set for agreeing to a new constitution, which he knew had not been met. Finally, he reiterated that since the bill involved renegotiation of a treaty between sovereign states he would be flying to the capital to discuss matters with Indira Gandhi herself.

But even as he was on the plane to Delhi further signs of what he was up against emerged. In Gangtok, events unfolded in just the way the American embassy had predicted. On 25 and 26 June, protestors from south and west Sikkim and beyond, many of Nepali origin, started arriving in the capital to demonstrate. Few were in any doubt that the protestors, who had been gathered from villages, had been paid to be there.* The Kazi, who had now recovered his composure, addressed the hastily assembled crowd, demanding that Das call another Assembly meeting to finally ratify the bill. Meanwhile some of the major Indian newspapers obediently reported the government's charge that Thondup was stifling democracy in Sikkim by refusing to assent to the proposed constitution.

One newspaper went further, insinuating that there might be 'invisible foreign hands working from behind to influence the palace thinking'. Such allegations were easy for Indian policy hawks to substantiate – they only had to point to the report from the Xinhua news agency, which criticised India's 'expansionist ambition to annex Sikkim', alleging 'interference in the internal affairs of another state'.[19]

In Delhi, Thondup set up base in his favourite hotel, the Ashoka. On 27 and 28 June, he met with both Swaran Singh and Kewal Singh, haranguing them with his account of what had taken place. But they were both equally blunt: Swaran Singh advised him 'politely but firmly' that he should reach a settlement with the Assembly in Gangtok; Kewal Singh reiterated the message, 'with a bit more of a cutting edge'. They were giving Thondup 'the option of holding his nose and swallowing the new constitution'.[20]

But Thondup had by no means given up hope. Feeling like he was bashing his head against a brick wall with the Singhs, he demanded another meeting with Mrs Gandhi.

While Thondup was 'cooling his heels' in the Ashoka Hotel in Delhi, awaiting a meeting with Mrs Gandhi, Das called another meeting of the Assembly in Gangtok for 7 p.m. on the evening of Friday, 28 June. As a sop to procedure, he opened the session by reading out an earlier telegram from Thondup, outlining his three pre-conditions for the bill. The Kazi then took the floor. Decrying the 'nefarious activities' of the Palace and expressing shock 'at the tactics adopted by the Chogyal', the

---

* Confirmed to the author by a number of people, including a member of the Special Security Bureau operating out of nearby Haflong.

Kazi thundered that Thondup had 'one last chance to come to reason'.
He gave him 48 hours – *in absentia* – to agree to the new bill. The young
firebrand Khatiawara reiterated the ultimatum, warning that the Chogyal
had failed to see 'the writing on the wall'.

In his role as president of the Assembly, Das knew full well what he
was expected to achieve – the introduction of the bill.[21] The Assembly
members (31 of the 32 were present) duly obliged. But it had taken some
heavy tactics – Khatiawara would later write that many of the members
were 'threatened to support the bill or else face the consequences'.[22]

Meanwhile, in Delhi, Thondup finally got his meeting with Mrs Gandhi.
He found the Indian prime minister in an intransigent mood. In a desperate
throw of the dice, he threatened to resign as Chogyal in the hope that Mrs
Gandhi might baulk at the prospect of a chaotic power vacuum in Sikkim.
But the Indian prime minister was unmoved. P. N. Dhar, a member of her
inner circle, later recalled the icy ending to the meeting:

> He wanted the discussion to continue but Mrs Gandhi fell silent and looked
> aloof. She had perfected the use of silence as a negative response. After an
> oppressive moment in which nothing was said, the Chogyal stood up to
> leave. Mrs Gandhi bade him farewell with folded hands and an enigmatic
> smile, still without saying anything.[23]

Mrs Gandhi's silent message came as a bitter blow to Thondup. He
had always believed that, whatever else happened, she would honour
her father's commitments to Sikkim. Now it seemed that was not the
case. He sent out an acid press release to demonstrate his deep sense
of betrayal. In it he laid everything bare: he enclosed the correspondence from Bajpai on the 20th and the 23rd; he alleged that he had been
deliberately duped by the Indian government over timings; the press
had also been guilty of 'one-sided reporting and unrestrained attacks'
on him personally; worst of all, the bill was 'deficient, particularly
with regard to financial matters, and vested real executive and legislative power in the (Indian) Chief Executive, which was contrary to the
objectives of the reform'.[24]

But few were now listening. The press release was also – implicitly – an acknowledgement that he had been outplayed. Perhaps for the first time he recognised the enormity of the task of saving Sikkim.

Dejected and deflated, Thondup returned to Gangtok.

On 4 July 1974, in the presence of Indian Foreign Secretary Kewal Singh, Thondup 'held his nose' and gave his assent to the Government of Sikkim Bill. The Assembly had passed the bill the previous day; two days later, the bill came into force as an act.

'The Chogyal blinked,' wrote a US embassy officer, summing up the game of political poker that had taken place.[25] But many in Gangtok knew that it had been far more sinister. Ishbel Ritchie summed up the mood in her latest missive home:

> It looks as though sufficient people have been intimidated into supporting the proposals they'd protested about – or at least have been forced to keep quiet for now. I'm afraid the sellout is now complete, and there's little anyone can do now. It is very sad to see things done in this manipulated way.

Even as Thondup was signing the act into force, the Chinese Xinhua news agency went on the offensive, describing the whole thing as 'a mini-Czechoslovakia' incident and railing against the 'truculent and unjustified interference' by India in another country's affairs.[26]

It was water off a duck's back for the Delhi machine, which embarked on a charm offensive with its new docile Sikkimese politicians. The Kazi and his entire Assembly were flown to Delhi, where they were put up in the same hotel that Thondup had stayed in only days earlier. No expense was spared, as the group were whisked around the corridors of power, introduced to the President and the Vice President and cabinet members. Swaran Singh flattered them as 'the founders of the democratic set-up' in a private meeting. Later they were taken to see the Taj Mahal by moonlight and Varanasi's famous ghats.[27]

On the final day they were ushered into the presence of Mrs Gandhi. She smoothly reassured them that Sikkim's 'individuality' would be preserved, and that India's purpose was to support 'the unfolding of the "new great experiment" of democracy in Sikkim'. Now, she concluded, it was 'for the leaders and people of Sikkim to visualise the kind of Sikkim that they want ... India's "sympathy", "cooperation" and "good neighbourliness"' would be offered to Sikkim and its new politicians to help with this endeavour.[28]

They were warm words; but the American embassy, diligent as ever, noted a distinct change in tone in Delhi. As the Kazi boarded the plane for Gangtok, he pointedly told the press that the 'immediate' problem facing Sikkim was to draft a new constitution. Meanwhile Swaran Singh had subtly changed the tone of his language: what he had previously referred to as the 'Constitution Bill' had now become the 'Government of Sikkim Bill' that India would 'assist Sikkim in implementing'.

The embassy cabled Washington immediately. There was every indication, they concluded, that the events of June had been only the start and that 'a new or revised constitution – with Indian acquiescence – is in the offing'.*[29]

In the British High Commission, too, they were trying to work out what would come next and how they might respond. One of the officials, Chris Stitt, tried to provide some guidance for British policy makers in London. While admitting to feeling some 'human sympathy for the Chogyal', his analysis was brutally frank:

> In this sorry and confused story scarcely any of the participants emerges with any credit. Over the years the Chogyal has been extraordinarily inept in handling his own subjects ... A more skilful and less hidebound leader might have been able to manage not only relations with the Indian Government but also to keep his own people quiet or on his side, if necessary by calculated adjustments to the need for change. By the same token the Sikkim Congress appears to have gone overboard for hamstringing or removing the Chogyal even at the expense of near-integration into India,

---

* Despite the pressure that Thondup was under during this period, he still found time to attend to protocol. US officials in Delhi reported that the embassy had received a cable addressed to the ambassador from the Chogyal and Gyalmo, dated Gangtok, 4 July: 'Our sincere good wishes on the American National Day. Please convey our warmest greetings and felicitations to His Excellency the President of America on this occasion.' It echoed the British High Commission's surprise in April 1973 when they received a birthday greeting for the Queen at the height of the troubles.

perhaps under pressure from the younger, more radical elements. In the long run this may well prove an expensive error since they could find they have exchanged a relatively weak if stubborn master for a much more powerful and determined one.[30]

He went on to speculate, through what he admitted was a 'clouded glass', as to what the motives of the various parties were. For the Kazi and the Sikkim Congress,

> [it] may be that they are simply blindly opposed to the Chogyal; or perhaps that they see a pro-Indian stance as prudent until power is theirs; or equally possibly India may have quietly made clear that if the Chogyal is to go, then there is no possibility of a successor Sikkimese republic: the price of the Chogyal's head is absorption.

As for the Indians, while Stitt could see their 'main interest throughout has been preserving stability in an area of the utmost strategic sensitivity at a time when relations with China are still cool', he was 'quite prepared to believe that they have been unscrupulous and dishonest over some of the detailed steps' in achieving that stability. 'I have no doubt,' he wrote, 'that Indira Gandhi and her government will topple the Chogyal with the same ruthlessness with which they dealt with the rail strike,* if necessary in the teeth of international opinion. [. . .] They can rely on a malleable and chauvinistic Indian press to support them.'

'The Indian government handling of the crisis,' he concluded, 'while inept presentationally, is a further illustration of the distance Indira Gandhi has travelled from the ways of her father.'

---

* In May 1974, after Indian trade union leader George Fernandes had called a rail strike, Mrs Gandhi responded by arresting some 20,000 railway workers, crushing the strike within 20 days.

CHAPTER EIGHT

'How Can We Fight With India?'

1974

- 1 -

Thondup arrived back in Gangtok utterly dejected, bitter and angry about the way he had been treated in Delhi. During his thorough examination of the documents while in the capital, he and his legal advisers had noticed that one clause – Clause 30 – of the new act seemed to have been designed to allow for intervention in his country, by stating that 'the Sikkim Government may . . . seek participation and representation for the people of Sikkim in the political institutions of India'.

He still found it hard to believe that Mrs Gandhi would actually allow for the clause to be used, even if, as Thondup knew was likely, the Kazi had made the request. A week after returning from Delhi, he fired off a letter to her, perhaps more in hope than expectation:

> The events of the recent weeks have been disastrous to all of us. After much agony the Government of Sikkim Bill 1974 has received my assent since your Excellency advised me to give it a try, after my constitutional right of firmly placing my views before the Assembly had been completed. I still have fears over clause 30 of the Act which I pray, under your protection, will never be invoked to destroy our separate identity which has been given to us under the treaty and which has been reassured to us.[1]

But he could feel his lifelines disappearing. A few days later he wrote a morose letter to Martha Hamilton, Ishbel Ritchie's predecessor, with whom he maintained a correspondence relationship, enclosing voluminous documentation about what had taken place. 'We have been through a thoroughly bad eighteen months,' he wrote:

> What the External Affairs have done is despicable and shameful. When the whole of Gangtok from the Chief Secretary to Chaprassi, from drivers to school children, went on a peaceful demonstration they were teargassed etc., whilst other demonstrators were stopped by the CRP counter-demonstrators (mostly hired) and Border road coolies were allowed to come into Gangtok on a rampage. People were openly beaten up and some officers and their wives as well. M.S. Basnett, President of the National Party, was made to carry Congress flag and shout slogans against the Chogyal and everybody else. I feel it was only this massive demonstration by the Gangtokians that have saved us from merger. As you have always been interested in our affairs I am sending a complete set of papers which will give you the actual legal position. There is an absolute Chief Executive with an Assembly that enjoys less powers than the old Council and an enabling clause, so called, where Sikkim can be absorbed at any time.
>
> Hope, unfortunately, does not wish to return to Gangtok as life here is more mundane than aesthetic, moreover she has been openly attacked in public by the Congress. The family has not been spared in the vicious attacks on me, and the Western press seems to take up such tales as it is considered 'readable news'. We do stay together in New York whenever I am there. I was to go in September but the situation here is such that I think the children [from his first marriage] will have to return without me.

It was a plea for help – but he knew, deep down, that there was little Martha Hamilton could do. He was now on his own. The only thread he clung to was the existence of the 1950 treaty. His legal advisers were adamant that the treaty – which by definition was between two international parties, one of which he was still the titular head of – would prevent India changing Sikkim's status without consulting him.

But Clause 30 had been worded in a deliberately vague way so as to make it almost an 'enabling' document. If the Assembly made a request to India, so the clause suggested, then India had something close to an obligation to allow 'participation and representation for the people of Sikkim in the political institutions of India'. The only thing they required was the request.

And, for that, they had a willing accomplice in the Kazi.

In theory the act provided for the Chogyal to be kept informed of any further constitutional developments or changes. But this too had been cleverly worded: the act said that 'important matters' should be submitted to the Chogyal 'for his information and for his approval of the action proposed to be taken'.[2] What 'important matters' constituted was wide open to interpretation.

In any case over the next six weeks, theory counted for nothing. Pragmatism took over. No further Assembly resolutions were deemed necessary, despite this also being a requirement under the act. Instead a hasty direct request from the Kazi and four other newly appointed 'ministers' to activate Clause 30 arrived on Das's desk towards the end of July. Das forwarded the request to the Indian government; he also sent it to Thondup, who immediately challenged it. Under the 8 May Agreement, Thondup pointed out, his approval was still required for any matters which involved Indo-Sikkim relations. He received no answer from Das. On 29 July, Thondup wrote separately to Mrs Gandhi, expressing his 'strong objections to any step that might damage Sikkim's international identity and affect relations with India'[3] It was not until 28 August – a full month later – that he received an answer to this letter, and then only from the Foreign Minister, Swaran Singh. Singh's letter was dated 22 August; in it he said that the Indian government was 'looking into the legal and constitutional implications' of the Kazi's letter, adding that 'if it is found feasible to respond, we shall be happy to do so'. There was no mention of the 1950 treaty.[4]

On 29 August, the day after Thondup received Swaran Singh's letter, the reason for these delays and obfuscations became clear. Listening to a late-night news bulletin on All India Radio, Thondup and his adviser Jigdal Densapa could hardly believe their ears.[5] The report stated that Mrs Gandhi intended to introduce an 'Amendment Bill' to the Indian constitution in the Lok Sabha, the Lower House of the Indian parliament, with the aim of converting Sikkim into what was being termed an 'associate state'. Thondup was stunned. It seemed he was expected to believe that, only six short days after Swaran Singh had said they were looking into 'the legal and constitutional implications', a draft bill had been prepared and parliamentary time had been found for it to be discussed.

It was not only Thondup who was caught by surprise. If the Indian government thought that they could slip the bill through without any adverse reaction, they were mistaken. The popular *Hindustan Times* was vehement in its criticism of the government's actions. A leading article, entitled 'Kanchenjungha, Here We Come' (referencing the Sikkimese mountain), was accompanied by a cartoon entitled 'The Autumn Collection!' that depicted Indira Gandhi sashaying in an elaborate, long Himalayan dress emblazoned with the word 'Sikkim'.[6] The accompanying article was no less harsh:

> If it is not outright annexation, it comes close to it. To suggest anything else would be self-deception and compound dishonesty with folly . . . The worst suspicions about the manner in which the protector has seduced its helpless and inoffensive ward, with some genuine and much synthetic drama, will not find confirmation. No country or people voluntarily choose self-effacement, and the Indian Government is not going to be able to persuade the world that Sikkim's 'annexation' to India represents the will of the Sikkimese people. Indeed this issue has never been placed before them.[7]

But even the timing of the All India Radio announcement had been carefully planned, made late on a Thursday, leaving only one day before the weekend. First thing on Monday morning the bill was formally introduced in the Indian parliament. Foreign Minister Swaran Singh's opening statement left the MPs in no doubt about the nature of the action. The bill was, he said, 'a political matter and not a question of legal niceties'. But the growing opposition in the Lok Sabha to Indira Gandhi's autocratic government would not be silenced; MP after MP pointed out that, political matter or not, the bill opened up a constitutional can of worms: the Congress (O) accused the government of outright 'procedural and constitutional impropriety', calling the new status a 'disparate marriage between a republic and a monarchy'[8]; the Jana Sangh, a Hindu nationalist opposition party, criticised the bill for not going far enough, creating an unworkable and meaningless halfway house of 'associate state'. And, others asked, if the people had voted *for* this new status (the government was arguing that the 1974 elections were a vote for accession to the union), did that imply that they could later reverse it and *leave* the union by a further vote *against* it?

Awkward questions were asked about the wider impact, too. What were the implications for other troublesome border states: could the bill encourage separatist tendencies in other areas? What was to stop Nagaland, Mizoram or even Kashmir arguing that they too should qualify for this nebulous new 'associate' status within the union? What about the impact on relations with neighbouring countries? The CPM berated the government for not considering the inevitable adverse reaction from China; Mrs Gandhi's own MPs even expressed concern over the potential Nepali reaction.

All were valid questions – but all were brushed aside. Congress (R)'s substantial parliamentary majority ensured that the bill was pushed through that same day in the Lok Sabha; by Friday it had also passed the Rajya Sabha, the Upper House of the Indian parliament.[9]

An editorial in the *Hindustan Times* was one of the few that directly criticised the action in strong terms: 'Only the most blind or cynical will derive any satisfaction over the sorry progression of the Indian presence in Sikkim from that of friend to master.'[10]

Even as the parliament was making decisions on the future of his country, Thondup sought another meeting with Mrs Gandhi. This time she flatly refused to see him.

Depressed and worn down, Thondup flew to Calcutta instead to hold a press conference. He was well aware that the attention Mrs Gandhi's actions were receiving from the international press gave him an opportunity. Choosing his words carefully, he painted Sikkim as an innocent victim without the resources to adequately challenge the unilateral Indian action. 'Ours is a protectorate of India, a very small state,' he was reported as telling journalists. 'How can we fight with India?' To resolve the matter he would rely on India's 'sense of justice' rather than pursuing things 'at an International level'.

But many other Sikkimese felt that India's 'sense of justice' had now been casually cast aside. As the reality of what the bill meant seeped through into Sikkim, people began to realise how momentous the bill was and how it threatened the country's separate identity. What had started as a movement for democratic change within Sikkim had been hijacked and now threatened the very existence of Sikkim itself.

It was also now impossible for anyone to suggest that the opposition to Sikkim's new status as an associate state was solely from the Palace and the Chogyal's Bhutia community. It was a *Nepali* schoolmaster from Sikkim, Nar Bahadur Bhandari, who led a brave delegation to the Indian capital to meet with Mrs Gandhi. The angry delegates told her that they were vehemently opposed to the speed and the manner of events taking place in Delhi. But Mrs Gandhi reassured Bhandari and his ten colleagues that Sikkim's 'distinct personality' would be respected under the new legislation. Besides, she was able to point out, the act was merely a response to a request from the leader of a legitimate democratically elected Assembly.

There was very little Bhandari could say to that. The Indians had done their preparation well.

-2-

In Gangtok, Das and Bajpai were understandably concerned by what was now evidently the growing potential for violent confrontations.

After the troubles in June they decided they could take no chances. Security was tightened; they could not risk further protests. Indian Central Reserve Police suddenly became a prominent feature on the streets. Ishbel Ritchie, travelling to Darjeeling, found that the CRP were 'stopping all vehicles and are inclined to whack a piece of luggage when demanding to know what is in it'.

The febrile atmosphere even extended to her classroom:

The local students, mostly the Boys' School, and, I'm sorry to say, ours have been conducting an agitation of their own since Thurs. because they are upset about Sikkim's new status & are v confused and upset without really understanding why. They've got themselves well on the wrong side of the authorities (and I fear have probably cooked the school's goose well and truly thereby). They have not been helped by a lack of understanding in other quarters and the whole thing has fermented in a way that could probably have been avoided with more tact.

Everything came to a head a few days later, when the police visited the school and interrogated Ritchie herself:

> I feel as though I've been through a mangle . . . I personally was accused of 'engaging in political activities' and 'allowing my political sensitivities to influence the admin of the school.' (This presumably would mean, if it means anything, that I am encouraging a hotbed of Scottish nationalism! But it is not, I think, what it is intended to mean.) The evidence for this seems to be some vague answer of some of the children to loaded questions put to them about what they are taught in school, but I have not been able to get any direct answer on this.

Despite the press being kept out of Gangtok, US Ambassador Moynihan in Delhi had managed to stay on top of events in Sikkim. From his desk in Delhi, he and his team catalogued in meticulous detail what they could glean from their network of agents about events, recording the international reaction for digestion by Kissinger and the State Department in Washington. Since the nuclear test in May, Moynihan had redoubled his efforts to repair relations between the two countries, efforts that were to culminate in a visit by Kissinger himself to Delhi at the end of October. An ugly dispute over tiny Sikkim, Moynihan and Washington agreed, was in nobody's interest.

In case of awkward press enquiries, on 11 September Washington sent out to its embassies across South Asia a set of prepared questions and evasive answers. The Q&A demonstrated the extreme sensitivity that Washington attached to the matter – particularly the possibility of criticisms of double standards through comparisons with the American involvement in Vietnam:

> Q. Do you have anything to say about India taking over Sikkim, which is, apparently, a sovereign state of its own?

A: No, I don't have anything to say. That is one problem that we are not involved in.

Q. What about the principle, though, of a larger country taking over a smaller one?

A. I don't wish to comment on the affair between Sikkim and India here.

Q: Are you saying in effect we are not concerned when a large country takes over a small one?

A: This is a very complicated parliamentary question that is being taken up in New Delhi, and I don't wish to comment on the merits of it – nor on the deliberations of the National Assembly of Sikkim. I think you can read some of the details of that yourself.

END QUOTE. KISSINGER UNQUOTE. KISSINGER.[11]

If it was a calculated move to improve relations between the US and India, it had the desired effect. Two days later N. B. Menon from External Affairs wrote to the embassy 'to express appreciation of the sensitivity of the US Government to Government of India concerns on this issue.'[12]

Washington had also realised that their implicit recognition of India's rights to control Sikkim's affairs might be a useful bargaining chip in their broader relations with the Government of India. For some time, the Chinese had been pressurising the US to recognise their de facto control in the Himalayan border area of Aksai Chin, to the west of Nepal (that had been fought over in 1962), which, they noted, US government maps still showed as disputed territory, with competing Indian and Chinese claims.[13] Given that it was, in fact, standard US government policy to show 'de facto lines of control' rather than competing claims, Washington spotted an opportunity for some diplomatic manoeuvring.

They flew a kite past the embassies in Delhi, Kathmandu and Dhaka. To persuade the Indians to give up their notional claims to Aksai Chin (and thus allow the map change that the Chinese were seeking), Washington suggested it might be willing to consider that the 'dotted border and separate identification of Sikkim might (rpt might) also be eliminated'. The changes could be made after Kissinger's proposed visit. How did the embassies think their host countries might react?

Moynihan was cautious – the Aksai Chin change would 'annoy the Government of India and generate a continuing hum in our dealings', although he acknowledged that the Sikkim trade-off 'should help'. The Nepali ambassador's reply was quite different – and illustrated the competing agendas in the region. The Government of Nepal, he reported back, would have 'no problem' with US recognition of Aksai Chin per se; but they felt that 'US Government acknowledgement of the new Indo-Sikkimese relationship' would not only be 'unnecessary', but would also be 'likely to add to Nepali apprehensions and could resurrect past concerns, which over the years we have tried to dispel, that we see India's relations with its neighbours through Indian eyes'.

Whatever the rights or wrongs of the Indian action in Sikkim, recognition of the country's right to exist had now become a commodity to be traded within the larger context of Asian politics.

The years when Thondup assisted the CIA in the 1950s by running their messages to Lhasa counted for nothing.

Meanwhile, across the key Asian countries there was a vociferous reaction to India's action in making Sikkim an associate state.

In Pakistan, President Bhutto was quick to put his own spin on the events in Sikkim. The Indian government's actions were, he said publicly,

> simply the latest demonstration of their psychosis – a craze to dominate, to spread their wings . . . we stand vindicated in our analysis. They marched into Goa and took that. They have gone nuclear. And now they have swallowed up Sikkim. . . Dr Kissinger ought to consider Sikkim when he comes here. But this must be something he does on his own. We can't keep telling him what India's intentions are, showing the maps.[14]

Unless someone confronted India, Bhutto added, Bhutan would be next.* Privately, he was even more vehement; when he met with Kissinger during the latter's tour of the subcontinent at the end of the month, he again put Sikkim in a category with Bangladesh as providing clear evidence of India's hegemonistic desire in Asia. Kissinger agreed – he thought India 'had their eyes on Nepal' – but told Bhutto he still could not understand

---

* In fact, the Bhutanese themselves were 'quiet as mice', Moynihan reported. They knew full well that they had achieved what they needed already – the protection that came from being a member of the UN.

the rationale for what had taken place in Sikkim. 'Why did they do it?' Kissinger asked Bhutto. 'Didn't they already control the foreign policy of Sikkim?' Bhutto's reply put Sikkim firmly into his own grand narrative of the region. The Indians, he said, 'continue to get more arrogant. It's outside the scope of logic. They lie. It is the history of the Sub-Continent.'*

Reaction in Nepal to what had happened in Sikkim was far more visceral. Within days of the announcement of the constitutional amendment bill, there had been mass student demonstrations on the streets of Nepal against the Indian action. Government troops had to prevent protestors wielding banners with slogans such as 'Indira Gandhi stay home' and 'Indians out of Sikkim' from marching on the Indian compound.

But it was the Chinese press that attacked India most aggressively. On 4 September, within a couple of days of the introduction of the bill, the *Chinese People's Daily* condemned this 'despicable act of the Indian government' as a 'grave incident', an attempt to reduce Sikkim to a 'colony' which would shatter Sino-Indian relations. The Lok Sabha debate showed, they asserted, that the 'clumsy trick is crystal clear even to the Indians'. The blame lay fairly and squarely at the door of the Indian prime minister: 'Nehru and his daughter have always acted this way and Indira Gandhi has gone further.'†

They also issued a stark warning that 'India's expansionist and aggressive ambition is not limited to Sikkim' and were quick to make accusations of Indo-Soviet collusion:

> Facts have shown once again that Soviet revisionist social-imperialism and Indian expansionism constitute a serious threat to the independence and sovereignty of the South Asian Countries and are the main cause of the unstable situation in the South Asian sub-continent.[15]

The Indian expansionists and their Soviet protectors were 'blind men and fools'.

---

* Bhutto's indignation did not, however, prevent him from quietly taking over the area of Hunza only a few weeks later. Hunza, a Princely State in the northern areas of Pakistan, had survived beyond Indian independence, like Sikkim. Mrs Gandhi was quick to suggest that the action in Hunza was not much different from her own actions in Sikkim.

† Ironically it was this personal criticism of Indira Gandhi that caused the most concern to the Indian government, as it was seen as a departure from a long-established protocol not to personalise commentary on political affairs.

A few days later the Chinese Foreign Ministry went further by suggesting that India had 'inherited the mantle of imperialism' and had 'always pursued a colonialist policy towards Sikkim'. They reiterated their view that Soviet revisionist social-imperialism was 'the boss behind the scene as well as the abettor of Indian expansionism'.[16]

The accusations of imperialism in particular severely aggravated Mrs Gandhi – the idea that she was in some way an inheritor of the worst excesses of the British colonial tradition was one that annoyed her intensely.

But the Chinese showed no intention of letting up. They were determined to use events in Sikkim to demonstrate the 'danger' that India – supported by the Soviet Union – posed to the region. On 3 October they went as far as to raise the matter at the UN.

Finally, Thondup had the UN debate that he had sought for so long. The Chinese UN representative, Qiao Guanghua, explicitly called the action in Sikkim an 'annexation' (echoing the headline from the *Hindustan Times* a month earlier), adding that it was 'another naked act of expansionism perpetrated by the Indian Government after dismembering Pakistan by armed force'. Perhaps the most remarkable accusation, though, was reserved for the Soviet Union. Qiao raised the spectre that the action in Sikkim might be a new imperialist thrust by Soviet Russia. Reiterating the claim that the Soviets were 'the boss behind the scenes of Indian expansionism', he suggested that they were spurred by 'dreams of opening a corridor to the Indian Ocean', precisely the charge that had been levelled at the Russians a century before during an earlier period of intrigue. Events in Sikkim showed, Qiao was suggesting, that the Great Game was still alive and well in the Himalayas.[17]

In reality, the Chinese comments had little to do with compassion for the fate of Thondup and Sikkim, and far more to do with labyrinthine geopolitical manoeuvring. Moynihan's number two, David T. Schneider, was sure that the Chinese portrayal of the Soviets was simply part of a wider strategy to highlight Soviet influence in New Delhi. Not that he thought the Soviets would mind that – they would be 'almost certainly pleased at the blow-up over Sikkim which serves Soviet interests in arousing Indian concerns over Chinese intentions, and thus revives in many minds here the importance of the Indo-Soviet treaty link.'[18]

The Soviet 'information (or disinformation) mills', he added, had been 'operating full blast' to ensure that the Himalayas remained 'a wedge between the two Asian neighbors', going as far as to place newspaper stories that 'China was deploying nuclear rockets in Tibet "which would hurtle over Indian territory in test launchings."'

Schneider's boss Ambassador Moynihan noted that this complex dance between the Chinese and the Soviets left the Indians 'caught in a cleft stick'. The Sikkim issue, he pointed out in a broad assessment of the Asian scene in early October, was intricately bound up with India's economic crisis and with the question of arms supplies in the region:

[The Indians] do need Moscow. Chinese posturing over Sikkim, even if only that, has again raised the problem of the Chinese threat which precipitated the signing of the Friendship treaty in 1971. Soviet prices for military goods are high and the equipment not always what the Indian military wants. But it is available for rupees and European equipment is not. The trade relationship [with the Soviets] is not indispensable, but does pay the bills for military equipment and modest imports of badly needed commodities. Nor does Delhi want to risk Moscow's turning to woo Pakistan with cakes and missiles . . .[19]

The Americans were right: Asia had turned into a swirling mass of competing priorities, as countries emerging from the emasculation of the colonial era sought to reassert themselves. The Chinese attempt to raise Sikkim as an issue in the United Nations – which, unsurprisingly, came to nothing – was as much a test of the limits or otherwise of the newfound power of the People's Republic of China in the UN (only theirs since 1971) as it was a show of support for the tiny Himalayan kingdom.

But behind the Chinese bluster over Sikkim, the country's leader was in fact just as puzzled as everyone else over why India had moved so suddenly to convert Sikkim into an untried and untested status as an associate state. In a meeting between new Chinese Vice-Premier Deng Xiaoping and Kissinger in November, Deng admitted that he was mystified by Indian policy in general, and by the Indian action in Sikkim in particular. If it was prompted by fears of a conflict between India and China in the Himalaya, he said, that was plainly ludicrous: he knew that his own troops hated the Tibetan plateau and he found it hard to believe that India could have any strategic interest in such a forbidding place. It was an extraordinary exchange – and a demonstration of just how easy the relationship between the top echelons in the US and in China had now become:

Vice-Premier Deng: 'There is something very peculiar about Indian policy. For example, that little kingdom of Sikkim. They had pretty good control of Sikkim. Why did they have to annex it?'

Secretary Kissinger: 'It is a good thing India is pacifist. I hate to think [of what they would do] if they weren't.' [Laughter]

Vice-Premier Deng: 'Sikkim was entirely under the military control of India.'

Secretary Kissinger: 'I haven't understood Sikkim. It is incomprehensible.'

Vice-Premier Deng: 'After the military annexation, their military position was in no way strengthened.'

Secretary Kissinger: 'They had troops there already.'

Vice-Premier Deng: 'And they haven't increased their troops there. We published a statement about it. We just spoke up for the sake of justice.'

Secretary Kissinger: 'Is it true that you have set up loudspeakers to broadcast to the Indian troops on the border? It makes them very tense.' [Laughter]

Vice-Premier Deng: 'We have done nothing new along the borders, and frankly we don't fear that India will attack our borders. We don't think they have the capability of attacking our borders. There was some very queer talk, some said that the reason why the Chinese Government issued that statement about Sikkim was that the Chinese were afraid after Sikkim that India would complete the encirclement of China. Well, in the first place, we never feel things like isolation or encirclement can ever matter very much with us. And particularly with India, it is not possible that India can do any encirclement of China. The most they can do is enter Chinese territory as far as the autonomous Republic of Tibet, Lhasa. And Lhasa can be of no strategic importance to India. The particular characteristic of Lhasa is it has no air – because the altitude is more than 3,000 meters. During the Long March we did cross the region of Tibet.'

Secretary Kissinger: 'Really.'

Vice-Premier Deng: 'Not the Lhasa area, but the southern part. Our experience was that when we wanted to take one step further, we couldn't.'

Secretary Kissinger: 'It is a very dangerous area for drinking *mao tai*.'* [Laughter]

Vice-Premier Deng: 'Frankly, if Indian troops were able to reach Lhasa, we wouldn't be able to supply them enough air.' [Laughter][20]

Deng was able to dismiss the idea of any Indian threat to Lhasa so breezily because China was now fully confident that it had complete control of Tibet. In October 1974, two months before Deng and Kissinger's friendly exchange, they had also put an end once and for all to the Tibetan guerrilla base in the Mustang Valley.

Mao's Cultural Revolution of the late 1960s and early 1970s had seen a brutal crackdown on any resistance to Chinese rule. They had stripped the remnants of the Buddhist theocratic order of any pretence to autonomy. At the same time the people suffered a terrible famine. Internal resistance to the Chinese presence in Tibet had ended. But one pocket of active resistance had survived high up in the Mustang Valley on the Tibet–Nepal border. While the Americans and the Indians had long ago dropped their practical assistance for the Mustang Valley Tibetans,† Birendra's Nepali government, by turning a blind eye to their activities, had effectively continued to support them. This had understandably aggravated the Chinese. In December 1973 Chairman Mao had told Birendra bluntly that he could not tolerate this any longer. Birendra, who, in the wake of the events in Sikkim, wanted to keep China onside, agreed.

It was no coincidence, therefore, that it had been shortly after the Indians had forced through the Sikkim Government Bill in late June 1974 that the Nepali government finally issued a deadline of 26 July for the Khampa force to give up their weapons. When word reached the beleaguered guerrilla fighters, they were hopelessly split – some wanted

---

* A popular Chinese liquor.

† Many Tibetans believe that the US had dropped support for Tibet at the insistence of the Chinese during Nixon's talks in Beijing in February 1972. (Kraus, *Orphans of the Cold War*, p. 72)

to confront the Nepalis, who they felt had betrayed them; others were persuaded by a dramatic last-minute taped appeal from the Dalai Lama (who saw that continued resistance could only lead to bloodshed) to lay down their arms and accept the Nepali ultimatum. Two companies refused to surrender and fled in a daring march west towards the Indian border, hopping back and forth between Nepal and Tibet. Pursued, harassed and tricked by the Nepali Army, most of these either surrendered or were captured in late August.

By the second week of September, just 40 guerrillas on horseback were left. As the bedraggled group approached the 5,394-metre Tinkar Pass from western Nepal into India, the Nepali Army were waiting, ordered to prevent their escape to India. A sharp-eyed Nepali sergeant spotted them, shooting and killing two (including the infamous leader Wangdu) and wounding another. The rest made a frantic final dash across the border, clambering up a recess that hid them from view of the Nepali. On the Indian side, the American embassy later reported, '600 Indians had their toes on the border waiting to greet the Khampas'. Some reports said that Indian jets had violated Nepali airspace to provide air cover.[21]

The Khampas' two decades fighting for Tibet's freedom from the Mustang Valley were over. But these events also had other ramifications in the region. When combined with the riots in Kathmandu in early September, the whole episode reinforced the antagonism that had been developing between Indira Gandhi and the Nepali king, Birendra, and his royalist followers. Reports suggesting that some Khampas had also fled into Sikkim to support the Chogyal only exacerbated the situation.

It was hardly a surprise when Washington received a cable from the US embassy in Kathmandu in early October painting a dire picture of the prospects for the region:

In the aftermath of the Indian squeeze on Sikkim, the Nepalese are begin-ning to ask themselves whether Nepal is next on India's list. It would there-fore be prudent for us to ask ourselves whether Indo-Nepalese relations are taking on a fundamentally new shape which could shatter the tenuous Pax Himalaya which has obtained over the past decade.[22]

Back in Gangtok, few had thoughts for anything beyond the immediate. While Sikkim was discussed in Peking and Kathmandu, the reality on the streets was of continuing violence, and consequent repression.

Ishbel Ritchie continued to get some news out, despite the persistent attentions of the censors, whose efforts made sending letters to her mother a bit like 'shooting off arrows without knowing where or whether they will land'. To confuse the censors, she reverted to broad Scots again: 'Aiblins the fowk wi the lang nebs hae been owre eident,' she wrote, no doubt chuckling in the absolute certainty that no minor Indian official would have access to a Scots – let alone an Ulster Scots – dictionary.* Despite the 'lang nebs', she still found ways to communicate the facts to her mother: some of the disturbances were turning ugly, with stones and 'petrol-soaked sacks' being 'flung sporadically from a higher road'. The students at the school were continuing to conduct agitations, she wrote, resulting in attendances slipping to 20 per cent at one point.

The escalating violence left Thondup more and more depressed, 'clearly dejected that his kingdom has been "sold down the river"', an article in the *Far Eastern Economic Review* noted. He blamed himself for his country's woes, but he was also caught off-guard by Indian actions and was unsure how to react to such blatant disregard for the law. As the *Far Eastern Economic Review* correspondent wrote, even the protests were being wilfully misrepresented: there was a 'hollowness' to

> official Indian statements about 'popular movements in Sikkim for greater independence in India'. During two weeks here, the only 'popular move-ments' this correspondent witnessed were demonstrations against the Indian incorporation of Sikkim, which the Indian police ensured were brief and not to be repeated.[23]

Thondup still, however, refused to believe that Mrs Gandhi was respon-sible for what had happened. He was certain that in the final analysis it

---

* Translation from the Ulster Scots: 'Perhaps the people with the long noses have been over-diligent.'

could not have been her that let him down, and that her actions over the previous months had been 'the result of the incorrect advice she has been fed'. Kewal Singh, the Indian Foreign Secretary, was Thondup's prime suspect. He was convinced that Singh had led a conspiracy against him, orchestrating everything. In a long, accusatory legal letter, a copy of which found its way into the British Foreign Office's secret files (released in 2005 under the 30-year rule), he wrote bitterly to Singh that the peaceful Sikkimese demonstrators on 20 June (at the time of the Government of Sikkim Bill) had been 'brutally stoned, beaten and teargassed by the CRP [Central Reserve Police]'; that the Indian foreign ministry had consistently 'either ignored or have been completely misled on the true position in Sikkim'; and that members of the Sikkim Assembly were 'openly indulging in daylight kidnapping of opposition leaders, students and others even in the presence of the CRP'. But what Thondup resented most was the accusation that his family had been involved in creating and promoting a poster campaign against Mrs Gandhi herself:

It is alleged that vulgar and obscene posters attacking Mrs Gandhi have been printed under the instigation and supervision of my sister, Princess Coocoola, in her house. To attribute such behaviour to our family is utterly repulsive and shocks our conscience particularly in view of the position we hold in Sikkim. Whatever our faults may be, it must be conceded that we have not as yet found it necessary to indulge in vulgarity or obsceni-ties to express our differences of opinion against anybody least of all the Prime Minister of India. I can only state that these allegations against my family and myself are being made with the ulterior and malicious motive to give events in Sikkim an anti-Indian colour, so that vested interests can somehow force the Government of India to take an overt anti-Chogyal stand.[24]

Singh knew perfectly well whom Thondup meant when he referred to the 'vested interests' accused of taking an 'anti-Chogyal stand': the Kazi and his foster son, Khatiawara. Thondup was sure that the bogus poster campaign was just another of the radical positions that the 25-year-old Khatiawara was taking in his thirst for power, funded by carefully distrib-uted piles of cash.

But many who saw the posters on the walls of buildings around Sikkim were convinced that the posters had, in fact, been produced by sources linked to and funded by Indian intelligence – and therefore to the Indian government itself – in an effort to discredit Thondup.

Within two weeks of the passing of the constitutional amendment, K. Shankar Bajpai and B. S. Das had been shipped out of Sikkim. Bajpai had arrived in Sikkim in 1970, expecting a two-year posting – in the event, he had served four. By the time he left, his health was suffering; he was more than ready to go. Das was easily lured away by an offer to become chairman of the International Airports Authority of India.*

Their replacements underlined the seriousness with which Delhi now took Sikkim. Bajpai's successor was Gurbachan Singh, a man with strong connections with the Research and Analysis Wing of Indian intelligence. Das was replaced as chief executive by a wily and experienced professional administrator, B. B. Lal, a man of far greater stature than any of the Indian-appointed dewans, principal administrative officers, sidlons or chief executives that had come before him.† The advent of these two men – both known for their ruthless streak – was a clear sign of India's intentions.

The change in tone was immediately apparent.

Lal wasted no time in making sweeping changes throughout Sikkim. He started with the Namgyal family powerbase. Some of the actions were petty and seemed calculated to cause offence: the family's name was removed wherever it occurred. The Namgyal Institute of Tibetology, opened by the Dalai Lama and promoted by Nehru, became simply the 'Institute of Tibetology'; the Palden Thondup Institute became the 'Cottage Industries Institute'; Thondup was replaced by the Kazi as chairman of the Tashi Namgyal Academy, the school set up in honour of Thondup's own father. Other actions were aimed at stripping the family of their financial base: the palace budget was slashed by 75 per cent; none of the money that had traditionally been allotted to the Sikkim Guards

---

* He would later run Air India (then government-owned) as chairman-cum-managing director before moving into the private sector.

† In an interview in 2012, Bajpai chuckled as he recalled that Thondup was heard to say: 'Bajpai may have been a B------, but now they have sent me a Double B------!'

was released; the family money set aside for educating the children now in New York was refused.

These arrows aimed at Thondup's personal situation were nothing compared with the determined way in which Lal set about trying to change the way the law worked in Sikkim. Thondup knew that the judicial system was something that he had to defend with all his might – a vital symbol that would allow him, as long as it was independent of Indian law, to argue for Sikkim's distinct identity. Lal saw this too, and was just as determined to bring Sikkim's law within the ambit of New Delhi. The battle for the judicial system became a proxy for the two men's personal antipathy.

Thondup took advantage of the fact that the events of 1973 and 1974 had left the situation regarding Sikkim's legal system hopelessly confused. At the time of the disturbances in April 1973 Thondup had been in the midst of making major reforms to the judicial set-up, seeking to abolish an outdated and irregular system where four highly independent area judges operated their own fiefdoms to one where there was a centralised judiciary with a guaranteed independence from the executive. Some of the reforms had later been implemented, but the overall situation remained extremely confused. The agreement of 8 May 1973 offered one view of how justice should work; the Government of Sikkim Act of June 1974 offered another, completely different. How both were affected by Sikkim becoming an associate state of the union was completely unclear. Did Indian law apply? If so, in what cases? Lal's solution – that, as he was chief executive of Sikkim (and Sikkim was an associate state), the judiciary should report directly to him – was easy for Thondup to attack as a subversion of the fundamental building block of any functioning democracy: that executive and judicial powers should be separate. Thondup also argued that if the Indians were serious about him continuing as some form of 'constitutional monarch' then that should include a role as the apolitical head of the legal system.

But while Thondup searched for ways to challenge Lal's actions, an increasingly dark side to the new arrangements in Sikkim emerged. A demonstration by the Sikkim Students Association was broken up with a level of violence clearly designed to ensure there would be no reoccurrence. The Kazi claimed Thondup was involved in subversive activities against the state, accusing him and his son Tenzing of 'instigating and supporting anti-social and anti-democratic elements'. The palace was increasingly 'depicted as the nerve-centre of murderous activities'. In December, when explosives were found on a road in southern Sikkim on which the Kazi and Kazini had recently travelled, a whispering campaign suggested that it had been Thondup and Tenzing who had been plotting to kill them.

Within days, half a dozen young men were arrested under extraordinary security powers.

The noose was tightening.

CHAPTER NINE

'They've A' Gane Clean Gyte'*

1975

-1-

As 1975 dawned, Sikkim seemed to be caught in a kind of purgatory, a halfway house, neither in nor out of the Indian Union, neither with nor without a constitution. Thondup's position was entirely unclear; the Kazi was increasingly acting as the stooge of an all-powerful Indian chief executive; the Assembly were losing credibility with an electorate who had voted them in before the manipulated events of June and September 1974.

But internationally there were clear signs that Sikkim's claims to an identity separate from that of India were gently slipping away, not least in the actions of those organisations tasked with making the decisions on how to categorise a 'country'. The London-based *Statesman's Yearbook*, seen as the arbiter of such matters, wondered if now was the time for a change. The editor approached the Foreign Office for advice, wondering if at last

> events in Sikkim may well mean that the country should be placed in the Indian section as a dependency. It is only in recent years I have separated it because I received considerable pressure from the Chogyal, via his solicitors in London. It is possible that I made a mistake in bending to his wishes although a recent article in the *Times* does suggest that Sikkim is very much a dependency of India.[1]

---

* Translation from Scots: 'They've all gone completely crazy.'

In New York, the Freedom House organisation went even further in their January 1975 report, deleting 'the formerly independent state of Sikkim'. The report, picked up by the US embassy in Delhi, included its rationale:

> It is argued by some Indians that recent changes in the status of Sikkim should not be interpreted as incorporation, yet it seems to us that the State's inclusion in Indian Economic plans, its representation in parliament, and Indian acceptance of responsibility for its administration reduced Sikkim's sovereignty to that of the Isle of Guernsey within the United Kingdom . . . on the other hand, freedom may have been *increased* by Indian interference in Sikkim.[2]

But even if the world's almanac publishers and freedom promoters were giving up on the idea of an independent Sikkim, the two Indian administrators in India's new associate state – B. B. Lal and Gurbachan Singh – were well aware that they would never have total control until they resolved one critical issue: the future of Palden Thondup Namgyal, Chogyal of Sikkim. As long as he remained in Sikkim with a nebulous and ill-defined position, Indian authority would always be open to question. Some in India still argued that there could be a role for Thondup as constitutional head of Sikkim, but the awkward moniker of associate state made even this virtually impossible. In any case they were outweighed by those in Indira's circle who felt strongly that he had to go.

In February 1975, an opportunity arose to resolve the issue of the Chogyal once and for all.

Despite acceding to the throne of Nepal in 1972, the date for Birendra's coronation was not confirmed until early 1975. Invitations were sent out to the world's leaders, announcing that the event would take place on 24 February. Birendra planned a major celebration. He wanted it to become a showcase for presenting Nepal to the world. He also intended to use the occasion to propose that Nepal become an official 'Zone of Peace'.

When Mrs Gandhi heard of Birendra's 'Zone of Peace' proposal, she was appalled, convinced that it was a ploy to extricate Nepal from the security obligations to India under the 1950 treaty by placing its relations with India on a par with its relations with China. For that reason, she also saw the Nepali king's coronation as an opportunity to make a point.

To emphasise the subordinate nature of Nepal, she announced that only India's vice-president (not the president, as diplomatic protocol would have dictated) would attend. It was a clear snub and did not augur well: for the Bhutanese coronation the previous year, India had sent its president.

But it was Thondup's invitation, which arrived in Gangtok in the middle of January, that raised awkward questions. The most obvious of which was who should actually decide whether he attended or not, now that Sikkim was an associate state of the Indian republic. The External Affairs Ministry in Delhi was well aware that direct intervention would create a storm. Instead they made clear to the Nepali government that while it was Thondup's decision to attend, if he *were* to accept the invitation (and they assumed that he would) there would be trouble if the Nepali extended any 'sovereign courtesies' to him.[3]

Thondup briefly considered sending Tenzing and avoiding a fight. Nine days before the date of the coronation, he changed his mind. He informed Political Officer Gurbachan Singh that he himself would attend, accompanied by Captain Yongda of the Sikkim Guards* and two other aides. Singh had no choice but to give his blessing.

But on the morning of departure on 21 February, as the small party prepared to leave, Chief Executive Lal arrived at the palace. The Sikkimese cabinet, he announced, did not approve of Thondup attending the coronation. As such, it would be wrong to allow the trip to go ahead. When Thondup told Lal that he could not possibly cancel at such late notice, Lal responded roughly that if he decided to go, he 'would have to face the consequences'.[4] After some frantic discussions, Thondup decided to stick to his plan and to set off that afternoon, albeit with a reduced entourage – he would be accompanied by Captain Yongda but they would also take the Indian head of the Sikkim Police with them, an added protection that Lal, who knew the Indian government was still very much responsible for Thondup's safety, insisted upon. The Kazi was furious that Thondup should be representing Sikkim once again – and under Indian protection.

Even as they left Gangtok in the palace Mercedes they passed small groups of protestors loitering by the road. With Yongda in the front with the driver and the Chogyal in the back with the chief of police, they descended

---

* The monk I met at Pemayangtse in 2009 (see Introduction).

towards the border with West Bengal from where they intended to take the road west to the Nepali border. As they approached Singtam Bridge – still well inside Sikkim – there was a loud crack, as something hit the rim of the windscreen. As the driver swerved, Yongda, thinking that it was a bullet or a missile and they were under attack, shouted to the driver to stop so that they could cordon off the area and find out what had happened. The police chief in the back countermanded Yongda's order, yelling at him to speed up and get out of the area as fast as possible.

Shaken, the passengers in the Mercedes continued down the road, hoping that it had been an isolated incident. But as they approached the border post at Rangpo, there was a far more visible problem. Half a dozen bitumen barrels had been spread out to block the road. Fearing an ambush, Yongda told the driver to swing left onto the monsoon road that climbed up to Kalimpong. It was a long diversion, but Yongda knew that in Kalimpong they could pause in relative safety in the compound of the royal queen grandmother.

Just before nightfall they reached Kalimpong, where the local West Bengal Police promised to provide them with security for the drive to the Nepali border. None of them slept much that evening. They left Kalimpong at midnight, driving through the night to Siliguri and reaching the border crossing with some relief. A Nepali government escort took over. There was a distinct change in atmosphere: as they travelled through the east of Nepal to Kathmandu, they found that each district commissioner had organised a reception for them.[5]

At the coronation itself, Thondup immediately set about associating with as many foreign dignitaries as he could. News of the eventful journey from Gangtok started to spread. Thondup recounted the story of what had happened at Singtam Bridge – which rapidly became an 'assassination attempt' in the retelling – to as many people as possible, including Lord Mountbatten (representing the Queen) and Senator Charles Percy (attending on behalf of Gerald Ford, the new US President). The two Indian ministers and their officials watched nervously, reporting back to Delhi. Birendra, they also noted, spent more than an hour talking to Thondup in private, twice the time he spent with anyone else. When he was spotted not only conversing with a representative of Pakistan but also spending time with China's Vice-Premier Chen Hsi-lien, the rumour mills went into overdrive. The Indian press 'screamed that with the USA, Britain, China and Nepal behind him, he [the Chogyal] was going to appeal to the UN; All India Radio, an arm of the government mockingly called "All Indira radio", led the attack. The sinister aim, they said, was to convert Sikkim into a beachhead of Western Imperialism'.[6]

Thondup's presence at the coronation was fast becoming a more important talking point than the event itself. He did not help matters when he held a press conference after the ceremony. He would, he told the press, 'leave no stone unturned' in seeking to preserve Sikkim's identity, and dramatically challenged the legitimacy of the September 1974 constitutional amendment that had made Sikkim into an associate state of India. If the Indian government believed there was support for the Amendment, they should hold 'a free and fair referendum' in Sikkim to validate it. King Birendra, recognising the seriousness of what Thondup had just done – directly questioning the Indian government's actions of the previous September – suggested that Thondup should stay in Nepal at least until things settled down. But Thondup was determined to return to Sikkim. Abandoning the Mercedes in Kathmandu, he flew to Calcutta with Yongda, where Thondup repeated his call for a referendum in another press conference.

They remained in Calcutta for two days, staying with Karma Topden, Thondup's former head of intelligence, who now lived there. The day after the press conference, Topden warned them that he had heard reports that they were likely to be attacked on their way into Sikkim by protestors angry that the Chogyal had gone to Kathmandu.

Thondup was determined not to be intimidated. Accompanied by a West Bengal police escort, Thondup and Yongda set off across the plains for the Sikkim border.

While the coronation had been taking place in Kathmandu, the Kazi had gone on the attack in Gangtok, whipping up anti-Thondup sentiment. He was furious that his newfound position as elected leader in Sikkim had been undermined. The press conferences in Nepal and Calcutta, he fumed, were a sign that Thondup had lost all credibility and that the position of Chogyal had become a joke, an anomaly in the new world of Sikkim. He told reporters that there was now a complete breakdown of trust between the Government of Sikkim and the Chogyal. The suggestion that Thondup had been talking openly with the Chinese was evidence of the gravity of the situation. He said he would be writing to the new Foreign Minister in Delhi, demanding that the Chogyal be removed.

Others in Sikkim, in particular those of Nepali background, were just as aggravated by the reports of the Chogyal's activities in Kathmandu. Many had relatives or friends who were associated with the Nepal Congress Party, which had been banned by King Birendra for more than a decade; some felt a close political affinity with that movement. Some, in particular Assembly members, were doubly offended – not only had Thondup's claim to be speaking for Sikkim undermined the Assembly's authority but also he seemed to be positioning himself alongside Birendra, a man they associated with political repression of those in Nepal who they considered their ethnic kin. The alarmist Indian press coverage, painting Thondup as a Chinese fifth columnist, only worsened matters. Given the choice between China and India, very few would choose China.

The leader of the Youth wing of the Sikkim Congress, R. C. Poudyal (one of the two young men who had gone on hunger strike in April 1973), was one of those most vehement in his criticism of what had taken place in Kathmandu. He was determined to provoke a showdown. The reports that he was hearing had convinced him that the Chogyal had become a barrier to the democratic progress they were fighting for. Along with 40 Youth Congress members, he set off for the border to meet Thondup's convoy.

When Thondup and Yongda reached Rangpo, they therefore found the Sikkimese half of the bridge blocked. Poudyal and others were standing on the bonnet of a jeep, chanting slogans. The West Bengal government pilot car at the front of the escort drove onto the bridge. Without consulting Thondup, Yongda got out of the car and walked past the pilot car towards the crowd on the Sikkim half of the bridge. He knew Poudyal; even considered him a friend. His behaviour seemed irrational.

'RC, what are you doing? Have you gone mad?' Yongda asked.

Poudyal looked straight at him and told him excitedly that he could not pass, that they could not return to Sikkim.

Yongda told Poudyal he could not understand his actions. Did he really think he could prevent the Chogyal from returning to his homeland? There was a short scuffle as the protestors pushed forward before Yongda returned to the car. Thondup berated him sharply for going to confront

Poudyal without asking permission. Yongda could only mumble that it was his duty.

Up ahead the pilot vehicle beeped its horn and the few West Bengal police present tried to get the roadblock removed. Suddenly there was a commotion and Poudyal emerged towards the Chogyal's car showing his bare arm with blood on it. 'My hand has been cut by the security forces!' he shouted at the window of the car, brandishing his arm at Thondup and alleging that he had been assaulted. There was even an insinuation that Yongda might have caused the injury.[7] Some protestors, fearing a major confrontation, tried to clamber off the bridge or up the slope. Poudyal returned to the remaining protestors, who jumped into their jeeps and drove off, still shouting slogans. The road was now clear.

It was almost as if they had got what they wanted – further evidence of the danger that Thondup and his Guards posed.

Yongda and Thondup crossed to the Sikkim side of the bridge, where they linked up with a Sikkim Guards escort and started the long ascent to Gangtok and the palace.

The whole episode had taken less than ten minutes.

-2-

In Gangtok, B. B. Lal was also determined that it was time for a final showdown with the Chogyal. The display in Kathmandu had been a severe embarrassment to India, just the latest for Lal in a long and frustrating six months as chief executive. When Thondup and Yongda arrived in Gangtok, Captain Yongda was immediately questioned regarding the incident at Rangpo and put into an identification parade, but, with nothing to charge him with, no formal arrest could be made.[8]

That same day Lal pushed the inner cabinet of the Assembly to pass a resolution deposing the Chogyal and dissolving the Guards. But he miscalculated. While frustrated by Thondup's activities in Kathmandu and aware that in theory he might be a barrier to progress in Sikkim, a number of Assembly members were starting to realise that if he were deposed, it would deprive Sikkim of one of the few things that guaranteed Sikkim's distinct identity. The cabinet members – other than the Kazi – said they would agree to Lal's proposed resolution only if there was a guarantee that there would be an elected head of state in the Chogyal's place.

The fact that Lal refused to give such a commitment only served to increase the anxiety that there was another agenda at play. Some in the Assembly were starting to think that the Chogyal might be their only safeguard against losing Sikkim's identity completely.

With the Kazi the only one in the cabinet willing to consider stripping Thondup of his powers unconditionally, Lal could go no further.

The Kazi's open alliance with Lal and his position as the champion of Indian involvement in Sikkim was now leaving him increasingly isolated. Even the Kazini was beginning to doubt whether the way things were progressing could possibly end well. Since her triumphant entry into Sikkim in August of the previous year, she had struggled to settle in Gangtok. She found Sikkim dull compared to the cosmopolitan feel of Kalimpong. (One person she did seek out was the only other 'Scot' in town: Ishbel Ritchie. Ritchie immediately recognised the Kazini's strength of character; she wrote to her mother that her new acquaintance was 'certainly in the past a force to be reckoned with and to be handled with kid gloves'.)

It had also dawned on the Kazini that she had not quite got what she bargained for. Far from her husband becoming head of a democratic government of Sikkim as she had expected, Sikkim had merely swapped the Chogyal for Lal, a monarch for a chief executive. She had expected a role as the power behind the Kazi as the leader of a small Himalayan state; in fact, she found that her husband had little real grasp on power in Sikkim. It was not at all what she had anticipated, and the events in Rangpo convinced her that unless she were careful, her husband would be forever beholden to Mrs Gandhi and the Indian government, something which she did not believe would be in Sikkim's – or her own – interest.

Like her husband's colleagues in the Assembly, she was starting to realise that something had to be done urgently to ensure that Sikkim retained some measure of individuality. When she heard that Lal refused to countenance the idea of an elected head of state, she realised the implications. She had spent years lampooning Thondup from Kalimpong, but retaining him as Chogyal might be the only safeguard to ensure that her husband remained a big fish in the small Sikkimese pond.

Far better that, she thought, than a small one in the vast ocean of Indian politics.

Crown Prince Tenzing, Thondup's son, who was also in Gangtok, back from Cambridge, was also certain that his father was the key to Sikkim retaining its distinct identity. He was determined to rescue what he knew had become a desperate situation by trying to reconcile his father with the Kazi and restore Sikkim to equilibrium before it was too late. On 10 March he, therefore, took the extraordinarily bold step of heading to the Kazi's bungalow to try and discuss the deteriorating situation with the Chief Minister. The Kazi, recognising the complexity of the situation and feeling somewhat isolated, agreed to talk to Tenzing.

That afternoon the Kazini brokered the meeting. For three hours the two men talked, while she cajoled and encouraged her husband to listen to Tenzing. The Kazi took it all in, calculating his options. He was nothing if not a pragmatist, and had already sensed that the tide of opinion might be turning in Sikkim. He also knew that two legal challenges had been mounted against the September 1974 amendment to the Constitution Act – one in Sikkim and one in Delhi – threatening the validity of Sikkim's position as an associate state in India. If he did not come to some form of reconciliation with the Palace, he knew he was in danger of losing power altogether.

The Kazi offered Tenzing a deal. He laid down three conditions: if the Chogyal a) explicitly accepted the 1974 elections, b) recognised that the Sikkim Congress should, therefore, be the party in power, and c) confirmed the Kazi himself in office, then – and only then – could the two men work together. He would accept the Chogyal had a continued role as a – limited – constitutional monarch. If Tenzing could agree, the Kazi said he would approach New Delhi to get them to rethink the situation.

Tenzing, relieved, told the Kazi that he would return the following night once he'd had time to speak to his father, who he was sure would accept the conditions.

It was a remarkable turnaround.

In Gangtok it was hard to keep anything secret. Within hours, news of the clandestine meeting somehow reached Political Officer

Gurbachan Singh. He exploded. The following day he summoned the Kazi to the Residency, accusing him of 'deceit and treachery'. He could not countenance such intrigue, Singh told the Kazi. He refused to let him leave and demanded that the Kazini should also be brought to the Residency to explain herself. When the Kazini, not used to taking orders from anyone, point-blank refused, Singh demanded that the CRP guard on the bungalow be increased to prevent Tenzing from visiting again.

Tenzing, meanwhile, unaware of the Kazi's dressing-down from Singh, returned to the Kazi and Kazini's bungalow in his jeep in the evening. He was in a buoyant mood – his father was willing to compromise. He was surprised to find the gate guarded by Central Reserve Policemen who would not open the gate to let him in.

The Kazini refused to be cowed. When she heard the jeep pull up, she bustled out, telling Tenzing to ignore the guards and vault the gate. When Tenzing did so, he found half-a-dozen rifles pointed at him. The Kazini, alive as ever to the drama of the situation, flung her arms round Tenzing to protect him. Seeing this sign of apparent affection, the guards were understandably perplexed, wondering who they were protecting from whom. They dropped their rifles.[9]

The Kazini explained what was happening to Tenzing. The Crown Prince left to update his father.

Meanwhile, the Kazi was given permission by Singh to return to his house.

If other Assembly members had been in any doubt about Indian intentions to tighten their grip on Sikkim and to prevent a reconciliation between the Palace and the politicians, the events of 10 and 11 March put those doubts to rest. K. C. Pradhan, one of the Kazi's inner cabinet members*, now decided that something had to be done – urgently – to reverse the unsustainable 'associate state' situation and create a new future for Sikkim. He approached the beleaguered Kazi (now back in the bungalow) to let him know the strength of opinion on the matter. Retaining Sikkim's individuality was vital, he told the Kazi. Many of the

---

* The same K. C. Pradhan who had been arrested in April 1973 by Thondup for 'fomenting communal strife'.

other Assembly members agreed. If the Chogyal needed to be retained as a symbol of that individuality, so be it.

The Kazi realised he had no option but to agree that, given the strength of opinion, resolutions should be drawn up stating what the Assembly wanted.

They quickly put together a document outlining their new position. The thrust was clear: the chief executive was to be merely an adviser to Sikkim; Indian appointments to the Sikkim civil service were to be limited; the judicial system needed an overhaul; and – crucially – the Assembly welcomed the Chogyal's desire for 'a dialogue with the Chief Minister'. The drafters agreed that, once the other Assembly members had signed the new resolutions, they should be sent directly to the Indian prime minister herself, with a covering letter. This should come to her via the Kazi as chief minister, Lal as chief executive and Gurbachan Singh as political officer.

Eighteen of the Assembly members signed that afternoon – four copies were typed to be taken to the remaining 11 signatories needed.

But it was not just the Assembly members who were preparing for confrontation. That same day, Political Officer Singh fired a letter off to the Chogyal with an extraordinary set of accusations – and a clear warning:

It has been brought to my notice that, as Maharajkumar Tenzing was leaving the chief minister's residence at about 9pm on 11 March, an object dropped from his baku which was picked up by the chief minister's bodyguard. The object could conceivably be a type of explosive device. There have, as you know, been two earlier occasions when explosives have been found buried in roads along which the chief minister was expected to travel.

This incident, especially following upon the earlier two, is indeed most serious, and I cannot express strongly enough my concern and, needless to add, disapproval of this evident resort to violence as a method to overcome political problems.

Public opinion in the state is incensed enough, particularly over the Rangpo incident last week. Now we have a direct indication of your son's intentions which will, if remaining unchecked, most certainly lead to consequences which the government of India does not desire. Nor, I am sure, does the government of Sikkim and, I should sincerely like to hope, that it is not your desire either . . .

A further very disturbing report came to me last night which, again, concerns a visit to the chief minister's residence by the Maharajkumar. He is reported to have been accompanied by three vehicles containing personnel of the Sikkim Guards. As I have pointed out earlier, both in conversation and in writing, the function of the Sikkim Guards is essentially for palace duties. They are not meant to be used as a show of strength on any occasion that your son chooses to go visiting around town. Even if it were considered necessary for him to be accompanied by a bodyguard, surely one person would suffice. Three vehicle-loads can hardly be termed a bodyguard.

The path you appear to have chosen to follow is a path which, I fear, will surely lead to a collision. In this case, the sole responsibility for the serious consequences which would inevitably result would be yours. I say this in all earnestness and with all emphasis at my command.

I regret to have to write this letter but developments over the last several days leave me no option and I should be failing in my duty if I were not to communicate to you my grave concern and serious misgivings.[10]

The allegations were not hard to dismiss as fabricated: Tenzing had been wearing jeans, not the Sikkimese *kho*, as alleged; the 'explosive device' was a felt-tip pen that the Crown Prince had lost, which he now realised he must have dropped in the grounds of the Kazi's house; there had been one jeep with three guards, not 'three vehicle-loads'. They were certainly serious allegations, Thondup accepted in a reply immediately sent back to the political officer, but that did not change the fact that they were also farcical and untrue. So much so that he would have ignored them 'if it were not for the fact that I am now convinced that a plot is being laid to somehow remove the Chogyal from Sikkim, and what could be a better excuse than to somehow involve me or the Crown Prince in an attempt to do away with the Chief Minister'.[11]

The following day, the extent of the control that Lal now had in Gangtok became clear. One of the copies of the letter that the Assembly members were trying to collect signatures for before sending to Mrs Gandhi somehow fell into his hands. No one knew who had given it to him, but Lal acted immediately: once again the Kazi was summoned to one of the government offices.

This time Lal went further than before. The kind of machinations suggested by the letter could not be tolerated.

The Kazi should remember from where his authority came. If he did not sort things out soon, Lal warned, his very job was at stake.

-3-

Mrs Gandhi knew nothing of the petty detail of what was going on in Gangtok. She was, however, highly irritated by the reports emerging from Sikkim. She felt that Thondup was refusing to face up to the reality of the situation.

Her irritation did not stem out of the events in Sikkim itself, but rather from the knowledge that the question of the Himalayan state's future only added to her mounting domestic problems. For months, she had been under severe political pressure. J. P. Narayan, the leader of the malcontents, had united all the factions railing against Indira (for many disparate reasons) under a single banner. Among JP's charges was that she wanted to establish 'a Soviet-backed dictatorship' in India. Indira countered with an accusation that Narayan himself was financed by the CIA. The 'JP movement' was no minor political irritant: by the early months of 1975, Narayan was attracting huge crowds wherever he went, portraying himself as the messiah of a new age true to the values of Mahatma Gandhi, calling for a 'total revolution – political, economic, social, educational, moral and cultural' throughout the country.

Indira's sense of persecution only increased. She was convinced that JP was involved in a plot against her, somehow financed and backed by the Americans. Other events were seen in this context. At the end of February the new US President, Gerald Ford, completely lifted the embargo on arms sales to South Asia, a move designed to boost President Bhutto (whose need for a source of arms to compete in the South Asian arms race would ensure a brisk trade) while also challenging the Indians to decide if they wanted to continue receiving all their arms from the Soviets. Mrs Gandhi immediately held a press conference: the US decision 'reopened old wounds', she said, and was plainly anti-Indian. Relations between India and the US plumbed new depths, as anti-American feeling ran riot. Bill Saxbe, appointed to replace Pat Moynihan as US Ambassador, had to delay his arrival by a week; his first journey into Delhi on 2 March was far from the grand entrance he had imagined, being smuggled in under cover of night as a precaution against rioting.[12] He was shocked to see anti-CIA banners, sponsored by the Congress Party.*

But if Indira's relations with the US were poor, those with China were worse, exacerbated by a series of outbursts in the Chinese press regarding events in Sikkim. On 12 March, an article appeared that threw a new level of vitriol at the Indian government. Charging the 'Indian expansionists' with turning 'questions of international affairs into "internal affairs"', the article cited the 'annexation of Sikkim', the 1971 'dismemberment of Pakistan', and the Government of India's continuing assistance to 'Nepalese anti-national elements' and to 'Chinese Tibetan rebels' as evidence. 'In short,' the Xinhua news agency railed, 'the Indian expansionists will take any place by force whenever they can. The robber has the cheek to say the spoils belong to him. This is purely the gangster's logic.'[13]

The timing of the article was, some in Delhi remarked, suspicious. The Chinese had splashed the issue on their front pages just as the Sikkim Assembly's loyalties seemed to be moving towards defending the Chogyal's position – and only days after the Chogyal had met with the Chinese while at Birendra's coronation in Kathmandu. Indira went on the counter-attack. In a newspaper interview a few days later, she made a snide reference to Tibet, saying that the Chinese statements on Sikkim 'seem odd to us considering what they have done'. She also sought to justify her own actions in Sikkim the previous year: the situation had been 'just building up' when India had acted. 'While we could perhaps have tried to hold back the (Sikkimese) people,' she said, 'I think that would only have led to a different type of explosion later on.'[14] And, she reiterated

---

* Saxbe wrote extensively about Mrs Gandhi's attitude to the USA and the CIA. 'She was often to repeat . . . that "they" wanted to do her in. She took care never specifically to identify who "they" were. But by innuendo and insinuation, she left little doubt that the accusing finger pointed to the CIA, if not to the Government of the United States.' (Saxbe, *I've Seen the Elephant*, p. 223)

pointedly, 'nobody reacted in the US and China' when Pakistan had 'very quietly swallowed up' Hunza in October 1974, within weeks of her own actions in Sikkim.

In Gangtok, meanwhile, Lal had reasserted Indian control. His dressing-down of the Kazi had worked beautifully.

On the 16th, the Kazi called another meeting of the Assembly. It was only four days since the 18 Assembly members had signed a letter demanding a complete rethink of the administrative arrangements in Sikkim. But in the intervening period money had been distributed, promotions had been promised, threats had been made, all in the cause of ensuring that those who had signed the 12 March resolutions understood exactly where their best interests lay: squarely with Lal, Singh and the Indian government. Lal knew which buttons to press. Sunanda Datta-Ray, who was one of the few Indian journalists with close access to those in Sikkim at the time, wrote later about the intimidation that took place. One member was assured there would be something 'in the ministry or as a Member of Parliament in Delhi' if he acquiesced. The Kazi himself was

> summoned again and threatened once more with the loss of his job. He was warned too that his wife's inner line and residence permits* would be revoked. Without them she would not be able to set foot in Kalimpong, leave alone play at being first lady in Gangtok. She could even be deported. All the signatories were individually interviewed. Some were similarly warned of New Delhi's severe displeasure. Others were promised rewards.[15]

A new set of resolutions was drafted, rescinding everything that had been written on the 12th. That meeting, the latest set of resolutions declared, had been 'illegal', and the suggestion that negotiations should be opened with the Chogyal had been 'anti-democratic and anti-people'. One resolution in particular contained the harshest condemnation of those who supported the idea of a continuing monarchy:

> The whole world knows that it is the Chogyal who has, throughout his life, been the greatest obstacle in the smooth functioning of the democratic

---

* Inner Line permits were required to access most areas of Sikkim; Residence permits were required for foreigners to live in India.

government, and his latest actions have proved beyond a shadow of a doubt that the Chogyal is unable to reconcile himself to the loss of his absolute powers and the changes brought about by the mass upsurge of April-May 1973. He and his agents have been doing everything in their powers to discredit and weaken the party and the government led by it so that they can regain their lost powers. With this end in view, they have sent their agents into the ranks of the party to carry out their subversive activities, and it is these infiltrators who have succeeded in misleading some party members and ministers in attending an illegally constituted meeting called without the knowledge and consent of the party leader and president.[16]

With the Assembly back into line, Lal immediately tightened up on the administration and instituted a security crackdown across Sikkim. The effect was highly noticeable. On the same Sunday that the Assembly performed its volte-face, Ishbel Ritchie sat down to write a letter to her mother, as she did after church every week. What she was hearing on the street was worse than ever. But she knew that hardly any letters were evading the censor. She made a decision – she would give the letter to a friend in Calcutta and get it sent from there. 'I do hope you are now receiving my letters,' she began in a letter that gives an extraordinary insight into the doom-laden atmosphere pervading Sikkim:

It is exasperating to send them and then not get them delivered.

We seem to be running short of a lot of things – white flour hasn't been obtainable for a little while and sugar is v variable in supply – Thuli reports that our regular grocer is also short of tinned things – an order I put in yesterday has resulted in 2 items out of 6 being sold. I don't know whether this is due to general shortages in India or a bit of policy, since it was hinted by one of the officials (or so I hear) that they could easily make folk here toe the line by such a policy.

I'm going to get this posted in Cal. – please don't comment on the contents in your reply. Things are getting pretty bad & it seems that a total absorption by our 'big brother' is only a matter of weeks or months off, but the methods being used are <u>most</u> inept & calculated to build up bitterness most unnecessarily. H.R.H. is being physically prevented fm. seeing the Chief Min, and vice versa which is a sorry state. They are both prepared to talk in the best interests of their country but big brother doesn't think it is in his interests – though no one can make out what b.b.* thinks his interests are – his actions are weird. Our folk get more & more bewildered – & in some cases more & more angry, especially those who'd genuinely looked for improvements & more freedom after the upheavals ... The whole atmosphere is surrealistic at times ...

A week later she wrote that the situation had worsened: 'the iron hand is becoming more & more evident with the velvet glove gone almost entirely'.

She was right – the Indian administration had given up on the 'light touch' approach. They had realised that as long as the Chogyal was there, Sikkim would always retain the characteristic of separateness. In the para-noid world of 1975 politics, that constituted a security threat.

The Chogyal would have to go.

-4-

In New York, Hope Cooke was staying in close touch with events in Sikkim. Since her return to the US she had found it hard to strike a balance between moving on to a new life and respecting the fact that she still – in theory at least – retained a duty to Sikkim as Gyalmo. As the situation worsened in early 1975, she had persuaded a friend, John Train, to form an organisation, Friends of Sikkim.† Train's cousin, Claiborne Pell, was a US senator, a Democrat well known for his opposition to the war in Vietnam and his support for unusual causes. Meeting in the front room of Train's New York apartment, Hope Cooke and the Friends of Sikkim readied themselves for any trouble there might be to come.[17]

But the events of early March crystallised another pressing problem in her mind. On the eve of her marriage in 1963 she had given up her American citizenship for an 'Indian Protected Person' passport, the category that

---

* 'Big Brother', 'b.b.' and 'B.B.Lal' had by now become interchangeable terms.
† John Train had an unusual career – he was one of the founders of the *Paris Review* and would go on to have great success as an investment banker, as well as serving as a part-time adviser to three presidents.

applied to people from Sikkim with a need to travel outside India. On her return to the US a decade later – with no certainty about her own future – she had postponed the thorny issue of her nationality, officially remaining in the US only as a visitor. But by the spring of 1975 she realised that if things deteriorated further in Sikkim – if Sikkim even disappeared off the face of the map – she could be left in limbo, in a state-less hinterland.

To regain US citizenship, she now discovered, was a complex process, which would require a special bill to be passed in both the Houses on Capitol Hill. She approached two old friends, Senator Mike Mansfield and Congressman James Symington, to argue her cause. But it was not that easy – the bill was a most unusual one, and some feared the precedent that her case might set.

Her citizenship prospects looked extremely poor, as did the prospects of resident-alien status.

The official alternative, she realised, was deportation. But if something happened to Sikkim, where on earth would she – let alone her children – be deported to?

After the pen-bomb fiasco, the Palace in Gangtok had gone on the offensive. Thondup challenged the political officer in writing three times for substantive evidence of the allegations that had been laid against him and his son. None was forthcoming, presumably because there was none. But the pen-bomb plot was nothing more than a sideshow – the bitter battle over control of the judicial system in Sikkim was of far greater significance.

Tarachand Hariomal, Chief Judge of the Central Court of Sikkim in 1975, had been in Sikkim since 1968. An Indian by birth, he had become deeply enamoured with the Himalayan kingdom. As Chief Judge, Hariomal had worked with Thondup during the early 1970s to update the outmoded judicial system. The reforms, which would have been Hariomal's crowning glory, were supposed to have been introduced in April 1973. Instead, Hariomal had watched with increasing dismay as the Chogyal had been marginalised. Some of the changes had, in fact, been belatedly introduced in 1974, but as first the Government of Sikkim Act in July and then the constitutional amendment in September were introduced, Hariomal became concerned not only for the Chogyal but also for the propriety of the judicial system itself.

Hariomal found himself at the heart of the battle with Lal. In early January he angered Lal by being party to a decision to release a group of young men accused of plotting to blow up the Kazi; in March he tested Lal's patience yet further when he saw no reason to pursue Yongda over the Rangpo 'stabbing' incident. There was a dispute at a more fundamental level, too. Lal was demanding that judicial files should be sent directly to him as chief executive. Hariomal refused to do so, arguing that the 1974 act had made no provisions for judicial authority to rest with the chief executive and that, in any case, it was the Chogyal as constitutional monarch who should be the guarantor of the independence of the judicial system.

In late March matters came to a head. M. M. Rasaily, an administrator in Sikkim close to the Palace, dropped a bombshell by mounting a legal challenge to the validity of the constitutional amendment of 1974 that had made Sikkim an associate state of India.

There had always been doubts over the amendment, many of them voiced at the time by MPs in the debate. But now not only was Rasaily mounting a challenge in Sikkim's courts but another ambitious young Indian lawyer had also mounted a challenge in the Central Courts in Delhi. Both picked holes in what was without doubt a poorly drafted and ill-thought-through piece of legislation. The Delhi case challenged the amendment 'on the grounds that admission of a foreign monarchy destroyed the unitary basis of India's constitution'; but it was Rasaily's Gangtok case that concerned Lal more. Rasaily's argument rested on a defence of the 1950 treaty – India's weak point. Since the 1950 treaty was still in existence, Rasaily said, any change in the relationship between the two parties to the treaty – India and Sikkim – required the assent of both sides. Since neither Sikkim's people nor its Assembly had formally given their assent, the unilateral constitutional amendment passed in Delhi had no legal basis. Only a referendum in Sikkim would provide this assent. Furthermore, Rasaily said, the status quo ante the September constitutional amendment should be reinstated: representatives should not be sent from Sikkim to the Delhi parliament until a referendum had been held; and the Assembly should be forbidden from discussing issues regarding the Chogyal forthwith.

Lal and the Kazi – who, as head of the Assembly, was a co-defendant in the Gangtok case – were determined that the case should be thrown out. It was nothing more than semantic rubbish, they argued, which would have the effect of stifling the Sikkimese voice in the Indian parliament. But Hariomal refused to be cowed. He would not throw the case out. Instead, he announced that the hearing should be postponed until the end of April. But he ruled that in the interim Rasaily should be considered right: since it was the 1974 act that was under discussion, the situation prior to that was the one that should exist until the hearing at the end of April: thus he effectively forbade the Assembly from sending representatives to Delhi – or from discussing the Chogyal.[18]

Unsurprisingly, Lal was furious.

On 1 April he told the Chogyal in no uncertain terms that New Delhi had made a decision: that 'the head of the judicial department shall submit to the chief executive all cases pertaining to the judicial department which require high level orders' because 'the chief executive, as the head of the administration in Sikkim, had full control over this department'.[19]

There was now no escaping the showdown. The chief executive had expressly contradicted the Chief Judge. Such a situation could not be allowed to continue.

In Sikkim, 4 April had always been a special day, a holiday dedicated to celebrating the Chogyal's birthday across the country. But on the 3rd the Sikkim government hurriedly declared it was now to be 'Martyrs' Day' in memory of '"those who lost their lives" in the "people's uprising against the autocratic rule of the Chogyal" in 1973,' Ishbel Ritchie wrote home in a deeply sarcastic tone. Even the school was ordered to toe the line:

> Since nobody I've encountered (a) knows of anyone who was killed at that time (except one of C's [the Chogyal's] supporters in the district who may have been murdered for private reasons), [and] (b) really believes that the whole country rose, [so] it was rather difficult to carry out the peremptory orders that we got from the Educn. Dept. to hold a morning Assembly to mourn the 'martyrs'. However, we managed to hold a 'prayer meeting' where we sang suitable hymns and had prayers for all who suffer, whether mistakenly or not, for sincerely held beliefs.

All the Government officers had been forbidden to offer the traditional scarves to the Chogyal – tho' a special request had been put in by the Chief Secretary on behalf of all of them & was turned down by the Chief Executive. It made the gathering at the Palace v. odd because there were all the representatives of the Government of India presenting their greetings as usual & no local officials.

Kewal Singh, the Indian Foreign Secretary, was one of those at the gathering in the Palace representing the Government of India. But he was not there out of respect for the Chogyal. His real purpose was to assess the tense situation and report back to Delhi. On 6 April he returned to the Indian capital and gave a detailed briefing to the prime minister's Political Affairs Committee.[20] The situation was grave, he told them – beyond repair. Everyone agreed it was time to act: decisively.

The first step was to remove potential pockets of resistance.

Since his release on bail following the Rangpo 'stabbing' incident, Captain Yongda had been watching all these developments carefully. As a member of the Sikkim Guards, he took his duty to protect the lives of the royal family seriously, a task the Guards had been carrying out since the 1960s on behalf of the Indian government.

On 6 April, the day that Mrs Gandhi was conferring with her Political Affairs Committee, Yongda worked late into the evening in his office in the Palace. Since the Rangpo incident, the Chogyal had given him a bedroom in the Palace so that he could stay close. At 11 p.m. that night, the Commanding Officer of the Sikkim Guards, Colonel Gurung, came to his door and updated him on what he knew. Gurung was an Indian Army officer deputed to the Sikkim Guards whom Yongda trusted. The two men had been discussing privately for some time what they would do if the situation came to the worst. With reports coming in that something was in the offing, they decided to wake Thondup for an urgent discussion.

Yongda and Gurung sat by the Chogyal's bed and discussed the situation with him. Over the past few days, there had been a significant increase in the army presence in Gangtok. The Indian Army had informed them that it was simply preparations for a major Eastern Division exercise in case of a Chinese attack on Sikkim. But the two men said they were not going to take any chances. Yongda outlined the options to the Chogyal. First, they advocated bringing the entire Sikkim Guard into the palace compound. Second, they said that they had already devised a plan of escape, taking him in monk's clothing across the border to Nepal. Third, Yongda said, if India were to attack he believed they could hold the Palace for 15 minutes to half an hour. But that might just be long enough to buy them enough time to inform China and Pakistan about what was happening, which might bring diplomatic support – possibly more.

Thondup simply smiled at his young Captain. He was convinced, he told them, that India, as a peace-loving nation, would never attack Sikkim. Even if they did attack he could never give an order for the Sikkim Guards to open fire on Indian troops. First, as a Buddhist king it would be against his every precept*; second, as an honorary Major-General in the Indian Army, he could find himself facing a court-martial; third, he would have no truck with any action that could unleash forces that might be cata-strophic for Sikkim and the wider Asian region.

He told the two men to leave and sleep – they would see what the morning brought.[21]

-5-

The following day, 7 April, the Indian government moved.

In Gangtok, a warrant was issued for the arrest of Captain Yongda. The charge was that he had conspired to assassinate the Kazi and his government, and that he had opened the Sikkim Guards armoury and distributed weapons. When Colonel Gurung heard of the charges, he opened the armoury to demonstrate to the General of the 17th Mountain Division that all the weapons were still there. But the reports of the charge had already appeared in the newspapers that morning. There was little that could be done. That afternoon Yongda was taken into custody. He

---

* Yongda recalled being deeply impressed by the Buddhist logic of Thondup's reasoning: most Indian soldiers had joined the army out of necessity rather than a desire to fight; and any injury to an Indian soldier would not just harm the soldier – it would also have a knock-on effect on the welfare of the soldier's family and community.

would later be taken to a jail in a town well outside Gangtok, where he was detained for 15 days. The man considered most likely to lead resistance to the forthcoming Indian action had been removed from the scene.

Next was Hariomal, the Central Court judge. In the previous days, Hariomal had railed against the chief executive, even threatening to resign. Realising that such a resignation would have left a chaotic situation, Lal had persuaded Hariomal to retract it. Instead, he arranged for the judge to take ten days' emergency leave of absence in New Delhi. Hariomal, worn down and feeling every one of his 70 years, accepted.[22]

Although no one realised it at the time, a carefully thought-through plan was being executed. All potential troublemakers were being sidelined. Another government official, Keshab Pradhan (brother to Krishna Chandra Pradhan), recalled nearly 40 years later that he too had been summoned to Lal's office. He was flattered to be told that he was suddenly in line for a major promotion and would be needed in Delhi. When he questioned what the job was, he was told that he would find out when he got there. He also left willingly.

Princess Coocoola, too, was quietly and efficiently kept away from Gangtok. She was in Delhi on the 7th, where she had been staying in Sikkim House for a few days, intending to return to Gangtok that same day. She received an unexpected invitation to Kewal Singh's home. For two hours, Singh and a colleague grilled her 'on the Chogyal's supposed Chinese contacts, whom she had met in Hong Kong two years previously, and about American interest in Sikkim'.[23] When she returned to Sikkim House, she found Central Reserve Police guards on the lawn, nominally for her protection. Once inside, she discovered the telephone lines were dead. She was told firmly that she was to stay in Sikkim House for her own protection.

Even Nari Rustomji, the Indian who had served so successfully as dewan in the late 1950s, forming a strong friendship with Thondup, was considered a threat. After receiving a request from Thondup to come to Gangtok, he contacted Kewal Singh. It was, Singh warned him, 'highly inadvisable' to visit. Rustomji took the hint and obediently stayed away.[24]

The following day press reports about Sikkim started to appear in the Indian newspapers. Yongda had 'confessed and implicated several other plotters', they said[25]; a separate plot to blow up the Kazi was supposedly uncovered after a 'bomb-like object was found hidden under the back seat of his jeep'.[26] Speculation and rumour about what was happening in Sikkim was rife; but with no foreign press allowed access to the country and Indian press access severely limited, it was easy to paint the picture of a deteriorating situation that needed urgent resolution.

Meanwhile the army continued to pour into Sikkim. 'Indian soldiers in full battle dress manoeuvred trucks, jeeps, radio cars with tags on their aerials, and ambulances' made their way through the steep, narrow streets.

In the Palace, the Chogyal called the Political Officer, Gurbachan Singh, to ask what was happening. It was only a military exercise, Singh told him, adding that Mrs Gandhi had asked to see the Chogyal in Delhi on the 10th to discuss what would be happening next. Arrangements had been made, Singh added, for him to fly with two advisers the following morning.

The meeting with Mrs Gandhi never took place. Singh cancelled it on the morning of the 9th on the basis that VIP transport out of Sikkim was fully booked. It seemed an odd reason to give, but Thondup had by now given up on trying to see reason in what was happening.

On that same morning Colonel Gurung, the commander of the Sikkim Guards, was summoned to an urgent meeting with divisional headquarters. With Yongda also imprisoned, it left a young man, Captain Roland Chhetri, in nominal control of the Guards.

At around 12.45 p.m., Chhetri was locking up the barracks and caught sight of Indian soldiers on the ridge just above him. The journalist Sunanda Datta-Ray talked to Chhetri about what he saw that day:

Two rows of men in CRP uniform stood on the ridge above. Bowling down the road from India House was a steady stream of one-ton military trucks and jeeps with lowered hoods. Soldiers in battle fatigues crammed the vehicles. The convoy stopped at the pavilion where men poured out to begin the advance. One file doubled towards the triple gateway. The other branched off to clamber down the ravine into the Guards area from where Chhetri watched in horrified disbelief.[27]

And then he heard the orders for covering fire from the prayer ground above the palace.

The curtain was about to fall on over three centuries of Namgyal rule in Sikkim.

It took no more than a few bursts of gunfire to overpower the palace compound. Right up till the last moments, no one had really believed there would be a military confrontation. When it came, it was short and sharp. The Sikkim Guards were not in any sort of positions to resist attack; the only real defence of the palace was at the two sentry boxes by the gates.

One of the sentries, Basant Kumar Chhetri, 'levelled his rifle at the attackers' and was shot dead. The other was hit in the right arm. The arm would later be amputated.[28]

Thondup, hearing the gunfire, ran out of the palace to a cottage nearby on the grounds. Panicking, he grabbed the phone and called the Political Officer, Gurbachan Singh. 'What the hell are you doing?' he shouted down the phone line. Singh put General Kullar of the Mountain Division on the line. Kullar advised Thondup to order his men to lay down arms and surrender.

As soon as Thondup put the phone down, it rang again. This time it was Roland Chhetri, but before they could agree a plan the line went dead. The whole operation had been conducted quickly and efficiently. The remainder of the Guards, most of whom had been resting, had by now been 'lined up in the football field with their hands above their heads like criminals'.

It had taken about 20 minutes, with one fatality and one serious injury, to disarm the Sikkim Guards.

When Colonel Singh of the First Paratroopers arrived with a small squad of soldiers, they found Thondup and his son Tenzing in the palace. Both father and son realised that as soon as the firing started things had changed forever. When Singh demanded that they give up any weapons they had, they handed over the motley collection of guns: '18 in all: eight .303 rifles left over from World Wars I and II, several hunting rifles and shotguns that had been presented by visiting potentates, two or three broken down carbines, and three sub-machine-guns'. Some had been buried in the garden by Tenzing; they too were handed over.

General Kullar also came to the palace, apparently embarrassed by what had taken place. Even if Thondup's rank of Major-General in the Indian Army was only honorary, Kullar knew it made Thondup the senior man. He apologised for what he knew had been a dirty little action. But there was no mistaking that Thondup was now under effective house arrest. Around the edge of his lawns stood Indian Army soldiers with machine guns and rifles at 50-yard intervals along all the paths.

Later in the afternoon, Political Officer Gurbachan Singh visited. The Chogyal, still trying to get his head around what had happened, gave him short shrift. 'You have the bloody gumption to show your face here after what you've done?' Thondup asked him angrily.

'If you want me to leave, I will,' Singh replied.

'Please do,' Thondup spat out.

As evening fell, Thondup donned his full Sikkim Guards uniform and made his way to the sentry boxes. There, alone, he made his own homage to the dead Guardsman. He took pride in the fact that it was a Sikkimese Nepali who had defended him to the last.

Like all leaders for whom men lay down their lives, he must have wondered whether the price paid by Chhetri had, in the end, been worth anything.[29]

Later that evening Thondup and Tenzing sat in the palace under effective house arrest. Nominally the soldiers stationed outside were for their 'protection', but no one was under any illusions about the situation. The phone lines were also dead.

Then they both suddenly remembered that they had a lifeline. In the spare room downstairs sat the only amateur radio transmitter in Sikkim, call sign AC3PT. They rarely used it, but perhaps...

They went to the room, brought the set to life and started to transmit.

-6-

Horst Geerken, a German telecoms engineer with Telefunken in Jakarta and a well-known ham radio enthusiast in Asia, was the first to hear the transmission. The details were clear: AC3PT was stating that his country had been attacked, that communications had been cut, and was calling for the story to be told to the world. The transmission went on for 8–10 minutes before the line went abruptly dead.[30]

Geerken sat back, a little non-plussed. He had just established that AC3PT was Palden Thondup Namgyal (address: The Palace, Gangtok, Sikkim) when Swedish ham Thomas Schell SM6AFH called through to say he had overheard the transmission. Another Swede, Stig Parrson SM4JPN, broke in to say he too had overheard it. They all decided to do something about it. While Schell was informing Swedish radio outlets, Geerken contacted a journalist friend of his own in Germany, who recorded Geerken's report and sent it to Norddeutscher Rundfunk (North-German Broadcasting) and other news agencies.[31] In Japan, Nobuyasu Itoh went as far as to record it. Others too, including John Clarke in Kent,* would report hearing transmissions.

The following morning, just before the story started appearing on newspaper front pages around the world, Richard Helms, US Ambassador in Tehran, sent an urgent cable to Bill Saxbe, the Ambassador in Delhi. Helms too had received a report from an Iranian ham. Under the subject line 'Reported Coup in Sikkim', the cable read:

1. Local Ham operator has just picked up transmission from Sikkim's only registered Ham station (T Namgyal, The Palace, Gangtok, Sikkim) following report which we are unable to evaluate: coup d'etat is in progress. Indian army has surrounded palace and is holding Namgyal and others inside building hostage. One Plane has been shot down and there is considerable shooting in the area. Namgyal has asked that word be transmitted to world press as Indian authorities were controlling all communications.

2. As above was being dictated, AP ticker item from New Delhi arrived indicating opposition of Chogyal to Sikkim constitution promulgated last July which gives effective power to Indian-nominated Chief Executive. Although embassy is uninformed about Himalayan affairs, ticker item lends credence to Ham operator's claim that there is political trouble in Sikkim.[32]

Indian soldiers were eventually sent into the palace to confiscate the radio set – but by then it was too late. If the Indians had hoped they could stop

---

* See prologue.

information coming out by banning journalists from Sikkim, they were sorely mistaken.

Ham radio, managing to circumvent the journalist ban, had got the word out about what was happening in Sikkim.

With the Chogyal safely under 'protective custody' in the palace and hundreds of soldiers on the street, Chief Executive Lal announced an emergency Assembly on 10 April. He made absolutely sure before the session began that he could be certain of the outcome.

Two resolutions were prepared. The first was that 'the institution of the Chogyal is hereby abolished and Sikkim shall henceforth be a constituent unit of India, enjoying a democratic and fully responsible government'. There was no pretence: Delhi had decided that Sikkim must become part of India – and that could only happen with the Chogyal removed from the scene. No one even mentioned that it clearly breached the provisions of the Assembly's own constitutional document prepared the previous July, which forbade the Assembly from discussing any matters relating to the Chogyal. The second resolution provided for an immediate referendum on the first.

Khatiawara later recalled that the Assembly members were 'rounded up and, under threat, were escorted to the Assembly . . . and made to sign on the dotted line'.[33]

The referendum poll, it was announced, would be held four days later, on Monday, 14 April.

'Rarely in its history since Independence,' Rustomji later noted, 'had Delhi operated with such phenomenal dispatch.'

In New York, Hope Cooke received the news from Sikkim with some trepidation. She still cared deeply for the Chogyal and for the country, despite all that had happened. Moreover, her own citizenship status was still unresolved.

The Friends of Sikkim group that had been set up a few weeks earlier quickly galvanised into action. On 10 April, Mr Tung of Debevoise, Plimpton, called on the US representative at the UN.[34] He had, he told them, legal opinion from around the world to support the case that Sikkim was not an internal Indian affair. The case should, therefore, be brought before the Security Council immediately to discuss these international 'acts of aggression'. The request for a UN appeal was quickly dismissed, but Tung's visit did highlight the tricky situation that the US and the UK now faced. How should they respond, particularly in the face of a possible request for asylum from the Chogyal himself? Advice was immediately issued from Kissinger to London and the Asian embassies:

Q: Would the US grant political asylum to the Chogyal if he requests it?

A: That's a hypothetical question which I am not prepared to address at this time. (If pressed on US policy on asylum: Without reference to any specific case you know that our policy is to give prompt consideration to requests for political asylum. The Department's recommendations in such cases are sent to the US immigration and naturalization service which has the legal authority for the final decision.)[35]

The legal implications of such a request from a country that some argued had never existed were unprecedented.

Kissinger's team at the State Department must have prayed that it would not happen.

The Indian authorities were well prepared for the inevitable reaction from the other regional powers. The Pakistan government railed against this 'annexation by force', which they said should be of 'great concern to the world and in particular to states of this region ... what the world feared might be India's real intention has been confirmed'. The *Peking People's Daily* repeated the charge that Mrs Gandhi had 'long cherished the ambition to annex Sikkim' and framed the Soviets as the real force behind the action.

But Mrs Gandhi's government had a plan in place.

On 11 April Foreign Minister Chavan addressed the Indian parliament in a prepared statement. The action had been necessary because the Chogyal had shown himself 'determined to obstruct the functioning of the democratically elected government through all means at his disposal'. As evidence they cited 'his statements questioning the validity of the democratic process, and even the Government of Sikkim Act, his propaganda campaign, and efforts to intimidate, terrorise, threaten and even physically harm political leaders and common people in Sikkim in a bid to disrupt law and order, obstruct the functioning of the government and subvert the democratic process'. The demand for the abolition of the position of Chogyal was 'being studied' by the government; in the meantime the referendum would, he said, settle the matter of India's relations with Sikkim once and for all.[36]

Over the next two days, Gangtok descended once more into a frightening melee of protestors brought in from outside the town to create an atmosphere of intimidation. Sunanda Datta-Ray, the Calcutta-based journalist who was one of those given access to the Sikkimese capital, interviewed bystanders who were convinced that 'the rhythm and the accents of the cheer-leaders indicated they were professional trade union organisers from the Darjeeling tea gardens and road repair gangs'. Datta-Ray, horrified by the mounting violence, carefully 'counted 54 Sikkimese Nationalised Transport trucks packed with Nepali in the convoy that wound its way through the streets, the chant of "Palden Namgyal, Sikkim *chorr!*" (Palden Namgyal, leave Sikkim) clearly audible from the palace'.[37]

'They've a' gane clean gyte here,'* wrote Ishbel Ritchie to her mother, quoting Sir Walter Scott's novel *Waverley*. 'Any news or reports you may have (or will get) really need only the additional comment: aye pu' the ither yin.'† She again used Scots words to convey her coded message to avoid the censor's pen: the school was closed for safety, she wrote, due to 'processions and demos all over the place – mostly skellums from South and West districts – jeep-loads of banshees in the night coming right down to the hostel'.‡ Harold Wilson – who had just declared that he would be holding a referendum on EU membership in the UK – 'has got a lot to learn from here', she wrote sarcastically.

Despite 2,000 CRP soldiers, 450 police and an estimated 25,000 soldiers in and around Sikkim, key figures considered close to the palace over the past three decades were dragged into the bazaar, she added. 'This is what happens when you are leal,'** she added bitterly. One elderly man, Athing-la, who had been key adviser to Tashi, the Chogyal until 1964,

---

* Translation: 'They've all gone completely crazy.'
† Translation: 'Oh yes, pull the other one.'
‡ Translation: 'skellums' and 'banshees' = hoodlums and mad people.
** Translation: 'loyal'.

was 'hauled out of his house while four CRP men, ostensibly looking after his safety, watched placidly'.[38] He was hauled through the streets and forced to carry a Sikkim Congress flag. The Kazini, horrified by the level of violence that was being meted out (and perhaps feeling some guilt for her own role in creating the trouble), confronted the protestors to get the old man back into her own bungalow and to safety.

Little of this was known to the US embassy, which had to rely mostly on the carefully controlled information coming out of the Indian press. A primary concern was the health of the Chogyal, whose fate no one really knew. 'The Chogyal remains secluded in his palace, allegedly "ill with flu"', was all that they could confirm to Washington. With no reliable official information, they could only report what they read. 'The Chief Minister Kazi Dorji,' they went on, 'was said by the Indian press to have presided over the largest public meeting in Sikkim history at Singtam on April 11, where over 15,000 Sikkimese reportedly "endorsed the Assembly's resolution".'[39]

All this was just the warm-up act for the day of the referendum.

-7-

Fifty-seven polling stations had been set up in record quick-time for the hastily arranged referendum on 14 April 1975. Each polling station was manned by Central Reserve Police. There was no question posed to the estimated 95,000 registered voters. Instead the Assembly resolution of 10 April was printed on pink slips of paper in three languages: English, Nepali and Sikkimese. It was, of course, a single resolution covering two completely unrelated subjects, deliberately conflated to ensure both were passed by those wanting one or the other: the removal of the Chogyal, and accession to India. Voters, many of them illiterate, were confronted with two boxes. One, marked 'FOR', was in the same shade of pink as the slips. The other box marked 'AGAINST' was white. 'Voting' was done in full view of everyone in the polling station; in some, the 'AGAINST' box was carefully placed at the far end of the room from the entrance, making it crystal clear that a vote against would be noted.[40] Ishbel Ritchie later found out that one of her staff hadn't cast his vote and she enquired why.

He looked at her with beaten eyes. 'They would have known who I was voting for,' he replied.

As the votes were being cast, the Indian administration arranged for the Chogyal to be allowed to hold a press conference. By now he was a shadow of his former self, resigned to the inevitability of the surreal events happening around him. In the sitting room of the palace, he tried to summon the motivation to fight for his country for one last time. The sheer volume of abuses made it hard for him to remain coherent. The referendum poll, he said under the harsh lights of the Indian press, would only have legitimacy if it were conducted under a 'neutral agency'; the Indian election commission, he added, could hardly be termed neutral. The poll was 'illegal and unconstitutional', he continued, since it was based on an Assembly resolution that clearly breached the stipulation in the 1974 Government of Sikkim Act, which forbade them from discussing matters regarding the Chogyal and the royal family. The elections of 1974 that had created the Assembly (where the Sikkim Congress had won 31 out of 32 seats) were in any case 'fantastic', possible only 'in a police state'.[41] As for the personal charges against him (that he had been involved in an assassination conspiracy and that he was obstructing the democratic process), he challenged anyone to provide evidence or cite a specific instance of either charge. He had managed to use a radio transmitter to get the truth out of the country, he said, despite the outrageous ban on reporting.

Sunanda Datta-Ray later recalled the performance as a 'faltering defence'. But for Gurbachan Singh, the Indian Political Officer, it had served 'a propaganda purpose'. The press conference showed, he said in follow-up interviews, that allegations that the Chogyal was under house arrest were clearly wrong. In any case, he added, the Chogyal had not expressed any desire to leave the palace.

'Official sources' even found a way to brush aside the stories of the radio broadcast. If they were true, they said in a final insult (the irony of which was not lost on the Chogyal), they were 'an affront to the 1950 treaty, which gave India exclusive rights over communications to India'.[42]

The Chogyal was well and truly beaten.

The results of the referendum were announced less than 48 hours after the polling booths were closed: 59,637 slips had been deposited in the pink box; 1,496 in the white box, a margin of support that the US embassy wryly commented was 'about the same 97% margin' as the 1974 elections.[43]

The Kazi was triumphant, carried on a special Air Force plane to Delhi to oversee what he termed 'the final completion of an act that should have occurred in 1947'.

Mrs Gandhi, challenged to respond to Peking's accusations of annexation, repeated her earlier criticism of China's apparent double-standards: 'China has been saying many things,' she said haughtily, 'but they did not say anything when Pakistan moved into Hunza.'

In any case, she asked newsmen, drawing an unfortunate parallel, 'What have they done to Tibet?'[44]

On 16 April, Henry Kissinger held his staff meeting in Washington as normal. Proceedings were dominated by discussions of the ignominious evacuation of personnel from Cambodia as the Vietnam War dragged to an end. But in the final moments, the niggling issue of Sikkim arose once again.

> MR ATHERTON: The next step in the disappearance of Sikkim has taken place. There was a plebiscite and as expected they asked to join India as a constituent state.
> SECRETARY KISSINGER: What is the Indian obsession with annexing Sikkim?
> MR ATHERTON: It is their obsession with the Himalayan frontier.
> SECRETARY KISSINGER: Then why not Nepal? Is that next?
> MR ATHERTON: That would be a little more difficult. They are a member of the United Nations. In fact, I don't think they really wanted to take this last step, until the Chogyal started to assert more authority than he had. And he made some statements at the coronation of the King of Nepal publicly, which upset the Indians. So they just finally decided that they had gone too far, and disarmed his palace guard. The Sikkim Assembly voted to request inclusion – a plebiscite. And it will become just another Indian state. And the Chogyal will probably – you may well get a request from him to come here since his wife is here.

SECRETARY KISSINGER: We will accept it, won't we?

MR ATHERTON: I think so. It has a nice esoteric complication, because his wife gave up her citizenship to marry him.

SECRETARY KISSINGER: I think the country can stand the Chogyal of Sikkim.

MR ATHERTON: There are enough people in Congress interested in this.

SECRETARY KISSINGER: Is Pell in on this? Who handles Sarawak? That's Habib. Pell wants 200,000 South Vietnamese to go to Sarawak . . .[45]

It would prove to be the very last time Henry Kissinger had to think seriously about the Himalayan kingdom that had so frequently and unexpectedly cropped up in conversations with world leaders, from Zhou Enlai to President Bhutto.

The conversation moved on. There were other pressing matters to worry about.

A few days later, two British news publications wrote opinion pieces about what had taken place in Sikkim. *The Observer*'s editorial, entitled 'Imperial India', ended with a sharp jab at Indira Gandhi's troubled government: 'The high democratic principles used to defend the takeover of Sikkim sound no more convincing in Indian mouths than they did in an earlier age when used by the British Raj.'[46]

But it was *The Economist*'s that produced a dry, and accurate, analysis of the future:

Whether swallowing Sikkim will be a good thing for India is a question which several opposition parties have raised in parliament. Whether it will be a good thing for Sikkim is something only China, Nepal and Pakistan raised, for their own obvious purposes, the last time round.

Soon there may be no one asking that question.[47]

They were right.

The fight for an independent Sikkim was, to all intents and purposes, well and truly over.

CHAPTER TEN

Death Must Follow Birth

1975–82

-1-

Mrs Gandhi and her government moved quickly to legitimise their actions in Sikkim. Armed with the 97 per cent result of the rigged referendum, they announced on 18 April that a constitutional amendment bill would be introduced in the Indian parliament. This time there were to be no halfway houses. On 21 April, the Indian parliament would be asked to make Sikkim a 'constituent unit of India', thus making it a fully fledged Indian state, the 22nd in the union.

The speed with which these events took place left little doubt that the whole process had been a long time in planning. Less than two weeks after the referendum, the bill was passed by the Lok Sabha on 23 April and the Raja Sabha three days later.

The Indian government was conscious, too, of the need to ensure that coverage of the events in Sikkim in the media was strictly controlled. Their answer was to ban foreign journalists and to ensure that Indian journalists in Sikkim were always chaperoned. To a large extent, it worked. Many in the domestic press argued that the internal pressure for change, combined with the threat of Chinese infiltration in Sikkim, was severe enough to justify the actions that had been taken, however egregious. One brave dissenting voice was the *Hindustan Times*, which argued strongly against the rationale for – and the execution of – what had taken place:

If anything has discredited Sikkim's demand for merger with India, it is the so-called referendum which demonstrably could not have been held and completed in a fair or reasonable manner within 72 hours . . . The fact that the referendum was conducted with such incredible speed must produce scepticism . . . The procedures followed were of questionable constitutional validity. The only justification for this can be the argument of revolutionary legality. But if the will of the people had to find expression outside and beyond the assembly, there was no need to diminish its sanctity by staging a mock referendum. And this is in the India of Gandhi and Nehru.[1]

The *Indian Express*, too, questioned the legitimacy of the referendum, though on a different basis: 'One wonders how many of the state's largely illiterate population had time to understand the significance of the issue.'[2]

Controlling coverage in overseas media outlets was more of a challenge. The government tried to combat the damage done by the Chogyal's dramatic ham radio message with a New Delhi wire service report; 'SIKKIM DUMPS MONARCHY' was the headline. In New York, Hope Cooke was frustrated to see the piece run without alteration in most of the newspapers across the States.*

The Indian government was also aware of the need to try and influence the diplomatic channels. In Delhi they were quick to respond to a request for information from the Acting British High Commissioner, Oliver Forster, sending External Affairs Minister N. B. Menon to meet him. Menon treated Forster to 'a historical exposition designed to show that India's only interest was peace and order', making further unsubstantiated claims that Thondup had been communicating with the Chinese via his sister Princess Coocoola. He also hinted at involvement from other foreign governments, saying he was 'suspicious of the very quick reaction from Pakistan'. But when Forster asked him how a referendum could be organised so quickly, Menon was 'clearly embarrassed'. It was, he sheepishly admitted, perhaps more of an 'opinion poll' than a referendum.[3]

Menon also used the meeting to probe Forster as to whether there was likely to be 'a United Kingdom reaction to all this'. Forster replied that he doubted there would be any official line but pointed out 'the Chogyal

---

* 'Only the Boston Globe made any point that Sikkim had been taken over, erased.' (Cooke, *Time Change*, p. 279)

had friends in London and might be able to stimulate an MP to ask a question but no more than that'. Forster was right. A few days later the MP and leader of the Liberal Party, Jeremy Thorpe, scribbled a handwritten note to the Foreign Secretary, Jim Callaghan, saying, 'I believe the annexation of Sikkim has been quite outrageous,'[4] But, as Forster had predicted, with every politician in the United Kingdom knee deep in campaigning on one side or the other of their own referendum – on membership of the European Common Market – the small matter of the disappearance of Sikkim hardly registered.

In the US, too, the minds of the political class were far away – watching the ignominious final retreat from Vietnam, as the last Americans were evacuated from Saigon on 28 April. In New York, the Friends of Sikkim, the organisation set up by John Train and other friends of Hope Cooke, did try and raise the issue. Having failed to get the US representative in the United Nations to take notice of Sikkim's plight, they turned to Ivor Richard, the British Ambassador to the UN, instead.[5] Their plea – for intervention from an international team of UN observers – fell on deaf ears. The *New York Times* was one US publication that did try to bring the matter to public attention. Their editorial began with a quote from Dr Sarvepalli Radhakrishnan, the respected Indian philosopher-politician: 'What does it profit a man if he gains the whole world but loses his own soul?' – which he had once asked Stalin, quoting the Bible. The editorial ended with a sombre critique of what had happened:

India's cynical absorption last week of the tiny Himalayan kingdom of Sikkim is a betrayal of values that gained India worldwide respect through the teachings of such men as Dr. Radhakrishnan and the late Mahatma Gandhi, leader of India's own long struggle against imperial rule. Imperial India is a diminished India.[6]

But US press interest in Sikkim had only ever really been linked to the story of Hope Cooke herself. In early May, *Time* magazine penned a piece entitled 'Fairy Tale's End':

Ten years ago, when Prince Palden Thondup Namgyal was crowned Chogyal (King) of Sikkim, his young wife, Sarah Lawrence Graduate

Hope Cooke, became 'Queen of the Happy Valley' and 'Consort of the Deities.' Together they pledged to make the tiny storybook kingdom 'a paradise on earth.' They also hoped to make Sikkim, an Indian protectorate since 1950, more economically and politically independent. That was a fairy tale not to be.

It was a different matter in the US embassy in New Delhi. The new Ambassador, Bill Saxbe, was a man of quite different character from the liberal intellectual Pat Moynihan. Saxbe's first experience of India had been a journey under cover of darkness to the embassy to try and avoid the possibility of anti-American riots. He was a plain-talking Cold War warrior, a man who would spend much of his time in India seeking out rare opportunities for hunting and trout fishing in Kashmir. He revelled in the fact that his new posting 'was a communications center for much of Asia, clear up into the Mediterranean – top secret operations.'[7] Saxbe's concern about the events in Sikkim was simple: he was well aware of the Soviet Union's deep penetration of the Indian government and wanted to know how far the action in Sikkim had been prompted by Soviet pressure.* His suspicions were increased by a piece in *The Patriot*, a newspaper allied to the Communist Party of India which had 'strong links with Moscow.'[8] Saxbe reported that *The Patriot* had written a 'lengthy commentary' (on the day of the referendum itself) in which it painted Thondup as 'an American gadfly out to besmirch India's name', accusing him of 'following his masters in Washington backed by Peking' in order to 'create destabilisation in one of the strategically sensitive spots'. Thondup's removal, they added, had 'assumed urgency because of Chinese intrigues in neighboring Bhutan in which the US is conniving.'[9] A few days later the newspaper continued to play up Thondup's alleged foreign contacts:

---

* In his autobiography, Saxbe talked of the open and frank espionage that took place in Delhi, prompted mainly by the desire of both the USSR and the USA to supply arms to India: 'We had a very close relationship with our neighbors the Russians. They entertained us and we entertained them. At the same time, we listened to them and they listened to us. That was one way to get information and to establish relationships, to know what their potential was, to know what their military situation was, to know what equipment they were selling to countries on the subcontinent. We were competing with Russia, of course, to supply American equipment.'

his radio had been fitted by 'two Americans', *The Patriot* alleged, darkly hinting at the involvement of Peter Burleigh, the US consular official in Calcutta who had two years earlier been accused of similar 'crimes'. Saxbe also noted that the Communist Party of India weekly, *New Age*, had 'chimed in by alleging that the Chogyal's palace had become "a rendezvous of plotters and would-be assassins" after the Chogyal's trip to the Kathmandu coronation and that he was intending to internationalise the issue "with the help of the Chinese and others."'[10]

In fact, Chinese reaction to the events in Sikkim had been muted at first. But days after the constitution had been amended to incorporate Sikkim as the 22nd state of India, they held back no longer. Their press statement was unequivocal:

Statement of the Government of the People's Republic of China
29th April 1975
Recently the Indian Government, in disregard of the strong opposition of the people and Chogyal of Sikkim, brazenly sent its troops to forcibly disband the palace guards of the Chogyal of Sikkim and directed the Sikkimese traitors it long nurtured to come forward and stage at the point of Indian bayonets a farce of so-called 'referendum' requesting the deposition of the Chogyal and turning Sikkim into a state of India. Now the Indian Parliament has passed a resolution 'legalising' the annexation of Sikkim. It is indeed presumptuous to the extreme for the Indian Government to swallow up a neighbouring country in so flagrant a fashion today, in the 70s of the 20th century. The Chinese Government and people express their utmost indignation and strong condemnation against this expansionist action on the part of the Indian Government.

The Indian Government long harboured an ambition to annex Sikkim. It brutally trampled on Sikkim's sovereignty all along. It used force to impose on the Sikkimese people the status of a 'protectorate'. Taking one step further, it used its puppets to forge 'popular will' and turned Sikkim into a so-called 'associate state' of India. Now, it has resorted outright to complete annexation. It has outdone old-line colonialism in arrogance and in the vileness of tactics. This has fully exposed the ugly features of Indian expansionism which attempts to play the supreme lord in South Asia. The Chinese Government solemnly states once again that it absolutely does not accept India's illegal annexation of Sikkim and firmly supports the people of Sikkim in their just struggle for national independence and in defence of state sovereignty against Indian expansionism.

Inheriting the mantle of colonialism, Indian expansionism has, over the past 20 and more years, indulged in the fond dream of a great Indian empire and been subjecting neighbouring countries to its control, interference, subversion and bullying . . . Throughout the process of the Indian Government's annexation of Sikkim, Soviet revisionist social-imperialism has set its propaganda machine in motion to give constant cheers. This is ample proof that Soviet revisionist social-imperialism is the behind-the-scenes boss of Indian expansionism and that it is the main threat to the independence and sovereignty of the South Asian countries and the most dangerous enemy of the people in South Asia.

The fact that India has annexed Sikkim so hastily with Soviet support sounds an alarm for India's other neighbouring countries. Sikkim today, whose turn tomorrow? [. . .]

The Chinese Government and people will, as always, firmly stand on the side of the Sikkimese people, and we are convinced that victory will surely belong to the Sikkimese people, no matter how many hardships and setbacks they may have to encounter. In the end, Indian expansionism and its backer will be severely punished by history.[11]

Despite its strong tone, the statement was considered relatively measured by Western diplomats used to these periodic Chinese outbursts. US Ambassador Bill Saxbe knew the Chinese were blustering and would not act, but the question of the extent of Soviet involvement remained a pressing matter. He quietly probed his contacts in the Soviet embassy for more information. His cable to Washington on the subject is a classic of the Cold War era, betraying the extent to which the Soviet–US relationship infused decision-making around the world in the 1970s:

With respect to Chinese concern about the Soviets deriving advantage from Sikkim's absorption into India two points are worth noting. Since the Government of India has traditionally exercised strict control over its inner line and borderland areas, we do not expect that the Soviets will have any greater access to Sikkim or sensitive areas within Sikkim . . . With respect to Soviet interest in Sikkim, we would only note that Soviet officials here had not to our knowledge traveled or even sought to travel to or around Sikkim in recent years. (This is what the Ministry of External Affairs as well as individual Soviet and East European diplomats have told us in various conversations in past months.) Our exchanges with Soviets here suggest that in fact conditions in Sikkim have attracted no more attention on their part than conditions in other Indian borderlands, for example, in the North-West Frontier area where the Chinese have contacts with dissident elements. All the above is not to say that the Soviets may not maintain covert contacts there although we have no evidence that this is so. Or that they are not pleased that the Government of India has prevented a possible political gain by the PRC in Sikkim by now moving to clarify its status once and for all. But on the basis of information now available here, we do not think the Soviets have a notably active interest in Sikkim or for that matter, Bhutan, at this time.[12]

-2-

While the Chinese, Soviets and Americans investigated what had happened in Sikkim, the country itself limped into the next phase of its existence. In his palace, Thondup remained under effective house arrest; outside, it slowly dawned on the people of Gangtok that Sikkim's independence was gone forever. 'Folk here are feeling a bit battered and sorrowfully resigned to their fate,' Ishbel Ritchie wrote to her mother five days after the poll.

The only thing Thondup could do was to try to galvanise international opinion. David Astor, editor of *The Observer* and the man who Hope Cooke and Coocoola had consulted in 1965 at the time of the border crisis, was keen to help, publishing the article 'Sikkim's Prisoner King' by Indian journalist Sunanda Datta-Ray, who had access to Sikkim in this period on 20 April. Datta-Ray did not hold back. He called events in Sikkim 'the most phony revolution that history has ever recorded'. The Kazini, far from being the leading light in the movement, Datta-Ray reported, was struggling to comprehend what she had done, with a strong feeling that she had been duped. 'This is not what I fought for,' she told him. Her husband had been manipulated and was now 'in a daze. He is a tortured man . . . the leadership of the party has passed to a Marxist Nepali chauvinist group who will be far more dangerous than the Chogyal ever was.' In fact, her husband remained Chief Minister, but the danger she was referring to came from the Young Pretender, Nar Bahadur Khatiawara, once her adopted son, now her arch-enemy. One thing was for sure: she knew now that with Sikkim's incorporation into India, her hope of being a big fish in a small pond was over – forever. She and the Kazi would be answerable only to Delhi in the coming years.

Thondup's 22-year-old second son Wongchuk, studying in London University at the time, also tried to publicise Sikkim's plight. Both he and David Astor called separately on the US embassy, but were stonewalled. Wongchuk had more success getting a series of letters into the pages of *The Times* in London.[13] Given most of the letter writers had connections with Sikkim, it is highly likely they were carefully coordinated.

The first letter appeared on 25 April. The author was Brian Crozier, a London-based journalist and historian with unashamedly hard-line anti-communist views, who had been an acquaintance of Thondup in the early 1950s. The letter dramatically denounced the Indian action as an '*Anschluss*'.* Days later an Indian PhD student at Wolfson College, Cambridge, backed up Crozier, charging that India's actions smacked of the worst sort of imperial expansionism. Major General Alec Bishop, one of Britain's foremost soldiers, lent his support to Crozier the very next day.

Bishop and Crozier were both acquainted with Wongchuk, who himself wrote to *The Times* on 1 May. 'I have been very pleased to see letters saying what I cannot say without easily being accused of self-interest,' he wrote, 'namely that my father, the Chogyal of Sikkim, is the very opposite of a feudal and outdated monarch ruthlessly suppressing the people of Sikkim.' The referendum poll, he wrote (citing Jeremy Thorpe in support of his view) was 'a gross distortion of the truth [designed] to give a superficial legality to a series of actions over the past year and a

---

* *The Guardian*'s obituary painted Crozier as 'a political vigilante who unashamedly cultivated a close, mutually beneficial, relationship with MI6, MI5 and the CIA'. The Telegraph wrote of his proud claim that he was the KGB's 'public enemy number one'.

half by a country which in the past has been the first to condemn imperial ambitions in the actions of others'. His father had always wanted friendly relations with India, but had – understandably – 'stopped short of jumping right into the tiger's mouth'.

Amid this stream of organised support for Thondup, two dissenting voices also wrote in to *The Times*. The first was G. S. Bhargava, then a research associate at the Institute of International Strategic Studies who would go on to become an eminent Indian journalist and a government officer in the late 1970s. Bhargava acknowledged the 'crudeness' of the Indian action, but defended the Indian government, who could not be expected to tolerate the Chogyal's discussions in Nepal about a 'Himalayan Federation'. The second was John Lall, the man who had been the first dewan of Sikkim. He also tried to defend the Indian position in the face of Wongchuk's tightly argued accusations. What had taken place was simply 'the accession of the state [of Sikkim] twenty five years too late'. It had been 'Delhi's folly', he said, to tolerate the Chogyal's nation-building in the 1960s, in particular allowing him 'to recruit three companies of palace guards, when a squad or at most a small platoon was all that his security demanded'.

The last word in *The Times* correspondence was from Hugh Richardson, the man who had been the last British resident in Tibet. He refuted Lall's letter and brought discussion to a halt with a typically pithy and precise response, coruscating the Indian government for being party to 'proceedings [which] call up the ghosts of Hyderabad and Goa'.*

It was a telling jab in the ribs for the Indian leadership.

None of these protests could change the facts of the matter. Mrs Gandhi's government had gambled – and won. It had created the appearance of a Sikkimese appeal to be part of the Indian Union; and it had calculated that since Sikkim had no seat at the UN, the issue would never come under discussion there. The incorporation of Sikkim appeared to be a fait accompli, just one among many examples of Indira Gandhi's increasingly autocratic style of government. During the first half of 1975, she had become the focus of mass discontent across the country. Her political

---

* The accessions of Hyderabad (1948) and Goa (1961) to the Indian Union had both required a level of military force that had earned considerable condemnation.

opponent J. P. Narayan organised a mass rally in Delhi calling for her resignation, while Morarji Desai went on hunger strike to protest at her failure to hold elections in Gujarat. In March she appeared in court in a case in which she was accused of electoral malpractice.

It was not just at home that she was coming under pressure. Relations with the Americans, too, were at such a low ebb that some in India had alleged that American's presence on the Indian Ocean island of Diego Garcia might presage an invasion by sea. Bill Saxbe, the US Ambassador, chose an interview with the *New York Times* correspondent in Delhi to make his frank views known. The interview was soon picked up by the *Hindu* newspaper. If India continued to treat the US in such a 'brittle way', Saxbe said, the US Congress and administration 'may begin asking why they should bother about India'. 'I have been here two months,' he continued,

> and I have yet to see any official or press reference to the US as a friendly nation. You have a curious combination of factors here. When I call on cabinet ministers, they all love to talk about their sons and daughters and sons-in-law in the US and how well they like it there. The next thing I read in the papers is that these same people are denouncing the US . . . It is not easy to understand. I do not think it is personal – I hear all kinds of stories – there are people who write in the press that it is all a build-up for a campaign. But because it is a necessary condition for Indian politicians, should we adjust to abuse?[14]

If such negative sentiment from his Indian counterparts continued, Saxbe said, the US would have to consider cancelling a forthcoming visit from President Ford. He also suggested darkly to the interviewer that 'in Washington, US officials now openly say that though they have withheld comment on Sikkim so far, they may not do so any longer'.

But despite the fighting words, the US had no real intention of raising Sikkim's status as an issue. Washington would never change its position – to have 'no position' – on Sikkim.

Especially after politics in India took a dramatic and unprecedented turn towards the end of June.

On 25 June 1975, Indira Gandhi declared a countrywide Emergency under Article 352 of the Indian constitution.*

Her problems had come to a head two weeks earlier on 12 June 1975, when she learnt that she had been found guilty of electoral malpractice in the 1971 election. The charge was a minor one, but her opponents were clear on what was required – she must resign as prime minister. Thinking she could ride out the protests by appealing the verdict, Indira delayed. Her political opponents were outraged. On the 24th, her intelligence advisers told her that her old foe, J. P. Narayan, was going to 'call upon the police and army in Delhi to mutiny' the following day.[15] She told her allies that she feared chaos on the streets. Worse, she told the Chief Minister of Bengal that the intelligence reports had implicated the CIA. She was 'genuinely afraid that she would be overthrown and destroyed in the same way Chile's CIA-backed Augusto Pinochet had staged a coup against Salvador Allende in 1973'.[16]

Technically, the country had been under an Emergency since the Bangladeshi crisis in 1971, but she argued that the 1971 Emergency was only an external one. Now she declared an internal one as well, which gave her almost unlimited powers of legislation. It was a devastating move against her opponents: over the next 24 hours thousands were arrested, including J.P. Narayan and Morarji Desai.

Six weeks earlier, the Constitutional Amendment Bill making Sikkim the 22nd state had passed its final hurdle, being ratified by 13 states and receiving presidential assent on 15 May.

The Emergency, therefore, came into force in Sikkim just as it did across the rest of India, but there was still no universal clarity across the branches of the Indian government as to the status of Sikkim. In his letter to *The Times* in June, shortly before the declaration of the Emergency, Hugh Richardson, reminded readers that before 1947 Sikkim had been dealt with by the Foreign, and not the Political, department. In the period

---

* Technically, the declaration came from the Indian President Fakhruddin Ali Ahmed after a request from Prime Minister Gandhi.

from 1947 to 1975 Sikkim hovered in a twilight world between Home and Foreign departments. After the Constitutional Amendment had been passed, there should in theory have been no doubt: Sikkim was a state of India.

But confusion persisted. A week after Sikkim's status had been finalised under Indian law, Simon Abrahams (who later married Thondup's daughter Yangchen) went to the Indian embassy to apply for a visa. He was told that since Sikkim was a restricted area approval could only be given by the Ministry of External Affairs. As late as December 1978, when Nari Rustomji called 180, the number for connecting to local calls within India, he was told to ring 186, the number for international calls. When he did so, he was 'informed that I should know that Sikkim is in India and not waste everyone's time by calling 186'. It took him four days to get through.[17]

One area where there was less confusion was in the Indian intelligence services. After May 1975, it was the Intelligence Branch (the home intelligence service) that was given the job of 'strengthening the post-merger relationship between Delhi and Gangtok and to consolidate the gains of the merger'. The man posted to Gangtok on 5 June 1975 as 'Officer on Special Duty' was Maloy Krishna Dhar.[18] He had recently completed an assignment dealing with the separatist movement in the north-east Indian state of Nagaland.

Dhar promptly set about understanding the situation in Sikkim. He immediately saw that the Kazi was deeply conflicted. The Kazi 'had reluctantly committed himself to the merger of Sikkim with India . . . Once caught into the web of Delhi's design [he] had no option but to drift along, though he did not want outright abolition of the identity of Sikkim.' Dhar watched the Kazi struggle as the kingdom was suddenly 'flooded with money, from plan and non-plan budgetary allocations'. Corruption mushroomed, reaching every corner of the state. The Kazini too, Dhar noticed, was deeply unhappy despite her public proclamations of loyalty to Delhi:

> As I penetrated closer to the hearts and thoughts of the Kazi I was left in no doubt that Kazi Lhendup [Dorji] and Kazini Eliza Maria had not really bargained for the merger of Sikkim with India. They wanted the Chogyal

out and continuation of Sikkim as a protectorate of Indian with a democratically elected government and at worst a constitutional monarchy.[19]

Here was the tragedy of Sikkim: there was virtually no one in Sikkim itself
who believed in what had taken place in April 1975.

As soon as the Emergency commenced in June, the pressure on the
Chogyal was deliberately increased. Dhar found himself 'asked by the
Governor* to submit regular reports on the activities of the Chogyal,
Crown Prince and the members of the gentry close to him'. When he
was later asked by a senior officer in Delhi to submit reports on 'the
pro-Chinese activities of the former king and CIA operations in Sikkim
from its Calcutta and Kathmandu bases', he 'declined to oblige, as I had
no clue about such CIA and Chinese operations in Sikkim'. Dhar could
not help but feel sympathy for Thondup. Everyone knew that Thondup
had 'played his cards wrong' and that he had been 'no match for the wily
games of the Foreign Office, RAW and the huge presence of the Indian
army'.

In Delhi, Bill Saxbe – in between rounds of golf† – was still trying to
understand the true implications of Mrs Gandhi's Emergency. The
Americans, along with many other nations, were flummoxed by the
reaction from the Indian public. Although there were those who decried
Indira's actions, the overall impression was that many in India welcomed
the strength of leadership she had shown.

Saxbe noticed an unexpected shift, too, in Mrs Gandhi's attitude to the
US. In a long cable to Washington entitled 'The Prime Minister: She loves
us; She loves us not?', he expressed some surprise at a series of 'favourable
gestures' towards the Americans since the Emergency had been declared.
But he cautioned against over-optimism: 'Lest we become giddy with
success, there is some balance as always with the US on the receiving end
of some slanderous attacks in the local Communist press which appears
to remain largely unchecked by censorship.' Even the accusations of

---

* The governor was B. B. Lal, who had been asked after Sikkim became a state of India to
switch from chief executive to this role.
† In his autobiography, Saxbe proudly related that he got his first hole-in-one at the Delhi
Golf Club on 17 August 1975 on a 140-yard par-3, celebrating by singing 'Ace in the Hole!'

CIA involvement in South-east Asian affairs had blessedly receded: Mrs Gandhi, who had been open about alleging interference in the past, now reduced her rhetoric by saying merely that 'sometimes there are presences which cannot be proved'.[20]

With signs of an unexpected upturn in Indo-US relations, Saxbe felt no need to pursue the question of Sikkim. But he came under some pressure to do so, particularly from Senator Claiborne Pell, cousin to John Train (the friend of Hope Cooke's running the Friends of Sikkim), and a long-standing member of the influential Senate Foreign Relations Committee. Pell assiduously sought to understand what had really happened in Sikkim. In August, he was a member of a Committee delegation visiting Beijing. During a meeting with Deng Xiaoping, the Chinese Vice-Premier, Pell asked pointedly why the Chinese had failed to bring the matter up with the UN. Deng replied, with typical pragmatism, that he didn't think the Security Council had the wherewithal to deal with such a matter; besides, he felt that 'labeling India's action as a clear act of aggression sufficed'. But, he added mischievously, he thought it was a 'good thing, because it revealed the nature of the Gandhi government'.[21]

More worrying for Saxbe and President Ford's US administration was when Pell brought up the matter during a bridge-building visit from Indian Foreign Minister Chavan in October, asking some 'sharp questions on Sikkim'. When Kissinger's Department of State subsequently pushed – under pressure from Pell again – for Saxbe to find out more about Thondup's welfare from the Ministry of External Affairs, Saxbe brusquely brushed them away, telling them:

> Frankly, we have no peg on which to hang further enquiries about the Chogyal other than his being married to an American citizen, and we are not getting any enquiries from her. Indeed, the Indians know of Pell's interest in the Chogyal and Sikkim but they also know it is a political interest. The MEA's Political Officer in Sikkim has closed down his office and communications with the MEA on Sikkim are referred to the Home Ministry for response. Are you sure you want us to pursue the Chogyal's 'current situation' with the Home Ministry?[22]

*

Britain's politicians, meanwhile, had their own problems to worry about. Events in a small corner of the Himalayas that was once a lynchpin in the northern frontier of its Indian Empire were of little practical concern as the Wilson Government focused on its own survival amid global economic turmoil and the surprising outcome of the vote on the European Common Market, in favour of continued membership. Nevertheless, Jim Callaghan, the Foreign Secretary who would soon take up the cudgels as Prime Minister, requested a political report on Sikkim. The resulting document – running to 31 pages – was drafted by Oliver Forster, the acting British High Commissioner, a man who, according to a colleague, 'always liked to please'. Forster, who would end his career as Her Majesty's Ambassador to Pakistan, saw the report as an opportunity to show what he could do. It was, he wrote, 'self-evident' that Mrs Gandhi could have prevented the events that had taken place. But, he added, 'as an exercise in realpolitik, India's handling of the Sikkim situation must be a cause of moderate self-satisfaction for those concerned'.[23] Britain's attitude to Sikkim in the post-colonial world was summed up in the final paragraph:

> All in all, the world may be a little worse off for the loss of a Shangrila, ruled benignly but in the interests of a small minority by a Buddhist prince with an American wife and a liking for alcohol. The Indian action may seem a little crude and Indian self-justification somewhat nauseating, but no British interests were involved, no deep moral issues were at stake and only one life was lost, probably accidentally. In the days of British India we would have done just the same, and frequently did with recalcitrant Maharajahs, though one may hope a little earlier and with fewer exclamations at our own virtues. In the event, we successfully kept out of the whole business and such support as the Chogyal has received in the correspondence columns of *The Times* has not been sufficient to offend Indian sensitivities.[24]

A couple of months after Forster's report, an opportunity unexpectedly arose to understand a little more about what was going on in Sikkim when a British Army officer, Brigadier Sinclair, found himself diverted there during an Indian National Defence College programme. His Indian hosts decided to demonstrate the progress they were making in their newest state.

'The tour programme was a masterpiece of security,' he wrote, tongue-in-cheek. Over six days, it included:

- three briefings
- two interviews
- three visits to monasteries
- one golf match
- twelve very heavy mess luncheons and dinners where drink was dispensed with aggressive hospitality [and]
- a visit to a distillery without which no tour by Indian officers is complete.

Sinclair continued: 'The briefing at 17 Mountain Division by the GOC [General Officer Commanding] took four full minutes followed by the inevitable tea, biscuits and cashew nuts for the remaining twenty six minutes.'

His report contained valuable military intelligence about the border area, under headings such as 'Picquets and Patrols', 'Tactical Positions' and 'Modern Ground sensors,' but towards the end of the tour he was given an unexpected chance to meet the Kazi and Kazini, about whom he had heard so much. The short interview confirmed much that the British intelligence agencies already knew about the emasculated new Chief Minister of Sikkim – and the woman behind him:

Throughout the interview the use of first person singular by her was most evident, and one wonders to what extent she runs Sikkim and not her husband. He obviously was very wise about Sikkim's internal affairs, but when any question turned on state affairs with Delhi or Indian affairs generally then she answers with no reference to her husband. She is an Indian chauvinist par excellence! Her views on the Chogyal, the CIA, Western Intelligence Agencies, Dr Henry Kissinger, President Ford, Pakistan and the legacy of the British Raj are not worth repeating in this report, but one is forced to wonder how a person who reputedly has a special relationship with Mrs Gandhi is so unbalanced.[25]

In Gangtok, Thondup cut a sorry figure. His main occupations were now playing football and mowing grass.[26] He let his hair lengthen, and grew a small, wispy beard. Since the Indian government had never admitted he was ever under house arrest in the first place, they could not release him from the same. But access to the Palace was carefully monitored. Captain Yongda, for instance, who had been released in late April (no charges were ever brought against him, making a mockery of his arrest), was unable to see the man he had once served.

Gradually, however, Thondup was allowed to lead a more normal life. He found his new circumstances hard to take, in particular as it dawned on him that if he had removed himself from the picture Sikkim might have had a greater chance of surviving as a permanent entity. The imposition of the Emergency vindicated his suspicions of Mrs Gandhi's intentions. He resigned himself to focusing on agreeing a settlement with the Indian government about his own future to protect his family's interests. Shortly after the Constitutional Amendment, his lands had passed to the Sikkim government, but the question of family's right to financial compensation would rumble on for decades.

Once he had the freedom to move about, Thondup found solace in his flat in Wood Street in Calcutta, from where he could see friends and supporters, including the journalist Sunanda Datta-Ray, and get medical help for an increasing number of illnesses. But it was a strange existence: Datta-Ray later recalled the harsh surveillance during the Emergency: 'Very few people could see him then; and a formidable circle of intelligence officials surrounded him always on visits to Calcutta or New Delhi. They kept constant watch at the door of his Wood Street flat, drove dinner guests away from his table in the Grand Hotel, and set up a watching post when he ate in the Calcutta Club.'[27] The restrictions were often petty, but somehow Thondup found ways to maintain his dignity. When his Indian minders in Calcutta refused to let him fly the Sikkim flag on his car, he responded in typical style: he told them he would walk while they drove. An assistant walked alongside him, carrying the Sikkim flag.

As the months passed, Thondup became more and more concerned about his own – and his family's – financial future. There had been no talk of a settlement for him, and, with the Emergency still in force, he was understandably anxious.

In November 1975, an opportunity arose to discuss the matter with Indira Gandhi. The Indian prime minister had gone from strength to strength during the first five months of the Emergency, cultivating a more personal style of leadership than ever. Her birthday in November offered an opportunity to consolidate her gains with a suitably regal celebration. But few expected her to choose Gangtok in Sikkim as a venue for the celebrations.

In the US embassy, Bill Saxbe (who was now, like his predecessor, adept at the piquant 'telegram from Delhi') captured the sense of majesty surrounding the carefully choreographed visit. His cable was entitled, with high irony, 'Let us all praise Indira, particularly on her birthday'.

We are struck by the contrast as we review accounts of the low-key 1974 observance of Mrs Gandhi's birthday with this year's 'Glorianna' tributes. Officially the Prime Minister spent a 'quiet birthday' in Sikkim yesterday along with members of her family. Actually Sikkim Chief Minister Dorji and his cabinet colleagues called and presented bouquets. Gangtok was elaborately festooned for her arrival, and large crowds appeared to greet her according to press accounts. Meanwhile in New Delhi President Ahmed addressed an invited audience at the Rashtrapati Bhavan where he released post birthday commemoration publications: a cartoon biography, a pictorial album, a special collection of tributes . . . The President said that Mrs Gandhi's popularity was increasing every day in spite of the 'calumnies' by her enemies. The Congress Party organs vied with each other in producing pledges and observances to mark the day while, according to the press, in most state capitals Chief Ministers extolled Mrs Gandhi's leadership and achievements. Information Minister V.C. Shukla paid perhaps the most fulsome tribute, declaring 'It would not be out of place to say that Indira Gandhi is one of the greatest leaders of present times, and again, that the formative stage of her mental development was when she was in her teens.'

While the president and the Emergency's ministers were piling on the tributes, Mrs Gandhi gave a press conference in Gangtok in which she attempted – not so subtly – to justify the takeover earlier in the year by talking up the threat from China. 'We have always sought amity and good relations even with our enemy,' she said, painting herself as a rejected lover. 'But unfortunately our hands of friendship have so far been spurned.' On her return from a helicopter flight up to forward areas to meet with Indian soldiers on the northern border with Tibet, she re-emphasised the dangerous possibility for subversion: 'In any border state like Sikkim,' she warned, 'it is not just a question of invasion but there are other ways of influencing the situation.'

It was the kind of bravura performance that Thondup would once have mocked over dinner with friends. But now he was reduced to meeting privately with Indira to try and resolve the question of his finances. The American embassy received a report of what had transpired from Karma Topden, Thondup's former intelligence chief, now resident in Calcutta and in regular contact with the US consular officer. Mrs Gandhi, perhaps trying to scotch once and for all the possibility that Thondup could become a figurehead for protest, offered the former ruler a deal. If he would 'assent' to the incorporation of Sikkim into India, he could be 'assured of financial assistance'. Thondup turned the offer down, particularly when Mrs Gandhi mentioned 'an American girl' who she said she knew he had met in Calcutta 'and warned him against continuing his contacts with the CIA and being a trouble-maker'.[28] He refused point-blank to stoop to such blackmail. He had no intention of letting Mrs Gandhi interfere with his active social life.

The following day there were persistent attempts from foreign journalists in Gangtok trying to find out what had happened in the meeting. The *New York Times* reporter managed to get him to stop his car. In an article entitled 'Sikkim's Ex-King Virtual Prisoner', he reported that Thondup wound down the window to tell him that he was 'under instructions not to make any public comments'. Moreover, he added, rumours that he was becoming an 'alcoholic recluse' were unfounded.

'I'm well and I'm not drunk,' he protested.[29]

While Thondup protested his sobriety in Gangtok, his former wife Hope Cooke was fretting more than ever over the question of her nationality.

The renunciation of her US citizenship in 1963 in favour of a putative Sikkimese one had seemed sensible at the time; now it looked like a grave error. The bill she had persuaded her old friends Senate Majority Leader Mike Mansfield and Congressman James Symington to sponsor had passed easily through the Senate on 30 October. But when it got bogged down for eight months in Congress, Hope felt 'mortified that my beloved country was doing this to me. I felt that in Sikkim I'd upheld some of the best traits of the Americans, and since returning I had been almost reverently grateful for our asylum.'[30]

The problem for some Congressmen was the bizarre nature of what she was asking: House consideration of a bill that concerned a single American – and of a matter of nationality that many felt she had brought upon herself.

It took a further six months to resolve the difficulties. Finally, on 15 June 1976, Private Law 94-52 received the assent of President Ford. Thirteen years earlier an article in *McCall's* about her wedding had started with the words: 'I remember how I felt when I realised that I was no longer an American.'[31] Now, at the age of 36, all Hope Cooke felt was relief as she was 'lawfully admitted to the United States for permanent residence' once more.

A couple of days later, she gave an interview to the *New York Times* from the New York apartment that had become her new home. Dressed in 'chocolate-coloured t-shirt, white cotton slacks and canvas espadrilles' and speaking in her trademark 'low, whispery voice', she told the newspaper that she was now just a 'regular New Yorker', relived to be 'no longer in a state of suspense'. Her children, the reporter noticed, were 'thoroughly Americanised. Yesterday morning, dressed in shorts, sneakers and Captain Marvel and Washington Redskins t-shirts, they chatted in unaccented English about the lemonade stand they plan to open on the sidewalk.'

Asked if she had plans to return to Sikkim, she was unequivocal: 'I can't go back. I live here now. I am rooted here now.'[32]

-5-

In February 1976, Mrs Gandhi postponed the planned elections and declared that the Emergency would continue to 'consolidate the gains' that had been won since it was first declared eight months previously.

Many suspected the influence of her headstrong son Sanjay in the decision to 'suspend democracy' for a prolonged period.

A few days later the American embassy reported that it had heard Thondup had been given '100,000 rupees (about $11,500) to pay outstanding bills and salaries'. They assumed that 'the Chogyal has adopted the type of cooperative attitude that he was advised by Mrs Gandhi to take during her visit to Sikkim'. In fact, Thondup was getting increasingly morose about the parlous state of his own finances while he watched Delhi's money pour into Sikkim. It was galling, too, to watch a huge army parade on 4 April, the day that had always been a national day of celebration of his own birthday; no less soul-destroying for Thondup was the inaugural 'National Integration Day' held in May on the anniversary of the date that Sikkim had joined the Indian Union.

By September, Thondup was thoroughly depressed. Nari Rustomji, his old friend who had been dewan in the 1950s, was acting as a go-between in an effort to help him find a settlement but was finding it hard to persuade Thondup to agree to anything. But for Thondup the matter was one of principle: 'It is demeaning having to beg for money but maybe that is the way it is fixed. It is not shameful as they are "on account" payments, whatever that means, pending our settlement. But it does put us in one big fix.'[33]

Matters came to an ugly head in October. On the evening of the 18th, Thondup was found unconscious by one of his servants, who immediately shouted for Crown Prince Tenzing and the family doctor. The doctor knew straight away that he was witnessing an overdose of barbiturates and alcohol. Thondup was flown immediately to Calcutta, where he spent a week convalescing in Bellevue Nursing Home while the Indian media speculated on what had happened. Whether the overdose was planned or not, it was undoubtedly a reflection of his troubled state of mind.

Within a week Thondup had made a full recovery, but his mental fragility had been splashed across the Indian newspapers, now clear for all to see.

As Thondup recovered from his overdose, he wrote to Rustomji that his financial situation was now 'critical, with literally no money in the kitty'. His main concern was for his children, for whom the Government of

India deliberately held back foreign exchange so that he could fund 'only 25% of their needs'. Desperate to see the two youngest again after he had made a full recovery, he petitioned the Government of India for renewal of his passport (as Chogyal he had always travelled on a diplomatic one) and for permission to travel to the United States. He was turned down. As Hope was – understandably – not keen to let them travel to Sikkim, Thondup had no option but to accept effective estrangement from the children of his second marriage.

It was not easy either for Thondup to watch the mess that was developing politically in Sikkim – and across India. The Kazi, following a meeting with Indira Gandhi during her November 1975 birthday visit to Sikkim, had been persuaded to merge his party with Indira Gandhi's Indian National Congress in late 1975. If it was intended to legitimise his actions, it had the opposite effect, only increasing the taunts in the Gangtok bazaar that the Kazi and his government were '*desh bechoa*' (sellers of the nation).

Maloy Dhar, the Indian Intelligence Branch officer in Gangtok, almost felt sorry for the Sikkimese leader, now well into his seventies:

> Two indomitable women, Indira and Elisa Maria [the Kazini] had put [the] Kazi on a tiger and he did not know how to disembark. He was left with no option but to swim along with the current that flowed from Delhi. He turned to Delhi for everything and started neglecting the Nepali forces that had the potential of challenging his actions.[34]

Those Nepali forces, of course, were equally worrying for Indira's government. Delhi, therefore, also sought to neutralise Khatiawara – who was now bitterly opposed to the Kazi and Kazini, and could emerge as a rival. When Indira and her family visited Gangtok again to celebrate her 59th birthday, her son Sanjay (by now as much, if not more, in control of the reins of government as his mother) tried to persuade Khatiawara to become 'an important functionary in the Indian Youth Congress', which he was now running.* It was a move that Dhar, who knew Khatiawara's reputation, advised against. He was right: the move backfired, instead providing Khatiawara with the 'connections to build up a firewall' against

---

* Widely despised, Sanjay had a simple 'five-point plan' for India; one of the points was forced sterilisation to ensure that India's population was brought under control.

the Kazi, which, by early 1977, he turned into support for a new party, Congress for Democracy.

Behind the scenes, the Kazini despaired of the horribly confused situation. She had now built up an unlikely friendship – based on a shared nationality – with Ishbel Ritchie. By December 1976, Ishbel was writing to her mother of the increasing number of visits and the Kazini's obvious distress. 'I think it does her good to unburden herself to a sympathetic ear . . . both she and the Kazi-sahib are over-working,' she wrote.

By February 1977 even Indira Gandhi realised that time was up on the Emergency. She announced prime ministerial elections for March. The Congress Party was badly beaten. By prolonging the Emergency the previous year, Mrs Gandhi had rapidly lost the trust of the Indian people. The Janata Party, led by the elderly Morarji Desai, trounced her, winning 299 seats to 153 for Congress.

The Janata victory across India prompted the Kazi to perform another remarkable act of political prostitution. The word soon filtered through from Delhi that the funds that had been pouring into the state would dry up unless the Kazi joined Janata. He duly did so within days of the general election announcement, calculating that this would take the wind out of the sails of Khatiawara and his new party – which it did.

But the suspension of the Emergency had much bigger consequences for Sikkim – and for the Kazi. In Delhi, despite Janata's comprehensive victory, Morarji Desai was well aware that he needed to exorcise Indira Gandhi and consign her to political exile for ever. He explored every avenue to do so and soon alighted on what he felt was a very obvious symbol of all that had been wrong with Indira's government even before she had declared the Emergency: her actions in Sikkim.

It did not take long for word to reach Gangtok that something was in the offing.

Suddenly Thondup had a new lease of life. He sped down to Calcutta to sound out his friends about what might be possible. Many tried to calm him down, warning that it would be a 'tough road' to get back what had been lost. But no one could deny that there was hope in the air. C. R. Irani, the editor of the *Statesman* newspaper and a friend to Thondup, promised to sound out Desai.

Meanwhile in London, Wangchuk – who was proving to be highly astute and politically minded – arranged to meet with the old campaigner J. P. Narayan. He then persuaded the *Daily Express* in London to run an article reporting that in their brief conversation Narayan had told him that 'he had always felt that Sikkim should be treated differently from other states' and that, while he was not in government, he would help by trying 'to prevail upon the existing administration to that effect'.[35]

But it was not only the Namgyal family who were wondering if the change of government in Delhi might affect the situation in Sikkim. Khatiawara, the man who had been the main driver behind the agitation in 1973 and a leading light in arranging the circumstances for the takeover in 1975, now calculated that it was time to tell the truth.

In August 1977, Khatiawara wrote an extraordinary memo to the new Indian Prime Minister Morarji Desai. In it, he and nine others revealed just how contrived the events between 1973 and 1975 had been. He went through the events stage by stage, admitting that the assembly had been 'forced' to pass the important bills in June 1974, and that in the referendum itself most people had believed they were only voting on the future of the Chogyal, not on the question of merging with India. The referendum in April 1975 had been 'unconstitutional and illegal' and the Sikkimese people had been 'befooled and deceived'. The 'Merger with India', he concluded, 'imposed on us a political trickery and debauchery, for no one, however meek or small, has ever in the entire history of the world, signed away his country as has been made to appear to have been done by the Sikkimese leaders.'

The document was deeply politically motivated – Khatiawara had high ambitions. But no one could now dispute that the merger had been forced on the Sikkimese people through duplicity.

The following month, in September 1977, 81-year-old Morarji Desai set up the Shah Commission to inquire into 'excesses, malpractices and misdeeds during the Emergency or in the days immediately preceding [it]'.[36] He thought he had an embarrassment of riches with which to pursue Mrs Gandhi. No one was in any doubt that the Commission's main aim was to end her political career for good.

But the process was badly handled. Shortly before she was due to appear at the enquiry, Mrs Gandhi was arrested on separate spurious charges. Her lawyers made short shrift of them. When they were dismissed, she managed to portray herself as a victimised martyr, being persecuted for taking the decisions that she had felt to be right at the time. She used the sympathy generated to force another split in the Congress Party. Now, Congress was split again: this time into Congress (I) – for Indira – and Congress (S).[37] When Justice Shah eventually got her to appear in front of the Commission in January 1978, her lawyer told the hearings that since they were 'illegal and unconstitutional', she would not be testifying. With its *raison d'être* gone, the Commission packed up on 20 February 1978. The whole thing had been a fiasco.

Still searching to find a way to beat his old political foe, Desai returned to the issue of Sikkim.

On 7 March 1978 he took the extraordinary step of admitting that India should not have annexed the tiny Himalayan kingdom of Sikkim in 1975. The *New York Times* ran the story the following day under the headline 'Desai Deplores Annexation of Sikkim, But Says He Cannot Undo It':

> It was 'not a desirable step' said the Prime Minster, in an interview, of India's absorption of Sikkim. 'But it has been accomplished, and most of the people there wanted it,' he went on. He said the reason was that the former ruler or Chogyal of Sikkim, 53-year-old Palden Thondup Namgyal, was not popular with his people.
>
> Nevertheless, Mr Desai said: 'It is wrong for a big country to do that. Many of the neighbouring states were bothered about it because they are smaller, and they thought it could be done to others. But I cannot undo it now.'

The rider on Desai's faux-sympathetic move left Sikkim with nowhere to go. One Asian journal, the *Economic and Political Weekly*, criticised the 'hypocritical rationalisation' of Desai's statement as a prime example of 'pharasaism . . . the ability to sound virtuous while rationalising every form of weakness'. Desai came in for heavy criticism in parliament too, where opposition 'joined in a blistering attack on Mr Desai for what they called "treasonable" statements that "questioned the integrity and sovereignty" of the country'.[38]

Once more Sikkim had become a political football – but in Gangtok, Thondup's spirits soared at the possibilities. Within three days of Desai's admission, however, Thondup's euphoria was replaced with tragic grief.

On the morning of 11 March 1978, Crown Prince Tenzing played football on the academy football ground before getting into the Palace Mercedes to drive to a petrol station on the road leading out of Gangtok. Halfway down the road, he encountered a truck driving too fast, swerved to avoid it and plunged off the road into the valley below. He was killed instantly. Ishbel Ritchie, who happened to be driving on the same road an hour later, was stopped by the police. 'One could see the skid mark on the road,' she wrote. 'There was the merest dent on the truck bumper where the car had glanced off it. The car went straight – and I mean straight, it is perpendicular there – 300 feet down the hillside, & I understand Tenzing was thrown through the windscreen, or that the windscreen was dislodged & he went on down on to the hillside.'

Thondup was heartbroken. Some called it the curse of the Namgyals – for the third generation, an elder son had been killed. But Tenzing had been special – headstrong as a boy, increasingly intelligent as a young man, looking as if he might mature into a leader that transcended the political mess in Sikkim.

As Thondup wearily made preparations for the funeral, he could sense that the event was turning into a symbolic opportunity to highlight all that had happened in Sikkim over the past decade. Some in Sikkim worried when he optimistically 'made arrangements to feed 10,000 mourners'.

Not even Thondup expected the nearly 20,000 who turned out on the streets to pay their last respects.[39]

-6-

For the people of Sikkim, Tenzing's death was a catalyst. It allowed them to articulate a number of pressing problems. There was deep resentment at the volume of immigration of 'outsiders' – most from Bengal – since 1975, an issue that united the Sikkimese Nepalis and Bhutia-Lepchas alike. Moreover the Governor, B. B. Lal (who had been chief executive at the time of the annexation), was overbearing and difficult. Many shared Khatiawara's scathing description from the previous August: that Lal's 'callous attitude towards the Sikkimese recalls the humiliating, snobbish and brutal attitudes of the civil servants of the British Raj'. Lal's reputation sank further when he refused to allow a proposed vote of sympathy and two minutes' silence in the Sikkim Assembly following Tenzing's death. He also forbade discussion of Morarji Desai's admission about the events of 1975 in the same forum.

For Thondup, his eldest son's death was just the latest blow in a life of tragedy. In a note to Nari Rutsomji, he tried to be philosophical: 'Death must follow birth, but it is so cruel a fate to lose Tenzing who was in the prime of life shouldering his responsibilities and was a source of strength and our hope for the future.'

His eldest daughter Yangchen, too, was seriously ill in New York. Now under severe financial pressure, Thondup asked Nari Rustomji to accompany him to Delhi to finalise a settlement. Rustomji agreed, despite anticipating that Thondup would be reluctant to compromise. 'The Delhi visit taxed my nerves to the utmost,' Rustomji later recalled, 'and it was only after a demonstration of temper that I could prevail upon, or rather bully the Prince into giving an assurance on the strength of which the Government of India would release funds and foreign exchange for his children's medical and educational expenses.' Even then, the assurance that Thondup gave in writing to Morarji Desai was mealy-mouthed:

> I can assure you that, in the changed circumstances of the day, I would not act in any way contrary to the existing constitutional position, but would give my co-operation to the Government of India in the interests of promoting the welfare of the people of Sikkim.[40]

With that, Thondup accepted that the fight was no longer his.

But there were others emerging in Sikkim who would show, in the election the following year, that they were willing to take up the cudgels.

While Tenzing's death had reminded many in Sikkim of what they had lost in April 1975, there were plenty who had gained since the country had become an Indian state.

The change of government did not stop the money pouring into Sikkim in the form of aid. The sheer volume of funds – far more than any other state – was bound to lead to corruption. As one commentator noted in early 1979, 'the cost of each project is generously inflated and palms are generously greased all down the line'.[41] This only served to increase the disparity between the booming Sikkim economy and the declining hill towns to the south – Darjeeling, Kalimpong and others – which had for so long relied on itinerant British migrants.

The result was that Sikkim became increasingly attractive, in particular to those of Nepali origin in the hill-town area, 'drawn by the tales of Central Largesse circulating in Sikkimese hands'. But it also meant that those already living in Sikkim became protective of their newfound position as recipient of Delhi's funds. Even more noticeable was the significant increase in 'plainspeople', i.e. Bengalis and other Indians, who started to make their presence known in Gangtok and some of the other towns around Sikkim. A whole new set of tensions crept into the political make-up of the state.

The reality was, however, that Sikkim was now an Indian state. As such there was a process of Indianisation that was bound to occur. Although Sikkim had been granted a certain degree of 'special dispensation' in the Constitutional Amendment of 1975, there was an inevitable move towards normalising the state and making it fit better with the whole tenor of the Indian Republic.

A very significant change came with the decision in late 1978 to declare the Bhutia-Lepchas – perhaps as a sop from Morarji Desai after his faux-apology – as a 'Scheduled Tribe'. Scheduled Tribes and Scheduled Castes are denominations that hark back to the days of the Raj (when the British government called them 'Depressed classes'); they had been used since Indian independence, along with another term created in 1953, 'Other Backward Classes', to enable positive discrimination for disadvantaged groups. But the decision had one bizarre consequence: the ex-ruling group in Sikkim – including the Namgyal family – was now classified as coming from a 'tribe' that deserved the central Indian government's assistance, financial and otherwise.

If the Nepali population in Sikkim thought this was bad enough, far worse was to come the following year, when the Indian government proposed a bill reforming the seat reservation within Sikkim. In April

1974, B. S. Das had created a system that allowed for 50 per cent Bhutia-Lepcha seats and 50 per cent Nepali seats – 15 each – albeit elected on a one man, one vote basis. Now, in early 1979, the Indian government proposed that the Bhutia-Lepchas – as a Scheduled Tribe – should be given 12 out of the 30 seats. Rather than reserve any other seats, all others should be 'general', i.e. available for anyone to stand in.

Immediately, the Nepali community smelt a rat. Two, in fact: first, the proportion of seats being given to the Bhutia-Lepchas (40 per cent) was still far beyond their numerical representation in Sikkim (nearer 20 per cent); second, the Sikkimese Nepali population had not only lost its seat reservation but also realised that, with increased immigration of plainspeople, they could end up being marginalised even further. Some suspected that the Indian government knew all of this only too well and had devised the bill as a way to counteract the possibility of a strong, difficult Nepali grouping in the Sikkim parliament which might even look to link with the nascent 'Gorkhaland' movement in Darjeeling district. R. C. Poudyal, the man who had confronted Captain Yongda and the Chogyal in 1975 on their way back from King Birendra's coronation, broke from the Kazi government in which he was serving to form a party campaigning on this issue. There were also serious complaints over the voters roll.

By the middle of 1979, the Kazi was not only losing support – but he had also lost all credibility in Sikkim. 'The Chief Minister travels with even greater panoply than the Chogyal ever did,' wrote a columnist in India's *Economic and Political Weekly*, noting that he had even bought a Mercedes saloon – the car that Thondup had used – and taken over the 'SIKKIM' number plate that the Namgyals had used. Not only was he considered to be one of the '*desh bechoa*' (sellers of the nation), but he was also seen as overseeing increasing corruption and as being unable to stand up to the 'deputationists' of the Delhi government, which was now in Sikkim in large numbers. The criticism from the columnist extended to the entire assembly, who had all become known for their 'extravagant forays into the fleshpots of Calcutta's best hotels . . . Where Sikkim had only one Chogyal there are now 32,' he wrote, adding acidly that the Kazi's 'most important asset in wooing voters' was 'to be able to dangle before the populace the hope of attaining similar grandeur at the Indian taxpayers' expense'.

In August 1979, Governor B. B. Lal, alarmed at the growing potential for unrest in Sikkim, declared President's rule. Within weeks, the Scheduled Tribe Bill became law and elections were declared. The Kazi's electoral support completely evaporated – he was left without a single seat. But the winner was not the Nepali Poudyal or the inconsistent Khatiawara, who had also lost credibility. Instead, Nar Bahadur Bhandari, the schoolteacher who had led a protest delegation to Delhi in 1974 after the Government of Sikkim Act passed that year, was returned in 16 out of 30 seats. All candidates had campaigned on an anti-Kazi, anti-merger, anti-plainsmen platform, but only Bhandari was able to claim distance from the murky events of 1975 and appeal across community boundaries.

Many in Sikkim, including Sonam Yongda, who had vigorously supported Bhandari, thought they had a new saviour. But the following year would see the return of the woman who many still associated directly with the country's annexation.

Mrs Gandhi was about to rise from the ashes of the Janata government.

Morarji Desai's Janata Government in Delhi had been doomed from the start – a coalition of interests, it had only really been held together by the desire to oust Mrs Gandhi and to experience what it felt like to exercise power.

Mrs Gandhi, on the other hand, was able to play the victim in the run-up to the general election in India in January 1980. She pulled off a remarkable victory by reminding the electorate what they had been missing – strong, positive leadership. On 14 January, less than three years after the Emergency had ended, she resumed her position at the helm of India as prime minister.

Her second period in office – from 1980 until her assassination in 1984 – was to be characterised, like the first, by major challenges. But this time most of them were domestic rather than international. 'At the beginning of the 1980s,' her biographer Katherine Frank wrote, 'India was threatening to deconstruct.' Tensions were emerging that seemed to be ripping the whole idea of India asunder. In Kashmir, Punjab, the north-east, and the southern Tamil states, she faced separatist movement led by men with varying degrees of attachment to violence.

In that context, Sikkim – ironically – became a minor issue, easy to manage. Unlike the sprawling masses of some of India's larger states, Sikkim was small and self-contained, with a disproportionate military presence, thanks to its geopolitical situation. The precedent for a massive flow of funds from Delhi to Sikkim had already been set during the previous five years and, given the tiny size of the state, the actual amount of financial support was rarely questioned – even though it was, per capita, far in excess of any other state in India. New Chief Minister Bhandari found himself inheriting a situation where kickbacks and bribes dominated both the economics and the politics of the state. Even with the best of intentions it was virtually impossible for him to do anything but continue with the same. The economy of the state continued to grow, but there were soon rumours that Bhandari was becoming an integral part of a system designed to ensure that the Sikkimese remained quiescent. He quickly pulled back from his earlier call for a rethink on the merger with India.

In New Delhi, Mrs Gandhi soon reinstituted her idiosyncratic and highly personal style of rule. The people might have voted her out in 1977, but they had voted her back in.* Her son Sanjay, now an elected MP but still deeply unpopular for his role in the worst excesses of the Emergency, was soon made General Secretary of the All India Congress Committee. But on 23 June 1980, Indira Gandhi suffered the same fate as Thondup two years earlier. Her beloved son Sanjay was killed while performing acrobatic stunts in a newly acquired two-seater aeroplane. Although a great personal tragedy for Indira, 'a wave of indefinable relief blew right across the country'[42] Politically, Sanjay had been something of a liability.

Sanjay's death left her once again isolated, and more conspicuous than ever as the towering figure of Indian politics. The immediate problem facing her was serious unrest in Assam, only a few hundred miles from Sikkim. As soon as the trouble flared, she returned to the familiar trope of implicating the Chinese, blaming it on a 'foreign hand'.[43] But the truth was that China had moved on significantly in five years. Deng Xiaoping, once

---

* 'Immediately after the election, when a Scandinavian journalist asked Indira how it felt to be India's leader again, she replied angrily, "I have always been India's leader."' (Frank, *Indira*, p. 441)

vilified by Mao, had succeeded him, intent on opening up China at a slow and steady pace and determined to engage with the world. In February 1979, he had acknowledged that China had, in the past, supported rebels in the north-east but assured the Indian foreign minister that it was no longer the case.

In fact, despite the vague accusations she had made, Mrs Gandhi too was keen to rebuild the broken Indo-Chinese relationship. In May 1980, she met with Chinese Premier Hua Guofeng to open up discussions, in particular with reference to the border areas disputed between the two countries since the war of 1962. The following year Deng, in a meeting with an Indian MP, revived the 20-year-old offer of a package deal to solve the dispute, making minor changes in the border alignment in both the Tawang (in the east) and the Aksai Chin (in the west) to satisfy both parties.

It would take eight years (and eight rounds of talks) for any progress to be made, but one area that Deng immediately asserted was not on the table was Sikkim. The Chinese government still vigorously disputed that Sikkim was Indian territory and while Deng agreed that he would 'not make an issue' of Sikkim in the talks, he made a point of saying that he was still 'thoroughly disappointed' with Indian actions in 1975.*

While China and India appeared to be edging towards a rapprochement, Mrs Gandhi's tortuous relationship with the Americans continued. There had been a brief flowering after the straight-talking Saxbe left (when Gerald Ford lost the American presidency to Jimmy Carter) and was replaced by the Indian-born academic Robert Goheen. Carter's visit to India in 1978 had helped to rebuild relations further. But with the United States backing Pakistan strongly after the Soviet invasion of Afghanistan in 1979, Mrs Gandhi once again conjured up images of a Washington–Islamabad–Beijing axis ranged against her. Matters were not helped by ex-Hollywood actor Ronald Reagan's victory in November 1980; Reagan was a man who Mrs Gandhi saw as intellectually vacuous.

Indo-US relations would flounder for another decade.

---

* While this sounded like a concession, it was in reality a tactic to hold recognition of Sikkim as a bargaining chip, as John Garver pointed out in his book *Protracted Contest: Sino-Indian Rivalry in the Twentieth Century* (p. 175)

In New York, Hope Cooke had finally found some peace. By the late 1970s, separation from Thondup had become inevitable. But she could not resist the urge to reflect on her experiences in Sikkim through writing about them.

When her autobiography *Time Change* was published in 1980, Thondup wrote to Rustomji asking if he might consider helping him to write his own version of what had happened. But time was catching up with Thondup. Although not yet 60, he was starting to fade. He found it hard to be in Gangtok. So many people said they regretted what had happened. But everyone knew that nothing was going to change. He found it difficult, too, to witness the gradual encroachment of the Indian way of life into Gangtok, such as the pointedly over-enthusiastic celebrations of Independence Day each 15 August. Even visits to Calcutta, where private dinners were still sometimes interrupted by the police, were painful.[44]

In the summer of 1981 Thondup approached Hope to arrange for the children to visit. He already knew he was ill. After a messy battle (Hope had 'obtained a court injunction against such a visit on the grounds that their lives would be in danger'[45]), Thondup finally got Palden and Hope Leezum to Sikkim in August. Hoping to show them something of the country he loved – and that they had left as young children – he went through the ignominy of applying to Delhi for permits to take them to a restricted area on a trek. The Indian government turned him down. 'I think,' he wrote to Rustomji, 'it was to put pressure on me to show the Govt can be uncooperative if they chose. Foolish, as don't I know it!' Instead he joined the increasing number of Indian tourists and took them on a bus tour. Despite the obstructions placed in his way, he wrote happily to Rustomji that the Palace – for the first time in a long time –was once again 'full of life'.

In September doctors in Calcutta confirmed that he had epidermoid carcinoma of the esophagus. He was immediately flown to New York for treatment to start chemotherapy. Against advice from the Dalai Lama, he went ahead with an operation, after which it became clear he would not recover.

On the morning of 29 January 1982, Chogyal Palden Thondup

Namgyal was finally released from the wheel of life 'to the accompaniment of prayers recited by his personal lama'.

There had been rumours in Gangtok for a few days that the Chogyal had died when the news was finally confirmed. When Ishbel Ritchie heard, she spotted the potential for trouble even in death:

> It would appear he will be accorded full honours and a state funeral – folk here wouldn't stand for anything else probably, but, of course, as far as the Central Govnt. is concerned he has become officially an ordinary person. I was told this morning that the Govnt of Bhutan will take on some of the responsibility and expense.

In the event, the Bhutanese had no need to foot the bill. Indira Gandhi was well aware of the challenging circumstances and immediately agreed to pay for a ceremonial funeral, also making arrangements for the body to be transported from New York to Gangtok.*

With 19 February fixed as the date for the funeral, the coffin lay in state at the Tsuklakhang monastery next to the palace for days, guarded by four Sikkim Armed Police on each corner with reversed rifles. 'The weather seems to be in mourning for the Chogyal too,' Ishbel Ritchie wrote. A constant stream of people made their way through the rain and hail, laying khadas (silk scarves) over the small, carved table that in life Thondup had always used to receive them. Chief Minister Bhandari had no hesitation in announcing that the funeral would be a 'national occasion'. Even the Kazi laid a khada, telling the press: 'I may have battled against him, but Sikkim is the poorer by his death.' But in Delhi, Mrs Gandhi could not help but claim Thondup as one of India's, referring to him by the Indian honorific 'Shri Palden Thondup Namgyal', adding that he was 'a sensitive man with concern for his state'.[46]

At 5 a.m. on 19 February 1982, Thondup's coffin was brought out of the chapel, where it lay for four hours, draped with a growing mountain of khadas. At 9 a.m. red-robed monks began the slow procession from the

---

* It was a complex operation, as Sunanda Datta-Ray recalled: 'Mrs Indira Gandhi's government had arranged to have his body flown back from New York, laid on an airforce Avro to transport the coffin to Bagdogra, and an MI-8 helicopter for the last lap to Gangtok.'

chapel to the royal burial ground six miles further up towards the Tibetan border. The Chogyal's family walked by the coffin, which was carried by bearers taken from various sections of Sikkim's community. In the vast shuffling column that followed there were government officials, clerks, schoolchildren, teachers, visitors from overseas, groups from every part of Sikkim. In a sign of just how far things had come, even Khatiawara was in the procession.

Ishbel Ritchie estimated the crowd at 20,000, probably more: 'one would have had to be in a helicopter to see it properly'. At the cremation ground itself the last post, lama's prayers and the sounds of volleys from the Sikkim Armed Police mixed as the pyre was lit. In a typewritten account, which she sent back to her predecessor Martha Hamilton, Ishbel Ritchie somehow found solace in the sight:

> It all seemed right and not mixed up. And when the clouds of smoke billowed on and on through the pyre they really seemed to be taking the last of a friend as well as a king on and up and beyond in just the right way. And all around crowds of his subjects and friends.

Epilogue

In early February 1982, a few days after Thondup's funeral, his old friend Nari Rustomji penned a short obituary in the *Indian Express*, ending with this sad – but accurate – summary:

> It was his misfortune that, try as he might, he could not get people to understand that small can be beautiful. Nor could he allow himself to be convinced that others did not see Sikkim as he saw her, that Sikkim's existence was, for the rest of the world, a non-event. His principles might have been unrealistic and all wrong, but he was not prepared, to the very last, to compromise with them. He was intoxicated by his passion for his land and his people.[1]

In the days following the Chogyal's funeral, the journalist Sunanda Datta-Ray made a similar observation in his obituary in the *Observer* newspaper, writing that 'the torments of [Thondup's] kingship were matched by his personal unhappiness'.[2]

Thondup certainly had more than his fair share of personal challenges – he had only become heir to Sikkim's kingdom after the death of his elder brother in an aeroplane crash; then he lost his first wife, his best friend Jigme Dorji and his own son to early deaths. But he was also unable to disentangle his personal commitment to Sikkim from the political realities that he had to face as a ruler. It was this stubbornness that gave his life the arc of Greek tragedy.

In Sikkim, over 30 years after his death, Thondup remains a talking point. Sikkim's politics has moved on since the 1980s, but when the Chogyal arises in conversation those who remember freely offer opinions on the merits of his actions. Everyone portrays him as a good man caught up in a difficult, some would say impossible, situation. That does not stop people pointing out the mistakes they feel he made – many of which, they add, may not have helped Sikkim's cause. Some note that it might have been easier if the Namgyals had been more realistic about Sikkim's future in 1947 and had brokered entry to the union at that stage, perhaps in the agreement of 1950. Others bemoan the effect of the 'play-acting' during the 1960s and early 1970s, when the court at Sikkim attracted more than its fair share of international press coverage, sometimes for the wrong reasons. Many say that if he had ceded more power to the politicians of Sikkim, even as late as the early 1970s, things might have been different. But, ultimately, everyone agrees that Sikkim's sensitive geopolitical position dealt Thondup an almost unplayable hand.

As Rustomji would later write, 'By a kind of inescapable necessity, he annihilated himself.'

Thondup was not the only one, of course, who had invested emotionally in the future of Sikkim. Hope Cooke, too, had embraced the tiny kingdom, risking her nationality in the process.

As I researched her story, I constantly had to remind myself that she had first arrived in Sikkim at the age of 18; that a month before her 23rd birthday she married a widower 17 years her senior; that by the age of 33 she had left Sikkim for the last time. It is hardly surprising that some of her actions appear naive. In India the legacy of the press coverage during the mid-1970s means that there are still those who are convinced that she was in the employ of the CIA, an accusation that K. S. Bajpai dismisses today as 'utter bilge'. It is undeniable, however, that her marriage to Thondup greatly influenced events in Sikkim. As one former courtier candidly admitted over dinner in Gangtok, 'the marriage brought western attention, and we lapped it up'. In his book, *A Himalayan Tragedy*, Rustomji went further, suggesting that Hope Cooke, as the main driving force behind Sikkim's appeal for greater international recognition, had been a significant contributory factor in the rift with Indira Gandhi's government. It was a view that Rustomji gave Hope a chance to refute, which she did in a reply which he published in the same book:

> What I really wanted to rebut, if I still may, is the suggestion that I got Thondup in over his head with regard to sovereignty. I had a big mouth, Nari, and was indiscreet, but I don't think I gave Thondup his ideas. They were an obsession with him both at a deep, substantial level and trivial. What I enjoyed doing was the fleshing out of the myth (cause I do think that nationalism is somewhat a myth, more positive than negative) . . .[3]

K. S. Bajpai, too, had some sympathy for her when I met him in Delhi in 2012. Hope had not been 'the driving force', he told me, but had merely been 'able to articulate what [Thondup] wanted, and give it a philosophical, one might say historical, context'. Thondup had recognised that her 'American connections' might be invaluable in achieving his goal of ensuring Sikkim remained an independent entity. There can be little doubt, however, that the press coverage that the couple courted, particularly in the USA, had the unintended – and devastating – consequence of aggravating public opinion in India, not least that of the Indian prime minister herself.

After Thondup's death in 1982, Hope Cooke remained in New York. In 1989 she made a brief appearance on *Oprah*, billed as 'the intellectual's Grace Kelly'. She retains a strong affinity for Sikkim but has never returned. She still lives in New York today.

Thondup's children, too, have chosen their own paths. In the immediate aftermath of the funeral, Wangchuk, Thondup's second son, was recognised by some in Sikkim as the next Chogyal. Realising the impossibility of the situation, Wangchuk has always resisted becoming actively involved in Sikkim's politics. He has spent much of the last 30 years 'in meditation and spiritual activities in Bhutan and Nepal'. On his 60th birthday in 2013, he reconfirmed that he would be unlikely to return to Sikkim.[4]

Yangchen, Wangchuk's younger sister, settled in London with her husband. Palden, Hope and Thondup's son, lives in New York. Only Thondup's youngest daughter, Hope Leezum, who has married a Sikkimese man, now lives in Gangtok, where she helps to operate the

Tsuklakhang Trust, set up after Thondup's death to manage the palace and the accompanying monastery in Gangtok. The trust has recently completed a superb renovation of the monastery.

As the decades passed, some of the Chogyal's adversaries had the chance to reflect on events.

After the Kazi's ignominious defeat in 1979, he retreated, with the Kazini, to Kalimpong, the West Bengali town just to the south of Sikkim that had once been called a 'nest of spies'. Ishbel Ritchie remained in touch with both during the 1980s, visiting her fellow Scot, the Kazini, frequently as she went into a sad decline. While she never lost her acid humour and sharp tongue, the Kazini was clearly troubled by what had taken place in Sikkim and perhaps her own role in it, and considered a return to Scotland. But her age made such a trip impossible; by the mid-1980s she was suffering from dementia, and accusing people of trying to poison her. On one of Ishbel Ritchie's last visits, the Kazini grabbed her arm, held her eye and pleaded once more to be taken back to her country of birth. The Kazini died, in Kalimpong, in 1989. She was 85.

Six years later, in 1995, the Kazi made an astonishing volte-face by expressing regret for his own role in the Indian annexation of 1975. Saddened by the continuing corruption resulting from state aid and false incentives, he called for 'de-merger' at a ceremony arranged by the state government to mark 20 years of Sikkim's Indian statehood. Instead of celebrating Sikkim's status, he put out a statement to journalists:

> At the very old age of 91, in the capacity of a signatory of the May 8, 1973 Agreement and the first Chief Minister of Sikkim, I am compelled to demand and call upon the Union Government to immediately restore to us – the people of Sikkim – the status of 'Protectorate State' guaranteed to the Sikkimese people by the Indo-Sikkim treaty of 1950, thereby abrogating all the instruments of merger like the 35th Constitutional Agreement Act, 1975 that reduced us to a part of India. This is because we have waited long enough and eventually lost our patience. We, therefore, feel confident that we are competent to govern ourselves better according to our political genius and outside the framework of the Constitution of India.[5]

In 2002, he went even further, admitting openly for the first time the role that the Indian Intelligence Bureau had played in Sikkim. 'The people from IB used to visit me twice or thrice a year,' he told the journalist, even naming an agent who 'used to hand over money to me personally'.[6]

The Kazi eventually died in July 2009. He was 103.

In January 2011, I tracked down Nar Bahadur Khatiawara, the young firebrand fostered by the Kazi and Kazini in the early 1970s who played such a crucial role in organising the demonstrations against the Chogyal in the period between 1973 and 1975. Today, Khatiawara is a lawyer. He continues to strongly defend the rights of Nepalis in Sikkim and across the hills in West Bengal.

It was clear he had moved on: the walls of his house, a few miles down the main road into Gangtok, are adorned with pictures of the graduation ceremonies and marriages of his five successful children. But he was still willing to talk about the events of the 1970s. I asked him about his relationship with the Kazi and Kazini, and how far he was responsible for the troubles.

'Oh, Kazini was much more than my foster mother – she was my teacher, my philosopher, my guide,' he said with a hint of wistfulness. 'I would read anything – the French Revolution, Russian Revolution, anything. I was certainly a little troublemaker. I would fight with Kazi, I would fight with Kazini, my foster mother. But Kazi needed a lieutenant, and I became that man; while the Kazini protected my courage and inspired me. All I wanted was freedom of thought and expression. Whatever I thought, I said. Of course, I fought with the Chogyal too – I told him his system would ruin him.'

I could sense that part of him still believed that what he had done was right, even if the consequences were not what he had expected. As our metaphor-laden conversation continued, I saw a hint of his old oratorical skill.

'India made hay while the sun shines!' he told me. 'They were beating about the bush – so yes, I did suggest they should annex. But today we have just exchanged Chogyalocracy for Indian democracy! Nevertheless, I'm proud of what we have today.' He shrugged, and added with a weak smile, 'Maybe a little hurt that we are not separate.'

Something flashed in his eyes. 'If you shut the door on a cat and chase it around the room, it will eventually turn on you,' he said with a flourish.

It was not hard to see how this man's rhetoric and hyperbole might have inspired others.

Thondup's greatest misfortune, of course, had been to find himself dealing with Indira Gandhi, one of India's most ruthless strategic thinkers, at a time when her concerns about her country's security were at their height. Her assassination in late 1984 came in the midst of a traumatic and turbulent decade for the country. The fact that her ashes were scattered over the Himalayas gives some indication of the importance she attached to the country's northern borderlands. After her son Rajiv succeeded her as prime minister, he and his Chinese counterpart, Deng Xiaoping, finally found the space in which to rebuild relations between their countries without interference.

The first step was to resolve the long-standing territorial disputes in the Himalayas, bequeathed by British India's 1914 negotiation of the McMahon Line, which had brought India and China to war nearly 50 years later. By the late 1980s, both countries were 'interested in groping towards a solution'.[7] In 1988, Rajiv Gandhi made the important formal concession that Tibet was an 'internal matter for China'. The following year he was studiously quiet at the time of the Tiananmen Square uprising. After Rajiv Gandhi was also assassinated, in 1991, repairing the Sino-India relationship again dropped down the priority list. But from around the millennium, as both countries started to experience unprecedented levels of economic growth, relations continued to steadily improve to the level of cautious cordiality that exists today.

Until only a decade ago, however, one issue remained resolutely off the table. Each year the Chinese Foreign Ministry published their almanac with a single line entry under the heading 'China's Relations with Sikkim'. It read: 'The Chinese Government does not recognise India's illegal annexation of Sikkim.'[8] Chinese maps, too, persisted in showing the line between Sikkim and India as an international boundary. It wasn't until 2003, as relations with India improved, that China signalled its intention to change policy by announcing that the position on Sikkim was 'an inheritance of history'.[9]

Finally, in 2005, the Chinese government recognised Sikkim as part of India.

Slowly, piece by piece, the hangovers of British imperial policy in this part of the Himalayas were disappearing. There was one final act required of the British to wash their hands completely of the Sikkim–Tibet saga. In 2008 the British Foreign Secretary, David Miliband, slipped out an announcement that the UK government accepted that China had 'sovereign' rights in Tibet, blithely referring to Britain's previous position on Tibet as an 'anachronism'.[10]

In 2006, as part of the package deal that included the Chinese recognition of Sikkim, the Indian and Chinese governments agreed to reopen trade through the Nathu La pass. It had been closed for more than five decades, since before the outbreak of hostilities between the two countries in the brief war of 1962.

Although the move was more symbolic than pragmatic (trade was severely limited – 29 products were allowed for export from Sikkim, and a further 15 allowed for import)[11] – traders in Sikkim maintain hopes that the Nathu La might one day become a vital land trading route.*

In February 2015, the new Indian Prime Minster, Narendra Modi, announced that he had reached an agreement to allow pilgrims to use the route to travel to Mount Kailash.

Two themes continue to dominate Sikkim's politics today: the question of Sikkim's actual status, and the relative position of ethnic community groups.

Bhandari, the Chief Minister who beat the Kazi in the election of 1979, survived till 1994. Many never forgave him for forming an alliance with Indira Gandhi in 1981 and retreating from the strong anti-merger position he had taken in order to oust the Kazi. In 1994 he appeared on the cusp of gaining an income tax exemption for Sikkim's citizens, but when it became clear that this would be granted initially only to the

---

* Locals say that the limited list represents only a tiny percentage of the illegal trade that takes place across the porous border.

Bhutia-Lepchas (on account of their new tribal status) and not to his bedrock Nepali community, he drew back. The income tax affair left no one satisfied, opening the way for a young politician-poet of Nepali background, Pawan Chamling, who appealed more directly than before for the support of the toiling Nepalis in the south of Sikkim. He has proved a tenacious and adept politician, with an effective party network that ensures he gets the votes he needs. His Sikkim Democratic Front party have won the last four elections. In the 2009 poll, they secured all 32 seats in the Assembly. In 2014, he faced down his first serious challenge. If he lasts for the whole of this term, he will have been chief minister for a quarter of a century.

Chamling is not shy of taking on the central government on behalf of Sikkim. So much so that one local journalist chuckled that he suspected that the irony of India's takeover in 1975 is that it probably actually loosened India's grip on the state.

Money continues to pour into the state from the central government in New Delhi, making Sikkim far and away the greatest recipient of aid (in per capita terms). Allegations abound that this has led to a culture of corruption, particularly in relation to a number of hydroelectric schemes; there have been large-scale protests against these projects by indigenous Lepchas, who feel their sacred connection to the land has been wilfully ignored. Despite the fact that these objections have twice resulted in hunger strikes, the building continues unabated.

Sikkim's political future is increasingly hard to disentangle from the pressure for a separate Gorkhaland in the north of West Bengal. Some in the Gorkhaland movement look longingly north at the central government subsidies that come from living in Sikkim and posit the possibility of a greater Gorkhaland encompassing Sikkim. But even the Nepalis in Sikkim are not keen on such a solution: in 2008, all holders of the Sikkim Subjects Certificate – including Nepalis – were granted income tax exemption, making getting one of these prized certificates – introduced by Thondup in 1961 – extremely worthwhile. It is a benefit that those in Sikkim now guard jealously.

Each time I return to Sikkim, I am struck by the rapid development that Gangtok and other towns in the state are undergoing. Both the central government in Delhi and the state government in Gangtok frequently boast of Sikkim as an economic success story. Chief Minister Pawan Chamling, in power for nearly two decades, has never been shy of proudly claiming that there are two pillars on which Sikkim's success stands: hydroelectricity and tourism.

The efforts to promote tourism have borne fruit: in late 2013, Lonely Planet declared the state as the most desirable place to travel in the world in 2014. Western tourists continue to come to Sikkim, but they are vastly outnumbered by Indian ones. Largely funded by central government, Sikkim has become a mecca for India's growing middle class. They love the central bazaar, one of the cleanest in India, with its piped music, bright lights and choice of Indian cuisine. There are still some traditional stalls lining the immaculately paved pedestrianised street, but they are dominated by the signs of wealth and success that characterise the state in the twenty-first century. Well-dressed locals hustle back and forth between the smart restaurants. Beautifully tended flowers line the central aisle, which culminates in the ubiquitous statue of Mahatma Gandhi found in towns and cities across India. Outside Gangtok, there has been a significant expansion in 'eco-tourism' in Sikkim, which attracts higher-spending clients. But the state's wild beauty will also never be tamed – the trekking agencies that operate out of Darjeeling and Gangtok lead tourists into the heart of the Himalayas (albeit with the appropriate government-issued passes for the Inner Line or Restricted Access areas).

Despite some inevitable packaging of Sikkim's Buddhist heritage, many of the hilltop monasteries still maintain the old traditions against the backdrop of the snow-capped peaks to the north, as I was reminded when I returned to Pemayangtse Monastery in February 2012, to watch the Guru Dragmar chaam dances that take place at the end of the Tibetan year.

As the Masked Dancers performed their ancient ritual to drive out evil spirits, I thought back to my first meeting with Sonam Yongda three years earlier, when he had asked me how much I knew about Sikkim. I realised there is so much more to know. I remembered too, that, but for my grandfather, I might not have discovered this story.

As I finalised this book in late 2014, I took one final trip to Sikkim, visiting Yongda in his house alongside the monastery where I had first come across the story. I set up a camera to record the interview.

As we drew towards the end of our conversation, I asked him what he would want people to remember Sikkim for. He paused to take a drink from his chang and rearranged his robe, reminding me that Buddhists believe that Padmasambhava, known as Lotus-born Buddha, identified Sikkim as a beyul, a hidden valley for Buddhists to retreat to in times of strife.

'Lotus-born Buddha has claimed that this is his own land, and he has created it as a pure land to benefit all sentient beings, particularly the people of the world. So I hope, one day, the leaders of India would realise this, and would really respect and honour . . .' He paused briefly, leaving the words hanging in the air. 'And leave this land to its own way.'

At that moment the electricity failed, throwing us into darkness once more. The tiny blue LED light that I had set up for the interview cast an eerie glow over Yongda's face.

'OK,' I said, as I got up, presuming that this was the end of the interview.

'Just wait . . . the light will come,' Yongda said.

I took my seat. There was another pause.

'I think,' said Yongda after a few seconds, 'India is not happy with my statement!'

We broke into laughter. The lights flickered back on.

❀

Endnotes

PROLOGUE

17. Private conversations with Brian Smith, who was also a partner at the firm of Murton, Clarke & Murton-Neale

18. The National Archives of the UK FCO 37/1674: Political Situation in Sikkim, fol.86, 26 August 1975

CHAPTER ONE: A BRITISH LEGACY

1. B. Gould, *The Jewel in the Lotus* (Chatto & Windus, London, 1957), p. 178

2. N. Rustomji, *A Himalayan Tragedy* (Allied Publishers Private Ltd, India, 1987), p. ix

3. N. Rustomji, *Enchanted Frontiers* (OUP, London, 1971), p. 3

4. Rustomji, *Enchanted Frontiers*, p. 21

5. Rustomji, *Enchanted Frontiers*, pp. 28–9

6. F. Maraini, *Secret Tibet* (Hutchison, London, 1952), p. 47

7. A. Hopkinson, memoir typed by his daughter-in-law (IOR MSS/EUR/D998/58, British Library)

8. Hopkinson (IOR MSS/EUR/D998/58, British Library)

9. Hopkinson (IOR MSS/EUR/D998/58, British Library)

10. S. Cutting, *The Fire Ox and Other Years* (Collins, London, 1947), p. 182

11. Rustomji, *Enchanted Frontiers*, p. 25

12. Sikkim state admin report, 1932–3 (IOR V/10/1980, British Library)

13. Hopkinson (IOR/MSS/EUR/D998/16, British Library)

14. A. von Tunzelmann, *Indian Summer* (Simon & Schuster, London, 2007), p. 137

15. A. Singh, *Himalayan Triangle* (British Library, London, 1988), p. 257

16. von Tunzelmann, *Indian Summer*, p. 218, quoting Mountbatten correspondence

17. Singh, *Himalayan Triangle*, p. 261, quoting 16 July meeting between Thondup and V. P. Menon, among others

18. Personal interview with C. D. Rai, 2010
19. All events concerning C. D. Rai collected in personal interviews with him in 2010
20. Interview with C. D. Rai, 2010
21. H. H. Risley, *The Gazetteer of Sikkim* (Bengal Secretariat Press, Calcutta, 1894), p. xxi
22. L. Rose, 'Modernizing a Traditional Administrative System' in James Fisher (ed.), *Himalayan Anthropology*, pp. 216–7
23. Rustomji, *A Himalayan Tragedy*, p. 27

CHAPTER TWO: UNDER THE SHADOW OF TIBET
1. J. K. Knaus, *Orphans of the Cold War* (Perseus Books Group, USA, 1999), pp. 34–6
2. Knaus, *Orphans of the Cold War*, p. 78
3. Knaus, *Orphans of the Cold War*, p. 78
4. Rustomji, *A Himalayan Tragedy*, p. 28
5. Rustomji, *A Himalayan Tragedy*, p. 37
6. Rustomji, *A Himalayan Tragedy*, p. 37
7. Rustomji, *A Himalayan Tragedy*, p. 151
8. Rustomji, *A Himalayan Tragedy*, p. 28
9. Knaus, *Orphans of the Cold War*, p. 73
10. Knaus, *Orphans of the Cold War*, n.34, p. 344
11. Rustomji, *A Himalayan Tragedy*, p. 34
12. Knaus, *Orphans of the Cold War*, p. 85
13. G. Patterson, *Patterson of Tibet* (Longriders Guild, Scotland, 2005), p. 186
14. Knaus, *Orphans of the Cold War*, p. 106
15. Knaus, *Orphans of the Cold War*, p. 105
16. K. Conboy and P. Morrison, *The CIA's Secret War in Tibet* (University Press of Kansas, USA, 2002), p. 21
17. H. Harrer, *Beyond Seven Years in Tibet: My Life Before, During and After* (Labyrinth Press, UK, 2007), p. 145
18. Conboy and Morrison, *The CIA's Secret War in Tibet*, p. 22
19. Maraini, *Secret Tibet*, pp. 48–51 *passim*
20. Maraini, *Secret Tibet*, p. 220
21. A. Balicki-Denjongpa, 'Princess Pema Tseuden of Sikkim (1924–2008)' in *Bulletin of Tibetology*, (Vol. 44, No. 1 & 2, 2008), p. 197
22. Conboy and Morrison, *The CIA's Secret War in Tibet*, p. 24
23. Conboy and Morrison, *The CIA's Secret War in Tibet*, p. 25
24. Rustomji, *Enchanted Frontiers*, p. 143
25. Rustomji, *Enchanted Frontiers*, p.152
26. Patterson, *Patterson of Tibet*, pp. 214–15
27. Rustomji, *A Himalayan Tragedy*, p. 48
28. Rustomji, *A Himalayan Tragedy*, p. 39

29. Rustomji, *A Himalayan Tragedy*, p. 38
30. Rustomji, *Enchanted Frontiers*, p. 145
31. J. Sack, *Report from Practically Nowhere* (Authors Guild Backinprint.com, 2000) p. 231
32. Rustomji, *Enchanted Frontiers*, p. 148
33. A. Pant, *Mandala: An Awakening* (Orient Longman, Bombay, 1978), pp. 60–2
34. Sack, *Report from Practically Nowhere*, pp. 217–18
35. Sack, *Report from Practically Nowhere*, p. 219
36. Rustomji, *A Himalayan Tragedy*, p. 42
37. Rustomji, *A Himalayan Tragedy*, p. 54
38. See M. Goldstein, *A History of Modern Tibet Volume 3, 1955–57: The Storm Clouds Descend* (Univ. of California Press, 2014), for the full debrief report
39. Rustomji, *A Himalayan Tragedy*, p. 52
40. Knaus, *Orphans of the Cold War*, p. 134
41. S. K. Datta-Ray, *Smash and Grab: The Annexation of Sikkim* (Tranquebar Press, Delhi, India, 2013), p. 141; Patterson, *Patterson of Tibet*, pp. 163–4; Knaus, *Orphans of the Cold War*, p. 171
42. Conboy and Morrison, *The CIA's Secret War in Tibet*, p. 30
43. M. Goldstein, *A History of Modern Tibet Volume 2, The Calm Before the Storm, 1951–1955* (Berkeley: University of California Press, 2007), p. 349
44. Conboy and Morrison, *The CIA's Secret War in Tibet*, p. 46
45. Rustomji, *A Himalayan Tragedy*, p. 115
46. Rustomji, *A Himalayan Tragedy*, p. 69
47. J. Avedon, *In Exile from the Land of the Snows* (Harper Perennial, UK, 1994), p. 48
48. M. Dunham, *Buddha's Warriors* (Penguin India, 2005), pp. 202–3
49. Roger McCarthy, quoted in Dunham, *Buddha's Warriors*, p. 205
50. Dunham, *Buddha's Warriors*, p. 314
51. Dunham, *Buddha's Warriors*, p. 298
52. Dunham, *Buddha's Warriors*, p. 304
53. Rustomji, *Enchanted Frontiers*, p. 254
54. 'Sikkim: Land of the Uphill Devils', *Time*, 12 January 1959

CHAPTER THREE: WHERE THERE'S HOPE

1. 'To be a Princess', *McCall's* magazine, September 1963, p. 162
2. H. Cooke, *Time Change: An Autobiography* (Simon & Schuster, New York, 1980), p. 72
3. I first contacted Hope Cooke for an interview in May 2010. She agreed, but only on the basis that she would provide me with 'cultural context'. We arranged to meet in New York. Two weeks later she emailed me to say that she had spoken to her children and they had reminded her that she had said she would never speak about her time in Sikkim, beyond her autobiography, *Time Change*. Shortly before publication she got back in touch via Martha Hamilton, with whom she

was in regular contact. All the details of her earlier life are taken from *Time Change*, and from an article in *McCall's* magazine, published in September 1963

4. Cooke, *Time Change*, p. 18
5. 'To be a Princess', *McCall's*, p. 166
6. Cooke, *Time Change*, p. 72
7. Knaus, *Orphans of the Cold War*, p. 176
8. Knaus, *Orphans of the Cold War*, p. 188, p. 194, p. 205
9. Knaus, *Orphans of the Cold War*, p. 181
10. Various sources have helped in putting together a picture of the Kazini's life. These include Datta-Ray, *Smash and Grab*, pp. 144–6; M. Shedden, *Orwell: The Authorized Biography* (HarperCollins, 1991), pp. 109–10; and extensive research printed on the internet by Claire Jordan, who claims descent from the Kazini, available at http://members.madasafish.com/~cj_whitehound/family/Ethel_Maud_Shirran_b1904.htm, retrieved 11 January 2012
11. Knaus, *Orphans of the Cold War*, p. 134
12. 'To be a Princess', *McCall's*, p. 163
13. 'To be a Princess', *McCall's*, p. 163
14. Cooke, *Time Change*, p. 89
15. Cooke, *Time Change*, pp. 88–9
16. 'To be a Princess', *McCall's*, p. 164
17. Cooke, *Time Change*, p. 84
18. Cooke, *Time Change*, p. 87–8
19. Rustomji, *A Himalayan Tragedy*, p. 58
20. 'To be a Princess', *McCall's*, p. 168
21. Martha Hamilton, private letters
22. Knaus, *Orphans of the Cold War*, pp. 217–18
23. Knaus, *Orphans of the Cold War*, p. 238
24. Knaus, *Orphans of the Cold War*, p. 245
25. Knaus, *Orphans of the Cold War*, p. 246
26. N. Maxwell, *India's China War* (Jonathan Cape, London, 1970), p. 84
27. D. Malone and R. Mukherjee, 'India and China: Conflict and Cooperation' in *Survival*, Vol. 52, No. 1, Feb–Mar 2010
28. Knaus, *Orphans of the Cold War*, p. 264
29. G. Patterson, *Peking Versus Delhi* (Faber and Faber, London, 1963), p. 243
30. Martha Hamilton, private letters
31. 'Sikkim, Tiny Himalayan Kingdom in the Clouds', *National Geographic*, Vol. 123, No. 3, March 1963
32. Cooke, *Time Change*, p. 104
33. Martha Hamilton, private letters
34. Martha Hamilton, private letters
35. Rustomji, *A Himalayan Tragedy*, p. 84
36. Cooke, *Time Change*, pp. 109–10

37. Rustomji, *A Himalayan Tragedy*, p. 84
38. Martha Hamilton, private letters
39. J. K. Galbraith, *Ambassador's Journals* (H. Hamilton, London, 1969), p. 559. The following morning, Galbraith 'inspected a company of soldiers on the rifle range and looked over numerous other troop dispositions', reporting that 'all of the soldiers – Sikhs, Dogras, Jats, Ghurkhas – looked very tough and professional, clean and well-fed, and one supposes they would make things difficult for the Chinese'.
40. 'Sikkim: Where There's Hope', *Time* magazine, 29 March 1963
41. Cooke, *Time Change*, pp. 114–15
42. Cooke, *Time Change*, p. 118
43. Cooke, *Time Change*, p. 121
44. S. Shukla, *Sikkim: The Story of Integration* (S. Chand, New Delhi, 1976), p. 65
45. Datta-Ray, *Smash and Grab*, p. 114
46. Conboy and Morrison, *The CIA's Secret War in Tibet*, p. 195
47. M. K. Dhar, *Open Secrets: India's Intelligence Unveiled* (Manas Publications, New Delhi, 2010), p. 95
48. Conboy and Morrison, *The CIA's Secret War in Tibet*, p. 191
49. J. Garver, *Protracted Contest: Sino-Indian Rivalry in the Twentieth Century* (University of Washington Press, 2001), p.62; Conboy and Morrison, *The CIA's Secret War in Tibet*, p. 199
50. Cooke, *Time Change*, p. 136
51. Cooke, *Time Change*, p. 136
52. Cooke, *Time Change*, p. 122
53. Garver, *Protracted Contest*, p. 127
54. Cooke, *Time Change*, p.127
55. Sikkim coronation booklet – 'Preparations for the Festival of the Coronation' section
56. Cooke, *Time Change*, p. 128
57. Rustomji, *A Himalayan Tragedy*, p. 75
58. 'Hope-la in Gangtok', *Time* magazine, 16 April 1965
59. Rustomji, *A Himalayan Tragedy*, p. 76
60. Speech recorded in official Sikkim coronation booklet
61. Shukla, *Sikkim*, p. 67
62. Garver, *Protracted Contest*, p. 191
63. Quoted in Garver, *Protracted Contest*, p. 194
64. Garver, *Protracted Contest*, p. 195
65. Garver, *Protracted Contest*, p. 199
66. Datta-Ray, *Smash and Grab*, p. 173
67. J. Hiltz, 'Constructing Sikkimese National Identity in the 1960s and 1970s', Jackie Hiltz, *Bulletin of Tibetology*, Vol. 39, No. 2, 2003
68. L. Rose, 'India and Sikkim: Redefining the Relationship' in *Pacific Affairs*, Vol. 42, No. 1, Spring 1969

69. Martha Hamilton, private letters
70. Martha Hamilton, private letters
71. Martha Hamilton, private letters
72. Cooke, *Time Change*, p. 138
73. Cooke, *Time Change*, p. 139
74. Garver, *Protracted Contest*, p. 202
75. Garver, *Protracted Contest*, p. 203

CHAPTER FOUR: A FRAGILE STATE
1. Cooke, *Time Change*, p. 142
2. Cooke, *Time Change*, p. 166
3. Cooke, *Time Change*, p. 168
4. Cooke, *Time Change*, p. 167
5. Cooke, *Time Change*, p. 159
6. V. Mehta, 'A Reporter at Large: Indian Journal, VI – The Himalayas: Towards the Dead Land' in *The New Yorker*, 26 July 1969, p. 45
7. K. Frank, *Indira: The Life of Indira Nehru Gandhi* (Harper Collins, London, 2002), p. 281
8. Mehta, 'A Reporter at Large' in *The New Yorker*, 26 July 1969, p. 45
9. Datta-Ray, *Smash and Grab*, p. 174
10. Datta-Ray, *Smash and Grab*, p. 169
11. Cooke, *Time Change*, p. 199
12. Frank, *Indira*, p. 297
13. Datta-Ray, *Smash and Grab*, p. 174
14. Datta-Ray, *Smash and Grab*, pp. 174–5
15. Private note from Sonam Wangdi, ex-Chief Secretary of Sikkim: 'Untold/ Unknown facts: In defence of the Study Forum'
16. J. Hiltz, 'Constructing Sikkimese National Identity in the 1960s and 1970s', p. 81
17. Frank, *Indira*, p. 305
18. R. Guha, *India after Gandhi: The History of the World's Largest Democracy* (Macmillan, London, 2007), p. 423
19. Guha, *India after Gandhi*, p. 443
20. R. Gupta, 'Sikkim: The Merger with India', *Asian Survey*, Vol. 15, No. 9 (Sept 1975), p. 789
21. J. Hiltz, 'Constructing Sikkimese National Identity in the 1960s and 1970s', p. 80
22. Datta-Ray, *Smash and Grab*, p. 176
23. Cooke, *Time Change*, p. 197
24. Cooke, *Time Change*, p. 196
25. Datta-Ray, *Smash and Grab*, p. 90
26. Datta-Ray, *Smash and Grab*, p. 178 (citing 'External Affairs ministry officials')
27. Extract from *Sikkim*, 6 August 1968, quoted in Datta-Ray, *Smash and Grab*, p. 175

28. Datta-Ray, *Smash and Grab*, pp. 183–4

29. All quotations from the Library of Congress 'American Memory' project: 'The Foreign Affairs Oral History Collection of the Association for Diplomatic Studies and Training'. Interviews available at: http://memory.loc.gov/ammem/collections/diplomacy/index.html, retrieved 26 January 2015

30. Frontline Diplomacy (Manuscript Division, Library of Congress, Washington DC)

31. 'A Queen Revisited', *Time*, May 1969

32. Cooke, *Time Change*, p. 178

33. Cooke, *Time Change*, p. 189

34. *Economic & Political Weekly*, 6 June 1970, pp. 901–2

35. The Foreign and Commonwealth Office files covering this period from 1971 to 1975 regarding Sikkim are available in the UK National Archives and are a remarkably rich source of material on the events of this period

CHAPTER FIVE: THE BIGGER PICTURE

1. Frank, *Indira*, p. 325

2. Frank, *Indira*, p. 327

3. As John Garver points out in his book *Protracted Contest*, Indira probably had little to worry about. Garver makes the point that China has always derived 'a *political* advantage from the existence of India-Pakistan enmity. As long as those two countries remain at loggerheads, foreign audiences automatically compare them with each other. China is left apart, in a separate category, either on a higher moral plane or in the category of a greater power. India's internecine feud with Pakistan pulls it down to Pakistan's level, to China's benefit.'

4. Quoted in C. Andrew, *The Mitrokhin Archive II* (Penguin, London, 2006), p. 321 (original source O. Kalugin, *Spymaster* (Perseus Books Group, London, 2009), p. 141)

5. H. Kissinger, *White House Years* (Weidenfeld and Nicholson and Michael Joseph, 1979), p. 848

6. Conboy and Morrison, *The CIA's Secret War in Tibet*, p. 245

7. B. Raman, *Kaoboys of R&AW* (Lancer Publishers, Illinois, USA, 2007), p. 9 inter alia

8. Garver, *Protracted Contest*, p. 214

9. Cooke, *Time Change*, p. 200

10. Cooke, *Time Change*, p. 201

11. *Washington Post*, 18 Nov. 1971, article by Dorothy Le Sueur

12. D. Cannadine, *Ornamentalism: How the British Saw their Empire* (Penguin, London, 2001), p. 156

13. TNA, FCO 37/982: Political Situation in Sikkim, 7 April 1972; see also Conboy and Morrison, *The CIA's Secret War in Tibet*, p. 265: 'According to one CIA officer

who forged contacts with the Sikkimese royals, the prince was a closet alcoholic. Interview with Kenneth Millian, 13 November 1999.'

14. Frank, *Indira*, p. 343
15. Guha, *India After Gandhi*, p. 463
16. Guha, *India After Gandhi*, p. 463
17. TNA, FCO 37/982: Political Situation in Sikkim, 2 November 1972
18. Cooke, *Time Change*, p. 226
19. Cooke, *Time Change*, p. 206
20. Cooke, *Time Change*, p. 207

CHAPTER SIX: A RAW DEAL

1. Datta-Ray, *Smash and Grab*, p. 210
2. Foreign relations of the United States, Volume XVIII, 1969–76 (China 1973–6), p. 165 ff. (record of conversation in Beijing, 18 Feb. 1973)
3. Foreign relations of the United States, Volume XVIII, 1969–76 (China 1973–6), p. 165 ff. (record of conversation in Beijing, 18 Feb. 1973)
4. 'Arms to Pakistan – Media and Parliamentary Reaction', (D. Moynihan), 14 March 1973, Wikileaks cable: 1973NEWDE02955_b, retrieved 26 Jan. 2015
5. 'Bhutto on Resumption U. S. Arms Sales to Pakistan', (S. Sober), 16 March 1973, Wikileaks cable: 1973ISLAMA02205_b, retrieved 26 Jan. 2015
6. Private interview with K. S. Bajpai, 2012
7. Recalled in a private interview with Karma Topden, 2014
8. P. N. Dhar, *Indira Ghandi, the 'Emergency' and Indian Democracy* (Oxford University Press, New Delhi, 2000), p. 276
9. Cooke, *Time Change*, p. 221
10. Private correspondence with K. S. Bajpai, 2013
11. Cooke, *Time Change*, p. 225
12. Datta-Ray, *Smash and Grab*, p. 233
13. Dhar, *Indira Ghandi: the 'Emergency' and Indian Democracy*, p. 278
14. 'Alarum in Cloudland', *Time*, 23 April 1973
15. Cooke, *Time Change*, pp. 224–31
16. Cooke, *Time Change*, p. 231
17. B. S. Das, *The Sikkim Saga* (Vikas Publishing, New Delhi, 1983), p. 2
18. Das, *The Sikkim Saga*, p. 2
19. Das, *The Sikkim Saga*, p. 3
20. Das, *The Sikkim Saga*, p. 3
21. Das, *The Sikkim Saga*, p. 1
22. 'Sikkim Crisis: Princess and PRC denounce India', (D. Osborn), 12 April 1973, Wikileaks cable: 1973HONGK03595_b, retrieved 26 Jan. 2015
23. TNA, FCO 37/1181: Political Situation in Sikkim, fol. 14, 13 April 1973
24. Pat Moynihan was an unusual appointment. A liberal intellectual who had formed an unexpected alliance with Nixon, he had been appointed to Nixon's cabinet in

1969, before being chosen as the Ambassador in Delhi in March. His cables from Delhi make great, if voluminous, reading. He quickly became frustrated by what he saw as an inadequate Foreign Service 'system' and the dominance of political considerations. At one point he became so depressed by the lack of interest in his detailed analyses that he wrote: 'To anyone who is still listening: let me report that bit by bit I am learning about our system: all winter long, cables were going out from New Delhi asking if we might get just a few more soybeans for the voluntary agencies under title II of PLK–Back came stern warnings against dogoodism. Last week however Senator Humphrey sent me a brief telegram, obviously drafted by some Antioch intern, asking what we were doing for the "starving Indians." Crash Bang came word from the department: approving extra food for same.'

25. 'Conversation with Senator Pell on Sikkim', (D. Moynihan), 12 April 1973, Wikileaks cable: 1973NEWDE04291_b, retrieved 26 Jan. 2015
26. 'Sikkim: Play of Events', (N. Thacher), 10 April 1973, Wikileaks cable: 1973 CALCUT00644_b, retrieved 26 Jan. 2015
27. 'Disturbances in Sikkim: Nepalese Views, Plus an Isolated Chinese One', (C. Coon), 12 April 1973, Wikileaks cable: 1973KATHMA01485_b, retrieved 26 Jan. 2015
28. Das, *The Sikkim Saga*, p. 4
29. Das also concluded in *The Sikkim Saga* that 'strong reactions in China, Pakistan and Nepal and a critical view abroad generally made Delhi change its strategy from confrontation to a negotiated settlement'.
30. There is no better evidence of the extent to which the Cold War infused Indo-US relations in this period than an event a couple of months later, in May 1973: US Ambassador Moynihan found himself dealing with accusations that one of his staff, Peter Burleigh – barely less than a year in the country – had been 'engaged in subversion within India, specifically the fomenting of civil disorders'. For Moynihan, it was another predictable turn of events and provoked him to threaten to resign as ambassador: 'I have told them that this is a dreary communist device which I cannot allow to influence me in any manner and that if they press it to the point where Burleigh goes home, I might well go with him. They have half withdrawn the half charge but the matter remains much on the Prime Minister's Mind.' (Moynihan, D. 'Indian charges of subversion against Vice Consul Burleigh', 11 May 1973, Wikileaks cable: 1973NEWDE05527_b, retrieved 26 Jan. 2015)
31. Das, *The Sikkim Saga*, p. 26
32. Das, *The Sikkim Saga*, p. 27
33. TNA, FCO 37/1181: Political Situation in Sikkim, fol. 29, 25 April 1973
34. Cooke, *Time Change*, p. 213
35. 'Sikkim: Queen of the Mountain', Loren Jenkin in *Newsweek*, 2 July 1973

CHAPTER SEVEN: WE ALSO WANT OUR PLACE IN THE SUN

1. *Volume E-8, Documents on South Asia, 1973–1976*, cable from New Delhi US Embassy, 5 May Foreign Relations, 1969–76, http://2001-2009.state.gov/r/pa/ho/frus/nixon/e8/97010.htm

2. TNA, FCO 37/1181: Political Situation in Sikkim, fol. 39, 2 August 1973

3. *Volume E-8, Documents on South Asia, 1973–1976*, cable from New Delhi US Embassy, 27 August Foreign Relations, 1969–76

4. Information on this meeting reported in Schneider, D. 'Sikkim: The Chogyal Visits Delhi', 22 Sept 1973, Wikileaks cable: 1973NEWDE11130_b, retrieved 26 Jan. 2015

5. 'Sikkim: The Chogyal Visits Delhi', (D. Schneider), 22 Sept 1973, Wikileaks cable: 1973NEWDE11130_b, retrieved 26 Jan. 2015

6. Das, *The Sikkim Saga*, p. 38

7. 'Ruler of Sikkim, Alone in Palace, Broods and Waits', *New York Times*, 23 April 1974

8. Dhar, *Indira Gandhi, the 'Emergency' and Indian Democracy*, p. 281

9. For details of this session and the resolutions, see Proceedings of the Sikkim Assembly, 10 May 1974, quoted in Das, *The Sikkim Saga*, pp. 119–28

10. S. Weisman (ed.) *Daniel Patrick Moynihan: A Portrait in Letters of an American Visionary* (Perseus Books Group, USA, 2010), p. 337

11. Quoted in Guha, *India after Gandhi*, p. 480

12. Das, *The Sikkim Saga*, p. 48

13. Das, *The Sikkim Saga*, pp. 50–1; Datta-Ray, *Smash and Grab*, pp. 284–6

14. Proceedings of the Sikkim Assembly held at 9.45 p.m. on Thursday, 20 June 1974, quoted in Das, *The Sikkim Saga*, pp. 129–32

15. Khatiawara memo, 'Sikkim's merger – A brief resume', quoted in Datta-Ray, *Smash and Grab*, p. 280

16. 'Constitutional Problems in Sikkim', (W. Annenberg), 25 June 1974, Wikileaks cable: 1974LONDON07986_b, retrieved 26 Jan. 2015

17. 'Sikkim Constitutional Crisis Continues', (D. Schneider), 24 June 1974, Wikileaks cable: 1974NEWDE08366_b, retrieved 26 Jan. 2015

18. 'Sikkim', (D. Schneider), 1 July 1974, Wikileaks cable: 1974NEWDE08716_b, retrieved 26 Jan. 2015; Datta-Ray, *Smash and Grab*, pp. 290–1

19. 'Sikkim: Foreign Hands (Invisible of Course)', (D. Schneider), 25 June 1974, Wikileaks cable: 1974NEWDE08416_b, retrieved 26 Jan. 2015

20. 'Sikkim: No solace for the Chogyal', (D. Schneider), 27 June 1974, Wikileaks cable: 1974NEWDE08558_b, retrieved 26 Jan. 2015

21. Proceedings of the Sikkim Assembly held at 7 p.m. on Friday, 28 June 1974, quoted in Das, *The Sikkim Saga*, pp. 133–8

22. Khatiawara memo, 'Sikkim's merger – A brief resume', quoted in Datta-Ray, *Smash and Grab*, p. 279

23. Dhar, *Indira Gandhi, the 'Emergency' and Indian Democracy*, p. 292

24. 'Sikkim', (D. Schneider), 1 July 1974, Wikileaks cable: 1974NEWDE08716_b, retrieved 26 Jan. 2015
25. 'Sikkim', (D. Schneider), 5 July 1974, Wikileaks cable: 1974NEWDE08934_b, retrieved 26 Jan. 2015
26. 'Weekly Review of the People's Republic of China, No. 28', (C. Cross), 10 July 1974, Wikileaks cable: 1974HONGK07742_b, retrieved 26 Jan. 2015; TNA, FCO 37/532: Political Affairs, Sikkim, 13 July 1974
27. Datta-Ray, *Smash and Grab*, p. 303
28. 'Sikkim Developments', (D. Schneider), 10 July 1974, Wikileaks cable: 1974NEWDE09170_b, retrieved 26 Jan. 2015
29. 'Sikkim Developments', (D. Schneider), 10 July 1974, Wikileaks cable: 1974NEWDE09170_b, retrieved 26 Jan. 2015
30. TNA, FCO 37/532: Political Affairs, Sikkim, fol. 15, 5 July 1974

Chapter Eight: 'How Can We Fight With India?'

1. Letter quoted in Datta-Ray, *Smash and Grab*, p. 302
2. The Government of Sikkim Act 1974, quoted in Das, *The Sikkim Saga*, p. 155
3. Datta-Ray, *Smash and Grab*, p. 309
4. Datta-Ray, *Smash and Grab*, p. 311
5. See unpublished note in TNA, FCO 37/1672: Political Situation in Sikkim, 17 October 1974
6. Cartoon received courtesy of Sanjoy Narayan, editor-in-chief, HT Media
7. Datta-Ray, *Smash and Grab*, p. 319
8. Dhar, *Indira Gandhi, the 'Emergency' and Indian Democracy*, p. 295
9. On India's statute book as the Constitution (Thirty Fifth Amendment) Act, See http://indiacode.nic.in/coinweb/amend/amend35.htm
10. *Himalayan Times*, quoted in *New York Times* editorial, 6 Sept. 1974
11. 'Department Press Briefing', (H. Kissinger), 11 Sept 1974, Wikileaks cable: 1974STATE197329_b, retrieved 26 Jan. 2015
12. 'Sikkim – State Department Press Briefing', (D. Moynihan), 11 Sept 1974, Wikileaks cable: 1974NEWDE12115_b, retrieved 26 Jan. 2015
13. Details of these discussions can be found in a series of Wikileaks cables between 26 September 1974 and 1 October 1974
14. 'Indian press reports of US reconsideration of Pak Arms', (D. Moynihan), 12 Sept 1974, Wikileaks cable: 1974NEWDE12193_b, retrieved 26 Jan. 2015
15. 'PRC Statement on Sikkim', (C. Cross), 13 Sept 1974, Wikileaks cable: 1974HONGK10183_b, retrieved 26 Jan. 2015
16. 'PRC Statement on Sikkim', (C. Cross), 13 Sept 1974, Wikileaks cable: 1974HONGK10183_b, retrieved 26 Jan. 2015
17. 'USUN Unclassified Summary, No. 32', 3 Oct 1974, Wikileaks cable: 1974USUNN03660_b, retrieved 26 Jan. 2015

18. 'Sino-Indian Relations', (D. Schneider), 13 Sept 1974, Wikileaks cable: 1974NEWDE13214_b, retrieved 26 Jan. 2015

19. 'Indo-Soviet Relations: Assessment on the eve of the Secretary's visit', (D. Moynihan), 11 Oct 1974, Wikileaks cable: 1974NEWDE13674_b, retrieved 26 Jan. 2015

20. Foreign relations of the United States, 1969–Vol XVIII, China 1973–6, pp. 616–17 (minutes of meeting in Beijing, 27 Nov. 1974)

21. 'Deterioration in Indian-Nepal Relations', (W. Cargo), 9 Oct 1974, Wikileaks cable: 1974KATHMA04166_b, retrieved 26 Jan. 2015

22. 'Deterioration in Indian-Nepal Relations', (W. Cargo), 9 Oct 1974, Wikileaks cable: 1974KATHMA04166_b, retrieved 26 Jan. 2015

23. 'The Pulse of India's Intentions', *Far Eastern Economic Review*, 11 Oct. 1974, p. 34

24. See unpublished note in TNA, FCO 37/1672: Political Situation in Sikkim, 17 October 1974

CHAPTER NINE: 'THEY'VE A' GANE CLEAN GYTE'

1. TNA, FCO 37/532: Political Situation in Sikkim, fol. 30, dated 13 Sept 1974

2. 'Freedom House Report on Political and Civil Liberty', (R. Ingersoll), 2 Jan. 1975, Wikileaks cable: 1975STATE000703_b, retrieved 27 Jan. 2015

3. Datta-Ray, *Smash and Grab*, p. 343

4. Datta-Ray, *Smash and Grab*, p. 344

5. Interview with Sonam Yongda, January 2012

6. Datta-Ray, *Smash and Grab*, p. 345

7. One member of the Indian parliament would later also allege that 'a member of the Chogyal's entourage' had caused the injury.

8. Datta-Ray, *Smash and Grab*, p. 348

9. Datta-Ray, *Smash and Grab*, pp. 366–7

10. Datta-Ray, *Smash and Grab*, pp. 368–9

11. Datta-Ray, *Smash and Grab*, p. 369

12. W. Saxbe, *I've Seen the Elephant* (Kent State University Press, USA, 2000), p. 214

13. 'PRC Media Condemns India on Kashmir Issue', (C. Cross), 12 Mar 1975, Wikileaks cable: 1975HONGK02564_b, retrieved 27 Jan. 2015

14. 'Prime Minister's Interview with UPI March 11', (W. Saxbe), 13 March 1975, Wikileaks cable: 1975NEWDE03523_b, retrieved 27 Jan. 2015

15. Datta-Ray, *Smash and Grab*, p. 374

16. Datta-Ray, *Smash and Grab*, pp. 374–5

17. Private email conversation with John Train

18. Datta-Ray, *Smash and Grab*, p. 354 ff.

19. Datta-Ray, *Smash and Grab*, p. 355

20. 'Sikkim', (W. Saxbe), 10 April 1975, Wikileaks cable: 1975NEWDE04815_b, retrieved, 27 Jan. 2015

21. The account of the events in the bedroom of the Chogyal is from a private interview with Sonam Yongda

22. Tarachand Hariomal's private note to Morarji Desai (15 April 1977, unpublished), as quoted in Datta-Ray *Smash and Grab*, pp. 356–7

23. Datta-Ray, *Smash and Grab*, pp. 390–1

24. Rustomji, *A Himalayan Tragedy*, p 103

25. 'Sikkim', (W. Saxbe), 10 April 1975, Wikileaks cable: 1975NEWDE04815_b, retrieved 27 Jan. 2015

26. 'Sikkim', (W. Saxbe), 10 April 1975, Wikileaks cable: 1975NEWDE04815_b, retrieved 27 Jan. 2015

27. Datta-Ray, *Smash and Grab*, p. 11

28. Datta-Ray, *Smash and Grab*, p. 13

29. Details of the events of 9 April are taken from Datta Ray, *Smash and Grab*, pp. 10–20

30. Private interview with Horst Geerken, and see H. Geerken, *A Gecko for Luck* (Bukitcinta, Germany, 2010), pp. 288–90

31. See http://hamgallery.com/qsl/deleted/Sikkim/ac3pt5.htm for full story, retrieved 24 Feb. 2015

32. 'Reported coup in Sikkim', (R. Helms), 10 April 1975, Wikileaks cable: 1975TEHRAN03252_b, retrieved 27 Jan. 2015

33. From Datta-Ray, *Smash and Grab*, pp. 382–3, quoting Khatiawara's later account of the 10 April Assembly session: 'On April 9, 1975, the Indian army deployed to annex Sikkim. All the Assembly members were once again rounded up and under threat were escorted to the assembly on April 10 and made to sign on the dotted line.'

34. 'American Friends of Sikkim', (W. Schaufele), 12 April 1975, Wikileaks cable: 1975USUNN01181_b, retrieved 27 Jan. 2015

35. 'Sikkim Press Guidance', (H. Kissinger), 11 April 1975, Wikileaks cable: 1975STATE083142_b, retrieved 27 Jan. 2015

36. 'Sikkim', (W. Saxbe), 11 April 1975, Wikileaks cable: 1975NEWDE04921_b, retrieved 27 Jan. 2015

37. Datta-Ray, *Smash and Grab*, p. 389

38. Datta-Ray, *Smash and Grab*, p. 388

39. 'Sikkim', (W. Saxbe), 14 April 1975, Wikileaks cable: 1975NEWDE04994_b, retrieved 27 Jan. 2015

40. 'Sikkim', (W. Saxbe), 14 April 1975, Wikileaks cable: 1975NEWDE04994_b, retrieved 27 Jan. 2015; and TNA, FCO 37/1672: Political Situation in Sikkim, fol. 26, 17 April 1975

41. 'Sikkim', (W. Saxbe), 16 April 1975, Wikileaks cable: 1975NEWDE05120_b, retrieved 27 Jan. 2015

42. 'Sikkim', (W. Saxbe), 16 April 1975, Wikileaks cable: 1975NEWDE05120_b, retrieved 27 Jan. 2015

43. 'Sikkim', (W. Saxbe), 16 April 1975, Wikileaks cable: 1975NEWDE05120_b, retrieved 27 Jan. 2015

44. 'Sikkim', (W. Saxbe), 15 April 1975, Wikileaks cable: 1975NEWDE05050_b, retrieved 27 Jan. 2015

45. Notes of 'The Secretary's, Principals' and Regionals' Staff Meeting, Wednesday, 16 April 1975, 8.00 a.m.', Department of State, US Government (retrieved from the Briish Library online archive)

46. 'Imperial India', *The Observer*, 20 April 1975

47. *The Economist*, 19 April 1975

CHAPTER TEN: DEATH MUST FOLLOW BIRTH

1. 'A Merger is Arranged', *Hindustan Times*, 15 April 1975, quoted in Datta-Ray, *Smash and Grab*, p. 393

2. *Indian Express*, quoted in 'Some in India Deplore Action on Sikkim', *New York Times*, 18 April 1975

3. TNA, FCO 37/1672: Political Situation in Sikkim, 15 April 1975

4. TNA, FCO 37/1673: Political Situation in Sikkim, fol. 37, 24 April 1975

5. TNA, FCO 37/1673: Political Situation in Sikkim, fol. 49, 23 April 1975

6. 'Imperial India', *New York Times*, 21 April 1975

7. Saxbe, *I've Seen the Elephant*, p. 216

8. Frank, *Indira*, p. 382

9. 'Sikkim', (W. Saxbe), 14 April 1975, Wikileaks cable: 1975NEWDE04994_b, retrieved 27 Jan. 2015

10. 'Sikkim', (W. Saxbe), 21 April 1975, Wikileaks cable: 1975NEWDE05359_b, retrieved 27 Jan. 2015

11. TNA, FCO 37/1673: Political Situation in Sikkim, fol. 52, 29 April 1975

12. 'Sikkim', (W. Saxbe), 16 April 1975, Wikileaks cable: 1975NEWDE05120_b, retrieved 27 Jan. 2015

13. For the letters, see *The Times*: 25, 28, 29 April; 1, 3, 12, 15, 29 May; and 7 June (all 1975)

14. Quoted in Saxbe, W. 'Indo-US relations', 29 April 1975, Wikileaks cable: 1975NEWDE05701_b, retrieved 27 Jan. 2015

15. Frank, *Indira*, p. 373

16. Frank, *Indira*, p. 375

17. Rustomji, *A Himalayan Tragedy*, p. 132–3

18. Quotations are from M. K. Dhar, *Open Secrets* (Manas Publications, New Delhi, 2010), p. 189–213

19. M. K. Dhar, *Open Secrets*, p. 196

20. 'The Prime Minister: she loves us; she loves us not?', (W. Saxbe), 30 August 1975, Wikileaks cable: 1975NEWDE11791_b, retrieved 27 Jan 2015

21. 'Teng Hsiao-Ping's [Deng Xiaoping] Remarks to Codel [Congress Delegate] Percy', (G. Bush), 12 August 1975, Wikileaks cable: 1975PEKING01503_b, retrieved 27 Jan. 2015

22. 'Sikkim', (W. Saxbe), 21 October 1975, Wikileaks cable: 1975NEWDE14022_b, retrieved 27 Jan. 2015

23. TNA, FCO 37/1674: Political Situation in Sikkim, 26 August 1975

24. TNA, FCO 37/1674: Political Situation in Sikkim, 26 August 1975

25. TNA, FCO 37/1674: Political Situation in Sikkim, 9 November 1975

26. 'Chogyal of Sikkim; Sino-Indian Border Clash', (W. Saxbe), 7 November 1975, Wikileaks cable: 1975NEWDE14806_b, retrieved 27 Jan. 2015

27. Datta-Ray: *Smash and Grab*, p. xlvii

28. 'Chogyal of Sikkim', (W. Saxbe), 17 December 1975, Wikileaks cable: 1975NEWDE16795_b, retrieved 27 Jan. 2015

29. 'Sikkim's Ex-King Virtual Prisoner', *New York Times*, 14 December 1975

30. Cooke, *Time Change*, p. 272

31. 'To be a Princess', *McCall's*, September 1963, p. 88

32. 'Hope Cooke: From Queen of Sikkim to "Regular" New Yorker', *New York Times*, 18 June 1975

33. Rustomji, *A Himalayan Tragedy*, p. 113

34. M. K. Dhar, *Open Secrets*, p. 215

35. Rustomji, *A Himalayan Tragedy*, p. 118–19

36. Frank, *Indira*, p. 421

37. Frank, *Indira*, p. 423–6

38. 'Desai Defends Criticism of Sikkim's Annexation', *New York Times*, 10 March 1978

39. Datta-Ray, article in *The Statesman*, 1978, quoted in Rustomji, *A Himalayan Tragedy*, p. 123

40. Rustomji, *A Himalayan Tragedy*, p. 128–9

41. *Economic and Political Weekly*, 10 March 1979

42. Quote from one of Indira Gandhi's closest friends and a seasoned commentator on Indian politics; cited by Katherine Frank in *Outlook India* magazine, 23 August 2004.

43. Frank, *Indira*, p. 453

44. Datta Ray, *Smash and Grab*, p. xlvii

45. Cooke, *Time Change*, p. 140

46. Datta-Ray, *Smash and Grab*, p. xlvi

Epilogue

1. *Indian Express*, 14 February 1982, quoted in Rustomji, *A Himalayan Tragedy*

2. 'Sikkim Defies Gandhi', *The Observer*, 28 February 1982

3. Letter from Hope Cooke to Rustomji, quoted in Rustomji, *A Himalayan Tragedy*, p. 97

4. 'Chogyal Unlikely to Return Home', *Himalayan Guardian*, 9 April 2013, see http://jigmenkazisikkim.blogspot.co.uk/2013/04/himalayan-guardian-wednesdayapril-3-9_12.html, retrieved 25 Feb. 2015

5. See http://www.darjeeling-unlimited.com/doc/Khangsarpa_Legacy.pdf, retrieved 25 Feb. 2015

6. See interview at http://blog.com.np/2013/01/31/the-pain-of-losing-a-nation-story-of-lhendup-dorji-and-sikkim/, retrieved 25 Feb. 2015

7. S. Ganguly, 'The Sino-Indian Border Talks, 1981–1989: A View from New Delhi', in *Asian Survey*, Vol. 29, No. 12 (Dec., 1989), pp. 1123–35

8. Garver, *Protracted Contest*, p. 175

9. T. Mathou, 'Tibet and its Neighbours: Moving Towards a New Chinese Strategy in the Himalayan Region', in *Asian Survey*, Vol. 45, No. 4 (Jul–Aug 2005), pp. 503–21

10. *Daily Telegraph*, 5 November 2008

11. See item list below:

EXPORT

1	Agriculture implements	
2	Blankets	
3	Copper products	
4	Clothes	
5	Cycles	
6	Coffee	
7	Tea	
8	Barley	
9	Rice	
10	Flour	
11	Dry Fruits	
12	Dry and fresh vegetables	
13	Vegetable oil	
14	Gur and Misri	
15	Tobacco	
16	Snuff	
17	Spices	
18	Shoes	
19	Kerosene oil	
20	Stationery	
21	Utensils	
22	Wheat	
23	Liquor	
24	Milk-processed product	
25	Canned Food	
26	Cigarettes	
27	Local herb	
28	Palm oil	
29	Hardware	

IMPORT

1	Goat skin
2	Sheep skin
3	Wool
4	Raw silk
5	Yak tail
6	Yak hair
7	China clay
8	Borax
9	Seabelyipe
10	Butter
11	Goat Kashmiri
12	Common salt
13	Horse
14	Goat
15	Sheep

⊛

Selected Timeline

1640s Namgyals dynasty established in Sikkim
1817 Treaty of Titalia (with East India Company)
1861 Treaty of Tulong (with British government)
1890 Anglo-Chinese Convention stating Sikkim is a British protectorate
1904 Younghusband Expedition reaches Tibetan capital of Lhasa
1914 Tashi Namgyal succeeds as Chogyal of Sikkim (on death of his brother Sidkeong)
1918 Tashi Namgyal granted full powers
1923 May: Birth of Thondup Namgyal
1939 14th Dalai Lama is enthroned in Lhasa, Tibet
1941 December: Death of Paljor Namgyal, Thondup's older brother
1944 Thondup Namgyal becomes head of State Council
1947 India gains independence from Britain
1949 May: India appoints dewan (prime minister) for Sikkim following disturbances
       October: Declaration of People's Republic of China
1950 October: Invasion of Tibet
       December: Indo-Sikkim Treaty
       December: Dalai Lama flees to Yatung in the south of Tibet
1953 Elections in Sikkim
1954 Nari Rustomji appointed Sikkim's dewan
1956 Dalai Lama visits Sikkim and India for Buddha's 2500th celebrations
1958 Elections in Sikkim

1959   March: Dalai Lama flees Tibet for exile
        September: Formation of Sikkim National Congress party
1961   March: US begins clandestine support of Tibetan rebels in Mustang Valley
1962   October: Sino-Indian Conflict, coinciding with the Cuban Missile Crisis
1963   March: Marriage of Thondup and Hope Cooke
        December: Death of Tashi Namgyal
1964   February: Birth (to Hope Cooke) of Palden Namgyal
        July: Death of Pandit Nehru, PM of India
1965   September–November: China tacitly supports Pakistan in Indo-Pakistani War, sending troops to Sikkim border
1966   January: Death of Lal Bahadur Shastri, PM of India
        January: Indira Gandhi appointed PM of India
1967   March: Elections in Sikkim: Sikkim National Congress emerge as largest single party winning 8 of 18 elected seats
        September: Clashes between Indian and Chinese troops on Sikkim–China border
1968   February: Birth (to Hope Cooke) of Hope Leezum Namgyal
1970   Elections in Sikkim: Sikkim National Party wins 8 of 24 seats in elections
1971   July: Secret Kissinger visit to China
        August: Indo-USSR Friendship Treaty
        October: PRC takes over Chinese seat on UN Security Council (from Taiwan)
        December: Bangladesh War
1973   January: Elections in Sikkim: Sikkim National Party emerges as leading party after winning 9 of 18 elected seats (disputed)
        March: Demonstrations for political reform in Gangtok
        April: Thondup asks for Indian support in controlling disturbances
        May: Tripartite Agreement (known as 8 May Agreement)
        August: Hope Cooke leaves Sikkim
1974   April: Elections in Sikkim: Sikkim National Congress wins in 31 of 32 constituencies; Kazi appointed Chief Minister
        May: India launches Smiling Buddha nuclear test
        June: Demonstrations in Gangtok

September: Sikkim made an 'associate state' of India
1975 April: Sikkim becomes 22nd state of India following takeover of palace and referendum
June: Indira Gandhi declares National Emergency
1976 February: Indira Gandhi postpones planned elections
1977 March: Indira Gandhi calls elections and loses; Morarji Desai becomes PM of India
August: Khatiawara releases 'Memo' on the events of 1975
1978 March: Death of Tenzing Namgyal
March: Indian PM Morarji Desai declares annexation of Sikkim 'not a desirable step'
1979 August: President's Rule declared
October: Elections in Sikkim: Sikkim Janata Parishad wins in 16 of 32 constituencies; Nar Bahadur Bhandari appointed Chief Minister
1980 January: Indira Gandhi elected PM of India for second time
1982 January: Death of Thondup Namgyal

Acknowledgements

Two days after I started this book from a cottage in Glenisla in the Angus Glens of Scotland my six-year-old nephew Robbie came across from my brother's cottage (next door) asking, 'Have you finished your book yet?' Such visits became a regular occurrence. Thank you to my seven nephews and nieces for keeping my feet on the ground, and for being patient enough to allow this book to mature alongside them. Thanks also to my brothers, Jim and Tom, and their other halves, Natalie and Aoife, for encouragement, comments and support over the last few years. Above all, thanks to my mum and dad, who have never put pressure on me, despite (I'm sure) being as eager as my nephews and nieces to see the book completed.

The Glenisla connection comes from my grandfather, David Inglis Duff, whose notes on Sikkim first inspired me to write this book. This book would not have been written if he hadn't cared enough to write notes and take photographs of his journey; nor would it have been possible without having Glenisla as a haven of peace in which to write. Thanks to both my grandparents, whose enthusiasm for India inspired my own.

It was in early 2010 that I first got in touch with Martha Steedman about her time as headteacher at the Paljor Namgyal Girls' School in Sikkim. Martha and her husband Robert were always unfailingly generous with their time, and a source of both help and inspiration. I was deeply saddened when Martha died only two months before publication of this book. Ishbel Ritchie, Martha's successor at the PNG School and now living in Dunfermline, has also always given me valuable insights. The two ladies' weekly letters home demonstrated their deep love for Sikkim, and brought the 1960s and 1970s to life. The realization that I had such a unique, contemporary perspective gave me the courage to keep going on this project.

Martha and Ishbel were vital in making introductions to many people in Sikkim who generously gave interviews and responded patiently to questions and requests for information. They include Sonam Yongda, Sonam Wangdi, Karma Topden, B. B. Gurung and family, Chandra Das Rai and family, Keshav Pradhhan and family, Jigme Kazi, Rinzing Chewang Kazi, Soden la and Jigme Wangchuk, Nar Bahadur Khatiawara, Nar Bahadur Bhandari and Primula Bhandari, Ringu Tulku, Pema Wangchuk, Vimal Khawas, Professor Mahendra Lama and the ever-helpful Raman Shresta at Rachna Books in Gangtok. Particular thanks to Tashi Densapa and Anna Balikci Denjongpa at the Namgyal Institute of Tibetology for their generosity in providing on-site accommodation during two separate visits, and being so helpful with access to material. Saul Mullard and Alex McKay also helped with understanding the early history of Sikkim. At the last minute, Tina Tashi came through with some brilliant photographs, which helped the book immeasurably. Many people in Sikkim have provided assistance in other ways: Thinley Densapa, the Gurung family in Chakung, Hope Leezum Namgyal and family. In Delhi, K. S. Bajpai gave a full and frank interview and helped greatly with follow up questions. One of the most remarkable interviews I conducted was with Ratu Ngawang, escort to the Dalai Lama during his flight from Tibet in 1959. Others in India who helped with information and background context include Kuldip Nayar, Soumitra Das, Brigadier Rai Singh, Rajeev Ranjan Chaturvedy, Gautam Shrestha and the staff at Adventures Unlimited, and Squadron Leader Rana T. S. Chhina. A special mention to Sonam at Sonam's Kitchen, whose Darjeeling breakfasts are unmissable. In the UK, thanks also to James and Bettine Scott, Elizabeth Preston, Peter de Vink, Krystyna Szumelukowa, Tom Drysdale, Malcolm Rust for help with introductions and with finding crucial information.

Sikkim could not have been written without reading Sunanda Datta-Ray's account, *Smash and Grab: Annexation of Sikkim,* and Hope Cooke's autobiography, *Time Change*. Both also generously allowed me to quote from their books, for which many thanks.

Writing a first book (and finding a publisher) requires sage advice and support. Michael Tobert is a brilliant critic and provided light during the dark periods. Others provided encouragement at critical points, often without realising it: John Keay, Jules Stewart, Patrick de Vink, Christopher MacLehose, Heather Adams, Giles Milton, Benedict Flynn, Richard Moore, Jonathan Foreman, Rick Maddocks and Barbara Lamplugh. Many others, too numerous to mention, gave beds, food, and lent a friendly ear when needed. A special mention to Linda Gillies, Kate Godfrey and Bill Everett, and other friends in Glenisla, including members of the Bridge Club, who provided much needed relief after long writing days. Thanks to Andrew and Jo Brydie for lending me their house in Carrbridge for a crucial month in the depths of winter 2013, to Ian Draper for putting me up in Delhi when he hardly knew me and allowing me to conduct an important interview in his sitting room, and to Richard Skinner and Jacqueline Crooks for letting me stay at their fabulous writers' retreat in Andalucia for two months. Also thanks to the team at consultancy Market Gravity, for periodic bouts of employment, and the Edinburgh MD Paul Bowman, who generously lent me his office during the final editing process.

Being assigned to a first-time author must be an editor's bad dream. Thanks to Debs Warner for being wonderfully patient and coping with my wanderings. Thanks also to the team at my publishers, Birlinn, for all their hard work.

Even in the days of instant internet access, libraries and archives remain vital for researching a book of this type. Thanks to the wonderful staff at the London Library, and in the Asia, Pacific and Africa collections of the British Library, who have always been diligent and helpful. Thanks also to the University of St Andrews Library, the Bodleian Library, the Tibetan Archives in Dharamsala and the Sikkim State Archives in Gangtok.

Finally, thanks to my wife, Louise, who has maintained a steadfast faith in me when my self-belief was severely challenged, and without whose comments and advice this book would have been much the poorer.

Andrew Duff
March 2015

Bibliography

OFFICIAL SOURCES
Foreign relations of the United States, Volume XVIII, 1969–76
India Office Records (IOR), in the British Library
The National Archives of the UK (TNA)
The Sikkim Code Vols I–V, Law Dept, Govt of Sikkim
Sikkim Coronation Booklet (Printed by Statesman Press, Calcutta, India)
Frontline Diplomacy: The Foreign Affairs Oral History Collection of the Association for Diplomatic Studies and Training (Manuscript Division, Library of Congress, Washington DC)

PRIVATE LETTERS AND OTHER SOURCES
Ishbel Ritchie, Private Letters
Martha Hamilton, Private Letters
Public Library of US Diplomacy (WikiLeaks)
Arthur Hopkinson, memoir (IOR MSS/EUR/D998/58)

PUBLISHED BOOKS
Adhikari, B. *Sikkim: The Wounds of History* (Biraj Adhikari, India, 2010)
Andrew, C. and Mitrokhin, V. *The Mitrokhin Archive II* (Penguin, London, 2006)
Avedon, J. *In Exile from the Land of the Snows* (Harper Perennial, UK, 1994)
Basnet, L. B. *Sikkim – a Short Political History* (S. Chand & Co, Delhi, India, 1974)
Bell, C. *Portrait of the Dalai Lama* (Collins, London, 1946)
Berry, S. *A Stranger in Tibet: The Adventures of a Wandering Zen Monk* (Collins, London, 1990)
Bhanja, K. C. *History of Darjeeling and the Sikkim Himalaya* (Gyan Books, New Delhi, 1993)

Brown, P. *Tours in Sikkim and the Darjeeling District* (W Newman & Co, Calcutta, 1917)

Cannadine, D. *Ornamentalism: How the British Saw Their Empire* (Penguin, London, 2001)

Coelho, V. H. *Sikkim and Bhutan* (Indian Council for Relations, India, 1967)

Conboy, K. and Hannon, P., *Elite Forces of India and Pakistan* (Osprey Publishing, London, 1992)

Conboy, K. and Morrison, P. *The CIA's Secret War in Tibet* (University Press of Kansas, USA, 2002)

Cooke, H. *Time Change: An Autobiography* (Simon & Schuster, New York, 1980)

Craig, M. *Kundun: A Biography of the Family of the Dalai Lama* (Harper Collins, London, 1997)

Crossette, B. *So Close to Heaven: The Vanishing Buddhist Kingdoms of the Himalayas* (Vintage Books, New York, 1996)

Curren, E. *Buddha's Not Smiling: Uncovering Corruption at the Heart of Tibetan Buddhism Today* (Alaya Press, USA, 2006)

Cutting, S. *The Fire Ox and Other Years* (Collins, London, 1947)

Das, B. S. *The Sikkim Saga* (Vikas Publishing, New Delhi, 1983)

Datta-Ray, S. K. *Smash and Grab: Annexation of Sikkim* (Tranquebar Press, Delhi, India, 2013)

Davis, W. *Into the Silence: The Great War, Mallory and the Conquest of Everest* (The Bodley Head, London, 2011)

Dhar, M. K. *Open Secrets: India's Intelligence Unveiled* (Manas Publications, New Delhi, 2010)

Dhar, P. N. *Indira Ghandi, the 'Emergency' and Indian Democracy* (Oxford University Press, 2000)

Doma, Y. *Legends of the Lepchas* (Tranquebar, Chennai, 2010)

Dunham, M. *Buddha's Warriors: The Story of the CIA-Backed Tibetan Freedom Fighters, the Chinese Communist Invasion, and the Ultimate Fall of Tibet* (Penguin India, 2005)

Frank, K. *Indira: The Life of Indira Nehru Gandhi* (Harper Collins, London, 2002)

French, P. *Younghusband: The Last Great Imperial Adventurer* (HarperCollins, London, 1994)

French, P. *Tibet, Tibet: A Personal History of a Lost Land* (Penguin, London, 2011)

Galbraith, J. K. *Ambassador's Journals: A Personal Account of the Kennedy Years* (H. Hamilton, London, 1969)

Garver, J. *Protracted Contest: Sino-Indian Rivalry in the Twentieth Century* (University of Washington Press, USA, 2001)

Goldstein, M. *A History of Modern Tibet Volume 2, The Calm Before the Storm, 1951-1955* (Berkeley: University of California Press, 2007)

Goldstein, M. *A History of Modern Tibet Volume 3, The Storm Clouds Descend, 1955-57* (Berkeley: University of California Press, 2014)

Gould, B. *The Jewel in the Lotus* (Chatto & Windus, London, 1957)

Goyal, *Political History of Himalayan States – Tibet, Nepal, Bhutan, Sikkim and Nagaland Since 1947*, 2nd edition (Cambridge Books, New Delhi, 1966)

Guha, R. *India after Gandhi: The History of the World's Largest Democracy* (Macmillan, London, 2007)

Harrer, H. *Seven Years in Tibet* (Harper Perennial, 2005)

Harrer, H. *Beyond Seven Years in Tibet: My Life Before, During and After* (Labyrinth Press, UK, 2007)

Harris, C. and Shakya, T. *Seeing Lhasa: British Depictions of the Tibetan Capital 1936–47* (Serindia, Chicago, 2003)

His Holiness the Dalai Lama *My Land and My People* (Weidenfeld & Nicolson, London, 1962)

Horne, A. *Kissinger: 1973, The Crucial Year* (Weidenfeld & Nicolson, London, 2009)

Geerken, H. *A Gecko for Luck* (Bukitcinta, Germany, 2010)

Kalugin, O. *Spymaster: My Thirty-Two Years in Intelligence and Espionage Against the West* (Perseus Books Group, London, 2009)

Kaul, T. *Diplomacy in Peace and War: Recollections and Reflections* (Vikas Publishing, India, 1979)

Kaul, T. *A Diplomat's Diary: The Tantalizing Triangle – China, India and USA* (Macmillan India, Delhi, 2000)

Kazi, J. *Inside Sikkim: Against the Tide* (Hill Media, Gangtok, Sikkim, India, 1993)

Kazi, J. *Sikkim for the Sikkimese* (Hill Media, Gangtok, Sikkim, India, 2009)

Kazi, J. *The Lone Warrior* (Hill Media, Gangtok, Sikkim, India, 2013)

Keay, J. *India: A History* (HarperCollins, London, 2000)

Keay, J. *Midnight's Descendants: A History of South Asia Since Partition* (William Collins, 2014)

Keegan, J. *Warpaths: Fields of Battle in Canada and America* (Key Porter Books, Toronto, 1995)

Kennedy, D. *The Magic Mountains: Hill Stations and the British Raj* (University of California Press, LA, 1996)

Kissinger, H. *On China* (Penguin Press, New York, 2011)

Kissinger, H., *White House Years* (Weidenfeld & Nicholson and Michael Joseph, New York, 1979)

Knaus, J. K. *Orphans of the Cold War: America and the Tibetan Struggle for Survival* (Perseus Books Group, USA, 1999)

Kux, D. *India and the United States: Estranged Democracies 1941–1991* (National Defense University Press, USA, 1992)

Laird, T. *The Story of Tibet: Conversations with the Dalai Lama* (Atlantic Books, London, 2006)

Lamb, A. *Tibet, China and India, 1914–1950: a history of imperial diplomacy* (Roxford Books, Hertingfordbury, 1989)

Lamb, A. *The McMahon Line: A Study in the Relations Between India China and Tibet, 1904 to 14* (Routledge & Kegan Paul, London, 1966)

Macdonald, D. *Twenty Years in Tibet* (Seeley, Service, London, 1932)

MacFarquhar, R. and Fairbank, J. K. (eds) *The Cambridge History of China Volume 15: The People's Republic, Part 2: Revolutions within the Chinese Revolution, 1966–1982* (Cambridge University Press, 1991)

Maraini, F. *Secret Tibet* (Hutchison, London, 1952)

Maxwell, N. *India's China War* (Jonathan Cape, London, 1970)

McKay, A. *Tibet and the British Raj: The Frontier Cadre 1904–47* (Curzon, London, 1997)

Meyer, K. and Bressac, S. *Tournament of Shadows: The Great Game and the Race for Empire in Asia* (Abacus Books, USA, 2001)

Moktan, R. *Sikkim and Darjeeling: Compendium of Documents* (R. Moktan, Darjeeling, 2004)

Moorhouse, G. *Calcutta* (Weidenfeld & Nicolson, London, 1971)

Mullard, S. *Opening the Hidden Land: State Formation and the Construction of Sikkimese History* (PhD Thesis, University of Oxford, 2009)

Mullard, S. and Wangchuk, P. *Royal Records: A Catalogue of the Sikkimese Palace Archive* (International Institute of Tibetan and Buddhist Studies, Andiast 2010)

Mullik, B. N. *The Chinese Betrayal: My Years with Nehru* (Allied Publishers, India, 1971)

Naher, G. *Wrestling the Dragon: In Search of the Boy Lama Who Defied China* (Ebury Press, London, 2004)

Neame, P. *Playing with Strife: The Autobiography of a Soldier* (George G. Harrap, London, 1947)

Neuhaus, T. *Tibet in the Western Imagination* (Palgrave Macmillan, Basingstoke, 2012)

Newall, D. *The Highlands of India strategically considered, with special reference to their colonization as reserve circles military, industrial and sanitary* (Harrison & Sons, London, 1882)

Nixon-Eisenhower, J. *Pat Nixon: The Untold Story* (Simon and Schuster, New York, 1986)

Norman, D. *Indira Gandhi: Letters to An American Friend, 1950–1984* (Weidenfeld & Nicolson, London, 1985)

O'Connor, F. *On the Frontier and Beyond* (John Murray, London, 1931)

Pant A. *Mandala: An Awakening* (Orient Longman, Bombay, 1978)

Pant, A. *Undiplomatic Incidents* (Sangam Books, Bombay, 1987)

Pant, A. *An Extended Family or Fellow Pilgrims* (Sangam Books, Bombay, 1990)

Patterson, G. *Peking Versus Delhi* (Faber and Faber, London, 1963)

Patterson, G. *Gods and Guerrillas: The International Collusion to Sacrifice Tibet* (Longriders Guild, Scotland, 2005)

Patterson, G. *Patterson of Tibet* (Longriders Guild, Scotland, 2005)

Peissel, M. *Cavaliers of Kham: The Secret War in Tibet* (William Heinemann, London, 1972)

Pemba, T. *Young Days in Tibet* (Jonathan Cape, London. 1957)

Philips (ed.) *The correspondence of Lord William Cavendish-Bentinck, governor-general of India 1828 to 1835* (OUP, Oxford, 1977)

Pinn, F. *The Road of Destiny: Darjeeling Letters 1839* (OUP, Oxford, 1986)

Pradhan, K. C. *The Life and Times of a Plantsman in the Sikkim Himalayas* (K. C. Pradhan, Sikkim, 2008)

Raina, A. *Inside RAW:* Story of India's Secret Service (Vikas Publishing, New Delhi, 1981)

Raman, B. *The Kaoboys of R&AW* (Lancer Publishers, Illinois, USA, 2007)

Rao, P. R. *India and Sikkim 1814–1970* (Stirling Publishers, India, 1972)

Rhodes, M. *The Final Curtsey: A Royal Memoir by the Queen's Cousin* (Birlinn, Edinburgh, 2012)

Rhodes, N. *A Man of the Frontier, S. W. Laden La: His Life & Times in Darjeeling and Tibet* (Mira Bose, Kolkata, 2006)

Richardson, H. *Tibet and its History* (Oxford University Press, London, 1962)

Richardson, H. *High Peaks, Pure Earth: Collected Writings on Tibetan History and Culture* (Serindia Publications, London, 1998)

Risley, H. H. *The Gazetteer of Sikkim* (Bengal Secretariat Press, 1894)

Ronaldshay, Earl of *Himalayan Bhutan, Sikkim and Tibet* (Constable, London, 1931)

Roselli, J. *Lord William Bentinck, The Making of a Liberal Imperialist, 1774–1839* (Chatto and Windus, London, 1974)

Rustomji, N. *Enchanted Frontiers: Sikkim, Bhutan and Indian's North-Eastern Borderlands* (OUP, London, 1971)

Rustomji, N. *Sikkim: A Himalayan Tragedy* (Allied Publishers Private Ltd, India, 1987)

Sack, J. *Report from Practically Nowhere* (Authors Guild Backinprint.com, 2000)

Salisbury, C. and A. Kandell *Mountaintop Kingdom: Sikkim* (W. W. Norton & Co, New York, USA, 1971)

Sangharakshita *Facing Mount Kanchenjunga* (Ibis Publications, Birmingham, 1991)

Sangharakshita *In the Sign of the Golden Wheel* (Ibis Publications, Birmingham, 1996)

Sangharakshita *Moving Against the Stream* (Ibis Publications, Birmingham, 2003)

Sangharakshita *Precious Teachers* (Ibis Publications, Birmingham, 2007)

Sangharakshita *Dear Dinoo: Letters to a Friend* (Ibis Publications, Birmingham, 2011)

Saxbe, W. *I've Seen the Elephant: An Autobiography* (Kent State University Press, USA, 2000)

Shor, T. *A Step Away from Paradise: A Tibetan Lama's Extraordinary Journey to a Land of Immortality* (Penguin Ananda, New Delhi, 2007)

Shukla, S. *Sikkim: The Story of Integration* (S. Chand, New Delhi, 1976)

Singh, A. *Himalayan Triangle: A Historical Survey of British India's Relations with Tibet, Sikkim and Bhutan, 1765–1950* (The British Library, London, 1991)

Singh, K. *Partition and Aftermath: Memoirs of an Ambassador* (Vikas Publishing, India, 1991)

Sinha, A. *Politics of Sikkim: A Sociological Study* (Thomson, India, 1975)

Sinha, S. *Operation Himalayas: To Defend Indian Sovereignty* (S. Chand & Co. (Pvt) Ltd, Delhi, India, 1975)

Spencer-Chapman, F. *Lhasa: The Holy City* (Chatto & Windus, London, 1938)

Varkey, F. A., *Contributions of French Missionaries in Kalimpong* (Loyola College of Education, Namchi, Sikkim, India, 2010)

von Tunzelmann, A. *Indian Summer: The Secret History of the End of an Empire* (Simon & Schuster, London, 2007)

Waddell, L. A. *The Buddhism of Tibet or Lamaism* (W. Heffer & Sons, Cambridge, 1894)

Waddell, L.A. *Among the Himalayas* (Mittal Publications, Delhi, India, 1899)

Wangchuk, P. and Zulca, M. *Khangchendzonga: Sacred Summit* (Pema Wangchuk, Gangtok, Sikkim, 2007)

Wangyal *Footprints in the Himalayas* (KMT Press, Phuentsholing, Bhutan, 2006)

Weisman, S. (ed.) *Daniel Patrick Moynihan: A Portrait in Letters of an American Visionary* (Perseus Books Group, USA, 2010)

Westmoreland, W. C. *A Soldier Reports* (Doubleday, New York, 1976)

Whelpton, J. *A History of Nepal* (Cambridge University Press, 2005)

White, C. *Sikkim and Bhutan: Twenty-One Years on the North-East Frontier 1897–1908* (N/K, London, 1909)

Williamson, M. *Memoirs of a Political Officer's Wife in Tibet, Sikkim and Bhutan* (Wisdom Publications, London, 1987)

ARTICLES

Academic

Balicki-Denjongpa, A. 'Princess Pema Tseuden of Sikkim (1924–2008)' in *Bulletin of Tibetology* (Vol. 44, No. 1 & 2, 2008)

Ganguly, S. 'The Sino-Indian Border Talks, 1981–1989: A View from New Delhi' in *Asian Survey* (Vol. 29, No. 12, December 1989)

Gupta, R. 'Sikkim: The Merger with India' in *Asian Survey* (Vol. 15, No. 9, September 1975)

Hiltz, J. 'Constructing Sikkimese National Identity in the 1960s and 1970s' in *Bulletin of Tibetology* (Vol. 39, No. 2, 2003)

Lall, J. 'Sikkim' in J. S. Lall and A. D. Moddie (eds.) *The Himalaya, aspects of change* (Oxford University Press, 1981)

Malone and Mukerjhee, 'India and China: Conflict and Cooperation' in *Survival* (Vol. 52, No. 1, Feb–Mar 2010)

Mathou, T. 'Tibet and its Neighbours: Moving Towards a New Chinese Strategy in the Himalayan Region' in *Asian Survey* (Vol. 45, No. 4, Jul–Aug 2005)

Maxwell, N. 'Forty years of folly: What caused the Sino-Indian Border War and Why the Dispute is Unresolved' in *Critical Asian Studies* (Vol. 35, No. 1, March 2003) pp. 99–112

Mehta, V. 'Royalty' (Talk of the Town) in *The New Yorker* (3 October 1964), pp. 45–7

Mehta, V. 'A Reporter at Large: Indian Journal, VI – The Himalayas: Towards the Dead Land' in *The New Yorker* (26 July 1969), pp. 40–8

Rose, L. 'India and Sikkim: Redefining the Relationship' in *Pacific Affairs* (Vol. 42, No. 1, Spring 1969)

Rose, L. 'Modernizing a Traditional Administrative System' in Fisher James F. (ed.), *Himalayan Anthropology: The Indo-Tibetan Interface* (Mounton Publishers, The Hague, 1978), pp. 205–26

Rustomji, N. K. 'Sikkim, Bhutan and India's northeastern borderlands: problems of change' in J. S. Lall and A. D. Moddie (eds) *The Himalaya, aspects of change* (Oxford University Press, 1981)

Vandenhelsken, M. 'Secularism and the Buddhist Monastery of Pemayangtse in Sikkim' in *Bulletin of Tibetology* (May 2003)

Vibha, A. 'Roots and the Route of Secularism in Sikkim'in *Economic and Political Weekly* (Vol. 41, No. 38, 23–29 September 2006)

Newspaper and Magazines

'Sikkim: Land of the Uphill Devils', *Time* magazine (12 January 1959)

'To be a Princess', *McCall's* magazine (September 1963)

'Sikkim: Where There's Hope', *Time* magazine (29 March 1963)

'A Queen Revisited', *Time* magazine (29 March 1963)

'Hope-la in Gangtok', *Time* magazine (16 April 1965)

'Sikkim: A Midget Awakes' in *Far Eastern Economic Review* (21 October 1972)

'Wary Chogyal' in *Far Eastern Economic Review* (23 April 1973)

'Alarum in Cloudland', *Time* magazine (23 April 1973)

'The Long Journey Home' in *Far Eastern Economic Review* (23 April 1973)

'Nominal Chogyal' in *Far Eastern Economic Review* (21 May 1973)

'Sikkim: Queen of the Mountain', *Newsweek* (2 July 1973)

'Ruler of Sikkim, Alone in Palace, Broods and Waits', *New York Times* (23 April 1974)

'The Pulse of India's Intentions', *Far Eastern Economic Review* (11 October 1974)

'It's not "Good Neighbourliness" but Aggression and Expansion' in *Peking Review*, Vol. 17, No. 47 (22 November 1974), pp. 16–19

'A Merger is Arranged', *Hindustan Times* (15 April 1975)

'Some in India Deplore Action on Sikkim', *New York Times* (18 April 1975)

'Imperial India', *The Observer* (20 April 1975)

'Hope Cooke: From Queen of Sikkim to "Regular" New Yorker', *New York Times* (18 June 1975)

'Sikkim's ex-King a Virtual Prisoner', *New York Times* (14 December 1975)

'Desai Deplores Annexation, but Says He Cannot Undo It Now', *New York Times* (8 March 1978)

'Desai Defends Criticism of Sikkim's Annexation', *New York Times* (10 March 1978)

'Sikkim Defies Gandhi', *The Observer* (28 February 1982)

'Chogyal unlikely to return home', *Himalayan Guardian* (9 April 2013)

Index